1957

CATHERINE HIMES

THE LOEB CLASSICAL LIBRARY

EDITED BY

E. CAPPS, Ph.D., LL.D.   T. E. PAGE, Litt.D.   W. H. D. ROUSE, Litt.D.

SENECA'S TRAGEDIES

II

SENECA'S TRAGEDIES

WITH AN ENGLISH TRANSLATION BY
FRANK JUSTUS MILLER, Ph.D., LL.D.
PROFESSOR IN THE UNIVERSITY OF CHICAGO

IN TWO VOLUMES
II

AGAMEMNON   THYESTES
HERCULES OETAEUS   PHOENISSAE
OCTAVIA

LONDON : WILLIAM HEINEMANN
NEW YORK : G. P. PUTNAM'S SONS
MCMXVII

CONTENTS

ARGUMENT

THE *blood-feud between Atreus and Thyestes was not ended with the terrible vengeance which Atreus wreaked upon his brother. It was yet in fate that Thyestes should live to beget upon his own daughter a son, Aegisthus, who should slay Atreus and bring ruin and death upon the great Atrides, Agamemnon.*

The Trojan war is done. And now the near approach of the victorious king, bringing his captives and treasure home to Argos, has been announced. But little does he dream to what a home he is returning. For Clytemnestra, enraged at Agamemnon because he had sacrificed her daughter Iphigenia at Aulis to appease the winds, and full of jealousy because he brings Cassandra as her rival home, estranged also by the long-continued absence of her lord, but most estranged by her own guilty union with Aegisthus, is now plotting to slay her husband on his return, gaining thus at once revenge and safety from his wrath.

AGAMEMNON

THYESTIS VMBRA

Opaca linquens Ditis inferni loca
adsum profundo Tartari emissus specu,
incertus utras oderim sedes magis—
fugio Thyestes inferos, superos fugo.
en horret animus et pavor membra excutit :
video paternos, immo fraternos lares.
hoc est vetustum Pelopiae limen domus ;
hinc auspicari regium capiti decus
mos est Pelasgis, hoc sedent alti toro
quibus superba sceptra gestantur manu,   10
locus hic habendae curiae—hic epulis locus.

    Libet reverti.   nonne vel tristes lacus
incolere satius, nonne custodem Stygis
trigemina nigris colla iactantem iubis ?
ubi ille celeri corpus evinctus rotae
in se refertur, ubi per adversum irritus
redeunte totiens luditur saxo labor,
ubi tondet ales avida fecundum iecur,
et inter undas fervida exustus siti
aquas fugaces ore decepto appetit   20
poenas daturus caelitum dapibus graves.
sed ille nostrae pars quota est culpae senex ?
reputemus omnes quos ob infandas manus

4

AGAMEMNON

GHOST OF THYESTES

Leaving the murky regions of infernal Dis, I come,
sent forth from Tartarus' deep pit, doubting which
world I hate the more—Thyestes flees the lower, the
upper he puts to flight. Lo, my spirit shudders, my
limbs quake with fear; I see my father's, nay more,
my brother's house. This is the ancient seat of
Pelops' line; here 'tis the custom of the Pelasgians
to crown their kings; on this throne sit high lords
whose proud hands wield the sceptre; here is their
council-chamber—here they feast.[1]

12 Fain would I turn me back. Is it not better to
haunt even the gloomy pools, better to gaze upon
the guardian of the Styx, tossing his three-fold neck
with sable mane? where one,[2] his body bound on
the swift-flying wheel, is whirled back upon himself;
where vain uphill toil[3] is mocked as the stone rolls
ever backward; where a greedy bird tears at the
liver[4] constantly renewed; and the old man,[5] thirst-
parched midst waters, catches at fleeing waves with
cheated lips, doomed to pay dearly for the banquet[6]
of the gods. But how small a part of my offence is
his? Let us take count of all whom for their

[1] He is reminded of his own horrid banquet in this very
place.
[2] Ixion.   [3] Of Sisyphus.   [4] Of Tityus.
[5] Tantalus.   [6] See Index s.v. "Pelops."

5

quaesitor urna Cnosius versat reos :
vincam Thyestes sceleribus cunctos meis.
a fratre vincar, liberis plenus tribus
in me sepultis ; viscera exedi mea.

Nec hactenus Fortuna maculavit patrem,
sed maius aliud ausa commisso scelus
natae nefandos petere concubitus iubet.   30
non pavidus hausi dicta, sed cepi nefas.
ergo ut per omnes liberos irem parens,
coacta fatis nata fert uterum gravem,
me patre dignum.   versa natura est retro ;
avo parentem, pro nefas ! patri virum,
natis nepotes miscui—nocti diem.

Sed sera tandem respicit fessos malis
post fata demum sortis incertae fides ;
rex ille regum, ductor Agamemnon ducum,
cuius secutae mille vexillum rates   40
Iliaca velis maria texerunt suis,
post decima Phoebi lustra devicto Ilio
adest—daturus coniugi iugulum suae.
iam iam natabit sanguine alterno domus :
enses secures tela, divisum gravi
ictu bipennis regium video caput ;
iam scelera prope sunt, iam dolus, caedes, cruor—
parantur epulae.   causa natalis tui,
Aegisthe, venit.   quid pudor vultus gravat ?
quid dextra dubio trepida consilio labat ?   50
quid ipse temet consulis, torques, rogas,
an deceat hoc te ?   respice ad matrem ; decet.

---

[1] Minos.   [2] *i.e.* Thyestes.

[3] *i.e.* Thyestes acted by direction of an oracle, which declared that by this means he might gain vengeance on
Atreus' line.

[4] It will not be his branch of the family that shall suffer
this time.

6

impious deeds the Cretan judge[1] with whirling urn condemns; all of them by my crimes shall I, Thyestes, conquer. But by my brother shall I be conquered, full of my three sons buried in me; my own flesh have I consumed.

[28] Nor thus far only has Fortune defiled the sire,[2] but, daring greater crime than that committed, she bade him seek his daughter's incestuous embrace. Fearlessly and to the dregs did I drain her bidding, but 'twas an impious thing I did. And therefore, that a father's power might extend o'er all his children, my daughter, forced by fate,[3] bore child to me, worthy to call me father. Nature has been confounded; father with grandsire, yea, monstrous! husband with father, grandsons with sons, have I confused—and day with night.

[37] But at length, though late and coming after death, the promise of dim prophecy is fulfilled to me, worn with my woes; that king of kings, that leader of leaders, Agamemnon, following whose banner a thousand ships once covered the Trojan waters with their sails, is now at hand,—to give his throat into his wife's power. Now, now shall this house swim in blood other than mine;[4] swords, axes, spears, a king's head cleft with the axe's heavy stroke, I see; now crimes are near, now treachery, slaughter, gore —feasts are being spread. The author of thy birth has come, Aegisthus.[5] Why dost hang thy head in shame? Why doth thy trembling hand, doubtful of purpose, fall? Why dost take counsel with thyself, why turn the question o'er and o'er whether this deed become thee? Think on thy mother; it becomes thee well.

[5] These and the remaining lines of the paragraph are addressed to Aegisthus, seemingly as if he were present.

Sed cur repente noctis aestivae vices
hiberna longa spatia producunt mora,
aut quid cadentes detinet stellas polo?
Phoebum moramur? redde iam mundo diem.

CHORUS

O regnorum magnis fallax
Fortuna bonis, in praecipiti
dubioque locas nimis excelsos.
numquam placidam sceptra quietem   60
certumve sui tenuere diem ;
alia ex aliis cura fatigat
vexatque animos nova tempestas.
non sic Libycis syrtibus aequor
furit alternos volvere fluctus,
non Euxini turget ab imis
commota vadis unda nivali
vicina polo,
ubi caeruleis immunis aquis
lucida versat plaustra Boötes,   70
ut praecipites regum casus
Fortuna rotat. metui cupiunt
metuique timent, non nox illis
alma recessus praebet tutos,
non curarum somnus domitor
pectora solvit.
Quas non arces scelus alternum
dedit in praeceps? impia quas non
arma fatigant? iura pudorque
et coniugii sacrata fides   80
fugiunt aulas. sequitur tristis
sanguinolenta Bellona manu
quaeque superbos urit Erinys,

⁵³ But why suddenly is the summer night prolonged to winter's span? or what holds the setting stars still in the sky? Are we delaying Phoebus? [*Preparing to go.*] Give back the day now to the universe. [*Ghost vanishes.*]

CHORUS

O Fortune, who dost bestow the throne's high boon with mocking hand, in dangerous and doubtful state thou settest the too exalted. Never have sceptres obtained calm peace or certain tenure; care on care weighs them down, and ever do fresh storms vex their souls. Not so on Libyan quicksands does the sea rage and roll up wave on wave; not so, stirred from their lowest depths, surge Euxine's waters, hard by the icy pole, where, undipped in the azure waves,[1] Boötes follows his shining wain, as does Fortune roll on the headlong fates of kings. To be feared they long, and to be feared they dread; kindly night gives them no safe retreat, and sleep, which conquers care, soothes not their breasts.

⁷⁷ What palace has not crime answering crime[2] hurled headlong? What palace do impious arms not vex? Law, shame, the sacred bonds of marriage, all flee from courts. Hard in pursuit comes grim Bellona of the bloody hand, and she who frets the

[1] *i.e.* the Northern constellations never set beneath the sea.
[2] *i.e.* waged by one member of a royal house against another.

    nimias semper comitata domos,
quas in planum quaelibet hora
tulit ex alto.
    Licet arma vacent cessentque doli,
sidunt ipso pondere magna
ceditque oneri Fortuna suo.
vela secundis inflata notis   90
ventos nimium timuere suos,
nubibus ipsis inserta caput
turris pluvio vapulat Austro,
densasque nemus spargens umbras
annosa videt robora frangi ;
feriunt celsos fulmina colles,
corpora morbis maiora patent
et cum in pastus armenta vagos
vilia currant, placet in vulnus
maxima cervix.   100
    Quidquid in altum Fortuna tulit,
ruitura levat.   modicis rebus
longius aevum est ; felix mediae
quisquis turbae sorte quietus
aura stringit litora tuta
timidusque mari credere cumbam
remo terras propiore legit.

CLYTAEMNESTRA

    Quid, segnis anime, tuta consilia expetis ?
quid fluctuaris ?   clausa iam melior via est.
licuit pudicos coniugis quondam toros   110
et sceptra casta vidua tutari fide ;
periere mores ius decus pietas fides—
et qui redire cum perit nescit pudor.
da frena et omnem prona nequitiam incita ;
per scelera semper sceleribus tutum est iter.

10

proud, Erinys, forever dogging homes too high,
which any hour brings low from high estate.

[87] Though arms be idle and treachery give o'er,
great kingdoms sink of their own weight, and Fortune gives way 'neath the burden of herself. Sails
swollen with favouring breezes fear blasts too
strongly theirs; the tower which rears its head to
the very clouds is beaten by rainy Auster; the
grove, spreading dense shade around, sees ancient
oak-trees riven; 'tis the high hills that the lightnings
strike; large bodies are more to disease exposed,
and while common herds stray o'er vagrant pastures,
the head highest upreared is marked for death.

[101] Whatever Fortune has raised on high, she lifts
but to bring low. Modest estate has longer life;
then happy he whoe'er, content with the common
lot, with safe breeze hugs the shore, and, fearing to
trust his skiff to the wider sea, with unambitious oar
keeps close to land.

CLYTEMNESTRA

Why, sluggish soul, dost safe counsel seek? Why
waver? Already the better way is closed. Once
thou mightest have guarded thy chaste bed and thy
widowed sceptre with pure, wifely faith; gone are
good fashions, right doing, honour, piety, faith,—and
modesty, which, once 'tis gone, knows no return.
Fling loose the reins and, forward bent, rouse onward
all iniquity; through crime ever is the safe way for

tecum ipsa nunc evolve femineos dolos,—
quod ulla coniunx perfida atque impos sui
amore caeco, quod novercales manus
ausae, quod ardens impia virgo face,
Phasiaca fugiens regna Thessalica trabe ; 120
ferrum, venena ; vel Mycenaeas domos
coniuncta socio profuge furtiva rate.
quid timida loqueris furta et exilium et fugas ?
soror ista fecit ; te decet maius nefas.

NVTRIX

Regina Danaum et inclitum Ledae genus,
quid tacita versas quidve consilii impotens
tumido feroces impetus animo geris ?
licet ipsa sileas, totus in vultu est dolor.
proin quidquid est, da tempus ac spatium tibi :
quod ratio non quit saepe sanavit mora. 130

CLYTAEMNESTRA

Maiora cruciant quam ut moras possim pati ;
flammae medullas et cor exurunt meum,
mixtus dolori subdidit stimulos timor,
invidia pulsat pectus ; hinc animum iugo
premit cupido turpis et vinci vetat.
et inter istas mentis obsessae faces,
fessus quidem et devinctus et pessumdatus,
pudor rebellat. fluctibus variis agor,
ut cum hinc profundum ventus, hinc aestus rapit,
incerta dubitat unda cui cedat malo. 140
proinde omisi regimen e manibus meis—
quocumque me ira, quo dolor, quo spes feret,

---

¹ Medea.   ² Helen.

crime. Devise now in thine own heart a woman's wiles,—what any faithless wife, beside herself with blind passion, what step-mother's hands have dared, or what she dared, that maid [1] ablaze with impious love, who fled her Phasian realm in that Thessalian bark; dare sword, dare poison; or else flee from Mycenae with the partner of thy guilt, in stealthy bark. But why timidly talk of stealth, of exile, and of flight? Such things thy sister [2] did; thee some greater crime becomes.

NURSE

Queen of the Greeks, Leda's illustrious child, what ponderest thou in silence, what mad deed, ungoverned in thy purpose, art planning with restless soul? Though thou say no word, thy face discovers all thy anguish. Wherefore, whate'er it be, give thyself time and room; what reason cannot, delay has ofttimes cured.

CLYTEMNESTRA

Passions rack me too strong to endure delay; flames are burning my very marrow and my heart; here fear [3] blent with anguish plies the spur, and my breast throbs with jealousy; [4] there base love forces its yoke upon my mind and forbids me to give way. And midst such fires that beset my soul, shame, weary indeed and conquered and utterly undone, still struggles on. [5] By shifting floods am I driven, as when here wind, there tide harries the deep, and the waters halt uncertain to which foe they will yield. Wherefore I have let go the rudder from my hands—where wrath, where smart, where

---

[3] *i.e.* of Agamemnon's vengeance.
[4] Of Cassandra.   [5] *i.e.* against lust.

huc ire pergam ; fluctibus dedimus ratem.
ubi animus errat, optimum est casum sequi.

NVTRIX

Caeca est temeritas quae petit casum ducem.

CLYTAEMNESTRA

Cui ultima est fortuna, quid dubiam timet?

NVTRIX

Tuta est latetque culpa, si pateris, tua.

CLYTAEMNESTRA

Perlucet omne regiae vitium domus.

NVTRIX

Piget prioris et novum crimen struis?

CLYTAEMNESTRA

Res est profecto stulta nequitiae modus.   150

NVTRIX

Quod metuit auget qui scelus scelere obruit.

CLYTAEMNESTRA

Et ferrum et ignis saepe medicinae loco est.

NVTRIX

Extrema primo nemo temptavit loco.

CLYTAEMNESTRA

Rapienda rebus in malis praeceps via est.

hope shall carry me, there will I go; to the waves
have I given my bark. Where reason fails, 'tis best
to follow chance.

NURSE

Blind is he and rash who follows chance.

CLYTEMNESTRA

When fortune is at its worst, why fear its hazard?

NURSE

Safe is thy sin and hidden, if thou allow it so.

CLYTEMNESTRA

Open to view is a royal house's every sin.

NURSE

Dost repent the old crime, yet plan the new?

CLYTEMNESTRA

Surely 'tis folly to stop midway in sin.

NURSE

Whoso piles crime on crime, makes greater what
he dreads.[1]

CLYTEMNESTRA

Both knife and cautery oft take the place of drugs.

NURSE

Desperate remedies no one tries at first.

CLYTEMNESTRA

In midst of ills, we must snatch at headlong ways.

[1] *i.e.* the penalty.

15

NVTRIX

At te reflectat coniugi nomen sacrum.

CLYTAEMNESTRA

Decem per annos vidua respiciam virum ?

NVTRIX

Meminisse debes sobolis ex illo tuae.

CLYTAEMNESTRA

Equidem et iugales filiae memini faces
et generum Achillem ; praestitit matri fidem !

NVTRIX

Redemit illa classis immotae moras   160
et maria pigro fixa languore impulit.

CLYTAEMNESTRA

Pudet doletque—Tyndaris, caeli genus,
lustrale classi Doricae peperi caput !
revolvit animus virginis thalamos meae
quos ille dignos Pelopia fecit domo,
cum stetit ad aras ore sacrifico pater
quam nuptiales !   horruit Calchas suae
responsa vocis et recedentes focos.
o scelera semper sceleribus vincens domus !
cruore ventos emimus, bellum nece !   170
sed vela pariter mille fecerunt rates ?
non est soluta prospero classis deo :
eiecit Aulis impias portu rates.
sic auspicatus bella non melius gerit.
amore captae captus, immotus prece

NURSE

But let the hallowed name of wedlock turn thee back.

CLYTEMNESTRA

For ten years widowed, shall I still think on husband?

NURSE

Thine offspring of him thou shouldst remember.

CLYTEMNESTRA

I do remember my daughter's [1] wedding fires, my son-in-law, Achilles; true faith he [2] showed a mother!

NURSE

She freed our becalmed fleet from delay, and roused the sluggish sea from its deep repose.

CLYTEMNESTRA

Oh, shame! oh, anguish! I, child of Tyndarus, of heavenly lineage, have borne a sacrifice for the Grecian fleet! Once more in memory I see my daughter's wedding rites, which *he* made worthy of Pelops' house, when, with prayer on lip, this father stood before the altars as for nuptials! Calchas shuddered at his own oracles and at the recoiling altar-fires. O house that ever o'ertops crime with crime! With blood we purchased winds, and war with murder! But, say you, by this means a thousand ships spread sail together? 'Twas by no favouring god the fleet was freed; no! Aulis from port drave forth the impious ships. Thus beginning, not more happily did he wage the war. With love of a captive

---

[1] Iphigenia. [2] *i.e.* Agamemnon.

Zminthea tenuit spolia Phoebei senis,
ardore sacrae virginis iam tum furens.
non illum Achilles flexit indomitus minis,
non ille solus fata qui mundi videt,
(in nos fidelis augur, in captas levis),   180
non populus aeger et relucentes rogi.
inter ruentis Graeciae stragem ultimam
sine hoste victus marcet ac Veneri vacat
reparatque amores ; neve desertus foret
a paelice umquam barbara caelebs torus,
ablatam Achilli diligit Lyrnesida,
nec rapere puduit e sinu avulsam viri—
en Paridis hostem ! nunc novum vulnus gerens
amore Phrygiae vatis incensus furit,
et post tropaea Troica ac versum Ilium   190
captae maritus remeat et Priami gener !

    Accingere, anime ; bella non levia apparas.
scelus occupandum est. pigra, quem expectas diem ?
Pelopia Phrygiae sceptra dum teneant nurus ?
an te morantur virgines viduae domi
patrique Orestes similis ? horum te mala
ventura moveant, turbo quis rerum imminet.
quid, misera, cessas ? en adest natis tuis
furens noverca. per tuum, si aliter nequit,
latus exigatur ensis et perimat duos.   200
misce cruorem, perde pereundo virum ;
mors misera non est commori cum quo velis.

---

[1] Chryses, father of Chryseïs.
[2] Cassandra, his second infatuation.   [3] Calchas.
[4] *i.e.* Agamemnon believed him when he demanded the
death of Iphigenia, but not when he required the return of
Briseïs.

18

smitten, unmoved by prayer, he held as spoil the
child of Smynthean Apollo's aged priest,[1] then as
now mad with passion for a sacred maid.[2] Neither
Achilles, unmoved by threats, could bend him, nor
he[3] who alone sees the secrets of the universe, (for
me and mine sure seer, for slave-girls of no weight),[4]
nor the plague-smit people, nor the blazing pyres.
Midst the death-struggle of falling Greece, conquered,
but by no foe, he languishes, has leisure for love,
seeks new amours ; and, lest his widowed couch ever
be free from some barbaric mistress, he lusted for the
Lyrnesian maid,[5] Achilles' spoil, nor blushed to bear
her away, torn from her lord's embrace—he, the
enemy of Paris ! Now, wounded afresh, he rages
with passion for the inspired Phrygian maid ;[6] and
after Troy's conquest, after Ilium's overthrow, he
comes back home, a captive's husband and Priam's
son-in-law !

[193] Now gird thee up, my soul ; no trivial strife art
thou preparing. Crime must be forestalled.[7] Sluggish, what day dost thou await ? Till Phrygian
wives shall wield our Pelops' sceptre ? Do the virgin
daughters of thy house and Orestes, image of his
father, hold thee back ? Nay, 'tis the ills that
that threaten them that should urge thee on ; o'er
them a storm of woes hangs lowering. Why, wretched
woman, dost thou hesitate ? For thy children a mad
step-dame is at hand. Through thine own side, if
not otherwise it can be done, let the sword be driven,
and so slay two. Mingle thy blood with his, in thy
death destroy thy husband ; death hath no pang when
shared with whom thou wouldest.

[5] Briseïs.   [6] Cassandra.
[7] *i.e.* I must take revenge on Agamemnon before he does
the like to me.

NVTRIX

Regina, frena temet et siste impetus
et quanta temptes cogita ; victor venit
Asiae ferocis, ultor Europae, trahit
captiva Pergama et diu victos Phrygas.
hunc fraude nunc conaris et furto aggredi,
quem non Achilles ense violavit fero,
quamvis procacem torvus armasset manum,
non melior Aiax morte decreta furens,   210
non sola Danais Hector et bello mora,
non tela Paridis certa, non Memnon niger,
non Xanthus armis corpora immixtis gerens
fluctusque Simois caede purpureos agens,
non nivea proles Cycnus aequorei dei,
non bellicoso Thressa cum Rheso phalanx,
non picta pharetras et securigera manu
peltata Amazon ?   hunc domi reducem paras
mactare et aras caede maculare impia ?
victrix inultum Graecia hoc facinus feret ?   220
equos et arma classibusque horrens fretum
propone et alto sanguine exundans solum
et tota captae fata Dardaniae domus
regesta Danais.   comprime adfectus truces
mentemque tibimet ipsa pacifica tuam.

AEGISTHVS

Quod tempus animo semper ac mente horrui
adest profecto, rebus extremum meis.

---

[1] *i.e.* Ajax son of Telamon in contradistinction to Ajax the
son of Oileus, called Ajax " the Less."

AGAMEMNON

NURSE

O Queen, restrain thyself, check thine impetuous wrath and think what thou art daring; the conqueror of wild Asia is at hand, Europe's avenger, dragging in triumph captive Pergama and the Phrygians, long since subdued. Against him now with guile and stealth dost thou essay to fight, whom Achilles with his savage sword hurt not, though in grim wrath he armed his insolent hand, nor the better Ajax [1] raging and bent on death, nor Hector, sole bulwark against the warring Greeks, nor the sure-aimed shafts of Paris, nor swarthy Memnon, nor Xanthus, rolling down corpses and arms commingled, nor Simoïs, its waves running red with blood, nor Cycnus, snowy [2] offspring of the Ocean-god, nor warlike Rhesus and his Thracian horde, nor the Amazon, with her painted quiver, battle-axe in hand, and crescent shield? Him, home-returning, dost thou prepare to slay and to defile thine altars with slaughter impious? Will victorious Greece leave such a deed unavenged? Horses and arms, the sea studded with ships, set these before thine eyes, the ground flowing with streams of blood, and the whole fate of the captured house of Dardanus turned 'gainst the Greeks.[3] Control thy fierce passions, and do thou thyself set thine own soul at peace. [*Exit.*

[*Enter* AEGISTHUS.]

AEGISTHUS [*in soliloquy*]

The hour which always in my heart and soul I dreaded is here indeed, the hour of fate for me.

---

[2] He was changed into a snow-white swan.

[3] *i.e.* Agamemnon's death will be as terribly avenged as was the injury to Helen.

quid terga vertis, anime ?   quid primo impetu
deponis arma ?   crede perniciem tibi
et dira saevos fata moliri deos.   230
oppone cunctis vile suppliciis caput,
ferrumque et ignes pectore adverso excipe,
Aegisthe ; non est poena sic nato mori.
    Tu nos pericli socia, tu, Leda sata,
comitare tantum ; sanguinem reddet tibi
ignavus iste ductor ac fortis pater.
sed quid trementes circuit pallor genas
iacensque vultu languido optutus stupet ?

CLYTAEMNESTRA

    Amor iugalis vincit ac flectit retro :
referamur [1] illuc, unde non decuit prius   240
abire ; vel [2] nunc casta repetatur fides,
nam sera numquam est ad bonos mores via :
quem paenitet peccasse paene est innocens.

AEGISTHVS

    Quo raperis amens ?   credis aut speras tibi
Agamemnonis fidele coniugium ?   ut nihil
subesset animo quod graves faceret metus,
tamen superba et impotens flatu nimis
Fortuna magno spiritus tumidos daret.
gravis ille sociis stante adhuc Troia fuit ;
quid rere ad animum suapte natura trucem   250
Troiam addidisse ?   rex Mycenarum fuit,
veniet tyrannus ; prospera animos efferunt. [3]
effusa circa paelicum quanto venit

----

[1] referemus *E : Leo* referemur : *Gronovius, followed by
Richter,* referamur : remeemus *A.*
   [2] *So Peiper, following Gronovius : Leo with MSS.* sed.
   [3] *So the MSS. : Leo, following Buecheler,* efferant

Why, soul, dost fear to face it? Why at the first
onslaught dost lay down thy arms? Be sure that for
thee destruction and dread doom the pitiless gods
prepare. Then set thy vile life to face all punishments, and with confronting breast welcome both
sword and flame, Aegisthus; for one so born, 'tis no
penalty to die.

[*To* CLYTEMNESTRA]

234 Thou partner of my peril, thou, Leda's daughter,
be but my comrade still; then blood for blood shall
he repay to thee, this cowardly warrior and valiant
sire. But why does pallor o'erspread thy trembling
cheeks, and why in thy listless face is thine eye so
dull and drooping?

CLYTEMNESTRA

Love for my husband conquers and turns me back.
Return we thither whence 'twere well never to have
come away. E'en now let us reseek purity and
truth, for never too late is trod the path to honesty;
whoso repents his sin is well-nigh innocent.

AEGISTHUS

Whither art borne, mad one? Dost believe or hope
that Agamemnon is still true to his marriage vows?
Though there were nought in thine own heart to
rouse grave fears, still would his arrogant, immoderate,
o'er-inflated fortune swell his pride. Harsh to his allies
was he while Troy still stood; what thinkest thou
Troy.[1] has added to a spirit by its own nature fierce?
Mycenae's king he was; he will come back her
tyrant;—prosperity urges pride beyond itself. With
what magnificence the surging throng of harlots

---

[1] *i.e.* the fall of Troy.

turba apparatu ! sola sed turba eminet
tenetque regem famula veridici dei.
feresne thalami victa consortem tui ?
at illa nolet. ultimum est nuptae malum
palam mariti possidens paelex domum.
nec regna socium ferre nec taedae sciunt.

CLYTAEMNESTRA

Aegisthe, quid me rursus in praeceps agis   260
iramque flammis iam residentem incitas ?
permisit aliquid victor in captam sibi ;
nec coniugem hoc respicere nec dominam decet.
lex alia solio est, alia privato in toro.
quid quod severas ferre me leges viro
non patitur animus turpis admissi memor ?
det ille veniam facile cui venia est opus.

AEGISTHVS

Ita est ? pacisci mutuam veniam licet ?
ignota tibi sunt iura regnorum aut nova ?
nobis maligni iudices, aequi sibi   270
id esse regni maximum pignus putant,
si quidquid aliis non licet solis licet.

CLYTAEMNESTRA

Ignovit Helenae ; iuncta Menelao redit
quae Europam et Asiam paribus afflixit malis.

AEGISTHVS

Sed nulla Atriden Venere furtiva abstulit
nec cepit animum coniugi obstrictum suae.

24

comes! But one stands out among the throng and holds the king in thrall, the handmaid[1] of the fate-revealing god.[2] Wilt thou give up and endure a sharer in thy marriage bed? But *she* will not. A wife's utmost of woe is a mistress openly queening it in her husband's house. Nor throne nor bed can brook a partnership.

CLYTEMNESTRA

Aegisthus, why dost thou again drive me headlong, and fan to flame my wrath already cooling? Suppose the victor has allowed himself some liberty toward a captive maid; 'tis meet neither for wife nor mistress to take note of this. There is one law for thrones, one for the private bed. What? Does my own heart, itself conscious of base guilt, suffer me to pass harsh judgment on my husband? Let her forgive freely who forgiveness needs.

AEGISTHUS

Sayst thou so? Canst bargain for mutual forgiveness? Are the rights of kings unknown to thee or strange? To us harsh judges, partial to themselves, they deem this the greatest pledge of kingship, if whate'er to others is unlawful is lawful to them alone.

CLYTEMNESTRA

He pardoned Helen; joined to her Menelaüs she returns, who Europe and Asia to like ruin dashed.

AEGISTHUS

Aye, but no woman with stealthy love has stolen Atrides and captured his heart close-barred against

[1] Cassandra.   [2] Apollo.

iam crimen ille quaerit et causas parat.
nil esse crede turpe commissum tibi ;
quid honesta prodest vita, flagitio vacans ?
ubi dominus odit fit nocens, non quaeritur.   280
Spartamne repetes spreta et Eurotan tuum
patriasque sedes profuga ?   non dant exitum
repudia regum.   spe metus falsa levas.

CLYTAEMNESTRA

Delicta novit nemo nisi fidus mea.

AEGISTHVS

Non intrat umquam regium limen fides.

CLYTAEMNESTRA

Opibus merebor, ut fidem pretio obligem.

AEGISTHVS

Pretio parata vincitur pretio fides.

CLYTAEMNESTRA

Surgit residuus pristinae mentis pudor ;
quid obstrepis ?   quid voce blandiloqua mala
consilia dictas ?   scilicet nubet tibi,   290
regum relicto rege, generosa exuli ?

AEGISTHVS

Et cur Atrida videor inferior tibi,
natus Thyestae ?

his wife.[1] Already thy lord seeks charge against thee, intends cause of strife. Suppose no baseness has been done by thee; what boots an honest life and sinless? Whom a master hates is condemned of guilt unheard. Spurned away, wilt thou go back to Sparta and thy Eurotas, wilt flee to thy father's house? The rejected of kings have no escape. With false hope dost thou relieve thy fears.

CLYTEMNESTRA

None knows my guilt save one faithful friend.

AEGISTHUS

Faith never crosses the threshold of a king.

CLYTEMNESTRA

With wealth will I purchase, with bribes will I bind faith.

AEGISTHUS

Faith gained by bribes is overcome by bribes.

CLYTEMNESTRA

The remnant of my old time chastity revives; why dost thou cry against it? Why with cozening words dost give me evil counsel? Deserting the king of kings, shall I wed with thee, a high-born woman with an outcast?

AEGISTHUS

And wherefore less than Atreus' son do I seem to thee, who am Thyestes' son?

[1] *i.e.* in Menelaüs' case his heart was not already hardened against his wife by another mistress, as is the case with Agamemnon.

27

CLYTAEMNESTRA

Si parum est, adde et nepos.

AEGISTHVS

Auctore Phoebo gignor ; haud generis pudet.

CLYTAEMNESTRA

Phoebum nefandae stirpis auctorem vocas,
quem nocte subita frena revocantem sua
caelo expulistis ? quid deos probro addimus ?
subripere doctus fraude geniales toros,
quem Venere tantum scimus inlicita virum,
facesse propere ac dedecus nostrae domus   300
asporta ab oculis ; haec vacat regi ac viro.

AEGISTHVS

Exilia mihi sunt haud nova, assuevi malis.
si tu imperas, regina, non tantum domo
Argisve cedo : nil moror iussu tuo
aperire ferro pectus aerumnis grave.

CLYTAEMNESTRA

Siquidem hoc cruenta Tyndaris fieri sinam.
quae iuncta peccat debet et culpae fidem.
secede mecum potius, ut rerum statum
dubium ac minacem iuncta consilia explicent.

CHORVS

Canite, o pubes inclita, Phoebum !   310
    tibi festa caput
    turba coronat, tibi virgineas,
    laurum quatiens,

28

CLYTEMNESTRA

If that is not enough, say grandson, too.

AEGISTHUS

Phoebus was the source of my begetting; my birth shames me not.

CLYTEMNESTRA

Dost thou name Phoebus as source of an incestuous birth, whom, calling back his steeds in sudden night, you [1] drove from heaven? Why besmirch the gods? Thou, trained by guile to steal the marriage bed, depart at once, take from my sight the infamy of our house; this home is waiting for its king and lord.

AEGISTHUS

Exile is not new to me; I am used to woe. If thou commandest, O queen, not alone from home and Argos do I flee: I am ready at thy bidding to plunge sword into my heart, o'erweighed with grief.

CLYTEMNESTRA [aside]

Yet, should I, cruel daughter of Tyndareus, let this be done.
    [To AEGISTHUS.]
Who jointly sins owes also faith to crime. Come thou with me, that the dark and threatening state of our affairs joint plans may set in order.   [Exeunt.

CHORUS

Sing ye, O maids renowned, of Phoebus! To thee, Phoebus, the festal throng wreaths the head, to thee, waving laurel-bough, the Argive maid in wonted

[1] i.e. your house. At the horrid feast of Thyestes the sun veiled his face in darkness that he might not see.

de more comas innuba fudit
    stirps Inachia ;   315
quaeque Erasini gelidos fontes,   318
    quaeque Eurotan,
quaeque virenti tacitum ripa   320
    bibis Ismenon ;
tu quoque nostros, Thebais hospes,   316
    comitare choros,[1]   317
quam fatorum praescia Manto,   322
    sata Tiresia,
Latonigenas monuit sacris
    celebrare deos.
    Arcus, victor, pace relata,
    Phoebe, relaxa
umeroque graves levibus telis
    pone pharetras
resonetque manu pulsa citata   330
    vocale chelys.
nil acre velim magnumque modis
    intonet altis,
sed quale soles leviore lyra
    flectere carmen
simplex, lusus cum docta tuos
    Musa recenset.
licet et chorda graviore sones,
    quale canebas
cum Titanas fulmine victos   340
    videre dei,
vel cum montes montibus altis
    super impositi
struxere gradus trucibus monstris,
    stetit imposita
Pelion Ossa, pinifer ambos
    pressit Olympus.

[1] *Lines 316, 317 were transposed by Bothe.*

fashion spreads forth her virgin locks; and thou who drinkest of Erasinus' cool waters, who of Eurotas, and who of Ismenus drinkest, silently flowing along its green banks; thou, too, though stranger in Thebes, come join in our chorus, whom Manto, reader of fate, Tiresias' daughter, warned with due rites to worship the gods, offspring of Latona.

326 Thy bow, now peace has come back, all-conquering Phoebus, loose, and thy quiver, full of swift arrows, lay down from thy shoulder and let resound, smit by thy flying fingers, the tuneful lyre. No stern, high strains in lofty measures would I have it sound, but such simple song as 'tis thy wont to modulate on lighter shell, when the learned Muse surveys thy sports. 'Tis thy right, too, on heavier strings to sound such strain as thou sangest when gods saw Titans by thunder overcome, even when mountains, on lofty mountains set, furnished pathway for grim monsters, when Pelion stood on Ossa set beneath, and cloud-capped Olympus weighed on both.

Ades, o magni, soror et coniunx,
    consors sceptri,
regia Iuno!   tua te colimus   350
    turba Mycenae.
tu sollicitum supplexque tui
    numinis Argos
sola tueris, tu bella manu
    pacemque regis.
tu nunc laurus Agamemnonias
    accipe victrix.
tibi multifora tibia buxo
    solemne canit,
tibi fila movent docta puellae   360
    carmine molli,
tibi votivam matres Graiae
    lampada iactant,
ad tua coniunx candida tauri
    delubra cadet,
nescia aratri, nullo collum
    signata iugo.
    Tuque, o magni nata Tonantis,
    incluta Pallas,
quae Dardanias cuspide turres   370
    saepe petisti,
te permixto matrona minor
    maiorque choro
colit et reserat veniente dea
    templa sacerdos.
tibi nexilibus turba coronis
    redimita venit,
tibi grandaevi lassique senes
    compote voto
reddunt grates libantque manu   380
    vina trementi.
    Et te Triviam nota memores
    voce precamur:

³⁴⁸ Thou, too, be near, who as wife and sister sharest the sceptre's might, Juno the royal! We, thy chosen band, in Mycenae adore thee. Thou art the sole protector of Argos that calls on thee with anxious prayers; thou in thy hand holdest war and peace. Accept now the laurels of Agamemnon, victorious goddess. To thee the box-wood flute of many openings soundeth its solemn strains; to thee skilled maidens touch the strings in soothing melody; to thee Grecian mothers wave the votive torch; at thy shrines shall fall the bull's white mate, which the plough knows not, whose neck the yoke ne'er scarred.

³⁶⁸ And thou, child of the great Thunderer, glorious Pallas, who oft with thy spear didst attack the Dardanian towers, to thee in mingled chorus mothers, younger and older, kneel, and at thy coming the priest throws wide the doors of the temple. To thee the throng, crowned with woven wreaths, advances; to thee aged and spent old men, their petitions heard, give thanks and with trembling hand pour wine in libation.

³⁸² Thee, too, O Trivia,[1] with mindful hearts and prayer familiar we adore. Thou biddest thy natal

---

[1] *i.e.* Diana.

tu maternam sistere Delon,
    Lucina, iubes,
huc atque illuc prius errantem
    Cyclada ventis :
nunc iam stabilis fixa terras
    radice tenet,
respuit auras religatque rates   390
    assueta sequi.
tu Tantalidos funera matris
    victrix numeras ;
stat nunc Sipyli vertice summo
    flebile saxum,
et adhuc lacrimas marmora fundunt
    antiqua novas.
colit impense femina virque
    numen geminum.
    Tuque ante omnes, pater ac rector   400
    fulmine pollens,
cuius nutu simul extremi
    tremuere poli,
generis nostri, Iuppiter, auctor,
    cape dona libens
abavusque tuam non degenerem
    respice prolem.

Sed ecce, vasto concitus miles gradu
manifesta properat signa laetitiae ferens
(namque hasta summo lauream ferro gerit)   410
fidusque regi semper Eurybates adest.

EVRYBATES

Delubra et aras caelitum et patrios lares   392[a]1
post longa fessus spatia, vix credens mihi,

---

[1] *Leo in line notation has followed Gronovius except in the
chorus just ended, which Gronovius, with E, prints in dimeters,*

Delos to stand firm, Lucina,[1] erstwhile a Cyclad, drifting hither and yon at the will of the winds; now 'tis a stable land with root firm fixed, repels the winds and gives anchorage for ships, though wont to follow them. Victorious, thou countest o'er the corpses that their mother,[2] child of Tantalus, bemoaned; now on Sipylus' high top she stands, a weeping statue, and to this day fresh tears the ancient marble drips. Zealously both maid and man adore the twin divinities.[3]

[400] And thou before all others, father and ruler, god of the thunder, by whose mere nod the farthest poles do tremble, O Jove, thou author of our race, kindly accept our gifts, and with a father's care take thought for thine own progeny.

[408] But lo, a soldier, hurrying with huge steps, hastes hither with signs of joyful tidings clearly visible, (for his spear bears a laurel wreath on its iron tip,) and Eurybates, the ever faithful servant of the king, is here.

[*Enter* EURYBATES *with laurel-wreathed spear.*]

EURYBATES

Ye shrines and altars of the heavenly gods, ye household deities of my fathers, after long wanderings wearied, and scarce trusting mine own eyes, I humbly

---

[1] Diana.   [2] Niobe.   [3] *i.e.* Phoebus and Phoebe (Diana).

---

while A alternates dimeters with monometers. Leo follows A, and adopts the notation 392ª–410ª, " in order not to break with Gronovius throughout the remainder of the play."

supplex adoro.   vota superis solvite;
telluris altum remeat Argolicae decus
tandem ad penates victor Agamemnon suos.

CLYTAEMNESTRA

Felix ad aures nuntius venit meas!
ubinam petitus per decem coniunx mihi
annos moratur?   pelagus an terras premit?

EVRYBATES

Incolumis, auctus gloria, laude inclitus   400[a]
reducem expetito litori impressit pedem.

CLYTAEMNESTRA

Sacris colamus prosperum tandem diem
et si propitios attamen lentos deos.
tu pande vivat coniugis frater mei
et pande teneat quas soror sedes mea.

EVRYBATES

Meliora votis posco et obtestor deos;
nam certa fari sors maris dubii vetat.
ut sparsa tumidum classis excepit mare,
ratis videre socia non potuit ratem.
quin ipse Atrides aequore immenso vagus   410[a]
graviora pelago damna quam bello tulit
remeatque victo similis, exiguas trahens
lacerasque victor classe de tanta rates.

give reverence. [*To the people.*] Pay now your vows
to the high gods; the pride and glory of the Argive
land returns to his own house at last, Agamemnon,
victorious!

[*Enter* CLYTEMNESTRA *in time to hear the herald's concluding words.*]

CLYTEMNESTRA

Blessed news this that falls upon mine ears! But
where delays my husband whom I have sought
through ten long years? Rests he on sea, or land?

EURYBATES

Unharmed, increased in glory, illustrious with
praise, he hath set homeward foot upon the longed-
for shore.

CLYTEMNESTRA

With sacred rites let us hail the day, fortunate at
last, and the gods, even if propitious, yet slow in
granting our request. But tell me, thou, does my
husband's brother live, and where is my sister,[1] tell.

EURYBATES

Better than our hopes I pray and beseech the
gods; for the sea's dubious lot forbids to speak
certainty. When our scattered fleet met swollen
seas, one ship could scarce descry her sister ship.
Nay, e'en Atrides' self, on the boundless ocean wandering, endured losses heavier by sea than war, and
like a vanquished man, though victor, he returns,
bringing but few and shattered vessels from his
mighty fleet.

[1] Helen.

CLYTAEMNESTRA

Effare casus quis rates hausit meas
aut quae maris fortuna dispulerit duces.

EVRYBATES

Acerba fatu poscis, infaustum iubes
miscere laeto nuntium.   refugit loqui
mens aegra tantis atque inhorrescit malis.

CLYTAEMNESTRA

Exprome ; clades scire qui refugit suas
gravat timorem ; dubia plus torquent mala.   420

EVRYBATES

Vt Pergamum omne Dorica cecidit face,
divisa praeda est, maria properantes petunt.
iamque ense fessum miles exonerat latus,
neglecta summas scuta per puppes iacent ;
ad militares remus aptatur manus
omnisque nimium longa properanti mora est.
signum recursus regia ut fulsit rate
et clara laetum remigem monuit tuba,
aurata primas prora designat vias
aperitque cursus, mille quos puppes secent.   430
  Hinc aura primo lenis impellit rates
adlapsa velis ; unda vix actu levi
tranquilla Zephyri mollis afflatu tremit,
splendetque classe pelagus et pariter latet.
iuvat videre nuda Troiae litora,
iuvat relicti sola Sigei loca.
properat iuventus omnis adductos simul

38

AGAMEMNON

CLYTEMNESTRA

Tell what calamity has swallowed up my ships,
or what mishap by sea has dispersed the chiefs.

EURYBATES

A tale bitter in the telling thou demandest; thou
biddest me mix the unlucky message with the glad.
My sick mind shrinks from speech and shudders at
the thought of such disasters.

CLYTEMNESTRA

Tell on; who shrinks from knowledge of his
calamities but aggravates his fear; troubles half
seen do torture all the more.

EURYBATES

When all Pergamum fell 'neath the Doric fire, the
spoil was divided and in eager haste all sought the
sea. And now the warrior eases his side of the
sword's weary load, and unheeded lie the shields
along the high sterns; the oar is fitted to the warrior's
hands, and to their eager haste all tarrying seems
over long. Then, when the signal for return gleamed
on the royal ship, and the loud trumpet-blast warned
the glad rowers, the king's gilded prow, leading,
marked out the way, and opened up the course for a
thousand ships to follow.

431 A gentle breeze at first steals into our sails and
drives our vessels onward; the tranquil waves, scarce
stirring, ripple beneath soft Zephyr's breathing, and
the sea reflects the splendour of the fleet, hiding the
while beneath it. 'Tis sweet to gaze on the bare
shores of Troy, sweet to behold deserted Sigeum's
wastes. The young men all haste to bend the oars,

39

lentare remos, adiuvat ventos manu
et valida nisu bracchia alterno movet.
sulcata vibrant aequora et latera increpant   440
dirimuntque canae caerulum spumae mare.
ut aura plenos fortior tendit sinus,
posuere tonsas, credita est vento ratis
fususque transtris miles aut terras procul,
quantum recedunt vela, fugientes notat,
aut bella narrat : Hectoris fortis minas
currusque et empto redditum corpus rogo,
sparsum cruore regis Herceum Iovem.
tunc qui iacente reciprocus ludit salo
tumidumque pando transilit dorso mare   450
Tyrrhenus omni piscis exultat freto
agitatque gyros et comes lateri adnatat,
anteire naves laetus et rursus sequi ;
nunc prima tangens rostra lascivit chorus,
millesimam nunc ambit et lustrat ratem.

 Iam litus omne tegitur et campi latent
et dubia parent montis Idaei iuga ;
et iam, quod unum pervicax acies videt,
Iliacus atra fumus apparet nota.
iam lassa Titan colla relevabat iugo,   460
in astra iam lux prona, iam praeceps dies.
exigua nubes sordido crescens globo
nitidum cadentis inquinat Phoebi iubar ;
suspecta varius occidens fecit freta.

 Nox prima caelum sparserat stellis, iacent
deserta vento vela. tum murmur grave,
maiora minitans, collibus summis cadit

---

 [1] *i.e.* of Achilles, by which Hector's body was dragged.
 [2] Priam was slain at the altar of Hercean Jove (Ζεὺς
Ἑρκεῖος, protector of the courtyard) in the courtyard of his
palace.
 [3] The dolphin is so called here in remembrance of the

40

with strokes together, aid winds with hands and move
their sturdy arms with rhythmic swing. The fur-
rowed waters quiver, the vessel's sides hiss through
the waves and dash the blue sea into hoary spray.
When a fresher breeze strains the swelling sails, the
warriors lay by their oars, trust ship to wind and,
stretched along the benches, either watch the far-
fleeing land as the sails retreat, or rehearse their
wars—brave Hector's threats, the chariot[1] and his
ransomed body given to the pyre, Hercean Jove
sprinkled with royal blood.[2] Then, too, the Tyrrhene
fish[3] plays to and fro in the smooth water, leaps over
the heaving seas with arching back, and sports
around, now dashing about in circles, now swimming
by our side, now gaily leading and again following
after; anon the band in sheer wantonness touch the
leading prow, now round and round the thousandth
ship they swim.

[456] Meanwhile all the shore is hid and the plains
sink from view, and dimly the ridges of Ida's mount
appear; and now, what alone the keenest eye can see,
the smoke of Ilium shows but a dusky spot. Already
from the yoke Titan was freeing his horses' weary
necks; now to the stars his rays sink low, now day
goes headlong down. A tiny cloud, growing to a
murky mass, stains the bright radiance of the setting
sun, and the many coloured sun-set has made us
doubt the sea.[4]

[465] Young night had spangled the sky with stars;
the sails, deserted by the wind, hung low. Then
from the mountain heights there falls a murmur
deep, worse threatening, and the wide-sweeping

Tyrrhene pirates who under the wrath of Bacchus were
changed to dolphins. See *Oedipus*, 449 ff.
[4] This is one of numerous weather-signs.

tractuque longo litus ac petrae gemunt;
agitata ventis unda venturis tumet—
cum subito luna conditur, stellae latent,   470
in astra pontus tollitur, caelum perit.
nec una nox est; densa tenebras obruit
caligo et omni luce subducta fretum
caelumque miscet.   undique incumbunt simul
rapiuntque pelagus infimo eversum solo [1]
adversus Euro Zephyrus et Boreae Notus.
sua quisque mittit tela et infesti fretum
emoliuntur, turbo convolvit mare.
Strymonius altas Aquilo contorquet nives
Libycusque harenas Auster ac Syrtes agit;   480
nec manet in Austro: flat gravis nimbis Notus,
imbre auget undas, Eurus orientem movet
Nabataea quatiens regna et Eoos sinus.
quid rabidus ora Corus Oceano exerens?
mundum revellit sedibus totum suis,
ipsosque rupto crederes caelo deos
decidere et atrum rebus induci chaos.
vento resistit aestus et ventus retro
aestum revolvit; non capit sese mare
undasque miscent imber et fluctus suas.   490
nec hoc levamen denique aerumnis datur,
videre saltem et nosse quo pereant malo.
premunt tenebrae lumina et dirae Stygis
inferna nox est.   excidunt ignes tamen
et nube dirum fulmen elisa micat,
miserisque lucis tanta dulcedo est malae;
hoc lumen optant.

           Ipsa se classis premit
et prora prorae nocuit et lateri latus:

---

[1] *So A : Leo* infimum † everso polo *with* E, *conjecturing*
infimum venti polo, *and deleting l. 476.*

shore and rocky headlands send forth a moaning sound; the waves, lashed by the rising wind, roll high—when suddenly the moon is hid, the stars sink out of sight, skyward the sea is lifted, the heavens are gone. 'Tis doubly night; dense fog o'erwhelms the dark and, all light withdrawn, confuses sea and sky. From all sides at once the winds fall on and ravage the sea, from its lowest depths upturned, West wind with East wind striving, South with North. Each wields his own weapons, with deadly assault stirring up the deep, while a whirlwind churns the waves. Strymonian Aquilo sends the deep snow whirling, and Libyan Auster stirs up the sands of Syrtes;[1] nor stands the strife with Auster: Notus, heavy with clouds, blows up, swells waves with rain, while Eurus attacks the dawn, shaking Nabataean realms, and eastern gulfs. What wrought fierce Corus, thrusting forth his head from ocean? The whole universe he tears from its foundations, and you might think the very gods falling from the shattered sky, and black chaos enveloping the world. Flood strives with wind and wind backward rolls the flood. The sea contains not itself, and rain and waves mingle their waters. Then even this comfort fails their dreadful plight, to see at least and know the disaster by which they perish. Darkness weighs on their eyes, and 'tis the infernal night of awful Styx. Yet fires burst forth, and from the riven clouds gleams the dire lightning flash, and to the poor sailors great is the sweetness of that fearful gleam; even for such light they pray.

497 The fleet itself helps on its own destruction, prow crashing on prow and side on side. One ship the

[1] The Syrtes were shallow sand-bars off the northern coast of Africa.

illam dehiscens pontus in praeceps rapit
hauritque et alto redditam revomit mari ;   500
haec onere sidit, illa convulsum latus
submittit undis, fluctus hanc decimus tegit.
haec lacera et omni decore populato levis
fluitat nec illi vela nec tonsae manent
nec rectus altas malus antemnas ferens,
sed trunca toto puppis Icario natat.
nil ratio et usus audet ; ars cessit malis.
tenet horror artus, omnis officio stupet
navita relicto, remus effugit manus.
in vota miseros ultimus cogit timor   510
eademque superos Troes et Danai rogant.
quid fata possunt ! invidet Pyrrhus patri,
Aiaci Vlixes, Hectori Atrides minor,
Agamemno Priamo ; quisquis ad Troiam iacet
felix vocatur, cadere qui meruit manu,[1]
quem fama servat, victa quem tellus tegit.
" nil nobile ausos pontus atque undae ferunt ?
ignava fortes fata consument viros ?
perdenda mors est ? quisquis es nondum malis
satiate tantis caelitum, tandem tuum   520
numen serena ; cladibus nostris daret
vel Troia lacrimas. odia si durant tua
placetque mitti Doricum exitio genus,
quid hos simul perire nobiscum iuvat,
quibus perimus ? sistite infestum mare ;
vehit ista Danaos classis et Troas vehit."
nec plura possunt ; occupat vocem mare.

[1] So A : Leo gradu.

---

[1] Every tenth wave was supposed to be the greatest and
most destructive.
[2] i.e. in safety. The contrast here is between timorous
44

yawning deep sucks into the abyss, engulfs and spews
forth again, restored to the sea above ; one sinks
of its own weight, another turns its wrecked side to
the waves, and one the tenth[1] wave o'erwhelms.
Here, battered and stripped of all its ornament, one
floats, with neither sails nor oars nor straight mast
bearing the high sailyards, a broken hulk, drifting
wide on the Icarian sea. Reason, experience, are of
no avail ; skill yields to dire calamity. Horror holds
their limbs ; the sailors all stand stupefied, their
tasks abandoned ; oars drop from hands. To prayer
abject fear drives the wretches, and Trojans and
Greeks beg the same things of the gods. What can
near doom accomplish ? Pyrrhus envies his father,
Ulysses Ajax, the younger Atrides Hector, Agamemnon Priam ; whoever at Troy lies slain is hailed as
blessed, who by deeds of arms earned death, whom
glory guards, whom the land he conquered buries.
" Do sea and wave bear[2] those who have dared
naught noble, and shall a coward's doom o'erwhelm
brave men ? Must death be squandered ? Whoe'er
of heaven's gods thou art, not yet with our sore
troubles sated, let thy divinity be at last appeased ;
o'er our calamities e'en Troy would weep. But if
thy hate is stubborn, and 'tis thy pleasure to send
the Greek race to doom, why wouldst have those[3]
perish along with us, for whose sake we perish ?
Allay the raging sea : this fleet bears Greeks but it
bears Trojans too." They can no more ; the sea
usurps their words.

folk who have safely sailed the sea and these brave men
who must perish in it and throw away their lives for no
return.
    [3] *i.e.* the Trojans, on whose account, it is here assumed,
the destructive storm has been sent upon the Greeks.

Ecce alia clades ! fulmine irati Iovis
armata Pallas quidquid haut [1] hasta minax,
haut [1] aegide haut [2] furore Gorgoneo potest,   530
at [3] igne patrio temptat, et caelo novae
spirant procellae. solus invictus malis
luctatur Aiax. vela cogentem hunc sua
tento rudente flamma perstrinxit cadens.
libratur aliud fulmen ; hoc toto impetu
certum reducta Pallas excussit manu,
imitata patrem. transit Aiacem et ratem
ratisque partem secum et Aiacem tulit.
nil ille motus, ardua ut cautes, salo
ambustus extat, dirimit insanum mare   540
fluctusque rumpit pectore et navem manu
complexus ignes traxit et caeco mari
conlucet Aiax, omne resplendet fretum.
tandem occupata rupe furibundum intonat :
" superasse cuncta,[4] pelagus atque ignes iuvat,
vicisse caelum Palladem fulmen mare.
non me fugavit bellici terror dei,
et Hectorem una solus et Martem tuli ; [5]
Phoebea nec me tela pepulerunt gradu.
cum Phrygibus istos vicimus—tene horream ?   550
aliena inerti tela mittis dextera.
quid, si ipse mittat —" [6] plura cum auderet furens,

[1] *So M. Mueller emending ω, followed by Richter : Leo aut.*
[2] *et ω, emended by M. Mueller : Leo et.*
[3] *aut ω, emended by M. Mueller : Leo aut.*
[4] *So Richter : nunc E : nunc se A : iuvit, Leo conj.*
[5] *This line is properly deleted by Leo, as applicable to the
greater Ajax and not to the present speaker. Farnabius, however, allows the line to stand, as befitting the boastful, wild
words of Ajax Oileus.*
[6] *All editors read* quid si ipse mittat ? *a meaningless phrase.
I have changed the punctuation as indicated above, leaving the
sentence unfinished.*

[528] But lo! disaster on disaster! Pallas, armed with the bolt of angry Jove, threatening essays whate'er she may, not with spear, not with aegis, not with Gorgon's [1] rage, but with her father's lightning, and throughout the sky new tempests blow. Ajax [2] alone, undaunted by disaster, keeps up the struggle. Him, shortening sail with straining halyard, the hurtling lightning grazed. Another bolt is levelled; this, with all her might, Pallas launched true, with hand back drawn, in imitation of her father. Through Ajax it passed, and through his ship, and part of the ship with it, and Ajax it bore away. Then he, nothing moved, like some high crag, rises flame-scorched from the briny deep, cleaves the raging sea, with his breast bursts through the floods and, holding to his wrecked vessel with his hand, drags flames along, shines brightly midst the darkness of the sea and illumines all the waves. At last, gaining a rock, in mad rage he thunders: "'Tis sweet to have conquered all things, flood and flame, to have vanquished sky, Pallas, thunderbolt and sea. I fled not in terror of the god of war; both Hector at once and Mars did I with my sole arm withstand; nor did Phoebus' shafts force me to give way. Such warriors, together with their Phrygians, I conquered;—and shall I shrink from thee? Another's weapon with weakling hand thou hurlest. What, if he himself should hurl —?" [3] When in his madness he would

---

[1] The shield (*aegis*) of Minerva was set with the terrifying Gorgon's head given to her by Perseus.

[2] *i.e.* Ajax "the Less," son of Oileus. This scene recalls Vergil, *Aen.* i. 41 ff.

[3] Ajax apparently would have finished by saying—" his bolt, even then I would not fear."

tridente rupem subruit pulsam pater
Neptunus imis exerens undis caput
solvitque montem ; quem cadens secum tulit
terraque et igne victus et pelago iacet.

Nos alia maior naufragos pestis vocat.
est humilis unda, scrupeis mendax vadis,
ubi saxa rapidis clausa verticibus tegit
fallax Caphereus ; aestuat scopulis fretum   560
fervetque semper fluctus alterna vice.
arx imminet praerupta quae spectat mare
utrimque geminum.   Pelopis hinc oras tui
et Isthmon, arto qui recurvatus solo
Ionia iungi maria Phrixeis vetat,
hinc scelere Lemnon nobilem et Calchedona
tardamque ratibus Aulida.   hanc arcem occupat
Palamedis ille genitor et clarum manu
lumen nefanda vertice e summo efferens
in saxa ducit perfida classem face.   570
haerent acutis rupibus fixae rates ;
has inopis undae brevia comminuunt vada,
pars vehitur huius prima, pars scopulo sedet ;
hanc alia retro spatia relegentem ferit
et fracta frangit.   iam timent terram rates
et maria malunt.   cecidit in lucem furor ;
postquam litatum est Ilio, Phoebus redit
et damna noctis tristis ostendit dies.

CLYTAEMNESTRA

Vtrumne doleam laeter an reducem virum ?
remeasse laetor vulnus et regni grave   580

---

[1] *i.e.* of the women who killed all their men, except that
Hypsipyle saved her father, Thoas.

48

be daring more, father Neptune, pushing with his trident, o'erwhelmed the rock, thrusting forth his head from his waves' depths, and broke off the crag. This in his fall Ajax bears down with him, and now he lies, by earth and fire and billows overcome.

557 But us shipwrecked mariners, another, worse ruin challenges. There is a shallow water, a deceitful shoal full of rough boulders, where treacherous Caphereus hides his rocky base beneath whirling eddies; the sea boils upon the rocks, and ever the flood seethes with its ebb and flow. A precipitous headland o'erhangs, which on either hand looks out upon both stretches of the sea. Hence thou mayst descry thine own Pelopian shores, and Isthmus which, backward curving with its narrow soil, forbids the Ionian sea to join with Phrixus' waves; hence also Lemnos, infamous for crime,[1] and Calchedon, and Aulis which long delayed the fleet. Seizing this summit, the father of Palamedes with accursed hand raised from the high top a beacon-light and with treacherous torch lured the fleet upon the reefs. There hang the ships caught on jagged rocks; some are broken to pieces in the shallow water; the prow of one vessel is carried away, while a part sticks fast upon the rock; one ship crashes with another as it draws back, both wrecked and wrecking. Now ships fear land and choose the seas. Towards dawn the storm's rage is spent; now that atonement has been made for Ilium, Phoebus returns and sad day reveals the havoc of the night.

CLYTEMNESTRA

Shall I lament or rejoice me at my lord's return? I do rejoice to see him home again, but o'er our

lugere cogor.   redde iam Grais, pater
altisona quatiens regna, placatos deos.
nunc omne laeta fronde veletur caput,
sacrifica dulces tibia effundat modos
et nivea magnas victima ante aras cadat.

    Sed ecce, turba tristis incomptae comas
Iliades adsunt, quas super celso gradu
effrena Phoebas entheas laurus quatit.

CHORVS

    Heu quam dulce malum mortalibus additum
vitae dirus amor, cum pateat malis   590
effugium et miseros libera mors vocet
portus aeterna placidus quiete.
nullus hunc terror nec impotentis
procella Fortunae movet aut iniqui
flamma Tonantis.
pax alta nullos [1]
civium coetus timet aut minaces
victoris iras, non maria asperis
insana coris, non acies feras
pulvereamve nubem   600
motam barbaricis equitum catervis ;
non urbe cum tota populos cadentes,
hostica muros populante flamma,
indomitumve bellum.
perrumpet omne servitium
contemptor levium deorum,
qui vultus Acherontis atri,
qui Styga tristem non tristis videt
audetque vitae ponere finem.

---

[1] *This awkward duplication of half-lines Richter avoids,
while at the same time obtaining a presumably more logical*

realm's heavy loss am I forced to grieve. At last
O father, that dost shake the high-resounding heavens,
restore to the Greeks their gods appeased. Now
let every head be crowned with festal wreaths, let
the sacrificial flute give forth sweet strains, and the
white victim at the great altars fall.

586 But see, a mournful throng with locks unbound,
the Trojan women are here, while high above them
all, with proud step advancing, Phoebus' mad priestess
waves the inspiring laurel branch.

[*Enter band of Trojan women led by* CASSANDRA.]

CHORUS OF TROJAN WOMEN

Alas, how alluring a bane is appointed unto
mortals, even dire love of life, though refuge from
their woes opes wide, and death with generous
hand invites the wretched, a peaceful port of everlasting rest. Nor fear nor storm of raging Fortune
disturbs that calm, nor bolt of the harsh Thunderer.
Peace so deep fears no citizens' conspiracy, no victor's
threatening wrath, no wild seas ruffled by stormy
winds, no fierce battle lines or dark cloud raised by
barbaric squadrons' hoofs, no nations falling with
their city's utter overthrow, while the hostile flames
lay waste the walls, no fierce, ungovernable war.
All bonds will he break through, who dares scorn
the fickle gods, who on the face of dark Acheron, on
fearful Styx can look, unfearful, and is bold enough
to put an end to life. A match for kings, a match

---

*arrangement, by reading ll. 605–609 after l. 595. He then
prints l. 596 with a lacuna:* Alta pax . . . nullos.

par ille regi, par superis erit.   610
o quam miserum est nescire mori!
  Vidimus patriam ruentem nocte funesta,
cum Dardana tecta Dorici raperetis ignes.
non illa bello victa, non armis,
ut quondam, Herculea cecidit pharetra;
quam non Pelei Thetidisque natus
carusque Pelidae nimium feroci
vicit, acceptis cum fulsit armis
fuditque Troas falsus Achilles,
aut cum ipse Pelides animos feroces   620
sustulit luctu celeremque saltu
Troades summis timuere muris,
perdidit in malis
extremum decus fortiter vinci;
restitit quinis bis annis
unius noctis peritura furto.
  Vidimus simulata dona
molis immensae Danaumque
fatale munus duximus nostra
creduli dextra tremuitque saepe
limine in primo sonipes, cavernis   630
conditos reges bellumque gestans;
et licuit dolos versare ut ipsi
fraude sua caderent Pelasgi.
saepe commotae sonuere parmae
tacitumque murmur percussit aures,
ut fremuit male subdolo
parens Pyrrhus Vlixi.

  Secura metus Troica pubes
sacros gaudet tangere funes.
hinc aequaevi gregis Astyanax,   640

---

¹ Patroclus.
² *i.e.* at the death of Patroclus.

52

for the high gods will he be. Oh, how wretched 'tis to
know not how to die !

[612] We saw our country fall on that night of death,
when you, ye Doric fires, ravished Dardania's homes.
She, not in war conquered, not by arms, not, as
aforetime, by Hercules' arrows, fell ; her, not Peleus'
and Thetis' son o'ercame, nor he,[1] well-beloved by
overbrave Pelides, when in borrowed arms he shone
and drove Troy's sons in flight, a false Achilles ; nor,
when Pelides' self through grief[2] gave o'er his fierce
resentment,[3] and the Trojan women, from the ram-
parts watching, feared his swift attack, did she lose
amid her woes the crowning glory of suffering
conquest bravely ; for ten long years she stood, fated
to perish by one night's treachery.[4]

[627] We saw that feigned gift, measureless in bulk,
and with our own hands trustfully dragged along the
Greeks' deadly offering ; and oft on the threshold of
the gate the noisy footed monster stumbled, bearing
within its hold hidden chiefs and war. We might
have turned their guile against themselves, and
caused the Pelasgians by their own trick to fall.
Oft sounded their jostled shields, and a low muttering
smote our ears, when Pyrrhus grumbled, scarce
yielding to crafty Ulysses' will.

[638] All unafraid, the Trojan youth joy to touch the
fatal ropes.[5] Companies of their own age here

---

[3] *i.e.* against Agamemnon.
[4] *i.e.* by the trick of the wooden horse.
[5] With this whole passage compare Vergil's description,
and especially *Aen.* II. 239.

hinc Haemonio desponsa rogo
ducunt turmas, haec femineas,
ille viriles.   festae matres
votiva ferunt munera divis ;
festi patres adeunt aras,
unus tota est vultus in urbe ;
et, quod numquam post Hectoreos
vidimus ignes, laeta est Hecuba.
quid nunc primum, dolor infelix,
quidve extremum deflere paras ?   650
moenia, divum fabricata manu,
diruta nostra ?
an templa deos super usta suos ?
non vacat istis lacrimare malis—
te, magne parens, flent Iliades.
vidi, vidi senis in iugulo
telum Pyrrhi vix exiguo
sanguine tingui.

CASSANDRA

Cohibete lacrimas omne quas tempus petet,
Troades, et ipsae vestra lamentabili   660
lugete gemitu funera ; aerumnae meae
socium recusant.   cladibus questus meis
removete.   nostris ipsa sufficiam malis.

CHORVS

Lacrimas lacrimis miscere iuvat ;
magis exurunt quos secretae
lacerant curae, iuvat in medium
deflere suos ; nec tu, quamvis
dura virago patiensque mali,
poteris tantas flere ruinas.
non quae verno mobile carmen   670
ramo cantat tristis aedon

Astyanax leads, there she,[1] to the Thessalian pyre betrothed, she leading maids, he youths. Gaily do mothers bring votive offerings to the gods; gaily do fathers approach the shrines; each wears but one look the city o'er; and, what never we saw since Hector's funeral, Hecuba was glad. And now, unhappy grief, what first, what last, wilt thou lament? Walls by divine hands fashioned, by our own destroyed? Temples upon their own gods consumed? Time lacks to weep such ills—thee, O great father, the Trojan women weep. I saw, I saw in the old man's throat the sword of Pyrrhus scarce wet in his scanty blood.

CASSANDRA

Restrain your tears which all time will seek, ye Trojan women, and do you yourselves grieve for your own dead with groans and lamentations; my losses refuse all sharing. Cease then your grief for my disasters. I myself shall suffice for the woes of mine own house.

CHORUS

'Tis sweet to mingle tears with tears; griefs bring more smart where they wound in solitude, but 'tis sweet in company to bewail one's friends; nor shalt thou, though strong, heroic, and inured to woe, avail to lament calamities so great. Not the sad nightingale,[2] which from the vernal bough pours

---

[1] Polyxena. [2] Into which Philomela was changed.

Ityn in varios modulata sonos,
non quae tectis Bistonis ales
residens summis impia diri
furta mariti garrula narrat,
lugere tuam poterit digne
conquesta domum.   licet ipse velit
clarus niveos inter olores
Histrum cycnus Tanainque colens
extrema loqui, licet alcyones   680
Ceyca suum fluctu leviter
plangente sonent, cum tranquillo
male confisae credunt iterum
pelago audaces fetusque suos
nido pavidae titubante fovent ;
non si molles comitata viros
tristis laceret bracchia tecum
quae turritae turba parenti
pectora, rauco concita buxo,
ferit ut Phrygium lugeat Attin,—   690
non est lacrimis, Cassandra, modus,
quia quae patimur vicere modum.

Sed cur sacratas deripis capiti infulas ?
miseris colendos maxime superos putem.

CASSANDRA

Vicere nostra iam metus omnes mala.
equidem nec ulla caelites placo prece
nec, si velint saevire, quo noceant habent.
Fortuna vires ipsa consumpsit suas.
quae patria restat, quis pater, quae iam soror ?

---

[1] The swallow (*hirundo*) into which Procne was changed.
[2] Cycnus (see Index) is here conceived of as swan rather than man.

forth her liquid song, piping of Itys in ever changing
strains; not the bird [1] which, perching on Bistonian
battlements, tells o'er and o'er the hidden sins of
her cruel lord, will e'er be able, with all her passionate
lament, worthily to mourn thy house. Should bright
Cycnus' [2] self, haunting midst snowy swans Ister
and Tanaïs, utter his dying song; should halcyons
mourn their Ceyx midst the light wave's lapping,
when, though distrustful, boldly they trust once
more to the tranquil ocean, and anxiously on un-
steady nest cherish their young; should the sad
throng which follows the unmanned men [3] bruise
their arms along with thee, the throng which, by the
shrill flute maddened, smite their breasts to the
tower-crowned mother,[4] that for Phrygian Attis they
may lament,—not so, Cassandra, is there measure
for our tears, for what we suffer has outmeasured
measure.

[693] But why dost tear off the holy fillets from thy
head? Methinks the gods should be most reverenced
by unhappy souls.

CASSANDRA

Now have our woes o'ermastered every fear.
Neither do I appease the heavenly gods by any
prayer, nor, should they wish to rage, have they
wherewith to harm me. Fortune herself has exhausted all her powers. What fatherland remains?
What father? What sister now? Altars [5] and

---

[3] Priests of Cybele.   [4] Cybele.
[5] Both her brother Polites and her father Priam had been
slain at the altar of Hercean Jove. See *Aen.* II. 526 ff.

bibere tumuli sanguinem atque arae meum.   700
quid illa felix turba fraterni gregis?
exhausta nempe ! regia miseri senes
vacua relicti ; totque per thalamos vident
praeter Lacaenam ceteras viduas nurus.
tot illa regum mater et regimen Phrygum,
fecunda in ignes Hecuba fatorum novas
experta leges induit vultus feros :
circa ruinas rabida latravit suas,
Troiae superstes, Hectori, Priamo, sibi !

CHORVS

Silet repente Phoebas et pallor genas   710
creberque totum possidet corpus tremor ;
stetere vittae, mollis horrescit coma,
anhela corda murmure incluso fremunt,
incerta nutant lumina et versi retro
torquentur oculi, rursus immoti rigent.
nunc levat in auras altior solito caput
graditurque celsa, nunc reluctantes parat
reserare fauces, verba nunc clauso male
custodit ore maenas impatiens dei.

CASSANDRA

Quid me furoris incitam stimulis novi   720
quid mentis inopem, sacra Parnasi iuga,
rapitis ? recede, Phoebe, iam non sum tua,
extingue flammas pectori infixas meo.
cui nunc vagor vaesana ? cui bacchor furens ?
iam Troia cecidit—falsa quid vates ago ?

tombs[1] have drunk up my blood. What of that
happy throng of brothers? Gone, all! in the
empty palace only sad old men are left; and
throughout those many chambers they see all
women, save her of Sparta, widowed. That mother
of so many kings, queen of the Phrygians, Hecuba,
fruitful for funeral-fires, proving new laws of fate,
has put on bestial form:[2] around her ruined walls
madly she barked, surviving Troy, son, husband—
and herself!

CHORUS

The bride of Phoebus suddenly is still, pallor
o'erspreads her cheeks, and constant tremors master
all her frame. Her fillets stand erect, her soft locks
rise in horror, her labouring heart sounds loud with
pent murmuring, her glance wanders uncertain,
her eyes seem backward turned into herself, anon
they stare unmoving. Now she lifts her head into
the air higher than her wont, and walks with stately
tread; now makes to unlock her struggling lips, now
vainly tries to close them on her words, a mad
priestess fighting against the god.

CASSANDRA

Why, O Parnassus' sacred heights, do ye prick me
with fury's goads anew, why do you sweep me on,
bereft of sense? Away! O Phoebus, I am no
longer thine; quench thou the flames set deep
within my breast. For whose sake wander I now in
madness? for whose sake in frenzy rave? Now
Troy has fallen—what have I, false prophetess,
to do?

---

[1] Polyxena had been slain on Achilles' tomb.
[2] *i.e.* she was changed into a dog.

Vbi sum ? fugit lux alma et obscurat genas
nox alta et aether abditus tenebris latet.
sed ecce gemino sole praefulget dies
geminumque duplices Argos attollit domus.
Idaea cerno nemora ; fatalis sedet   730
inter potentes arbiter pastor deas.—
timete reges, moneo, furtivum genus ;
agrestis iste alumnus evertet domum.[1]
quid ista vaecors tela feminea manu
destricta praefert ? quem petit dextra virum
Lacaena cultu, ferrum Amazonium gerens ?—
quae versat oculos alia nunc facies meos ?
victor ferarum colla sublimis iacet
ignobili sub dente Marmaricus leo,
morsus cruentos passus audacis leae.—   740
quid me vocatis sospitem solam e meis,
umbrae meorum ? te sequor testis, pater,
Troiae sepultae ; frater, auxilium Phrygum
terrorque Danaum, non ego antiquum decus
video aut calentes ratibus exustis manus,
sed lacera membra et saucios vinclo gravi
illos lacertos ; te sequor, nimium cito
congresse Achilli Troile ; incertos geris,
Deiphobe, vultus, coniugis munus novae.
iuvat per ipsos ingredi Stygios lacus,   750
iuvat videre Tartari saevum canem
avidique regna Ditis ! haec hodie ratis
Phlegethontis atri regias animas vehet,
victamque victricemque. vos, umbrae, precor,
iurata superis unda, te pariter precor :

---

[1] *Wilamowitz conjectures that several lines have fallen out after l. 733, concerning the fates of Troy and the crimes of the Atridae. Lines 730–733 seem to Leo to be spurious.*

---

[1] These words have no logical connection with her previous utterance, and are a dark allusion to Aegisthus.

[726] Where am I? Fled is the kindly light, deep darkness blinds my eyes, and the sky, buried in gloom, is hidden away. But see! with double sun the day gleams forth, and double Argos lifts up twin palaces! Ida's groves I see; there sits the shepherd, fateful judge midst mighty goddesses.— Fear him, ye kings, I warn you, fear the child of stolen love;[1] that rustic foundling shall overturn your house. What means that mad woman with drawn sword in hand? What hero seeks she with her right hand, a Spartan in her garb,[2] but carrying an Amazonian axe?—What sight is that other which now employs mine eyes? The king of beasts with his proud neck, by a base fang lies low, an Afric lion, suffering the bloody bites of his bold lioness.— Why do ye summon me, saved only of my house, my kindred shades? Thee, father, do I follow, eye-witness of Troy's burial; thee, brother, help of the Phrygians, terror of the Greeks, I see not in thine old-time splendour, or with thine hands hot from the burning of the ships, but mangled of limb, with those arms wounded by the deep-sunk thongs; thee, Troilus, I follow, too early with Achilles met; unrecognisable the face thou wearest, Deiphobus,[3] the gift of thy new wife.[4] 'Tis sweet to fare along the very Stygian pools; sweet to behold Tartarus' savage dog and the realms of greedy Dis! To-day this skiff of murky Phlegethon shall bear royal souls,[5] vanquished and vanquisher. Ye shades, I pray; thou stream on which the gods make oath, thee no less I pray: for a little withdraw the

---

[2] She has a clairvoyant prevision of the act of Clytemnestra.
[3] See Vergil, *Aen.* VI. 494 ff.
[4] *i.e.* Helen.
[5] Her own and Agamemnon's.

reserate paulum terga nigrantis poli,
levis ut Mycenas turba prospiciat Phrygum.
spectate, miseri ; fata se vertunt retro.

    Instant sorores squalidae,
    sanguinea iactant verbera,   760
    fert laeva semustas faces
    turgentque pallentes genae
    et vestis atri funeris
    exesa cingit ilia,
    strepuntque nocturni metus
    et ossa vasti corporis
    corrupta longinquo situ
    palude limosa iacent.[1]
    et ecce, defessus senex
    ad ora ludentes aquas   770
    non captat oblitus sitim,
    maestus futuro funere ;
    exultat et ponit gradus
    pater decoros Dardanus.

CHORVS

Iam pervagatus ipse se fregit furor,
caditque flexo qualis ante aras genu
cervice taurus vulnus incertum gerens.
relevemus artus.   en deos tandem suos
victrice lauru cinctus Agamemnon adit,
et festa coniunx obvios illi tulit   780
gressus reditque iuncta concordi gradu.

AGAMEMNON

Tandem revertor sospes ad patrios lares ;
o cara salve terra.   tibi tot barbarae

---

[1] *Leo remarks upon the unintelligibility of ll. 766-768.*

covering of that dark world, that on Mycenae the
shadowy throng of Phrygians may look forth. Behold, poor souls; the fates turn backward on themselves.

759 They press on, the squalid sisters, their bloody
lashes brandishing; their left hands half-burned
torches bear; bloated are their pallid cheeks, and
dusky robes of death their hollow loins encircle;
the fearsome cries of night resound, and a huge
body's bones, rotting with long decay, lie in a slimy
marsh.[1] And see! that spent old man,[2] forgetting
thirst, no longer catches at the mocking waters,
grieving at death[3] to come; but father Dardanus
exults and walks along with stately tread.

CHORUS

Now has her rambling frenzy spent itself, and
falls, as before the altar with sinking knees falls the
bull, receiving an ill-aimed stroke upon his neck.
Let us lift up her body. But lo! at last to his own
gods, wreathed with victorious bay, Agamemnon
comes; his wife with joy has gone forth to meet
him, and now returns, joining her steps in harmony
with his.

[*Enter* AGAMEMNON. *He has been met and greeted by
his wife, who enters with him and goes on alone into
the palace.*]

AGAMEMNON

At length am I returned in safety to my father's
house. O dear land, hail! To thee many barbaric

---

[1] If Seneca wrote lines 766–768, he may have had some
definite reference in his mind unknown to us, or he may have
meant merely to add further gruesome detail to the picture.

[2] Tantalus.

[3] *i.e.* of Agamemnon, great-grandson of Tantalus.

dedere gentes spolia, tibi felix diu
potentis Asiae Troia summisit manus.—
quid ista vates corpus effusa ac tremens
dubia labat cervice ?   famuli, attollite,
refovete gelido latice.   iam recipit diem
marcente visu.   suscita sensus tuos !
optatus ille portus aerumnis adest.   790
festus dies est.

CASSANDRA

Festus et Troiae fuit.

AGAMEMNON

Veneremur aras.

CASSANDRA

Cecidit ante aras pater.

AGAMEMNON

Iovem precemur pariter.

CASSANDRA

Herceum Iovem ?

AGAMEMNON

Credis videre te Ilium ?

CASSANDRA

Et Priamum simul.

AGAMEMNON

Hic Troia non est.

CASSANDRA

Vbi Helena est Troiam puto.

---

[1] Cassandra.   [2] See Vergil, *Aen.* ii. 249.
[3] It was at the altar of Hercean Jove that Priam was
slain (*Aen.* ii. 512 ff.).

nations have given spoil, to thee proud Asia's Troy, long blest of heaven, has yielded.—Why does the priestess [1] there faint and fall tottering with drooping head? Slaves, lift her up, revive her with cool water. Now with languid gaze she again beholds the light. [*To* CASSANDRA.] Awake to life! that longed for haven from our woes is here; this is a festal day.

CASSANDRA

'Twas festal,[2] too, at Troy.

AGAMEMNON

Let us kneel before the altar.

CASSANDRA

Before the altar my father fell.

AGAMEMNON

To Jove let us pray together.

CASSANDRA

Hercean Jove?[3]

AGAMEMNON

Dost think thou lookst on Ilium?

CASSANDRA

And Priam, too.

AGAMEMNON

Here is not Troy.

CASSANDRA

Where a Helen [4] is, I think is Troy.

[4] *i.e.* an evil, adulterous woman such as Helen. Helen was not in Greece at this time. The reference is obviously to Clytemnestra.

65

AGAMEMNON

Ne metue dominam famula.

CASSANDRA

Libertas adest.

AGAMEMNON

Secura vive.

CASSANDRA

Mihi mori est securitas.

AGAMEMNON

Nullum est periclum tibimet.

CASSANDRA

At magnum tibi.

AGAMEMNON

Victor timere quid potest?

CASSANDRA

Quod non timet.

AGAMEMNON

Hanc fida famuli turba, dum excutiat deum,　800
retinete ne quid impotens peccet furor.
at te, pater, qui saeva torques fulmina
pellisque nubes, sidera et terras regis,
ad quem triumphi spolia victores ferunt,
et te sororem cuncta pollentis viri,
Argolica Iuno, pecore votivo libens
Arabumque donis supplice et fibra colam.

---

[1] Cassandra is supposed to be still under the influence of Apollo.

AGAMEMNON

AGAMEMNON

Fear thou no mistress, though a slave.

CASSANDRA

Freedom is near at hand.

AGAMEMNON

Live on, secure.

CASSANDRA

For me, death is security.

AGAMEMNON

For thee there is naught to fear.

CASSANDRA

But much for thee.

AGAMEMNON

What can a victor fear?

CASSANDRA

What he doth not fear.

AGAMEMNON

Ye faithful slaves, restrain her till she throw off
the god,[1] lest in her wild frenzy she do some harm.
But thee, O father, who the dire thunder hurlest,
and driv'st the clouds, who the stars and lands dost
rule, to whom in triumph victors bring their spoils;
and thee, sister of thine almighty lord, Argolian
Juno, gladly with votive flocks, with gifts [2] from
Araby, and with suppliant heart will I adore.

[*Exit into the palace.*]

[2] Incense.

CHORVS

Argos nobilibus nobile civibus,
Argos iratae carum novercae,
semper ingentes alumnos   810
educas, numerum deorum
imparem aequasti.   tuus ille
bis seno meruit labore
adlegi caelo
magnus Alcides, cui lege mundi
Iuppiter rupta geminavit horas
roscidae noctis iussitque Phoebum
tardius celeres agitare currus
et tuas lente remeare bigas,
pallida Phoebe ;
rettulit pedem
nomen alternis stella quae mutat   820
seque mirata est Hesperum dici ;
Aurora movit ad solitas vices
caput et relabens imposuit seni
collum marito.
sensit ortus, sensit occasus
Herculem nasci ; violentus ille
nocte non una poterat creari.
tibi concitatus substitit mundus,
o puer subiture caelum.

Te sensit Nemeaeus arto
pressus lacerto fulmineus leo   830
cervaque Parrhasis,
sensit Arcadii populator agri,

---

¹ *i.e.* to Juno, constantly angered by the children of Jove's
mistresses.

² Farnabius thus explains this curious statement : the
deification of Hercules (to which Juno at last consented)
added to the number, not of the great gods, who were

AGAMEMNON

CHORUS OF ARGIVE WOMEN

O Argos, ennobled by thy noble citizens, Argos, dear to the step-dame though enraged,[1] ever mighty sons thou fosterest and hast made even [2] the odd number of the gods. That hero of thine by his twelve labours earned the right to be chosen for the skies, great Hercules, for whom,[3] the world's law broken, Jove doubled the hours of dewy night, bade Phoebus more slowly drive his hastening car, and thy team to turn back with laggard feet, O pale Phoebe. Backward the star turned his steps, the star who changes from name to name,[4] and marvelled still to be called Hesperus, evening star. Aurora stirred at the accustomed hour of dawn, but, sinking back, laid her head and neck upon the breast of her aged husband.[5] The rising, yea, and the setting of the sun felt the birth of Hercules; a hero so mighty could not be begotten in a single night. For thee the whirling universe stood still, O boy, destined to mount the skies.

[829] The lightning-swift lion of Nemea felt thy power, crushed by thy straining arms, and the Parrhasian hind, the ravager [6] of Arcady's fields, felt

twelve in number, but of the gods of the second rank (*diis communibus*), three in number—Mars, Bellona, and Victoria —thus making even the number which had been odd.

[3] *i.e.* for his begetting. See *Herc. Fur.* ll 24 and 1158.

[4] *i.e.* it is now called Lucifer and now Hesperus, according as it is morning or evening star.

[5] Tithonus.

[6] The Erymanthian boar.

gemuitque taurus Dictaea linquens
horridus arva.
morte fecundum domuit draconem
vetuitque collo pereunte nasci,
geminosque fratres
pectore ex uno tria monstra natos
stipite incusso fregit insultans,
duxitque ad ortus Hesperium pecus,   840
Geryonae spolium triformis.
egit Threicium gregem,
quem non Strymonii gramine fluminis
Hebrive ripis pavit tyrannus ;
hospitum dirus stabulis cruorem
praebuit saevis tinxitque crudos
ultimus rictus sanguis aurigae.
vidit Hippolyte ferox
pectore e medio rapi
spolium, et sagittis
nube percussa Stymphalis alto   850
decidit caelo ;
arborque pomis fertilis aureis
extimuit manus insueta carpi
fugitque in auras leviore ramo.
audivit sonitum crepitante lamna
frigidus custos nescius somni,
linqueret cum iam nemus omne fulvo
plenus Alcides vacuum metallo.
tractus ad caelum canis inferorum
triplici catena tacuit nec ullo   860
latravit ore,
lucis ignotae metuens colorem.

---

[1] It was the nature of the hydra that as each head was cut
off two appeared in its place.

[2] *geminos* here = *trigeminos*, referring to the triple-man
monster, Geryon.

thee, too, and loud bellowed the savage bull, leaving
the fields of Crete. The hydra, fertile in death, he
overcame and forbade new births from each neck
destroyed;[1] the mated[2] brethren, springing three
monsters from a single body, he crushed, leaping on
them with his crashing club, and brought to the
east the western herd, spoil of the three-formed
Geryon. He drove the Thracian herd[3] which the
tyrant fed, not on the grass of the Strymon or on
the banks of the Hebrus; cruel, he offered his savage
horses the gore of strangers—and the blood of their
driver[4] was the last to stain red their jaws. Warlike
Hippolyte saw the spoil[5] snatched from about her
breast; and by his shafts down from the riven cloud
from high heaven fell the Stymphalian bird. The
tree, laden with golden fruit, shrank from his hands,
unused to such plucking, and the bough, relieved of
its burden, sprang into the air. The cold, sleepless
guardian[6] heard the sound of the clinking metal,
only when heavy laden Alcides was leaving the grove
all stripped of its tawny gold. Dragged to the upper
world by triple fetters, the infernal dog was silent,
nor with any mouth did he bay, shrinking from the
hues of unexperienced light. Under thy leader-

[3] The man-eating horses of Diomedes, tyrant of Thrace.
[4] *i.e.* Hercules gave Diomedes to his own horses to devour.
[5] The famous golden girdle.
[6] The dragon, set to guard the golden apples.

te duce succidit
mendax Dardanidae domus
et sensit arcus iterum timendos ;
te duce concidit
totidem diebus Troia quot annis.

CASSANDRA

Res agitur intus magna, par annis decem.
eheu quid hoc est ?   anime, consurge et cape
pretium furoris—vicimus victi Phryges !
bene est, resurgit Troia ; traxisti iacens,   870
parens, Mycenas, terga dat victor tuus !
tam clara numquam providae mentis furor
ostendit oculis ; video et intersum et fruor ;
imago visus dubia non fallit meos ;
spectemus.
        Epulae regia instructae domo,
quales fuerunt ultimae Phrygibus dapes,
celebrantur ; ostro lectus Iliaco nitet
merumque in auro veteris Assaraci trahunt.
en ipse picta veste sublimis iacet,
Priami superbas corpore exuvias gerens.   880
detrahere cultus uxor hostiles iubet,
induere potius coniugis fidae manu
textos amictus—horreo atque animo tremo !
regemne perimet exul et adulter virum ?
venere fata.   sanguinem extremae dapes
domini videbunt et cruor Baccho incidet.
mortifera vinctum perfide tradit neci
induta vestis ; exitum manibus negant

---

[1] In the time of Laomedon.
[2] The arrows of Hercules in the hands of Philoctetes
assisted in the final fall of Troy under Priam.
[3] She either stands where she can see the interior of the

ship fell the lying house[1] of Dardanus and suffered
the arrows, once again[2] to be feared; under thy
leadership in as many days Troy fell as it took years
thereafter.

CASSANDRA [*alone upon the stage*][3]

A great deed is done within, a match for ten years
of war. Ah! What is this? Rise up, my soul, and
take the reward of thy madness—we are conquerors,
we conquered Phrygians! 'Tis well! Troy has risen
again! In thy fall, O father, thou hast dragged
down Mycenae; thy conqueror gives way! Never
before did my mind's prophetic frenzy give sight to
mine eyes so clear; I see, I am in the midst of it, I
revel in it; 'tis no doubtful image cheats my sight;
let me gaze my fill.

[875] A feast is spread within the royal house and
thronged with guests, like that last banquet of the
Phrygians; the couches gleam with Trojan purple,
and their wine they quaff from the golden cups of
old Assaracus. Lo, he himself[4] in broidered vest-
ments lies on lofty couch, wearing on his body the
proud spoils of Priam. His wife bids him doff the
raiment of his foe and don instead a mantle her own
fond hands have woven—I shudder and my soul
trembles at the sight! Shall an exile[5] slay a king?
an adulterer[5] the husband? The fatal hour has
come. The banquet's close shall see the master's
blood, and gore shall fall into the wine. The deadly
mantle he has put on delivers him bound treacherously to his doom; the loose, impenetrable folds

palace, and describes what is going on within, or else she
sees it by clairvoyant power.
[4] Agamemnon.   [5] Aegisthus.

caputque laxi et invii claudunt sinus.
haurit trementi semivir dextra latus,   890
nec penitus egit; vulnere in medio stupet.
at ille, ut altis hispidus silvis aper
cum casse vinctus temptat egressus tamen
artatque motu vincla et in cassum furit,—
cupit fluentes undique et caecos sinus
disicere et hostem quaerit implicitus suum.
armat bipenni Tyndaris dextram furens,
qualisque ad aras colla taurorum popa
designat oculis antequam ferro petat,
sic huc et illuc impiam librat manum.   900
habet! peractum est! pendet exigua male
caput amputatum parte et hinc trunco cruor
exundat, illic ora cum fremitu iacent.
nondum recedunt; ille iam exanimem petit
laceratque corpus, illa fodientem adiuvat.
uterque tanto scelere respondet suis—
est hic Thyeste natus, haec Helenae soror.
stat ecce Titan dubius emerito die,
suane currat an Thyestea via.

ELECTRA

Fuge, o paternae mortis auxilium unicum,   910
fuge et scelestas hostium vita manus.
eversa domus est funditus, regna occidunt.
    Hospes quis iste concitos currus agit?
germane, vultus veste furabor tuos.

---

¹ *i.e.* Clytemnestra, daughter of Tyndareus.
² *i.e.* the wound. The formula is taken from the gladiatorial contests.

74

refuse outlet to his hands and enshroud his head.
With trembling right hand the half-man stabs at his
side, but hath not driven deep; in mid stroke he
stands as one amazed. But he, as in the deep woods
a bristling boar, though with the net entangled, still
tries for freedom, and by his struggling draws close
his bonds and rages all in vain,—he strives to throw
off the blinding folds all around him floating, and,
though closely enmeshed, seeks for his foe. Now
Tyndaris [1] in mad rage snatches a two-edged axe
and, as at the altar the priest marks with his eye the
oxen's necks before he strikes, so, now here, now
there, her impious hand she aims. He has it! [2] the
deed is done! The scarce severed head hangs by a
slender part; here blood streams o'er his headless
trunk, there lie his moaning lips. And not yet do
they give o'er; *he* attacks the already lifeless man,
and keeps hacking at the corpse; *she* helps him in
the stabbing. Each one in this dire crime answers
to his own kin—he is Thyestes' son, she, Helen's
sister. See, Titan, the day's work done, stands
hesitant whether his own or Thyestes' [3] course to run.

[*Remains beside the altar.*

[*Enter* ELECTRA, *leading her young brother,* ORESTES.]

ELECTRA

Fly, O sole avenger of our father's death, fly and
escape our enemies' miscreant hands. O'erthrown
is our house to its foundations, our kingdom fallen.

[913] But who is yonder stranger, driving his chariot
at speed? Come brother, I will hide thee 'neath my

---

[3] *i.e.* backward as on the occasion of Thyestes' banquet on
his own sons.

quid, anime demens, refugis ?   externos times ?
domus timenda est.   pone iam trepidos metus,
Oresta ; amici fida praesidia intuor.

STROPHIVS

Phocide relicta Strophius Elea inclutus
palma revertor.   causa veniendi fuit
gratari amico, cuius impulsum manu   920
cecidit decenni Marte concussum Ilium.
quaenam ista lacrimis lugubrem vultum rigat
pavetque maesta ?   regium agnosco genus.
Electra !   fletus causa quae laeta in domo est ?

ELECTRA

Pater peremptus scelere materno iacet,
comes paternae quaeritur natus neci,
Aegisthus arces Venere quaesitas tenet.

STROPHIVS

O nulla longi temporis felicitas !

ELECTRA

Per te parentis memoriam obtestor mei,
per sceptra terris nota, per dubios deos ;   930
recipe hunc Oresten ac pium furtum occule.

robe. Why, foolish heart, dost thou shrink away?
Strangers dost fear? 'Tis our home that must be
feared. Put away now thy trembling dread, Orestes;
the trusty protection of a friend I see.

[*Enter* STROPHIUS *in a chariot, accompanied by his son*
PYLADES.]

STROPHIUS

I, Strophius, had Phocis left, and now am home
returning, made glorious by the Elean palm. The
cause of my coming hither was to congratulate my
friend, o'erthrown by whose hand and crushed by
ten years of war has Ilium fallen. [*He notices*
ELECTRA'S *distress.*] But who is that yonder, watering
her sad face with tears, fear-struck and sorrowful?
One of the royal house I recognize. Electra! What
cause of weeping can be in this glad house?

ELECTRA

My father lies murdered by my mother's crime;
they seek the son to share in his father's death;
Aegisthus holds the throne by guilty love secured.

STROPHIUS

Alas! no happiness is of lengthened stay.

ELECTRA

By the memory of my father I beseech thee, by
his sceptre known to all the world, by the fickle
gods:[1] take this boy, Orestes, and hide the holy
theft.

---

[1] Who may bring quick downfall to thee also.

77

STROPHIVS

Etsi timendum caesus Agamemnon docet,
aggrediar et te, Oresta, furabor libens.
fidem secunda poscunt, adversa exigunt.[1]
cape hoc decorum ludicri certaminis,
insigne frontis ; laeva victricem tenens
frondem virenti protegat ramo caput,
et ista donum palma Pisaei Iovis
velamen eadem praestet atque omen tibi.
tuque o paternis assidens frenis comes,   940
condisce, Pylade, patris exemplo fidem.
vos Graecia nunc teste veloces equi
infida cursu fugite praecipiti loca.

ELECTRA

Excessit, abiit, currus effreno impetu
effugit aciem.   tuta iam opperiar meos
hostes et ultro vulneri opponam caput.
Adest cruenta coniugis victrix sui
et signa caedis veste maculata gerit.
manus recenti sanguine etiamnunc madent
vultusque prae se scelera truculenti ferunt.   950
concedam ad aras.   patere me vittis tuis,
Cassandra, iungi paria metuentem tibi.

CLYTAEMNESTRA

Hostis parentis, impium atque audax caput,
quo more coetus publicos virgo petis ?

> [1] *Leo deletes this line, following Peiper.*

---

[1] Of olive.   [2] Of palm.   [3] In the Olympic games.

AGAMEMNON

Although murdered Agamemnon warns me to beware, I will brave the danger and gladly, Orestes, will I steal thee off. Good fortune asks for faith, adversity demands it. [*Takes* ORESTES *into the chariot.*] Take thou this crown,[1] won in the games, as an ornament for thy head, and, holding this victor's bough [2] in thy left hand, shield thy face with its great branch, and may that palm, the gift of Pisaean Jove, afford thee at once a covering and an omen. And do thou, Pylades, who standest as comrade to guide thy father's car, learn faith from the example of thy sire. And now, do you, my horses, whose speed all Greece has seen,[3] flee from this treacherous place in headlong flight. [*Exeunt at great speed.*

ELECTRA [*looking after them*]

He has departed, gone, his car at a reckless pace has vanished from my sight. Now free from care shall I await my foes, and willingly oppose myself to death. [*She sees* CLYTEMNESTRA *approaching.*]
[947] Here is the bloody conqueror of her lord, with the signs of murder on her blood-stained robe. Her hands are still reeking with blood fresh-spilled, and her savage features bear tokens of her crime. I'll take me to the altar. Let me be joined, Cassandra, with thy fillets,[4] since I fear like doom with thee.

[*Enter* CLYTEMNESTRA.]

CLYTEMNESTRA

Foe of thy mother, unfilial and froward girl, by what custom dost thou, a maid, seek public gatherings?

[4] *i.e.* let me join her who with the sacred fillets on her head has taken refuge at the altar.

ELECTRA

Adulterorum virgo deserui domum.

CLYTAEMNESTRA

Quis esse credat virginem?

ELECTRA

Natam tuam?

CLYTAEMNESTRA

Modestius cum matre!

ELECTRA

Pietatem doces?

CLYTAEMNESTRA

Animos viriles corde tumefacto geris
sed agere domita feminam disces malo.

ELECTRA

Nisi forte fallor, feminas ferrum decet.   960

CLYTAEMNESTRA

Et esse demens te parem nobis putas?

ELECTRA

Vobis?   quis iste est alter Agamemnon tuus?
ut vidua loquere; vir caret vita tuus.

CLYTAEMNESTRA

Indomita posthac virginis verba impiae
regina frangam; citius interea mihi
edissere ubi sit natus, ubi frater tuus.

ELECTRA

Because I am a maid have I left the adulterers home.

CLYTEMNESTRA

Who would believe thee maid?

ELECTRA

A child of thine?[1]

CLYTEMNESTRA

More gently with thy mother!

ELECTRA

Dost thou teach piety?

CLYTEMNESTRA

Thou hast a mannish soul, a heart puffed up; but, tamed by suffering, shalt thou learn to play a woman's part.

ELECTRA

If perchance, I mistake not, a sword befits a woman.

CLYTEMNESTRA

And thinkest thou, mad one, thou art a match for us?

ELECTRA

For you? What other Agamemnon is that of thine? Speak thou as widow; lifeless is thy lord.

CLYTEMNESTRA

The unbridled tongue of an unfilial girl hereafter as queen I'll check; meanwhile be quick and tell where is my son, where is thy brother.

[1] *i.e.* surely no one, since I am thy child.

ELECTRA

Extra Mycenas.

CLYTAEMNESTRA

Redde nunc natum mihi.

ELECTRA

Et tu parentem redde.

CLYTAEMNESTRA

Quo latitat loco?

ELECTRA

Tuto quietus, regna non metuens nova ;
iustae parenti satis.

CLYTAEMNESTRA

At iratae parum.   970
morieris hodie.

ELECTRA

Dummodo hac moriar manu.
recedo ab aris.   sive te iugulo iuvat
mersisse ferrum, praebeo iugulum tibi ;
seu more pecudum colla resecari placet,
intenta cervix vulnus expectat tuum.
scelus paratum est ; caede respersam viri
atque obsoletam sanguine hoc dextram ablue.

CLYTAEMNESTRA

Consors pericli pariter ac regni mei,
Aegisthe, gradere.   nata genetricem impie
probris lacessit, occulit fratrem abditum.   980

ELECTRA

Far from Mycenae.

CLYTEMNESTRA

Restore me now my son.

ELECTRA

And do thou restore my father.

CLYTEMNESTRA

Where does he hide?

ELECTRA

In peace and safety, where he fears no new-made king; for a righteous mother 'tis enough.

CLYTEMNESTRA

But too little for an angry one. Thou shalt die this day.

ELECTRA

So but it be by this hand of thine. I leave the altar. If 'tis thy pleasure in my throat to plunge the sword, I offer my throat to thee; or if, as men smite sheep, thou wouldst cut off my neck, my bent neck waits thy stroke. The crime is ready; thy right hand, smeared and rank with a husband's slaughter, purge with this blood of mine.

[*Enter* AEGISTHUS.]

CLYTEMNESTRA

Thou partner equally in my perils and my throne, Aegisthus, come. My child undutifully insults her mother, and keeps her brother hidden.

83

AEGISTHVS

Furibunda virgo, vocis infandae sonum
et aure verba indigna materna opprime.

ELECTRA

Etiam monebit sceleris infandi artifex,
per scelera natus, nomen ambiguum suis,
idem sororis natus et patris nepos ?

CLYTAEMNESTRA

Aegisthe, cessas impium ferro caput
demetere ?   fratrem reddat aut animam statim.

AEGISTHVS

Abstrusa caeco carcere et saxo exigat
aevum, et per omnes torta poenarum modos
referre quem nunc occulit forsan volet.   990
inops egens inclusa, paedore obruta,
vidua ante thalamos, exul, invisa omnibus
aethere negato sero subcumbet malis.

ELECTRA

Concede mortem.

AEGISTHVS

Si recusares, darem.
rudis est tyrannus morte qui poenam exigit.

ELECTRA

Mortem aliquid ultra est?

AEGISTHUS

Mad girl, hold thy impious tongue, and speak not words unworthy thy mother's ears.

ELECTRA

Shall he e'en give instructions, the worker of an impious crime, one criminally begot, whom even his own parents cannot name, son of his sister, grandson of his sire?

CLYTEMNESTRA

Aegisthus, why dost hesitate to strike off her wicked head with the sword? Let her at once give up her brother or her life.

AEGISTHUS

Mured in a dark, rocky dungeon shall she spend her life and, by all kinds of tortures racked, perchance she will consent to give back him she now conceals. Resourceless, starving, in prison pent, buried in filth, widowed ere wedded, in exile, scorned by all, denied the light of day, then will she, though too late, yield to her doom.

ELECTRA

Oh, grant me death.

AEGISTHUS

Shouldst plead against, I'd grant. An unskilled tyrant he who punishes by death.

ELECTRA

Is aught worse than death?

AEGISTHVS

            Vita, si cupias mori.
abripite, famuli, monstrum et avectam procul
ultra Mycenas ultimo in regni angulo
vincite saeptam nocte tenebrosi specus,
ut inquietam virginem carcer domet.   1000

CLYTAEMNESTRA

At ista poenas capite persolvet suo
captiva coniunx, regii paelex tori.
trahite, ut sequatur coniugem ereptum mihi.

CASSANDRA

Ne trahite, vestros ipsa praecedam gradus.
perferre prima nuntium Phrygibus meis
propero—repletum ratibus eversis mare,
captas Mycenas, mille ductorem ducum,
ut paria fata Troicis lueret malis,
perisse dono feminae—stupro, dolo.
nihil moramur, rapite, quin grates ago.   1010
iam, iam iuvat vixisse post Troiam, iuvat.

CLYTAEMNESTRA

Furiosa, morere.

CASSANDRA

           Veniet et vobis furor.

AEGISTHUS

Yes, life, if thou longest to die. Away, ye slaves, with this unnatural girl; far from Mycenae bear her, and in the remotest corner of the realm chain her immured in the black darkness of a cell, that prison walls may curb the unmanageable maid. [ELECTRA *is dragged away.*]

CLYTEMNESTRA [*indicating* CASSANDRA]

But she shall pay her penalty with death, that captive bride, that mistress of the royal bed. Drag her away, that she may follow the husband whom she stole from me.

CASSANDRA

Nay, drag me not, I will precede your going. I hasten to be first to bear news unto my Phrygians— of the sea covered with the wrecks of ships, of Mycenae taken, of the leader of a thousand leaders (that so he might meet doom equal to Troy's woes) slain by a woman's gift—by adultery, by guile. Take me away; I hold not back, but rather give you thanks. Now, now 'tis sweet to have outlived Troy, 'tis sweet.

CLYTEMNESTRA

Mad creature, thou shalt die.

CASSANDRA

On you, as well, a madness is to come.[1]

---

[1] Referring to the madness of Orestes, who is later to slay both Aegisthus and Clytemnestra.

THYESTES

DRAMATIS PERSONAE

THYESTES, *brother of Atreus, in exile from his fatherland.*

THE GHOST OF TANTALUS, *doomed for his sins to come back to earth and inspire his house to greater sin.*

THE FURY, *who drives the ghost on to do his allotted part.*

ATREUS, *king of Argos, grandson of Tantalus, who has quarrelled with his brother and driven him into exile.*

AN ATTENDANT OF ATREUS.

THREE SONS OF THYESTES, *Tantalus, Plisthenes, and another, only one of whom, Tantalus, takes part in the dialogue.*

A MESSENGER.

CHORUS, *Citizens of Mycenae.*

THE SCENE is laid partly without the city of Argos, and partly within the royal palace.

ARGUMENT

Pelops, *the son of* Tantalus, *had banished his sons for the murder of their half-brother, Chrysippus, with a curse upon them, that they and their posterity might perish by each others' hands.   Upon the death of Pelops, Atreus returned and took possession of his father's throne.   Thyestes, also, claimed the throne, and sought to gain it by the foulest means.   For he seduced his brother's wife, Aërope, and stole by her assistance the magical, gold-fleeced ram from Atreus' flocks, upon the possession of which the right to rule was said to rest. For this act he was banished by the king.*

But Atreus has long been meditating a more complete revenge upon his brother ; and now in pretended friendship has recalled him from banishment, offering him a place beside himself upon the throne, that thus he may have Thyestes entirely in his power.

THYESTES

TANTALI VMBRA

Quis inferorum sede ab infausta extrahit
avido fugaces ore captantem cibos,
quis male deorum Tantalo vivas [1] domos
ostendit iterum?   peius inventum est siti
arente in undis aliquid et peius fame
hiante semper ?   Sisyphi numquid lapis
gestandus umeris lubricus nostris venit
aut membra celeri differens cursu rota,
aut poena Tityi qui specu vasto patens
visceribus atras pascit effossis aves   10
et nocte reparans quidquid amisit die
plenum recenti pabulum monstro iacet ?
in quod malum transcribor ?   o quisquis nova
supplicia functis durus umbrarum arbiter
disponis, addi si quid ad poenas potest
quod ipse custos carceris diri horreat,
quod maestus Acheron paveat, ad cuius metum
nos quoque tremamus, quaere.   iam nostra subit
e stirpe turba quae suum vincat genus
ac me innocentem faciat et inausa audeat.   20
regione quidquid impia cessat loci
complebo ; numquam stante Pelopea domo
Minos vacabit.

[1] *So A : Leo* visas, *with E :* invisas *N. Heinsius.*

THYESTES

THE GHOST OF TANTALUS

Who from the accursed regions of the dead haleth me forth, snatching at food which ever fleeth from my hungry lips? What god for his undoing showeth again to Tantalus the abodes of the living? Hath something worse been found than parching thirst midst water, worse than ever-gaping hunger? Cometh the slippery stone of Sisyphus to be borne upon my shoulders? or the wheel[1] stretching apart my limbs in its swift round? or Tityus' pangs, who, stretched in a huge cavern, with torn out vitals feeds the dusky birds and, by night renewing whate'er he lost by day, lies an undiminished banquet for new monsters? To what new suffering am I shifted? O whoe'er thou art, harsh judge of shades, who dost allot fresh punishments to the dead, if aught can be added to my sufferings whereat e'en the guardian of our dread prison-house would quake, whereat sad Acheron would be seized with dread, with fear whereof I, too, should tremble, seek thou it out. Now from my seed a multitude is coming up which its own race shall out-do, which shall make me seem innocent, and dare things yet undared. Whatever space is still empty in the unholy realm, I[2] shall fill up; never, while Pelops' house is standing, will Minos[3] be at rest.

[1] Of Ixion. [2] *i.e.* with my descendants.
[3] A judge in Hades.

FVRIA

Perge, detestabilis
umbra, et penates impios furiis age.
certetur omni scelere et alterna vice
stringatur ensis ; ne sit irarum modus
pudorve, mentes caecus instiget furor,
rabies parentum duret et longum nefas
eat in nepotes ; nec vacet cuiquam vetus
odisse crimen—semper oriatur novum,   30
nec unum in uno, dumque punitur scelus,
crescat.   superbis fratribus regna excidant
repetantque profugos ; dubia violentae domus
fortuna reges inter incertos labet ;
miser ex potente fiat, ex misero potens
fluctuque regnum casus assiduo ferat.
ob scelera pulsi, cum dabit patriam deus
in scelera redeant, sintque tam invisi omnibus,
quam sibi ; nihil sit ira quod vetitum putet :
fratrem expavescat frater et natum parens   40
natusque patrem, liberi pereant male,
peius tamen nascantur ; immineat viro
infesta coniunx, bella trans pontum vehant,
effusus omnes irriget terras cruor,
supraque magnos gentium exultet duces
Libido victrix.   impia stuprum in domo
levissimum sit ; fratris et fas et fides
iusque omne pereat.   non sit a vestris malis
immune caelum—cur micant stellae polo
flammaeque servant debitum mundo decus ?   50

---

[1] Let the brothers, Atreus and Thyestes, reign, fall, be
exiled and recalled, each in turn. In the present case Atreus
94

THYESTES

Onward, damned shade, and goad thy sinful house
to madness. Let there be rivalry in guilt of every
kind; let the sword be drawn on this side and on
that; let their passions know no bounds, no shame;
let blind fury prick on their souls; heartless be
parents' rage, and to children's children let the long
trail of sin lead down; let time be given to none to
hate old sins—ever let new arise, many in one, and
let crime, e'en midst its punishment, increase. From
haughty brothers' hands let kingdoms fall, and in
turn let them call back the fugitives;[1] let the wavering fortune of a home of violence midst changing
kings totter to its fall; from power to wretchedness,
from wretchedness to power—may this befall, and
may chance with her ever-restless waves bear the
kingdom on. For crimes' sake exiled, when God
shall bring them home, to crime may they return,
and may they be as hateful to all men as to themselves; let there be naught which passion deems un-
allowed; let brother brother fear, father fear son,
and son father; let children vilely perish and be yet
more vilely born; let a murderous wife lift hand
against her husband, let wars pass over sea, let
streaming blood drench every land, and over the
mighty chiefs of earth let Lust exult, triumphant.
In this sin-stained house let shameful defilement be
a trivial thing; let fraternal sanctity and faith and
every right be trampled under foot. By our sins let
not heaven be untainted—why do the stars glitter in
the sky? Why do their fires preserve the glory due
the world? Let the face of night be changed, let

is on the throne, and Thyestes, who has been exiled, is
recalled.

nox alia fiat, excidat caelo dies.
misce penates, odia caedes funera
arcesse et imple Tantalo totam domum.[1]
  Ornetur altum columen et lauro fores
laetae virescant, dignus adventu tuo
splendescat ignis—Thracium fiat nefas
maiore numero. dextra cur patrui vacat?
nondum Thyestes liberos deflet suos—
et quando tollet? ignibus iam subditis
spument aena, membra per partes eant   60
discerpta, patrios polluat sanguis focos,
epulae instruantur—non novi sceleris tibi
conviva venies. liberum dedimus diem
tuamque ad istas solvimus mensas famem;
ieiunia exple, mixtus in Bacchum cruor
spectante te potetur; inveni dapes
quas ipse fugeres—siste, quo praeceps ruis?

TANTALI VMBRA

  Ad stagna et amnes et recedentes aquas
labrisque ab ipsis arboris plenae fugas.
abire in atrum carceris liceat mei   70
cubile, liceat, si parum videor miser,
mutare ripas; alveo medius tuo,
Phlegethon, relinquar igneo cinctus freto.
  Quicumque poenas lege fatorum datas
pati iuberis, quisquis exeso iaces
pavidus sub antro iamque venturi times
montis ruinam, quisquis avidorum feros
rictus leonum et dira Furiarum agmina

[1] imple scelere Tantaleam domum A.

---

  [1] Procne and her wronged sister, Philomela, served up
Itys as a banquet to his father, Tereus, king of Thrace.
  [2] <i>i.e.</i> with the murder of three sons instead of one.

day fall from heaven. Embroil thy household gods, summon up hatred, slaughter, death, and fill the whole house with Tantalus.

⁵⁴ Adorn the lofty pillar and with laurel let the festal doors be green; let torches worthy of thine approach shine forth—then let the Thracian crime[1] be done with greater number.[2] Why is the uncle's[3] hand inactive? Not yet does Thyestes bewail his sons—and when will he lift his hand? Now set o'er the flames let cauldrons foam; let the rent members one by one pass in; let the ancestral hearth be stained with blood, let the feast be spread—to no novel feast of crime[4] wilt come as banqueter. To-day have we made thee free, have loosed thy hunger to the banquet yonder; go, feed full thy fasting, and let blood, with wine commingled, be drunk before thine eyes. I have found feast which thou thyself wouldst flee— but stay! Whither dost headlong rush?

GHOST OF TANTALUS

Back to my pools and streams and fleeing waters, back to the laden tree which shuns my very lips. Let me return to the black couch of my prison-house; let it be mine, if I seem too little wretched, to change my stream; in thy bed's midst, O Phlegethon, let me be left, hemmed round with waves of fire.

⁷⁴ Whoe'er thou art, by the fates' law bidden to suffer allotted punishment; whoe'er liest quaking beneath the hollowed rock, and fearest the downfall of the mountainous mass even now coming on thee;[5] whoe'er shudderest at the fierce gaping of greedy lions, and, entangled in their toils, dost shudder at

---

[3] *i.e.* Atreus.   [4] See Index *s.v.* Pelops.
[5] A common conception of punishment in Hades. See Vergil, *Aen.* VI. 601.

implicitus horres, quisquis immissas faces
semiustus abigis, Tantali vocem excipe   80
properantis ad vos : credite experto mihi,
amate poenas.   quando continget mihi
effugere superos ?

FVRIA

Ante perturba domum
inferque tecum proelia et ferri malum
regibus amorem, concute insano ferum
pectus tumultu.

TANTALI VMBRA

Me pati poenas decet,
non esse poenam.   mittor ut dirus vapor
tellure rupta vel gravem populis luem
sparsura pestis, ducam in horrendum nefas
avus nepotes.   magne divorum parens   90
nosterque, quamvis pudeat, ingenti licet
taxàta poena lingua crucietur loquax,
nec hoc tacebo ; moneo, ne sacra [1] manus
violate caede neve furiali malo
aspergite aras.   stabo et arcebo scelus—

Quid ora terres verbere et tortos ferox
minaris angues ?   quid famem infixam intimis
agitas medullis ?   flagrat incensum siti
cor et perustis flamma visceribus micat—
sequor.[2]   100

FVRIA

Hunc, hunc furorem divide in totam domum !
sic, sic ferantur et suum infensi invicem
sitiant cruorem.   sentit introitus tuos

<hr>

[1] *So A : Leo* sacras.   [2] *Leo deletes this word.*

the dread ranks of furies; whoe'er, half burned, shunnest their threatening torches, hear ye the words of Tantalus now hasting to you: believe me who know, and love your punishments. Oh, when shall it fall to me to escape the upper world?

THE FURY

First throw thy house into confusion dire, bring strife with thee, bring lust for the sword, an evil thing for rulers, and rouse to mad passion the savage breast.

GHOST OF TANTALUS

'Tis meet for me to suffer punishments, not be a punishment. I am sent as some deadly exhalation from the riven earth, or as a pestilence, spreading grievous plague among the people, that I a grandsire may lead my grandsons into fearful crime. O mighty sire of gods, my father, too, however to thy shame I say it, though to cruel punishment my tattling tongue be doomed, I will not hold my peace; I warn ye, defile not your hands with accursed slaughter, nor stain your altars with a madman's crime. Here will I stand and prevent the evil deed. [*To* THE FURY.] Why with thy scourge dost fright mine eyes, and fiercely threaten with thy writhing snakes? Why deep in my inmost marrow dost rouse hunger pains? My heart is parched with burning thirst, and in my scorched vitals the fire is darting—I follow thee.

THE FURY

This, this very rage of thine distribute throughout thy house! So, e'en as thou, may they be driven on, raging to quench their thirst each in the other's blood. Thy house feels thy near approach, and has

domus et nefando tota contactu horruit.
actum est abunde ! gradere ad infernos specus
amnemque notum ; iam tuum maestae pedem
terrae gravantur. cernis ut fontes liquor
introrsus actus linquat, ut ripae vacent
ventusque raras igneus nubes ferat?
pallescit omnis arbor ac nudus stetit 110
fugiente pomo ramus, et qua fluctibus
illinc propinquis Isthmos atque illinc fremit
vicina gracili dividens terra vada,
longe remotos litus exaudit sonos.
iam Lerna retro cessit et Phoronides
latuere venae nec suas profert sacer
Alpheos undas et Cithaeronis iuga
stant parte nulla cana deposita nive
timentque veterem nobiles Argi sitim.
en ipse Titan dubitat an iubeat sequi 120
cogatque habenis ire periturum diem.

CHORVS

Argos de superis si quis Achaicum
Pisaeasque domos curribus inclitas,
Isthmi si quis amat regna Corinthii
et portus geminos et mare dissidens,
si quis Taygeti conspicuas nives,
quas cum Sarmaticus tempore frigido
in summis Boreas composuit iugis,
aestas veliferis solvit Etesiis,
quem tangit gelido flumine lucidus 130
Alpheos, stadio notus Olympico,
advertat placidum numen et arceat,
alternae scelerum ne redeant vices
nec succedat avo deterior nepos

shrunk in utter horror from thine accursed touch.
Enough! more than enough! Go thou to the infernal
caves and well-known stream; now is the grieving
earth weary of thy presence. Seest thou how the
water, driven far within, deserts the springs, how
river banks are empty, how the fiery wind drives
away the scattered clouds? Every tree grows pale,
and from the bare branches the fruit has fled; and
where this side and that the Isthmus is wont to roar
with neighbouring waves, dividing near seas with
narrow neck of land, the shore but faintly hears the
far off sound. Now Lerna has shrunk back, the
Phoronean stream [1] has disappeared, the sacred Alpheus no longer bears his waters on, Cithaeron's
heights have lost their snows and nowhere stand
hoary now, and the lordly Argos fears its ancient
drought.[2] Lo! Titan himself stands doubtful whether
to bid day follow on, and, plying the reins, compel
it to come forth to its undoing.

CHORUS

If any god loves Achaian Argos and Pisa's homes
renowned for chariots; if any loves Corinthian
Isthmus' realm, its twin harbours, its dissevered
sea; if any, the far-seen snows of Mount Taÿgetus,
snows which, when in winter-time the Sarmatian
blasts have laid them on the heights, the summer
with its sail-filling Etesian breezes melts away; if
any is moved by the cool, clear stream of Alpheus,
famed for its Olympic course—let him his kindly
godhead hither turn, let him forbid the recurrent
waves of crime to come again, forbid that on his
grandsire follow a worse grandson, and greater crime

---

[1] *i.e.* the river Inachus.
[2] *i.e.* in the time of Phaëthon.

et maior placeat culpa minoribus.
tandem lassa feros exuat impetus
sicci progenies impia Tantali.
peccatum satis est ; fas valuit nihil
aut commune nefas. proditus occidit
deceptor domini Myrtilus, et fide   140
vectus qua tulerat nobile reddidit
mutato pelagus nomine ; notior
nulla est Ioniis fabula navibus.
exceptus gladio parvulus impio
dum currit patrium natus ad osculum,
immatura focis victima concidit
divisusque tua est, Tantale, dextera,
mensas ut strueres hospitibus deis.
hos aeterna fames persequitur cibos,
hos aeterna sitis ; nec dapibus feris   150
decerni potuit poena decentior.
　　Stat lassus vacuo gutture Tantalus ;
impendet capiti plurima noxio
Phineis avibus praeda fugacior ;
hinc illinc gravidis frondibus incubat
et curvata suis fetibus ac tremens
alludit patulis arbor hiatibus.
haec, quamvis avidus nec patiens morae,
deceptus totiens tangere neglegit
obliquatque oculos oraque comprimit   160
inclusisque famem dentibus alligat.
sed tunc divitias omne nemus suas
demittit propius pomaque desuper
insultant foliis mitia languidis
accenduntque famem, quae iubet irritas

---

[1] A retention of the rhetorical element in this line results
in an obscurity impossible to avoid in English. The meaning
is : Let not the descendants (*minoribus*) do worse sin than
their ancestor.

please lesser men.[1] Wearied at last, may the impious
race of thirsty Tantalus give o'er its lust for savagery.
Enough sin has been wrought; nothing has right
availed, or general wrong. Himself betrayed, fell
Myrtilus, betrayer of his lord, and, dragged down
by the faith which he had shown, he made a sea[2]
famous by its change of name; to Ionian ships no
tale is better known. While the little son[3] ran to
his father's kiss, welcomed by sinful sword, he fell,
an untimely victim at the hearth, and by thy right
hand was carved, O Tantalus, that thou mightest
spread a banquet for the gods, thy guests. Such
food eternal hunger, such eternal thirst pursues;
nor for such bestial viands could have been meted
penalty more fit.

[152] Weary, with empty throat, stands Tantalus;
above his guilty head hangs food in plenty, than
Phineus'[4] birds more elusive; on either side, with
laden boughs, a tree leans over him and, bending
and trembling 'neath its weight of fruit, makes sport
with his wide-straining jaws. The prize, though he
is eager and impatient of delay, deceived so oft, he
tries no more to touch, turns away his eyes, shuts
tight his lips, and behind clenched teeth he bars his
hunger. But then the whole grove lets its riches
down nearer still, and the mellow fruits above his
head mock him with drooping boughs and whet
again the hunger, which bids him ply his hands in

---

[2] The Myrtoan sea, that portion of the Aegean south of
Euboea. The name is here fancifully derived from Myrtilus.
For the whole incident see Index.

[3] Pelops.   [4] The Harpies.

exercere manus. has ubi protulit
et falli libuit, totus in arduum
autumnus rapitur silvaque mobilis.
instat deinde sitis non levior fame ;
qua cum percaluit sanguis et igneis   170
exarsit facibus, stat miser obvios
fluctus ore petens, quos profugus latex
avertit sterili deficiens vado
conantemque sequi deserit ; hic bibit
altum de rapido gurgite pulverem.

ATREVS

Ignave, iners, enervis et (quod maximum
probrum tyranno rebus in summis reor)
inulte, post tot scelera, post fratris dolos
fasque omne ruptum questibus vanis agis
iratus Atreus ? fremere iam totus tuis   180
debebat armis orbis et geminum mare
utrimque classes agere, iam flammis agros
lucere et urbes decuit ac strictum undique
micare ferrum. tota sub nostro sonet
Argolica tellus equite ; non silvae tegant
hostem nec altis montium structae iugis
arces ; relictis bellicum totus canat
populus Mycenis, quisquis invisum caput
tegit ac tuetur, clade funesta occidat.
haec ipsa pollens incliti Pelopis domus   190
ruat vel in me, dummodo in fratrem ruat.
age, anime, fac quod nulla posteritas probet,
sed nulla taceat. aliquod audendum est nefas
atrox, cruentum, tale quod frater meus
suum esse mallet. scelera non ulcisceris,
nisi vincis. et quid esse tam saevum potest

---

[1] Not because he failed, but because he almost succeeded.

vain. When he has stretched these forth and gladly [1] has been baffled, the whole ripe harvest of the bending woods is snatched far out of reach. Then comes a raging thirst, harder to bear than hunger; when by this his blood has grown hot and glowed as with fiery torches, the poor wretch stands catching at waves that seem to approach his lips; but these the elusive water turns aside, failing in meagre shallows, and leaves him utterly, striving to pursue; then deep from the whirling stream he drinks—but dust.

ATREUS [*in soliloquy*]

O undaring, unskilled, unnerved, and (what in high matters I deem a king's worst reproach) yet unavenged, after so many crimes, after a brother's treacheries, and all right broken down, in idle complaints dost busy thyself—a mere wrathful Atreus? By now should the whole world be resounding with thy arms, on either side thy fleets be harrying both seas; by now should fields and cities be aglow with flames and the drawn sword be gleaming everywhere. Let the whole land of Argolis resound with our horses' tread; let no forests shelter my enemy, nor citadels, built on high mountain tops; let the whole nation leave Mycenae and sound the trump of war; and whoso hides and protects that hateful head, let him die a grievous death. This mighty palace itself, illustrious Pelops' house, may it e'en fall on me, if only on my brother, too, it fall. Up! my soul, do what no coming age shall approve, but none forget. I must dare some crime, atrocious, bloody, such as my brother would more wish were his. Crimes thou dost not avenge, save as thou dost surpass them. And what crime can be so dire as to overtop his sin?

quod superet illum ?   numquid abiectus iacet ?
numquid secundis patitur in rebus modum,
fessis quietem ?   novi ego ingenium viri
indocile ; flecti non potest—frangi potest.   200
proinde antequam se firmat aut vires parat,
petatur ultro, ne quiescentem petat.
aut perdet aut peribit ; in medio est scelus
positum occupanti.

SATELLES

                    Fama te populi nihil
adversa terret ?

ATREVS

                    Maximum hoc regni bonum est,
quod facta domini cogitur populus sui
tam ferre quam laudare.

SATELLES

                    Quos cogit metus
laudare, eosdem reddit inimicos metus.
at qui favoris gloriam veri petit,
animo magis quam voce laudari volet.   210

ATREVS

Laus vera et humili saepe contingit viro,
non nisi potenti falsa.   quod nolunt velint.

SATELLES

Rex velit honesta : nemo non eadem volet.

ATREVS

Vbicumque tantum honesta dominanti licent,
precario regnatur.

106

Does he lie downcast? Does he in prosperity endure
control, rest in defeat? I know the untamable spirit
of the man; bent it cannot be—but it can be broken.
Therefore, ere he strengthen himself or marshal his
powers, we must begin the attack, lest, while we
wait, the attack be made on us. Slay or be slain will
he; between us lies the crime for him who first
shall do it.

ATTENDANT

Does public disapproval deter thee not?

ATREUS

The greatest advantage this of royal power, that
their master's deeds the people are compelled as
well to bear as praise.

ATTENDANT

Whom fear compels to praise, them, too, fear makes
into foes; but he who seeks the glory of true favour,
will wish heart rather than voice to sing his praise.

ATREUS

True praise even to the lowly often comes; false,
only to the strong. What men choose not, let them
choose.

ATTENDANT

Let a king choose the right; then none will not
choose the same.

ATREUS

Where only right to a monarch is allowed, sovereignty is insecure.

SATELLES

           Vbi non est pudor
nec cura iuris sanctitas pietas fides,
instabile regnum est.

ATREVS

              Sanctitas pietas fides
privata bona sunt; qua iuvat reges eant.

SATELLES

Nefas nocere vel malo fratri puta.

ATREVS

Fas est in illo quidquid in fratre est nefas.   220
quid enim reliquit crimine intactum aut ubi
sceleri pepercit?   coniugem stupro abstulit
regnumque furto; specimen antiquum imperi
fraude est adeptus, fraude turbavit domum.
est Pelopis altis nobile in stabulis pecus,
arcanus aries, ductor opulenti gregis.
huius per omne corpus effuso coma
dependet auro, cuius e tergo [1] novi
aurata reges sceptra Tantalici gerunt;
possessor huius regnat, hunc tantae domus   230
fortuna sequitur.   tuta seposita sacer
in parte carpit prata, quae claudit lapis
fatale saxeo pascuum muro tegens.
hunc facinus ingens ausus assumpta in scelus
consorte nostri perfidus thalami avehit.
hinc omne cladis mutuae fluxit malum;
per regna trepidus exul erravi mea,

·   [1] *Leo conjectures* tracto : *Wilamowitz*, texto.

---

[1] A ram with golden fleece, whose possession, according to
an oracle, guaranteed possession of the throne.   See Index
s. v. Thyestes.

THYESTES

Where is no shame, no care for right, no honour,
virtue, faith, sovereignty is insecure.

ATREUS

Honour, virtue, faith are the goods of common
men; let kings go where they please.

ATTENDANT

O count it wrong to harm even a wicked brother.

ATREUS

Whate'er is wrong to do unto a brother is right to
do to him. For what has he left untouched by
crime, or where has he failed to sin? My wife has
he debauched, my kingdom stolen; the ancient
token[1] of our dynasty by fraud he gained, by fraud
o'erturned our house. There is within Pelops' lofty
folds a lordly flock, and a wondrous ram, the rich
flock's leader. O'er all his body a fleece of spun
gold hangs, and from his back[2] the new-crowned
kings of the house of Tantalus have their sceptres
wreathed with gold. His owner rules; him does the
fortune of the whole house follow. Hallowed and
apart he grazes in safe meadows fenced with stone,
that guards the fated pasture with its rocky wall. Him
did the perfidious one,[3] daring a monstrous crime,
steal away, with the partner of my bed helping the
sinful deed. From this source has flowed the whole
evil stream of mutual destruction; throughout my
kingdom have I wandered, a trembling exile; no

---

[2] *i.e.* from the golden fleece upon it.
[3] Thyestes.

pars nulla generis tuta ab insidiis vacat,
corrupta coniunx, imperi quassa est fides,
domus aegra, dubius sanguis est—certi nihil   240
nisi frater hostis. quid stupes ? tandem incipe
animosque sume ; Tantalum et Pelopem—aspice ;
ad haec manus exempla poscuntur meae.
    Profare, dirum qua caput mactem via.

SATELLES

    Ferro peremptus spiritum inimicum expuat.

ATREVS

    De fine poenae loqueris ; ego poenam volo.
perimat tyrannus lenis ; in regno meo
mors impetratur.

SATELLES

Nulla te pietas movet ?

ATREVS

    Excede, Pietas, si modo in nostra domo
umquam fuisti. dira Furiarum cohors   250
discorsque Erinys veniat et geminas faces
Megaera quatiens ; non satis magno meum
ardet furore pectus ; impleri iuvat
maiore monstro.

SATELLES

Quid novi rabidus struis ?

ATREVS

    Nil quod doloris capiat assueti modus ;
nullum relinquam facinus et nullum est satis.

---

[1] *i.e.* by which the two brothers were to reign alternately.

part of my family is safe and free from snares; my wife seduced, our pledge[1] of empire broken, my house impaired, my offspring dubious—no one thing certain save my brother's enmity. Why standest inactive? At last begin, put on thy courage; Tantalus and Pelops—look on them; to work like theirs my hands are summoned.

[244] Tell thou, by what means I may bring ruin on his wicked head.

ATTENDANT

Slain by the sword, let him spew forth his hateful soul.

ATREUS

Thou speakest of punishment's completion; I punishment itself desire. Let the mild tyrant slay; in my dominion death is a boon to pray for.

ATTENDANT

Does piety move thee not?

ATREUS

Be gone, O Piety, if ever in our house thou hadst a place. Let the dread band of Furies come, the fiend Discord, and Megaera, brandishing her torches twain; not great enough the frenzy with which my bosom burns; with some greater horror would I be filled.

ATTENDANT

What strange design does thy mad soul intend?

ATREUS

Naught that the measure of accustomed rage can hold; no crime will I leave undone, and no crime is enough.

SATELLES

Ferrum?

ATREVS

Parum est.

SATELLES

Quid ignis?

ATREVS

Etiamnunc parum est.

SATELLES

Quonam ergo telo tantus utetur dolor?

ATREVS

Ipso Thyeste.

SATELLES

Maius hoc ira est malum.

ATREVS

Fateor.   tumultus pectora attonitus quatit   260
penitusque volvit; rapior et quo nescio,
sed rapior.   imo mugit e fundo solum,
tonat dies serenus ac totis domus
ut fracta tectis crepuit et moti lares
vertere vultum—fiat hoc, fiat nefas
quod, di, timetis.

SATELLES

Facere quid tandem paras?

ATREVS

Nescio quid animo maius et solito amplius
supraque fines moris humani tumet
instatque pigris manibus—haud quid sit scio,

ATTENDANT

The sword?

ATREUS

'Tis not enough.

ATTENDANT

Fire, then?

ATREUS

Still not enough.

ATTENDANT

What weapon, pray, will thy great anguish use?

ATREUS

Thyestes' self.

ATTENDANT

This plague is worse than passion.

ATREUS

I do confess it. A frantic tumult shakes and heaves deep my heart. I am hurried I know not whither, but I am hurried on. The ground rumbles from its lowest depths, the clear sky thunders, the whole house crashes as though 'twere rent asunder, and the trembling Lares turn away their faces—let it be done, let a deed of guilt be done whereat, O gods, ye are affrighted.

ATTENDANT

What, pray, wouldst do?

ATREUS

Some greater thing, larger than the common and beyond the bounds of human use is swelling in my soul, and it urges on my sluggish hands—I know not

113

sed grande quiddam est.   ita sit.   hoc, anime,
   occupa.   270
dignum est Thyeste facinus et dignum Atreo ;
uterque faciat.   vidit infandas domus
Odrysia mensas—fateor, immane est scelus,
sed occupatum ; maius hoc aliquid dolor
inveniat.   animum Daulis inspira parens
sororque ; causa est similis ; assiste et manum
impelle nostram.   liberos avidus pater
gaudensque laceret et suos artus edat.
bene est, abunde est.   hic placet poenae modus.
   Tantisper[1] ubinam est? tam diu cur innocens 280
versatur Atreus?   tota iam ante oculos meos
imago caedis errat, ingesta orbitas
in ora patris—anime, quid rursus times
et ante rem subsidis?   audendum est, age !
quod est in isto scelere praecipuum nefas,
hoc ipse faciet.

SATELLES

     Sed quibus captus dolis
nostros dabit perductus in laqueos pedem ?
inimica credit cuncta.

ATREVS

     Non poterat capi,
nisi capere vellet.   regna nunc sperat mea ;
hac spe minanti fulmen occurret Iovi,   290
hac spe subibit gurgitis tumidi minas
dubiumque Libycae Syrtis intrabit fretum,
hac spe, quod esse maximum retur malum,
fratrem videbit.

   [1] *All editors punctuate* modus | tantisper.   ubinam est ?
114

what it is, but 'tis some mighty thing. So let it be. Haste, thou, my soul, and do it. 'Tis a deed worthy of Thyestes, and of Atreus worthy; let each perform it. The Odrysian[1] house once saw a feast unspeakable—'tis a monstrous crime, I grant, but it has been done before; let my smart find something worse than this. Inspire my soul, O Daulian[2] mother, aye and sister,[3] too; my case is like to yours; help me and urge on my hand. Let the father with joyous greed rend his sons, and his own flesh devour. 'Tis well, more than enough. This way of punishment is pleasing.

[280] Meanwhile, where is he? Why does Atreus so long live harmless? Already before mine eyes flits the whole picture of the slaughter; his lost children heaped up before their father's face—O soul, why dost shrink back in fear and halt before the deed? Come! thou must dare it! What is the crowning outrage in this crime he himself shall do.

ATTENDANT

But with what wiles caught will he be led to set foot within our snares? He counts us all enemies.

ATREUS

He could not be caught were he not bent on catching. Even now he hopes to gain my kingdom; in this hope he will face Jove as he brandishes his thunder-bolt, in this hope will brave the whirlpool's rage and enter the treacherous waters of the Libyan sands; in this hope (what he deems the greatest curse of all), he will see his brother.

---

[1] *i.e.* Thracian. See Index.   [2] Procne.   [3] Philomela.

SATELLES

Quis fidem pacis dabit?
cui tanta credet?

ATREVS

Credula est spes improba.
natis tamen mandata quae patruo ferant
dabimus : relictis exul hospitiis vagus
regno ut miserias mutet atque Argos regat
ex parte dominus. si nimis durus preces
spernet Thyestes, liberos eius rudes   300
malisque fessos gravibus et faciles capi
prece commovebunt.   hinc vetus regni furor,
illinc egestas tristis ac durus labor
quamvis rigentem tot malis subigent virum.

SATELLES

Iam tempus illi fecit aerumnas leves.

ATREVS

Erras ; malorum sensus accrescit die.
leve est miserias ferre, perferre est grave.

SATELLES

Alios ministros consili tristis lege.

ATREVS

Peiora iuvenes facile praecepta audiunt.

SATELLES

In patre facient quidquid in patruo doces ;   310
saepe in magistrum scelera redierunt sua.

---

[1] *i.e.* other than Atreus' own sons.

ATTENDANT

Who will give him confidence in peace? Whose word will he so greatly trust?

ATREUS

Base hope is credulous. Still to my sons will I give a message to carry to their uncle: let the exiled wanderer quit strangers' homes, for a throne exchange his wretched state and rule at Argos, a partner of my sway. If too stubbornly Thyestes spurns my prayer, his sons, guileless and spent with hard misfortunes and easy to be entreated, will be moved. On this side, his old mad thirst for power, on that, grim want and unfeeling toil by their many woes will force the man, however stiff, to yield.

ATTENDANT

By now time has made his troubles light.

ATREUS

Not so; a sense of wrongs increases day by day. 'Tis easy to bear misfortune; to keep on bearing it a heavy task.

ATTENDANT

Choose other [1] agents of thy grim design.

ATREUS

To the worse schooling youth lends ready ear.

ATTENDANT

Toward their father they will act as toward their uncle thou instructest them; often upon the teacher have his bad teachings turned.

117

ATREVS

Vt nemo doceat fraudis et sceleris vias,
regnum docebit.   ne mali fiant times?
nascuntur.   istud quod vocas saevum asperum
agique dure credis et nimium impie,
fortasse et illic agitur.

SATELLES

               Hanc fraudem scient
nati parari?

ATREVS

       Tacita tam rudibus fides
non est in annis; detegent forsan dolos;
tacere multis discitur vitae malis.

SATELLES

Ipsosque per quos fallere alium cogitas   320
falles?

ATREVS

     Vt ipsi crimine et culpa vacent.
quid enim necesse est liberos sceleri meos
inserere?   per nos odia se nostra explicent.—
male agis, recedis, anime: si parcis tuis,
parces et illis.   consili Agamemnon mei
sciens minister fiat et patri sciens
Menelaus assit.   prolis incertae fides
ex hoc petatur scelere: si bella abnuunt
et gerere nolunt odia, si patruum vocant,
pater est.   eatur.—multa sed trepidus solet   330
detegere vultus, magna nolentem quoque
consilia produnt: nesciant quantae rei
fiant ministri.   nostra tu coepta occules.

---

¹ By Thyestes against Atreus.

THYESTES

ATREUS

Though none should teach them the ways of
treachery and crime, the throne will teach them.
Lest they become evil, fearest thou? They were
born evil. What thou callest savage, cruel, thinkest
is done ruthlessly, with no regard for heaven's law,
perchance even there [1] is being done.

ATTENDANT

Shall thy sons know that this snare is being laid?

ATREUS

Silent discretion is not found in years so in-
experienced; perchance they will disclose the plot;
the art of silence is taught by life's many ills.

ATTENDANT

Even those by whom thou plannest to deceive
another, wilt thou deceive?

ATREUS

That they themselves may be free even from
blame of crime. What need to entangle my sons in
guilt? By my own self let my hatred be wrought
out.—Thou doest ill, thou shrinkest back, my soul.
Let Agamemnon be the witting agent of my plan,
and Menelaus wittingly assist his father. By this deed
let their uncertain birth be put to proof: if they
refuse the combat, if they will not wage the war of
hate, if they plead he is their uncle, he is their sire.
Let them set forth.—But a troubled countenance oft
discloses much; great plans betray their bearer even
against his will; let them not know of how great a
matter they are the ministers. And do thou conceal
my plans.

SATELLES

Haud sum monendus; ista nostro in pectore
fides timorque, sed magis claudet fides.

CHORVS

Tandem regia nobilis,
antiqui genus Inachi,
fratrum composuit minas.[1]

    Quis vos exagitat furor,
alternis dare sanguinem   340
et sceptrum scelere aggredi?
nescitis, cupidi arcium,
regnum quo iaceat loco.
regem non faciunt opes,
non vestis Tyriae color,
non frontis nota regiae,
non auro nitidae fores[2];
rex est qui posuit metus
et diri mala pectoris,
quem non ambitio inpotens   350
et numquam stabilis favor
vulgi praecipitis movet,
non quidquid fodit Occidens
aut unda Tagus aurea
claro devehit alveo,
non quidquid Libycis terit
fervens area messibus,
quem non concutiet cadens
obliqui via fulminis,
non Eurus rapiens mare   360
aut saevo rabidus freto
ventosi tumor Hadriae,
quem non lancea militis,

---

[1] *Richter deletes 336–338.*   [2] trabes *A.*

THYESTES

No need to admonish me ; both fear and loyalty shall shut them in my heart, but rather loyalty.

CHORUS

At last our noble house, the race of ancient Inachus, hath quelled the brother's threats.

339 What madness pricks you on to shed by turns each others' blood, and by crime to gain the throne ? Ye know not, for high place greedy, wherein true kingship lies. A king neither riches make, nor robes of Tyrian hue, nor crown upon the royal brow, nor doors with gold bright-gleaming ; a king is he who has laid fear aside and the base longings of an evil heart ; whom ambition unrestrained and the fickle favour of the reckless mob move not, neither all the mined treasures of the West nor the golden sands which Tagus sweeps along in his shining bed, nor all the grain trod out on burning Libya's threshing-floors ; whom no hurtling path of the slanting thunderbolt will shake, nor Eurus, harrying the sea, nor wind-swept Adriatic's swell, raging with cruel wave ; whom no warrior's lance nor bare steel ever

non strictus domuit chalybs,
qui tuto positus loco
infra se videt omnia
occurritque suo libens
fato nec queritur mori.

    Reges conveniant licet
qui sparsos agitant Dahas,   370
qui rubri vada litoris
et gemmis mare lucidis
late sanguineum tenent,
aut qui Caspia fortibus
recludunt iuga Sarmatis,
certet Danuvii vadum
audet qui pedes ingredi
et (quocumque loco iacent)
Seres vellere nobiles—
mens regnum bona possidet.   380
nil ullis opus est equis,
nil armis et inertibus
telis quae procul ingerit
Parthus, cum simulat fugas,
admotis nihil est opus
urbes sternere machinis,
longe saxa rotantibus.
rex est qui metuit nihil,
rex est qui cupiet nihil.[1]
hoc regnum sibi quisque dat.   390

    Stet quicumque volet potens
aulae culmine lubrico ;
me dulcis saturet quies ;
obscuro positus loco
leni perfruar otio,
nullis nota Quiritibus
aetas per tacitum fluat.

[1] *Leo deletes lines 388, 389.*

mastered; who, in safety 'stablished, sees all things beneath his feet, goes gladly to meet his fate nor grieves to die.

³⁶⁹ Though kings should gather themselves together, both they who vex the scattered Scythians and they who dwell upon the Red Sea's marge, who hold wide sway o'er the blood-red main with its gleaming pearls, they who leave unguarded[1] the Caspian heights to the bold Sarmatians; though he strive against him, who dares on foot to tread the Danube's waves[2] and (wheresoe'er they dwell) to despoil the famous Serians[3]—'tis the upright mind that holds true sovereignty. He has no need of horses, none of arms and the coward weapons which the Parthian hurls from far when he feigns flight, no need of engines hurling rocks, stationed to batter cities to the ground. A king is he who has no fear; a king is he who shall naught desire. Such kingdom on himself each man bestows.

³⁹¹ Let him stand who will, in pride of power, on empire's slippery height; let me be filled with sweet repose; in humble station fixed, let me enjoy untroubled ease, and, to my fellow citizens[4] unknown, let my life's stream flow in silence. So when my

---

[1] Because they do not fear these enemies.

[2] *i.e.* the frozen surface.

[3] The poet here conceives of the Serians as near by Scythia.

[4] *Quirites* must be taken in a general sense. Specifically, it would be impossible, since it applies only to Roman citizens, who at this time had not come into existence.

  sic cum transierint mei
  nullo cum strepitu dies,
  plebeius moriar senex.   400
  illi mors gravis incubat
  qui, notus nimis omnibus,
  ignotus moritur sibi.

THYESTES

 Optata patriae tecta et Argolicas opes
miserisque summum ac maximum exulibus bonum,
tractum soli natalis et patrios deos
(si sunt tamen di) cerno, Cyclopum sacras
turres, labore maius humano decus,
celebrata iuveni stadia, per quae nobilis
palmam paterno non semel curru tuli   410
occurret Argos, populus occurret frequens—
sed nempe et Atreus. repete silvestres fugas
saltusque densos potius et mixtam feris
similemque vitam ; clarus hic regni nitor
fulgore non est quod oculos falso auferat ;
cum quod datur spectabis, et dantem aspice.
modo inter illa, quae putant cuncti aspera,
fortis fui laetusque ; nunc contra in metus
revolvor ; animus haeret ac retro cupit
corpus referre, moveo nolentem gradum. 420

TANTALVS

 Pigro (quid hoc est ?) genitor incessu stupet
vultumque versat seque in incerto tenet.

days have passed noiselessly away, lowly may I die
and full of years. On him does death lie heavily,
who, but too well known to all, dies to himself
unknown.

[*Enter* THYESTES, *returning from banishment, accompanied
by his three sons.*]

THYESTES

At last I see the welcome dwellings of my fatherland, the wealth of Argolis, and, the greatest and
best of sights to wretched exiles, a stretch of native
soil and my ancestral gods (if after all gods there
are), the sacred towers reared by the Cyclopes, in
beauty far excelling human effort, the race-course
thronged with youth, where more than once, lifted
to fame, have I in my father's chariot won the palm.
Argos will come to meet me, the thronging populace
will come—but surely Atreus too! Rather seek
again thy retreats in the forest depths, the impenetrable glades, and life shared with beasts and like to
theirs; this gleaming splendour of the throne is
naught that should blind my eyes with its false tinsel
show; when thou lookest on the gift, scan well the
giver, too. Of late midst such fortune as all count
hard, I was brave and joyous; but now I am returned
to fears; my courage falters and, eager to go back, I
move unwilling feet along.

TANTALUS [*aside*]

My father (what can it mean?) with faltering pace
goes as if dazed, keeps turning his face away, and
holds uncertain course.

THYESTES

Quid, anime, pendes quidve consilium diu
tam facile torques ?   rebus incertissimis,
fratri atque regno, credis ac metuis mala
iam victa, iam mansueta et aerumnas fugis
bene collocatas ?   esse iam miserum iuvat.
reflecte gressum, dum licet, teque eripe.

TANTALVS

Quae causa cogit, genitor, a patria gradum
referre visa ?   cur bonis tantis sinum   430
subducis ?   ira frater abiecta redit
partemque regni reddit et lacerae domus
componit artus teque restituit tibi.

THYESTES

Causam timoris ipse quam ignoro exigis.
nihil timendum video, sed timeo tamen.
placet ire, pigris membra sed genibus labant
alioque quam quo nitor abductus feror.
sic concitatam remige et velo ratem
aestus resistens remigi et velo refert.

TANTALVS

Evince quidquid obstat et mentem impedit   440
reducemque quanta praemia expectent vide.
pater, potes regnare.

THYESTES
                    Cum possim mori.

---

¹ *i.e.* made the best of by learning how to bear them.
² Blessings are being poured into his bosom and he will
not receive them.

THYESTES

THYESTES [*in soliloquy*]

Why O soul, dost hesitate, or why dost so long
turn o'er and o'er a plan so simple? Dost thou trust
to things most unsure, to a brother and to kingship?
Dost fear hardships already mastered, already easier
to bear, and dost flee from distresses well employed?[1]
'Tis sweet now to be wretched. Turn back, while
still thou mayest, and save thyself.

TANTALUS

What cause compels thee, father, to turn thee
back from sight of thy native land? Why from so
great blessings dost withhold thy bosom?[2] Thy
brother returns to thee with wrath given o'er, gives
thee back half the realm, unites the members of thy
sundered house, and to thyself restores thee.

THYESTES

My cause of fear, which I myself know not, thou
demandest of me. Naught to be feared I see, but
still I fear. Fain would I go, but my limbs totter
with faltering knees, and other-whither than I strive
to go am I borne away in thrall. Just so a ship,
urged on by oar and sail, the tide, resisting both oar
and sail, bears back.

TANTALUS

O'ercome thou whate'er opposes and thwarts thy
will, and see how great rewards await thee on thy
return. Father, thou canst be king.

THYESTES

Yea, since I can die.[3]

[3] The power to die is more precious than the power of
kings; since, therefore, he *can* die, Thyestes has indeed regal
power.

TANTALVS

Summa est potestas—

THYESTES

Nulla, si cupias nihil.

TANTALVS

Natis relinques.

THYESTES

Non capit regnum duos.

TANTALVS

Miser esse mavult esse qui felix potest?

THYESTES

Mihi crede, falsis magna nominibus placent,
frustra timentur dura.   dum excelsus steti,
numquam pavere destiti atque ipsum mei
ferrum timere lateris.   o quantum bonum est
obstare nulli, capere securas dapes   450
humi iacentem !   scelera non intrant casas,
tutusque mensa capitur angusta cibus ;
venenum in auro bibitur.   expertus loquor :
malam bonae praeferre fortunam licet.
non vertice alti montis impositam domum
et eminentem civitas humilis tremit
nec fulget altis splendidum tectis ebur
somnosque non defendit excubitor meos ;
non classibus piscamur et retro mare
iacta fugamus mole nec ventrem improbum   460
alimus tributo gentium, nullus mihi

THYESTES

TANTALUS

The height of power is—

THYESTES

Naught, if nothing thou desirest.

TANTALUS

To thy sons wilt thou bequeath it.

THYESTES

The throne admits not two.

TANTALUS

Would he wish wretchedness who can be blest?

THYESTES

False, believe me, are the titles that give greatness charm; idle our fears of hardship. While I stood high in power, never did I cease to dread, yea, to fear the very sword upon my thigh. Oh, how good it is to stand in no man's road, care-free to eat one's bread, on the ground reclining! Crime enters not lowly homes, and in safety is food taken at a slender board; poison is drunk from cups of gold. I speak that I do know: evil fortune is to be preferred to good.[1] The lowly citizen fears no house of mine set high and threatening on a mountain top; my towering roofs flash not with gleaming ivory, no guard watches o'er my slumbers; with no fleet of boats I fish, with no piled break-water do I drive back the sea; I gorge not my vile belly at the world's expense; for me no fields are harvested beyond the Getae and

[1] Having tried both, he comes to this conclusion.

129

ultra Getas metatur et Parthos ager ;
non ture colimur nec meae excluso Iove
ornantur arae ; nulla culminibus meis
imposita nutat silva nec fumant manu
succensa multa stagna nec somno dies
Bacchoque nox iungenda pervigili datur :
sed non timemur, tuta sine telo est domus
rebusque parvis magna praestatur quies.
immane regnum est posse sine regno pati.   470

TANTALVS

Nec abnuendum, si dat imperium deus,
nec appetendum est ; frater ut regnes rogat.

THYESTES

Rogat ?   timendum est.   errat hic aliquis dolus.

TANTALVS

Redire pietas unde submota est solet
reparatque vires iustus amissas amor.

THYESTES

Amat Thyesten frater ?   aetherias prius
perfundet Arctos pontus et Siculi rapax
consistet aestus unda et Ionio seges
matura pelago surget et lucem dabit
nox atra terris, ante cum flammis aquae,   480
cum morte vita, cum mari ventus fidem
foedusque iungent.

TANTALVS

                    Quam tamen fraudem times ?

THYESTES

Omnem ; timori quem meo statuam modum ?
tantum potest quantum odit.
130

the Parthians; no incense burns for me, nor are my shrines adorned in neglect of Jove; no planted grove waves on my battlements, nor does many a pool heated by art steam for me; my days are not given to sleep nor are my nights linked with wakeful revelry: but I am not feared, safe without weapons is my house and to my small estate great peace is granted. 'Tis a boundless kingdom,—the power without kingdoms to be content.

TANTALUS

Neither is empire to be refused if a god bestows it, nor needst thou seek it; thy brother invites thee to be king.

THYESTES

Invites? Then must I fear. Some trick strays hereabouts.

TANTALUS

Brotherly regard ofttimes returns unto the heart whence it was driven, and true love regains the vigour it has lost.

THYESTES

His brother love Thyestes? Sooner shall ocean bathe the heavenly Bears, and the devouring waves of the Sicilian tides stand still; sooner shall ripening grain spring from the Ionian sea, and dark night illume the world; sooner shall fire with water, life with death commingle, and winds join faith and treaty with the sea.

TANTALUS

And yet what treachery dost thou fear?

THYESTES

All treachery; to my fear what limit shall I set? His power is boundless as his hate.

131

TANTALVS

> In te quid potest?

THYESTES

Pro me nihil iam metuo ; vos facitis mihi
Atrea timendum.

TANTALVS

> Decipi cautus times?

THYESTES

Serum est cavendi tempus in mediis malis ;
eatur.   unum genitor hoc testor tamen :
ego vos sequor, non duco.

TANTALVS

> Respiciet deus
bene cogitata.   perge non dubio gradu.   490

ATREVS

Plagis tenetur clausa dispositis fera ;
et ipsum et una generis invisi indolem
iunctam parenti cerno.   iam tuto in loco
versantur odia.   venit in nostras manus
tandem Thyestes, venit, et totus quidem !
vix tempero animo, vix dolor frenos capit.
sic, cum feras vestigat et longo sagax
loro tenetur Vmber ac presso vias
scrutatur ore, dum procul lento suem
odore sentit, paret et tacito locum   500

132

TANTALUS

What power has he against thee?

THYESTES

For myself I have now no fear; 'tis you, my sons,
who make Atreus cause of dread to me.

TANTALUS

Dost fear to be entrapped if on thy guard?

THYESTES

'Tis too late to guard when in the midst of
dangers; but let us on. Yet in this one thing I
prove my fatherhood: I follow you, not lead.

TANTALUS

God will protect us if we heed well our ways.
With assured step haste thou on.

[*Enter* ATREUS. *Seeing* THYESTES *and his sons, he gloats
over the fact that his brother is at last in his power.*]

ATREUS [*aside*]

The prey is fast caught in the toils I spread; both
the sire himself and, together with the sire, the
offspring of his hated race I see. Now on safe
footing does my hatred fare. At last has Thyestes
come into my power; he has come, and the whole [1]
of him! Scarce can I control my spirit, scarce does
my rage admit restraint. So when the keen Umbrian
hound tracks out the prey and, held on a long leash,
with lowered muzzle snuffs out the trail, while with
faint scent he perceives the boar afar, obediently and

[1] *i.e.* sons and all.

rostro pererrat; praeda cum propior fuit,
cervice tota pugnat et gemitu vocat
dominum morantem seque retinenti eripit.
cum sperat ira sanguinem, nescit tegi;
tamen tegatur. aspice, ut multo gravis
squalore vultus obruat maestos coma.
quam foeda iaceat barba. praestetur fides—
fratrem iuvat videre. complexus mihi
redde expetitos. quidquid irarum fuit
transierit; ex hoc sanguis ac pietas die   510
colantur, animis odia damnata excidant.

THYESTES

Diluere possem cuncta, nisi talis fores.
sed fateor, Atreu, fateor, admisi omnia
quae credidisti. pessimam causam meam
hodierna pietas fecit. est prorsus nocens
quicumque visus tam bono fratri est nocens.
lacrimis agendum est; supplicem primus vides;
hae te precantur pedibus intactae manus:
ponatur omnis ira et ex animo tumor
erasus abeat. obsides fidei accipe   520
hos innocentes, frater.

ATREVS

A genibus manum
aufer meosque potius amplexus pete.
vos quoque, senum praesidia, tot iuvenes, meo
pendete collo. squalidam vestem exue
oculisque nostris parce et ornatus cape
pares meis laetusque fraterni imperi

with silent tongue he scours the field; but when the
game is nearer, with his whole strength of neck he
struggles, loudly protests against his master's loitering,
and breaks away from his restraint. When rage
scents blood, it cannot be concealed; yet let it be
concealed. See how his thick hair, all unkempt,
covers his woeful face, how foul his beard hangs
down. [*In bitter irony.*] Now let me keep my promise.[1] [*To* THYESTES.] 'Tis sweet to see my brother
once again. Give me the embrace that I have
longed for. Let all our angry feelings pass away;
from this day let ties of blood and love be cherished
and let accursed hatred vanish from our hearts.

THYESTES

I might excuse all my deeds wert thou not such as
this. But I confess, Atreus, I confess that I have
done all that thou believedst of me. Most foul has
thy love to-day made my case appear. Sinful indeed
is he who has been proved sinful toward so good a
brother. My tears must plead for me; thou art the
first to see me suppliant. These hands, which have
never touched man's feet, beseech thee: put away
all thy wrath and let swollen anger pass from thy
heart and be forgot. As pledge of my faith, O brother,
take these guiltless boys.

ATREUS

From my knees remove thy hand and come rather
into my embrace. And you, too, boys, all of you,
comforters of age, come cling about my neck. Thy
foul garments put off, spare my eyes, and put on
royal trappings equal to my own, and with glad

[1] Which he had made through his sons. See l. 296.

capesse partem.   maior haec laus est mea,
fratri paternum reddere incolumi decus ;
habere regnum casus est, virtus dare.

THYESTES

Di paria, frater, pretia pro tantis tibi   530
meritis rependant.   regiam capitis notam
squalor recusat noster et sceptrum manus
infausta refugit.   liceat in media mihi
latere turba.

ATREVS

Recipit hoc regnum duos.

THYESTES

Meum esse credo quidquid est, frater, tuum.

ATREVS

Quis influentis dona fortunae abnuit ?

THYESTES

Expertus est quicumque quam facile effluant.

ATREVS

Fratrem potiri gloria ingenti vetas ?

THYESTES

Tua iam peracta gloria est, restat mea ;
respuere certum est regna consilium mihi.   540

ATREVS

Meam relinquam, nisi tuam partem accipis.

heart share a brother's kingdom. Mine is the greater glory, to restore to a brother all unharmed ancestral dignity; wielding of power is the work of chance, bestowing of it, virtue's.

THYESTES

May the gods, my brother, fitly repay thee for so great deserts. The kingly crown my wretched state refuses, and the sceptre my ill-omened hand rejects. Let it be mine to hide amidst the throng.

ATREUS

Our throne has room for two.

THYESTES

I count, my brother, all of thine as mine.[1]

ATREUS

Who puts aside inflowing fortune's gifts?

THYESTES

Whoso has found how easily they ebb.

ATREUS

Dost forbid thy brother to gain great glory?

THYESTES

Thy glory is won already; mine is still to win: to refuse the throne is my fixed intent.

ATREUS

My glory must I abandon, unless thou accept thy share.

[1] But I will not take possession of it.

137

Accipio; regni nomen impositi feram,
sed iura et arma servient mecum tibi.

ATREVS

Imposita capiti vincla venerando gere;
ego destinatas victimas superis dabo.

CHORVS

Credat hoc quisquam? ferus ille et acer
nec potens mentis truculentus Atreus
fratris aspectu stupefactus haesit.
nulla vis maior pietate vera est;
iurgia externis inimica durant,   550
quos amor verus tenuit tenebit.
ira cum magnis agitata causis
gratiam rupit cecinitque bellum,
cum leves frenis sonuere turmae,
fulsit hinc illinc agitatus ensis
quem movet crebro furibundus ictu
sanguinem Mavors cupiens recentem—
opprimet ferrum manibusque iunctis
ducet ad Pacem Pietas negantes.
 Otium tanto subitum e tumultu   560
quis deus fecit? modo per Mycenas
arma civilis crepuere belli;
pallidae natos tenuere matres,
uxor armato timuit marito,
cum manum invitus sequeretur ensis,
sordidus pacis vitio quietae;
ille labentes renovare muros,
hic situ quassas stabilire turres,
ferreis portas cohibere claustris
ille certabat, pavidusque pinnis   570
anxiae noctis vigil incubabat—

THYESTES

I do accept; the name of king set on me will I wear; but unto thee shall laws and arms along with myself be subject.

ATREUS [*placing the crown upon his brother's head*]

This crown, set on thy reverend head, wear thou; but I the destined victims to the gods will pay. [*Exit.*

CHORUS

Such things are past belief. Atreus, there, the fierce and savage, reckless of soul and cruel, at sight of his brother stood as one amazed. There is no power stronger than true love; angry strife 'twixt strangers doth endure, but whom true love has bound 'twill bind for ever. When wrath, by great causes roused, has burst friendship's bonds and sounded alarms of war; when fleet squadrons with ringing bridles come; when the brandished sword gleams now here, now there, which the mad god of war, thirsting for fresh-flowing blood, wields with a rain of blows,—then will Love stay the steel, and lead men, even against their will, to the clasped hands of Peace.

560 This sudden lull out of so great uproar what god has wrought? But now throughout Mycenae the arms of civil strife resounded; pale mothers held fast their sons, the wife feared for her lord full armed, when to his hand came the reluctant sword, foul with the rust of peace; one strove to repair tottering walls, one to strengthen towers, crumbling with long neglect; another strove to shut gates tight with iron bars, while on the battlements the trembling guard kept watch o'er the troubled night—for worse

139

peior est bello timor ipse belli.
iam minae saevi cecidere ferri,
iam silet murmur grave classicorum,
iam tacet stridor litui strepentis ;
alta pax urbi revocata laetae est.
sic, ubi ex alto tumuere fluctus
Bruttium Coro feriente pontum,
Scylla pulsatis resonat cavernis
ac mare in portu timuere nautae   580
quod rapax haustum revomit Charybdis,
et ferus Cyclops metuit parentem
rupe ferventis residens in Aetnae,
ne superfusis violetur undis
ignis aeternis resonans caminis,
et putat mergi sua posse pauper
regna Laertes Ithaca tremente—
si suae ventis cecidere vires,
mitius stagno pelagus recumbit ;
alta, quae navis timuit secare,   590
hinc et hinc fusis speciosa velis
strata ludenti patuere cumbae,
et vacat mersos numerare pisces
hic ubi ingenti modo sub procella
Cyclades pontum timuere motae.

   Nulla sors longa est ; dolor ac voluptas
invicem cedunt ; brevior voluptas.
ima permutat levis hora summis.
ille qui donat diadema fronti,
quem genu nixae tremuere gentes,   600
cuius ad nutum posuere bella
Medus et Phoebi propioris Indus
et Dahae Parthis equitem minati,
anxius sceptrum tenet et moventes
cuncta divinat metuitque casus
mobiles rerum dubiumque tempus.

than war is the very fear of war. Now the sword's dire threats have fallen; now still is the deep trumpet-blare; now silent the shrill clarion's blast; deep peace to a glad city is restored. So, when the floods heave up from ocean's depths and Corus [1] lashes the Bruttian waters; when Scylla roars in her disturbed cavern, and mariners in harbour tremble at the sea which greedy Charybdis drains and vomits forth again; when the wild Cyclops, sitting on burning Aetna's crag, dreads his sire's [2] rage, lest the o'erwhelming waves put out the fires that roar in immemorial furnaces; and when beggared Laërtes thinks, while Ithaca reels beneath the shock, that his kingdom may be submerged—then, if their strength has failed the winds, the sea sinks back more peaceful than a pool; and the deep waters which the ship feared to cleave, now far and wide, studded with bellying sails, a beauteous sight, to pleasure-boats spread out their waves; and you may now count the fish swimming far below, where but lately beneath the mighty hurricane the tossed Cyclads trembled at the sea.

[596] No lot endureth long; pain and pleasure, each in turn, give place; more quickly, pleasure. Lowest with highest the fickle hour exchanges. He who wears crown on brow, before whom trembling nations bend the knee, at whose nod the Medes lay down their arms, and the Indians of the nearer sun, [3] and the Dahae who hurl their horse upon the Parthians, —he with anxious hand holds the sceptre, and both foresees and fears fickle chance and shifting time that change all things.

[1] The North-west wind.   [2] Neptune.
[3] The sun was supposed to be nearer to the oriental nations.

Vos quibus rector maris atque terrae
ius dedit magnum necis atque vitae,
ponite inflatos tumidosque vultus;
quidquid a vobis minor expavescit.   610
maior hoc vobis dominus minatur;
omne sub regno graviore regnum est.
quem dies vidit veniens superbum,
hunc dies vidit fugiens iacentem.
nemo confidat nimium secundis,
nemo desperet meliora lapsis:
miscet haec illis prohibetque Clotho
stare fortunam, rotat omne fatum.
nemo tam divos habuit faventes,
crastinum ut posset sibi polliceri: 620
res deus nostras celeri citatas
                    turbine versat.

NVNTIVS

Quis me per auras turbo praecipitem vehet
atraque nube involvet, ut tantum nefas
eripiat oculis?   o domus Pelopi quoque
et Tantalo pudenda!

CHORVS

Quid portas novi?

NVNTIVS

Quaenam ista regio est?   Argos et Sparte, pios
sortita fratres, et maris gemini premens
fauces Corinthos, an feris Hister fugam
praebens Alanis, an sub aeterna nive   630
Hyrcana tellus an vagi passim Scythae?
quis hic nefandi est conscius monstri locus?

---

¹ *i.e.* Castor and Pollux.   See *Phoenissae*, 128.

THYESTES

607 O you, to whom the ruler of sea and land has
given unbounded right o'er life and death, abate your
inflated, swelling pride; all that a lesser subject
fears from you, 'gainst you a greater lord shall
threaten; all power is subject to a weightier power.
Whom the rising sun hath seen high in pride, him
the setting sun hath seen laid low. Let none be
over-confident when fortune smiles; let none despair
of better things when fortune fails. Clotho blends
weal and woe, lets no lot stand, keeps every fate
a-turning. No one has found the gods so kind that
he may promise to-morrow to himself. God keeps
all mortal things in swift whirl turning.

[*Enter* MESSENGER *breathlessly announcing the horror
which has just been enacted behind the scenes.*]

MESSENGER

What whirlwind will headlong bear me through
the air and in murky cloud enfold me, that it may
snatch this awful horror from my sight? O house,
to Pelops even and to Tantalus a thing of shame!

CHORUS

What news bringst thou?

MESSENGER

What place is this? Is it Argos? Is it Sparta,
to which fate gave loving brothers?[1] Corinth,
resting on the narrow boundary of two seas? Or
the Ister, giving chance of flight to the barbarous
Alani? Or the Hyrcanian land 'neath its everlasting snows? Or the wide-wandering Scythians?
What place is this that knows such hideous crime?

CHORVS

Effare et istud pande, quodcumque est, malum.

NVNTIVS

Si steterit animus, si metu corpus rigens
remittet artus.   haeret in vultu trucis
imago facti !   ferte me insanae procul,
illo, procellae, ferte quo fertur dies
hinc raptus.

CHORVS

Animos gravius incertos tenes.
quid sit quod horres ede et auctorem indica.
non quaero quis sit, sed uter.   effare ocius.   640

NVNTIVS

In arce summa Pelopiae pars est domus
conversa ad austros, cuius extremum latus
aequale monti crescit atque urbem premit
et contumacem regibus populum suis
habet sub ictu ; fulget hic turbae capax
immane tectum, cuius auratas trabes
variis columnae nobiles maculis ferunt.
post ista vulgo nota, quae populi colunt,
in multa dives spatia discedit domus ;
arcana in imo regio secessu iacet,   650
alta vetustum valle compescens nemus,
penetrale regni, nulla qua laetos solet
praebere ramos arbor aut ferro coli,
sed taxus et cupressus et nigra ilice
obscura nutat silva, quam supra eminens
despectat alte quercus et vincit nemus.

144

CHORUS

Speak out and tell this evil, whate'er it is.

MESSENGER

When my spirit is composed, when numbing fear lets go its hold upon my limbs. Oh, but I see it still, the picture of that ghastly deed! Bear me far hence, wild winds, oh, thither bear me whither [1] the vanished day is borne.

CHORUS

More grievously dost thou hold our minds in doubt. Tell thou what is this thing which makes thee shudder, and point out the doer of it. I ask not who it is, but which. [2] Speak out and quickly.

MESSENGER

On the summit of the citadel a part of Pelops' palace faces south; its farthest side rises to mountainous height, and o'erlooks the city, having beneath its menace the people, insolent to their kings. Here gleams the great hall that could contain a multitude, whose gilded architraves columns glorious with varied hues upbear. Behind this general hall, which nations throng, the gorgeous palace stretches out o'er many a space; and, deep withdrawn, there lies a secret spot containing in a deep vale an ancient grove, the kingdom's innermost retreat. Here no tree ever affords cheerful shade or is pruned by any knife; but the yew-tree and the cypress and woods of gloomy ilex-trees wave obscure, above which, towering high, an oak looks down and overtops the grove. From

---

[1] *i.e.* to the other side of the world.
[2] It must be one of the two brothers.

hinc auspicari regna Tantalidae solent,
hinc petere lapsis rebus ac dubiis opem.
affixa inhaerent dona ; vocales tubae
fractique currus, spolia Myrtoi maris,   660
victaeque falsis axibus pendent rotae
et omne gentis facinus ; hoc Phrygius loco
fixus tiaras Pelopis, hic praeda hostium
et de triumpho picta barbarico chlamys.

   Fons stat sub umbra tristis et nigra piger
haeret palude ; talis est dirae Stygis
deformis unda quae facit caelo fidem.
hinc nocte caeca gemere ferales deos
fama est, catenis lucus excussis sonat
ululantque manes.   quidquid audire est metus   670
illic videtur ; errat antiquis vetus
emissa bustis turba et insultant loco
maiora notis monstra ; quin tota solet
micare silva flamma, et excelsae trabes
ardent sine igne.   saepe latratu nemus
trino remugit, saepe simulacris domus
attonita magnis.   nec dies sedat metum ;
nox propria luco est et superstitio inferum
in luce media regnat.   hinc orantibus
responsa dantur certa, cum ingenti sono   680
laxantur adyto fata et inmugit specus
vocem deo solvente.
                 Quo postquam furens
intravit Atreus liberos fratris trahens,
ornantur arae—quis queat digne eloqui ?
post terga iuvenum nobiles religat manus

this spot the sons of Tantalus are wont to enter on their reign, here to seek aid midst calamity and doubt. Here hang their votive gifts; resounding trumpets and broken chariots, spoils of the Myrtoan Sea,[1] and wheels o'ercome by treacherous axle-trees hang there, and memorials of the race's every crime; in this place is Pelops' Phrygian turban hung, here spoil of the enemy, and the embroidered robe, token of triumph o'er barbaric foes.

[665] A dismal spring starts forth beneath the shadow, and sluggish in a black pool creeps along; such are the ugly waters of dread Styx, on which the gods take oath. 'Tis said that from this place in the dark night the gods of death make moan; with clanking chains the grove resounds, and the ghosts howl mournfully. Whatever is dreadful but to hear of, there is seen; throngs of the long-since dead come forth from their ancient tombs and walk abroad, and creatures more monstrous than men have known spring from the place; nay more, through all the wood flames go flickering, and the lofty beams glow without help of fire. Oft-times the grove re-echoes with three-throated bayings; oft-times the house is affrighted with huge, ghostly shapes. Nor is terror allayed by day; the grove is a night unto itself, and the horror of the underworld reigns even at midday. From this spot sure responses are given to those who seek oracles; with thundering noise the fates are uttered from the shrine, and the cavern roars when the god sends forth his voice.

[682] When to this place maddened Atreus came, dragging his brother's sons, the altars were decked —but who could worthily describe the deed? Behind their backs he fetters the youths' princely

---

[1] See Index *s.v.* " Myrtilus."

et maesta vitta capita purpurea ligat;
non tura desunt, non sacer Bacchi liquor
tangensque salsa victimam culter mola.
servatur omnis ordo, ne tantum nefas
non rite fiat.

CHORVS

Quis manum ferro admovet?   690

NVNTIVS

Ipse est sacerdos, ipse funesta prece
letale carmen ore violento canit,
stat ipse ad aras, ipse devotos neci
contrectat et componit et ferro admovet[1];
attendit ipse—nulla pars sacri perit.
lucus tremescit, tota succusso solo
nutavit aula, dubia quo pondus daret
ac fluctuanti similis; e laevo aethere
atrum cucurrit limitem sidus trahens.
libata in ignes vina mutato fluunt   700
cruenta Baccho, regium capiti decus
bis terque lapsum est, flevit in templis ebur.
   Movere cunctos monstra, sed solus sibi
immotus Atreus constat atque ultro deos
terret minantes. iamque dimissa mora
adsistit aris, torvum et obliquum intuens.
ieiuna silvis qualis in Gangeticis
inter iuvencos tigris erravit duos,
utriusque praedae cupida quo primum ferat
incerta morsus (flectit huc rictus suos,   710
illo reflectit et famem dubiam tenet),
sic durus Atreus capita devota impiae
speculatur irae. quem prius mactet sibi

---

[1] *The full form of this technical phrase is seen in line 690.*

hands and their sad brows he binds with purple
fillets. Nothing is lacking, neither incense, nor
sacrificial wine, the knife, the salted meal to sprinkle
on the victims. The accustomed ritual is all ob-
served, lest so great a crime be not duly wrought.

CHORUS

Who lays his hand unto the knife?

MESSENGER

Himself is priest; himself with baleful prayer
chants the death-song with boisterous utterance;
himself stands by the altar; himself handles those
doomed to death, sets them in order and lays hand
upon the knife; himself attends to all—no part of
the sacred rite is left undone. The grove begins to
tremble; the whole palace sways with the quaking
earth, uncertain whither to fling its ponderous mass,
and seems to waver. From the left quarter of the
sky rushes a star, dragging a murky trail. The
wine, poured upon the fire, changes from wine and
flows as blood; from the king's head falls the crown
twice and again, and the ivory statues in the temples
weep.

⁷⁰³ These portents moved all, but Atreus alone,
true to his purpose, stands, and e'en appals the
threatening gods. And now, delay at end, he stands
before the altar with lowering, sidelong glance. As
in the jungle by the Ganges river a hungry tigress
wavers between two bulls, eager for each prey, but
doubtful where first to set her fangs (to the one she
turns her jaws, then to the other turns, and keeps
her hunger waiting), so does cruel Atreus eye the
victims doomed by his impious wrath. He hesitates

149

dubitat, secunda deinde quem caede immolet.
nec interest, sed dubitat et saevum scelus
iuvat ordinare.

CHORVS

Quem tamen ferro occupat?

NVNTIVS

Primus locus (ne desse pietatem putes)
avo dicatur: Tantalus prima hostia est.

CHORVS

Quo iuvenis animo, quo tulit vultu necem?

NVNTIVS

Stetit sui securus et non est preces   720
perire frustra passus; ast illi ferus
in vulnere ensem abscondit et penitus premens
iugulo manum commisit: educto stetit
ferro cadaver, cumque dubitasset diu,
hac parte an illa caderet, in patruum cadit.
tunc ille ad aras Plisthenem saevus trahit
adicitque fratri; colla percussa amputat;
cervice caesa truncus in pronum ruit,
querulum cucurrit murmure incerto caput.

CHORVS

Quid deinde gemina caede perfunctus facit?   730
puerone parcit an scelus sceleri ingerit?

within himself whom first to slay, whom next to sacrifice by the second stroke. It matters not, but still he hesitates, and gloats over the ordering of his savage crime.

CHORUS

Whom, for all that, does he first attack with the steel?

MESSENGER

The place of honour (lest you deem him lacking in reverence) to his grandsire [1] is allotted—Tantalus is the first victim.

CHORUS

With what spirit, with what countenance bore the lad his death?

MESSENGER

Careless of self he stood, nor did he plead, knowing such prayer were vain; but in his wound the savage buried the sword and, deep thrusting, joined hand with throat. The sword withdrawn, the corpse still stood erect, and when it had wavered long whether here or there to fall, it fell upon the uncle. Then Plisthenes to the altar did that butcher drag and set him near his brother. His head with a blow he severed; down fell the body when the neck was smitten, and the head rolled away, grieving with murmur inarticulate.

CHORUS

What did he then after the double murder? Did he spare one boy, or did he heap crime on crime?

[1] *i.e.* the boy, Tantalus, is named after his grandfather. This " place of honour " is a ghastly jest.

NVNTIVS

Silva iubatus qualis Armenia leo
in caede multa victor armento incubat
(cruore rictus madidus et pulsa fame
non ponit iras ; hinc et hinc tauros premens
vitulis minatur dente iam lasso piger)—
non aliter Atreus saevit atque ira tumet,
ferrumque gemina caede perfusum tenens,
oblitus in quem fureret, infesta manu
exegit ultra corpus ; ac pueri statim   740
pectore receptus ensis in tergo exstitit.
cadit ille et aras sanguine extinguens suo
per utrumque vulnus moritur.

CHORVS

O saevum scelus !

NVNTIVS

Exhorruistis ?   hactenus si stat nefas,
pius est.

CHORVS

An ultra maius aut atrocius
natura recipit ?

NVNTIVS

Sceleris hunc finem putas ?
gradus est.

CHORVS

Quid ultra potuit ?   obiecit feris
lanianda forsan corpora atque igne arcuit ?

NVNTIVS

Vtinam arcuisset ! ne tegat functos humus
nec solvat ignis !   avibus epulandos licet   750

THYESTES

E'en as a maned lion in the Armenian woods with much slaughter falls victorious on the herd (his jaws reek with gore, and still, though hunger is appeased, he rages on; now here, now there charging the bulls, he threatens the calves, sluggishly now and with weary fangs)—not otherwise Atreus raves and swells with wrath and, still grasping his sword drenched with double slaughter, scarce knowing 'gainst whom he rages, with deadly hand he drives clean through the body; and the sword, entering the boy's breast, straightway stood out upon his back. He falls and, staining the altar with his blood, dies by a double wound.

CHORUS

Oh, savage crime!

MESSENGER

Are you so horror-stricken? If only the crime stops there, 'tis piety.

CHORUS

Does nature admit crime still greater or more dread?

MESSENGER

Crime's limit deemst thou this? 'Tis the first step of crime.

CHORUS

What further could he do? Did he perchance throw the bodies to the beasts to tear, and refuse them fire?

MESSENGER

Would that he had refused! I pray not that earth cover or fire consume the dead! He may give them to the birds to feast upon, may drag them out as a

153

ferisque triste pabulum saevis trahat—
votum est sub hoc quod esse supplicium solet—
pater insepultos spectet! o nullo scelus
credibile in aevo quodque posteritas neget—
erepta vivis exta pectoribus tremunt
spirantque venae corque adhuc pavidum salit.
at ille fibras tractat ac fata inspicit
et adhuc calentes viscerum venas notat.

Postquam hostiae placuere, securus vacat
iam fratris epulis. ipse divisum secat   760
in membra corpus, amputat trunco tenus
umeros patentes et lacertorum moras,
denudat artus durus atque ossa amputat;
tantum ora servat et datas fidei manus.
haec veribus haerent viscera et lentis data
stillant caminis, illa flammatus latex
candente aeno iactat. impositas dapes
transiluit ignis inque trepidantes focos
bis ter regestus et pati iussus moram
invitus ardet. stridet in veribus iecur;   770
nec facile dicam corpora an flammae magis
gemuere. piceos ignis in fumos abit;
et ipse fumus, tristis ac nebula gravis,
non rectus exit seque in excelsum levat—
ipsos penates nube deformi obsidet.

O Phoebe patiens, fugeris retro licet
medioque ruptum merseris caelo diem,
sero occidisti. lancinat natos pater
artusque mandit ore funesto suos;
nitet fluente madidus unguento comam   780
gravisque vino; saepe praeclusae cibum
tenuere fauces. in malis unum hoc tuis
154

ghastly meal for ravenous beasts—oh, after what befell, one might pray for what is oft held punishment—unburied may the father gaze upon his sons ! O crime incredible to any age, which coming generations will deny—torn from the still living breasts the vitals quiver ; the lungs still breathe and the fluttering heart still beats. But he handles the organs and enquires the fates, and notes the markings of the still warm entrails.

759 When with the victims he has satisfied himself, he is now free to prepare his brother's banquet. With his own hands he cuts the body into parts, severs the broad shoulders at the trunk, and the retarding arms, heartlessly strips off the flesh and severs the bones ; the heads only he saves, and the hands that had been given to him in pledge of faith. Some of the flesh is fixed on spits and, set before slow fires, hangs dripping ; other parts boiling water tosses in heated kettles. The fire overleaps the feast that is set before it and, twice and again thrown back upon the shuddering hearth and forced to tarry there, burns grudgingly. The liver sputters on the spits ; nor could I well say whether the bodies or the flames made more complaint. The fire dies down in pitchy smoke ; and the smoke itself, a gloomy and heavy smudge, does not rise straight up and lift itself in air—upon the household gods themselves in disfiguring cloud it settles.

776 O all-enduring Phoebus, though thou didst shrink afar, and in mid-sky didst bury the darkened day, still thou didst set too late. The father rends his sons and with baleful jaws chews his own flesh ; with hair dripping with liquid nard he sits resplendent, heavy with wine ; oft-times the food sticks in his choking gullet. In the midst of these thy woes,

155

bonum est, Thyesta, quod mala ignoras tua.
sed et hoc peribit.   verterit currus licet
sibi ipse Titan obvium ducens iter
tenebrisque facinus obruat tetrum novis
nox missa ab ortu tempore alieno gravis,
tamen videndum est.   tota patefient mala.

CHORVS

Quo terrarum superumque parens,
cuius ad ortus noctis opacae   790
decus omne fugit, quo vertis iter
medioque diem perdis Olympo?
cur, Phoebe, tuos rapis aspectus?
nondum serae nuntius horae
nocturna vocat lumina Vesper;
nondum Hesperiae flexura rotae
iubet emeritos solvere currus;
nondum in noctem vergente die
tertia misit bucina signum;
stupet ad subitae tempora cenae   800
nondum fessis bubus arator.
quid te aetherio pepulit cursu?
quae causa tuos limite certo
deiecit equos?   numquid aperto
carcere Ditis victi temptant
bella Gigantes?   numquid Tityos
pectore fesso renovat veteres
saucius iras?   num reiecto
latus explicuit monte Typhoeus?
numquid struitur via Phlegraeos   810
alta per hostes et Thessalicum
Thressa premitur Pelion Ossa?

---

¹ *i.e.* the day's.   ² *i.e.* in mid-heaven, at noon.

156

THYESTES

Thyestes, this only good remains, that thou knowest
not thy woes. But even this will perish. Though
Titan himself should turn his chariot back, taking
the opposite course; though heavy night, rising at
dawn and at another's [1] time, with strange shadows
should bury this ghastly deed, still it must out.
There is no sin but it shall be revealed.

[*Unnatural darkness has settled over the world.*]

CHORUS

Whither, O father of the lands and skies, before
whose rising thick night with all her glories flees,
whither dost turn thy course and why dost blot out
the day in mid-Olympus? [2] Why, O Phoebus, dost
snatch away thy face? Not yet does Vesper,
twilight's messenger, summon the fires of night; not
yet does thy wheel, turning its western goal, bid free
thy steeds from their completed task; not yet as day
fades into night has the third trump sounded; [3] the
ploughman with oxen yet unwearied stands amazed at
his supper-hour's quick coming. What has driven
thee from thy heavenly course? What cause from
their fixed track has turned aside thy horses? Is
the prison-house of Dis thrown wide and are the
conquered Giants again essaying war? Doth sore-
wounded Tityos renew in his weary breast his ancient
wrath? Has Typhoeus thrown off the mountainous
mass and set his body free? Is a highway being built
by the Phlegraean [4] foe, and does Thessalian Pelion
press on Thracian Ossa?

[3] The Greek day was divided into three parts of four
hours each. The third trump sounding would indicate the
beginning of day's last third.
[4] *i.e.* the Giants, so called from Phlegra, a valley in Thrace,
where started their battle against the gods.

157

Solitae mundi periere vices;
nihil occasus, nihil ortus erit.
stupet Eoos, assueta deo
tradere frenos genetrix primae
roscida lucis, perversa sui
limina regni; nescit fessos
tinguere currus nec fumantes
sudore iubas mergere ponto.   820
ipse insueto novus hospitio
Sol Auroram videt occiduus,
tenebrasque iubet surgere nondum
nocte parata.   non succedunt
astra nec ullo micat igne polus,
non Luna graves digerit umbras.
    Sed quidquid id est, utinam nox sit!
trepidant, trepidant pectora magno
percussa metu:
ne fatali cuncta ruina   830
quassata labent iterumque deos
hominesque premat deforme chaos,
iterum terras et mare cingens
et vaga picti sidera mundi
natura tegat.   non aeternae
facis exortu dux astrorum
saecula ducens dabit aestatis
brumaeque notas, non Phoebeis
obvia flammis demet nocti
Luna timores vincetque sui   840
fratris habenas, curvo brevius
limite currens.   ibit in unum
congesta sinum turba deorum.
hic qui sacris pervius astris
secat obliquo tramite zonas
flectens longos signifer annos,
lapsa videbit sidera labens;

[813] Heaven's accustomed alternations are no more; no setting, no rising shall there be again. The dewy mother [1] of the early dawn, wont to hand o'er to the god his morning reins, looks in amaze upon the disordered threshold of her kingdom; she is not skilled [2] to bathe his weary chariot, nor to plunge his steeds, reeking with sweat, beneath the sea. Startled himself at such unwonted welcoming, the sinking sun beholds Aurora, and bids the shadows arise, though night is not yet ready. No stars come out; the heavens gleam not with any fires: no moon dispels the darkness' heavy pall.

[827] But whatever this may be, would that night were here! Trembling, trembling are our hearts, sore smit with fear, lest all things fall shattered in fatal ruin and once more gods and men be o'erwhelmed by formless chaos; lest the lands, the encircling sea, and the stars that wander in the spangled sky, nature blot out once more. No more by the rising of his quenchless torch shall the leader of the stars, guiding the procession of the years, mark off the summer and the winter times; no more shall Luna, reflecting Phoebus' rays, dispel night's terrors, and outstrip her brother's reins, as in scantier space [3] she speeds on her circling path. Into one abyss shall fall the heaped-up throng of gods. The Zodiac, which, making passage through the sacred stars, crosses the zones obliquely, guide and sign-bearer for the slow-moving years, falling itself, shall see the fallen

---

[1] Aurora.
[2] As is Tethys of the western sea.
[3] *i.e.* her monthly orbit.

hic qui nondum vere benigno
reddit Zephyro vela tepenti,
Aries praeceps ibit in undas,   850
per quas pavidam vexerat Hellen ;
hic qui nitido Taurus cornu
praefert Hyadas, secum Geminos
trahet et curvi bracchia Cancri ;
Leo flammiferis aestibus ardens
iterum e caelo cadet Herculeus,
cadet in terras Virgo relictas
iustaeque cadent pondera Librae
secumque trahent Scorpion acrem ;
et qui nervo tenet Haemonio   860
pinnata senex spicula Chiron,
rupto perdet spicula nervo ;
pigram referens hiemem gelidus
cadet Aegoceros frangetque tuam,
quisquis es, urnam ; tecum excedent
ultima caeli sidera Pisces,
Plostraque numquam perfusa mari
merget condens omnia gurges ;
et qui medias dividit Vrsas,
fluminis instar lubricus Anguis,   870
magnoque minor iuncta Draconi
frigida duro Cynosura gelu,
custosque sui tardus plaustri
iam non stabilis ruet Arctophylax.

---

¹ This lion and other monsters were said to have fallen
from the moon.
² Astraea.   See Index.
³ Chiron is Sagittarius in the constellations of the Zodiac.
⁴ Capricornus.
⁵ A reference to the Zodiacal sign, Aquarius, the "Water-
man," concerning whose identity ancient authorities have
not agreed.

constellations; the Ram, who, ere kindly spring has come, gives back the sails to the warm West-wind, headlong shall plunge into the waves o'er which he had borne the trembling Helle; the Bull, who before him on bright horns bears the Hyades, shall drag the Twins down with him and the Crab's wide-curving claws; Alcides' Lion, with burning heat inflamed, once more [1] shall fall down from the sky; the Virgin [2] shall fall to the earth she once abandoned, and the Scales of justice with their weights shall fall and with them shall drag the fierce Scorpion down; old Chiron,[3] who sets the feathered shafts upon Haemonian chord, shall lose his shafts from the snapped bowstring; the frigid Goat [4] who brings back sluggish winter, shall fall and break thy urn, whoe'er thou [5] art; with thee shall fall the Fish, last of the stars of heaven, and the Wain,[6] which was ne'er bathed by the sea, shall be plunged beneath the all-engulfing waves; the slippery Serpent which, gliding like a river, separates the Bears, shall fall, and icy Cynosura, the Lesser Bear, together with the Dragon vast, congealed with cold; and that slow-moving driver of his wain, Arctophylax,[7] no longer fixed in place, shall fall.

[6] Otherwise known as the "Bear." The constellation is unfortunately named here, since there was no mythological reason why the Wain should not be bathed in the Ocean, as was the case with the Bear.

[7] Seneca badly mixes his mythology here. Arctophylax, the "bear-keeper," is appropriate only if the Bear is mentioned in his connection; he should be Boötes if the companion constellation is thought of as the Wain.

Nos e tanto visi populo
digni premeret quos everso
cardine mundus?
in nos aetas ultima venit?
o nos dura sorte creatos,
seu perdidimus solem miseri,   880
sive expulimus!
abeant questus, discede, timor!
vitae est avidus quisquis non vult
mundo secum pereunte mori.

ATREVS

Aequalis astris gradior et cunctos super
altum superbo vertice attingens polum.
nunc decora regni teneo, nunc solium patris.
dimitto superos; summa votorum attigi.
bene est, abunde est, iam sat est etiam mihi.
sed cur satis sit? pergam et impleto patre [1]   890
funere suorum.[2] ne quid obstaret pudor,
dies recessit. perge dum caelum vacat.
utinam quidem tenere fugientes deos
possem et coactos trahere, ut ultricem dapem
omnes viderent! quod sat est, videat pater.
etiam die nolente discutiam tibi
tenebras, miseriae sub quibus latitant tuae.
nimis diu conviva securo iaces
hilarique vultu, iam satis mensis datum est
satisque Baccho; sobrio tanta ad mala   900
opus est Thyeste.
               Turba famularis, fores
templi relaxa, festa patefiat domus.

[1] *So L. Müller, followed by Richter: MSS.* implebo patrem
[2] *Leo deletes lines 890ᵇ, 891ᵃ.*

---

[1] Probably referring to the golden ram. See ll. 223 ff.
[2] *i.e.* I need make no more prayers to them.

THYESTES

875 Have we of all mankind been deemed deserving that heaven, its poles uptorn, should overwhelm us? In our time has the last day come? Alas for us, by bitter fate begotten, to misery doomed, whether we have lost the sun or banished it! Away with lamentations, begone, O fear! Greedy indeed for life is he who would not die when the world is perishing in his company.

[*Enter* ATREUS, *exulting.*]

ATREUS

Peer of the stars I move, and, towering over all, touch with proud head the lofty heavens. Now the glory[1] of the realm I hold, now my father's throne. I release the gods,[2] for the utmost of my prayers have I attained. 'Tis well, 'tis more than well, now 'tis enough even for me. But why enough? Nay, I will go forward, e'en though the father is full-fed with his dead sons.[3] That shame might not hold me back, day has departed. On! while heaven is tenantless. O that I might stay the fleeing deities,[4] might force and draw them hither that they all might see the avenging feast! But 'tis enough if but the father see. Even though daylight refuse me aid, I'll dispel the darkness from thee, beneath which thy woes are lurking. Too long thou liest at feast with care-free and cheerful countenance; now enough time has been given to tables, enough to wine; for such monstrous ills there needs Thyestes sober. [*To the slaves.*] Ye menial throng, open the temple doors, let the banquet-hall be disclosed. 'Tis

[3] The horror of the draught of blood and wine is still to follow.

[4] *i.e.* the stars which have fled in horror from the sky.

163

libet videre, capita natorum intuens
quos det colores, verba quae primus dolor
effundat aut ut spiritu expulso stupens
corpus rigescat.   fructus hic operis mei est.
miserum videre nolo, sed dum fit miser.
   Aperta multa tecta conlucent face.
resupinus ipse purpurae atque auro incubat,
vino gravatum fulciens laeva caput.   910
eructat.   o me caelitum excelsissimum,
regum atque regem !   vota transcendi mea.
satur est, capaci ducit argento merum—
ne parce potu ; restat etiamnunc cruor
tot hostiarum ; veteris hunc Bacchi color
abscondet.   hoc, hoc mensa cludatur scypho.
mixtum suorum sanguinem genitor bibat :
meum bibisset.   ecce, iam cantus ciet
festasque voces nec satis menti imperat.

THYESTES

    Pectora longis hebetata malis,   920
    iam sollicitas ponite curas.
    fugiat maeror fugiatque pavor,
    fugiat trepidi comes exilii
    tristis egestas rebusque gravis
    pudor afflictis ; magis unde cadas
    quam quo refert.   magnum, ex alto
    culmine lapsum stabilem in plano
    figere gressum ; magnum, ingenti

sweet to note, when he sees his children's heads,
what hue his cheeks display, what words his first
grief pours forth, how his body, breathless with the
shock, grows stiff. This is the fruit of all my toil.
To see him wretched I care not, but to see the
wretchedness come upon him.

[The doors are thrown open, showing THYESTES *at the
banquet-table.]*

⁹⁰⁸ The open hall with many a torch is gleaming.
There he himself reclines at full length on gold and
purple, propping his wine-heavy head on his left
hand. He belches with content. Oh, most exalted
of the gods am I, and king of kings! I have o'er-
topped my hopes. His meal is done; from the
great silver cup he quaffs the wine—spare not thy
drinking; there still remains the blood of all the
victims, and this the colour of old wine will well
disguise. With this, this goblet let the meal be
done. His sons' mingled blood let the father
drink; he would have drunk my own. Lo, now he
raises his joyous voice in song, nor well controls his
spirit.

*[*THYESTES *sits alone at the banquet-table, half overcome
with wine; he tries to sing and be gay, but, in spite
of this, some vague premonition of evil weighs upon
his spirits.]*

THYESTES

O heart, dulled with long miseries, now put aside
anxious cares. Away with grief, away with terror,
away with bitter want, the companion of hunted
exiles, and shame that weighs heavy on misfortune;
more matters it whence thou fallest, than to what.
'Tis a great thing, when fall'n from a lofty pinnacle,
to set foot firmly on the plain; great, midst the

strage malorum pressum fracti
pondera regni non inflexa   930
cervice pati nec degenerem
victumque malis rectum impositas
ferre ruinas.   sed iam saevi
nubila fati pelle ac miseri
temporis omnes dimitte notas ;
redeant vultus ad laeta boni,
veterem ex animo mitte Thyesten.

    Proprium hoc miseros sequitur vitium,
numquam rebus credere laetis ;
redeat felix fortuna licet,   940
tamen afflictos gaudere piget.
quid me revocas festumque vetas
celebrare diem, quid flere iubes,
nulla surgens dolor ex causa ?
quid me prohibes flore decenti
vincire comam ?   prohibet, prohibet
vernae capiti fluxere rosae,
pingui madidus crinis amomo
inter subitos stetit horrores,
imber vultu nolente cadit,   950
venit in medias voces gemitus.
maeror lacrimas amat assuetas,
flendi miseris dira cupido est.
libet infaustos mittere questus,
libet et Tyrio saturas ostro
rumpere vestes, ululare libet.
mittit luctus signa futuri
mens, ante sui praesaga mali ;
instat nautis fera tempestas,
cum sine vento tranquilla tument.   960
quos tibi luctus quosve tumultus
fingis, demens ?   credula praesta
pectora fratri.   iam, quidquid id est,

ruins of huge and crushing woes, with unbending
neck to endure a wrecked kingdom's weight, and
with soul heroic, by woes unconquered, erect to bear
the burden of misfortune. But now, banish the
clouds of bitter fate, and remove all marks of those
unhappy days; greet present happiness with joyful
countenance, and dismiss the old Thyestes from thy
thoughts.

938 But this peculiar failing dogs the wretched,
never to believe that happiness is here; though
lucky fortune come again, still they who have suffered
find it hard to smile. Why dost restrain me and
oppose my celebration of this joyful day? Why dost
bid me weep, O grief, that rises from no cause?
Why dost forbid with beauteous flowers to wreathe
my hair? It forbids, it does forbid! The spring
roses have fallen from my head; my hair, dripping
with precious nard, has started up in sudden horror,
a rain of tears falls down my unwilling cheeks, and
in the midst of speech comes groaning. Grief loves
her accustomed tears, and to the wretched comes an
ominous desire for weeping. Even so, I long to
utter ill-omened lamentation, I long to rend these garments, rich dyed with Tyrian purple, I long to shriek
aloud. My mind gives warnings of distress at hand,
presaging its own woe; oft does a fierce storm draw
nigh to mariners, when without wind the tranquil
waters heave. What distresses, what upheavals dost
thou imagine for thyself, thou fool? Let thy heart
trust thy brother. Already, whate'er it be, either

vel sine causa vel sero times.
nolo infelix, sed vagus intra
terror oberrat, subitos fundunt
oculi fletus, nec causa subest.
dolor an metus est? an habet lacrimas
magna voluptas?

ATREVS

Festum diem, germane, consensu pari   970
celebremus; hic est, sceptra qui firmet mea
solidamque pacis alliget certae fidem.

THYESTES

Satias dapis me nec minus Bacchi tenet.
augere cumulus hic voluptatem potest,
si cum meis gaudere felici datur.

ATREVS

Hic esse natos crede in amplexu patris;
hic sunt eruntque; nulla pars prolis tuae
tibi subtrahetur. ora; quae exoptas dabo
totumque turba iam sua implebo patrem.
satiaberis, ne metue. nunc mixti meis   980
iucunda mensae sacra iuvenilis colunt;
sed accientur. poculum infuso cape
gentile Baccho.

THYESTES

Capio fraternae dapis
donum; paternis vina libentur deis,
tunc hauriantur.—sed quid hoc? nolunt manus
parere, crescit pondus et dextram gravat;
admotus ipsis Bacchus a labris fugit

causelessly or too late thou fearest. I would fain
not be unhappy, but within me vague terror wanders,
sudden tears pour from mine eyes, and all for naught.
Is it from grief or fear? Or doth great joy hold
tears?

ATREUS
[*advancing to his brother with show of effusive affection*]

With mutual accord, brother, let us keep this
festal day; this is the day which shall make strong
my sceptre and bind firm the bonds of peace assured.

THYESTES [*pushing the remains of the feast from him*]

I have had my fill of food, and no less of wine.
My pleasure by this crowning joy can be increased,
if with my sons I may share my happiness.

ATREUS

Be sure that here, in their father's bosom, are thy
sons;—here now, and here shall be; no one of thy
children shall be taken from thee. Make request;
what thou desirest will I give, and wholly with his
family will I fill the sire. Thou shalt be satisfied,
have no fear of that. Just now, in company with
my own, at the children's table, they are sharing the
joyful feast; but I will summon them. Take thou
this cup, an heirloom, filled with wine.

THYESTES

I accept this bounty of my brother's feast; let wine
be poured to our ancestral gods, and then be quaffed.
—But what is this? My hands refuse their service,
and the cup grows heavy and weighs down my hand;
the lifted wine recoils from my very lips; around my

169

circaque rictus ore decepto fluit
et ipsa trepido mensa subsiluit solo.
vix lucet ignis ; ipse quin aether gravis   990
inter diem noctemque desertus stupet.
quid hoc ? magis magisque concussi labant
convexa caeli ; spissior densis coit
caligo tenebris noxque se in noctem addidit ;
fugit omne sidus. quidquid est, fratri precor
natisque parcat, omnis in vile hoc caput
abeat procella. redde iam natos mihi !

ATREVS

Reddam, et tibi illos nullus eripiet dies.

THYESTES

Quis hic tumultus viscera exagitat mea ?
quid tremuit intus ?   sentio impatiens onus   1000
meumque gemitu non meo pectus gemit.
adeste, nati, genitor infelix vocat,
adeste. visis fugiet hic vobis dolor—
unde obloxuntur ?

ATREVS

          Expedi amplexus, pater ;
venere.—natos ecquid agnoscis tuos ?

THYESTES

Agnosco fratrem. sustines tantum nefas
gestare, Tellus ? non ad infernam Styga
tenebrasque mergis rupta et ingenti via

---

¹ Time itself, as indicated by the heavens, is in suspense.

gaping jaws, cheating my mouth, it flows, and the very table leaps up from the trembling floor. The lights burn dim; nay, the very heavens, grown heavy, stand in amaze 'twixt day and night,[1] deserted.[2] What next? Now more, still more the vault of the shattered sky is tottering; a thicker gloom with dense shades is gathering, and night has hidden away in a blacker night; every star is in full flight. Whate'er it is, I beg it may spare my brother and my sons, and may the storm break with all its force on this vile head. Give back now my sons to me!

ATREUS

I will give them back, and no day shall tear them from thee. [*Exit.*

THYESTES

What is this tumult that disturbs my vitals? What trembles in me? I feel a load that will not suffer me, and my breast groans with a groaning that is not mine. O come, my sons, your unhappy father calls you, come; this pain will pass away at the sight of you—whence come their reproachful voices?

[*Re-enter* ATREUS *with a covered platter in his hands.*]

ATREUS

Now, father, spread out thine arms; they are here. [*He uncovers the platter, revealing the severed heads of* THYESTES' *sons.*] Dost recognize thy sons?

THYESTES

I recognize my brother. Canst thou endure, O Earth, to bear a crime so monstrous? Why dost not burst asunder and plunge thee down to the infernal

---

[2] *i.e.* by sun, moon, and stars.

171

ad chaos inane regna cum rege abripis ?
non tota ab imo tecta convellens solo   1010
vertis Mycenas ?   stare circa Tantalum
uterque iam debuimus.   hinc compagibus
et hinc revulsis, si quid infra Tartara est
avosque nostros, huc tuam inmani sinu
demitte vallem nosque defossos tege
Acheronte toto.   noxiae supra caput
animae vagentur nostrum et ardenti freto
Phlegethon harenas igneus totas agens
exilia supra nostra violentus fluat—
immota tellus pondus ignavum iacet,   1020
fugere superi.

ATREVS

      Iam accipe hos potius libens
diu expetitos.   nulla per fratrem est mora ;
fruere, osculare, divide amplexus tribus.

THYESTES

Hoc foedus ?   haec est gratia, haec fratris fides ?
sic odia ponis ?   non peto, incolumes pater
natos ut habeam ; scelere quod salvo dari
odioque possit, frater hoc fratrem rogo :
sepelire liceat.   redde quod cernas statim
uri ; nihil te genitor habiturus rogo,
sed perditurus.

ATREVS

      Quidquid e natis tuis   1030
superest habes, quodcumque non superest habes.

Stygian shades and, by a huge opening to void chaos,
snatch this kingdom with its king away? Why dost
not raze this whole palace to the very ground, and
overturn Mycenae? We should both of us long since
have been with Tantalus. Rend asunder thy prison-
bars on every side, and if there is any place 'neath
Tartarus and our grandsires,[1] thither with huge abyss
let down thy chasm and hide us buried beneath all
Acheron. Let guilty souls wander above our head,
and let fiery Phlegethon, with glowing flood down-
pouring all his sands, flow tempestuous above our
place of exile—but the earth lies all unmoved, an
insensate mass; the gods have fled away.

ATREUS

Now, rather, take these with joy, whom thou hast
so long desired. Thy brother delays thee not; enjoy
them, kiss them, divide thy embraces 'mongst the
three.

THYESTES

Is this thy bond? Is this thy grace, this thy
fraternal pledge? Thus puttest thou hate away?
I do not ask that I, a father, may have my sons unharmed; what can be granted with crime and hate
intact, this I, a brother, of a brother ask: that I may
bury them. Give me back what thou mayst see
burned at once. The father asks naught of thee
with hopes of having, but of losing it.

ATREUS

Whatever of thy sons is left, thou hast; whatever
is not left, thou hast.

[1] He means Tantalus alone, using the plural for the
singular by *enallage*.

THYESTES

Vtrumne saevis pabulum alitibus iacent,
an beluis servantur, an pascunt feras?

ATREVS

Epulatus ipse es impia natos dape.

THYESTES

Hoc est deos quod puduit, hoc egit diem
aversum in ortus.   quas miser voces dabo
questusque quos ?   quae verba sufficient mihi ?
abscisa cerno capita et avulsas manus
et rupta fractis cruribus vestigia—
hoc est quod avidus capere non potuit pater.   1040
volvuntur intus viscera et clusum nefas
sine exitu luctatur et quaerit fugam.
da, frater, ensem (sanguinis multum mei
habet ille); ferro liberis detur via.
negatur ensis ?   pectora inliso sonent
contusa planctu—sustine, infelix, manum,
parcamus umbris.   tale quis vidit nefas ?
quis inhospitalis Caucasi rupem asperam
Heniochus habitans quisve Cecropiis metus
terris Procrustes ?   genitor en natos premo   1050
premorque natis—sceleris est aliquis modus ?

ATREVS

Sceleri modus debetur ubi facias scelus,
non ubi reponas.   hoc quoque exiguum est mihi.
ex vulnere ipso sanguinem calidum in tua
defundere ora debui, ut viventium
biberes cruorem—verba sunt irae data

174

THYESTES

Do they lie a prey for the wild birds? Are they reserved for monsters? Are they food for beasts?

ATREUS

Thyself hast feasted on thy sons, an impious meal.

THYESTES

'Twas this that shamed the gods; this drove the day back against its dawning. What cries in my misery shall I utter, what complaints? What words will suffice for me? I see the severed heads, the torn-off hands, the feet wrenched from the broken legs—this much the father, for all his greed, could not devour. Their flesh is turning round within me, and my imprisoned crime struggles vainly to come forth and seeks way of escape. Give me thy sword, O brother, the sword reeking with my blood; by the steel let deliverance be given to my sons. Dost refuse the sword? Then let my breast resound, bruised by crushing blows—hold thy hand, unhappy man, let us spare the shades. Who ever beheld such crime? What Heniochian, dwelling on wild Caucasus' rough rocks, or what Procrustes, terror of the Cecropian land? Lo, I, the father, overwhelm my sons, and by my sons am overwhelmed—of crime is there no limit?

ATREUS

Crime should have limit, when the crime is wrought, not when repaid. E'en this is not enough for me. Straight from the very wound I should have poured the hot blood down thy throat, that thou mightst drink gore of thy living sons—my wrath was cheated

175

dum propero.   ferro vulnera impresso dedi,
cecidi ad aras, caede votiva focos
placavi et artūs, corpora exanima amputans,
in parva carpsi frusta et haec ferventibus   1060
demersi aenis, illa lentis ignibus
stillare iussi.   membra nervosque abscidi
viventibus, gracilique traiectas veru
mugire fibras vidi et aggessi manu
mea ipse flammas.   omnia haec melius pater
fecisse potuit, cecidit in cassum dolor :
scidit ore natos impio, sed nesciens,
sed nescientes !

THYESTES

          Clausa litoribus vagis
audite maria, vos quoque audite hoc scelus,
quocumque, di, fugistis ; audite inferi,   1070
audite terrae, Noxque Tartarea gravis
et atra nube, vocibus nostris vaca
(tibi sum relictus, sola tu miserum vides,
tu quoque sine astris), vota non faciam improba,
pro me nihil precabor—et quid iam potest
pro me esse ?   vobis vota prospicient mea.
tu, summe caeli rector, aetheriae potens
dominator aulae, nubibus totum horridis
convolve mundum, bella ventorum undique
committe et omni parte violentum intona,   1080
manuque [1] non qua tecta et immeritas domos
telo petis minore, sed qua montium
tergemina moles cecidit et qui montibus
stabant pares Gigantes,—haec arma expedi

---

[1] *So A : Leo, with E,* manumque.

by my haste. With the deep-driven sword I smote them; I slew them at the altars; with their offered blood I appeased the sacred fires; hewing their lifeless bodies, into small scraps I tore them, and some into boiling cauldrons did I plunge, and some before slow fires I set to drip. Their limbs and sinews I rent asunder while still they lived, and their livers, transfixed on slender spits and sputtering I saw, and with my own hand I fed the flames. All these things better the father might have done; my grief has fallen fruitless; with impious teeth he tore his sons, but unwittingly, but them unwitting.[1]

THYESTES

Hear, O ye seas, by shifting shores imprisoned, and ye, too, hear this crime, whithersoever you have fled, ye gods; hear, lords of the underworld; hear, lands, and Night, heavy with black, Tartarean fogs, give ear unto my cries; (to thee am I abandoned, thou only lookest on my woe, thou also forsaken of the stars;) no wicked pleas will I make, naught for myself implore—and what now can I ask in my own behalf? For you[2] shall my prayers be offered. O thou, exalted ruler of the sky, who sittest in majesty upon the throne of heaven, enwrap the whole universe in awful clouds, set the winds warring on every hand, and from every quarter of the sky let the loud thunders roll; not with what hand thou seekest houses and undeserving homes, using thy lesser bolts, but with that hand by which the threefold mass of mountains fell, and the Giants, who stood level with

[1] Atreus would have had both father and sons conscious of what they did and suffered.

[2] *i.e.* the gods of heaven, who have fled from the sight of crime, and whom he now addresses.

ignesque torque.   vindica amissum diem,
iaculare flammas, lumen ereptum polo
fulminibus exple.   causa, ne dubites diu,
utriusque mala sit ; si minus, mala sit mea :
me pete, trisulco flammeam telo facem
per pectus hoc transmitte.   si natos pater   1090
humare et igni tradere extremo volo,
ego sum cremandus.   si nihil superos movet
nullumque telis impios numen petit,
aeterna nox permaneat et tenebris tegat
inmensa longis scelera.   nil, Titan, queror,
si perseveras.

ATREVS

Nunc meas laudo manus,
nunc parta vera est palma.   perdideram scelus,
nisi sic doleres.   liberos nasci mihi
nunc credo, castis nunc fidem reddi toris.

THYESTES

Quid liberi meruere ?

ATREVS

Quod fuerant tui.   1100

THYESTES

Natos parenti——

ATREVS

Fateor et, quod me iuvat,
certos.

the mountains—these arms let loose and hurl thy fires. Make compensation for the banished day, brandish thy flames, and the light that was snatched from heaven with thy lightning's flash supply. Let the cause, lest long thou hesitate, of each one of us be evil; if not, let mine be evil; aim thou at me, through this heart send thy three-forked flaming bolt. If I their father would give his sons to burial and commit them to the funeral flames, I must myself be burned. But if naught moves the gods, and no divinity hurls darts against the impious, may night stay on for ever, and cover with endless darkness boundless crimes. No protest do I make, O sun, if thou continue steadfast.[1]

ATREUS

Now do I praise my handiwork, now is the true palm won. I had wasted my crime, didst thou not suffer thus. Now do I believe my children are my own, now may I trust once more that my marriage-bed is pure.

THYESTES

What was my children's sin?

ATREUS

That they were thine.

THYESTES

Sons to the father——[2]

ATREUS

Yea, and what gives me joy, surely thy sons.

[1] *i.e.* in hiding thy face, as at present.
[2] ——thou didst give to be devoured.

THYESTES

Piorum praesides testor deos.

ATREVS

Quin coniugales?

THYESTES

Scelere quis pensat scelus?

ATREVS

Scio quid queraris: scelere praerepto doles,
nec quod nefandas hauseris angit dapes;
quod non pararis.   fuerat hic animus tibi
instruere similes inscio fratri cibos
et adiuvante liberos matre aggredi
similique leto sternere.   hoc unum obstitit—
tuos putasti.

THYESTES

Vindices aderunt dei;   1110
his puniendum vota te tradunt mea.

ATREVS

Te puniendum liberis trado tuis.

THYESTES

THYESTES

I call on the gods who guard the innocent.

ATREUS

Why not the marriage-gods?

THYESTES

Who punishes crime with crime?

ATREUS

I know what thou complainst of: thou grievest that I have forestalled thee in the crime, and art distressed, not because thou hast consumed the ghastly feast, but because thou didst not offer it to me. This had been thy purpose, to prepare for thine unwitting brother a like feast, and with their mother's aid to assail his sons and lay them low in like destruction. This one thing stayed thee—thou didst think them thine.

THYESTES

The gods will be present to avenge; to them for punishment my prayers deliver thee.

ATREUS

To thy sons for punishment do I deliver thee.

HERCVLES OETAEVS

DRAMATIS PERSONAE

HERCULES, *son of Jupiter and Alcmena.*

HYLLUS, *son of Hercules and Deïanira.*

ALCMENA, *daughter of Electryon, king of Mycenae.*

DEÏANIRA, *daughter of Oeneus, king of Aetolia, and wife of Hercules.*

IOLE, *daughter of Eurytus, king of Oechalia.*

NURSE *of Deïanira.*

PHILOCTETES, *a prince of Thessaly, son of Poeas, and the faithful friend of Hercules.*

LICHAS, *the messenger* (persona muta) *of Deïanira to Hercules.*

CHORUS *of Aetolian women, faithful to Deïanira.*

CHORUS *of Oechalian maidens, suffering captivity in company with Iole.*

THE SCENE is laid, first in Euboea, and later at the home of Hercules in Trachin.

ARGUMENT

THE long, heroic life of Hercules has neared its end.
His twelve great tasks, assigned him by Eurystheus
through Juno's hatred, have been done. His latest
victory was over Eurytus, king of Oechalia. Him he
slew and overthrew his house, because the monarch would
not give him Iole to wife.

And now the hero, having overcome the world, and
Pluto's realm beneath the earth, aspires to heaven. He
sacrifices to Cenaean Jove, and prays at last to be
received into his proper home.

HERCVLES OETAEVS

Sator deorum, cuius excussum manu
utraeque Phoebi sentiunt fulmen domus,
secure regna ; protuli pacem tibi,
quacumque Nereus porrigi terras vetat.
non est tonandum ; perfidi reges iacent,
saevi tyranni.   fregimus quidquid fuit
tibi fulminandum.   sed mihi caelum, parens,
adhuc negatur ?   parui certe Iove
ubique dignus teque testata est meum
patrem noverca.   quid tamen nectis moras ?   10
numquid timemur ?   numquid impositum sibi
non poterit Atlas ferre cum caelo Herculem ?
quid astra, genitor, quid negas ?   mors me tibi
certe remisit, omne concessit malum
quod terra genuit, pontus aer inferi.
nullus per urbes errat Arcadias Ieo,
Stymphalis icta est, Maenali nulla est fera ;
sparsit peremptus aureum serpens nemus
et hydra vires posuit et notos Hebro
cruore pingues hospitum fregi greges   20

---

¹ East and West, or both hemispheres.
² The Arcadian stag. Its capture was the third labour of
Hercules.

186

HERCULES OETAEUS

[*In Euboea, near Oechalia, after the overthrow of Eurytus,
king of that city.*]

HERCULES

O SIRE of gods, hurled by whose hand both homes [1]
of Phoebus feel the thunderbolt, reign thou untroubled; peace have I 'stablished for thee wherever
Nereus forbids the land to extend its bounds. Thou
needst not thunder now; false kings lie low, and
cruel tyrants. I have crushed all who merited thy
bolts. But to me, father, is heaven still denied?
Of a surety have I everywhere proved worthy Jove;
and that thou art sire of mine my stepdame testifies.
Yet why dost still contrive delays? Am I cause of
fear? Will Atlas not avail to bear up Hercules
placed upon him together with the sky? Why, O
father, why dost thou deny the stars to me? Verily
hath death given me back to thee; and every evil
thing which earth, sea, air, the lower world, produced,
hath yielded to my might. No lion prowls amidst
Arcadia's towns; the Stymphalian bird is smitten;
the beast of Maenalus [2] is no more; the dragon,[3]
slain, hath sprinkled the golden orchard with his
blood; the hydra's [4] strength is gone; the herds,[5]
well known to Hebrus, fat with strangers' blood, have

---

[3] Which guarded the apples of the Hesperides.   See Index
s.v. "Hesperides."
[4] See Index.   [5] *i.e.* of Diomedes.

hostisque traxi spolia Thermodontiae.
vidi silentum fata nec tantum redi,
sed trepidus atrum Cerberum vidit dies
et ille solem. nullus Antaeus Libys
animam resumit, cecidit ante aras suas
Busiris, una est Geryon sparsus manu
taurusque populis horridus centum pavor.
quodcumque tellus genuit infesta occidit
meaque fusum est dextera ; iratis deis
non licuit esse.
          Si negat mundus feras   30
animum noverca,[1] redde nunc nato patrem
vel astra forti. nec peto ut monstres iter ;
permitte tantum, genitor ; inveniam viam.
vel si times ne terra concipiat feras,
properet malum quodcumque, dum terra Herculem
habet videtque ; nam quis invadet mala
aut quis per urbes rursus Argolicas erit
Iunonis odio dignus ? in tutum meas
laudes redegi, nulla me tellus silet.
me sensit ursae frigidum Scythicae genus   40
Indusque Phoebo subditus, cancro Libys.
te, clare Titan, testor : occurri tibi
quacumque fulges, nec meos lux prosequi
potuit triumphos, solis excessi vices
intraque nostras substitit metas dies.
natura cessit, terra defecit gradum :
lassata prior est. nox et extremum chaos

---

[1] *So Richter, with A : Leo* †animum novercam, *conjecturing*
tandem novercae.

---

[1] *i.e.* the golden girdle of Hippolyte, queen of the Amazons.
[2] The gods, in wrath, were supposed to have sent monsters
on the earth, and by slaying these Hercules has frustrated
that wrath.

I destroyed, and have brought away Thermodon's spoils[1] of war. The lot of the silent throng have I beheld; and not alone have I returned, but shuddering day hath seen black Cerberus, and he the sun. No longer doth the Libyan Antaeus renew his strength; before his own altars hath Busiris fallen; by my sole hand hath Geryon been o'erthrown, and the bull, dread terror of a hundred tribes. Whatever hostile earth hath 'gendered is fallen, by my right hand laid low; the anger of the gods hath been set at naught.[2]

[30] If the earth is done with monsters, if my stepdame is done with wrath, give back now the father to his son, yea, the stars unto the hero. I ask thee not to show the way to me; but grant thy permission, father, and the way I'll find. Or, if thou fearest that earth shall yet give birth to monsters, let the ill make haste, whate'er it be, while yet the earth doth hold and look on Hercules; for who else will attack evil things, or who, throughout the Argive cities, will be worthy Juno's hate? I have my honours safe bestowed; there is no land but sings my praise. The race that shivers 'neath the Scythian Bear[3] hath known me; the sun-scorched Indian and the tropic African. O glowing Sun, bear witness: I have encountered thee where'er thou shinest, nor could thy beams keep pace with my triumphant course; I have gone beyond the changes of the sun, and day hath halted far within my bounds. Nature hath yielded to me, and earth hath failed my feet; she hath been weary first.[4] Night and utter chaos have

---

[3] *i.e.* the Scythians, dwelling far north beneath the Bear.

[4] It is as if the whole earth, trying to keep pace with Hercules, and to give him new land to travel over, has become weary of the attempt.

in me incucurrit; inde ad hunc orbem redi,
nemo unde retro est.   tulimus Oceani minas,
nec ulla valuit quatere tempestas ratem   50
quamcumque pressi.   pars quota est Perseus mei?
iam vacuus aether non potest odio tuae
sufficere nuptae quasque devincam feras
tellus timet concipere nec monstra invenit.
ferae negantur; Hercules monstri loco
iam coepit esse.   quanta enim fregi mala,
quot scelera nudus!   quidquid immane obstitit,
solae manus stravere; nec iuvenis feras
timui nec infans.   quidquid est iussum leve est,
nec ulla nobis segnis illuxit dies.   60
o quanta fudi monstra quae nullus mihi
rex imperavit!   institit virtus mihi
Iunone peior.

             Sed quid inpavidum genus
fecisse prodest?   non habent pacem dei;
purgata tellus omnis in caelo videt
quodcumque timuit; transtulit Iuno feras.
ambit peremptus cancer ardentem plagam
Libyaeque sidus fertur et messes alit;
annum fugacem tradit Astraeae leo,
at ille, iactans fervidam collo iubam,   70
austrum madentem siccat et nimbos rapit.
invasit omnis ecce iam caelum fera
meque antecessit; victor e terris meos
specto labores, astra portentis prius

---

[1] *i.e.* he is the only unconquered creature left on earth—a
marvel, past the bounds of nature.
[2] On the very day of his birth he killed two huge snakes
which Juno sent against him.   [3] *i.e.* Eurystheus.

assailed me, and thence to this world have I come again whence none e'er returns. I have borne Ocean's threats, and no storm of his has availed to wreck the ship which I have weighted down. How trivial Perseus' deeds compared with mine! Now can the empty air no more suffice the hatred of thy wife, and earth fears to produce beasts for me to conquer, nor can she find monsters more. Beasts are at end; 'tis Hercules now begins to hold the place of monster.[1] For how great evils have I crushed, how many crimes, and all unarmed! Whatever monstrous thing opposed me, with but my hands I laid it low; nor was there ever savage thing which as youth or babe[2] I feared. All my commanded toils seem light, and no inactive day has ever dawned for me. Oh, how great monsters have I overthrown, which no king[3] bade me meet! My courage, more relentless than Juno's self, has urged me on.

[63] But what avails it to have freed the race of men from fear? Now have the gods no peace; the freed earth sees in the sky all creatures which she feared; for there hath Juno set them.[4] The crab I slew goes round the torrid zone, is known as Libya's constellation,[5] and matures her grain; the lion to Astraea gives the flying year;[6] but he, his burning mane upon his neck back tossing, dries up the dripping south-wind and devours the clouds. Behold, now has every beast invaded heaven, forestalling me; though victor, I gaze upon my labours from the earth; for to monsters first and to wild beasts has

[4] *i.e.* she has changed them to constellations in the sky.

[5] The zodiacal constellation of the Crab, in which the sun attains his summer solstice.

[6] *i.e.* the sun passes from Leo into Virgo. For Astrea see Index, *s.v.*

ferisque Iuno tribuit, ut caelum mihi
faceret timendum. sparserit mundum licet
caelumque terris peius ac peius Styge
irata faciat, dabitur Alcidae locus.
si post feras, post bella, post Stygium canem
haud dum astra merui, Siculus Hesperium latus   80
tangat Pelorus, una iam tellus erit ;
illinc fugabo maria. si iungi iubes,
committat undas Isthmos, et iuncto salo
nova ferantur Atticae puppes via.
mutetur orbis : vallibus currat novis
Hister novasque Tanais accipiat vias.
da, da tuendos, Iuppiter, saltem deos ;
illa licebit fulmen a parte auferas,
ego quam tuebor. sive glacialem polum,
seu me tueri fervidam partem iubes,   90
hac esse superos parte securos puta.
Cirrhaea Paean templa et aetheriam domum
serpente caeso meruit—o quotiens iacet
Python in hydra ! Bacchus et Perseus deïs
iam se intulere ; sed quota est mundi plaga
oriens subactus aut quota est Gorgon fera !
quis astra natus laudibus meruit suis
ex te et noverca ? quem tuli mundum peto.
    Sed tu, comes laboris Herculei, Licha,
perfer triumphos, Euryti victos lares   100
stratumque regnum. vos pecus rapite ocius

---

[1] *i.e.* Italian.
[2] The Isthmus of Corinth.

Juno given stars, that to me she might make the sky
a place of dread. Yet, though in her rage she scatter
them o'er the sky, though she make heaven worse
than earth, yea, worse than Styx, to Alcides shall
room be given. If after beasts, after wars, after
the Stygian dog, I have not yet earned the stars, let
Sicilian Pelorus touch the Hesperian [1] shore, and they
both shall become one land; thence will I put seas
to flight. If thou bidst seas be joined, let Isthmus [2]
give passage to the waves and on their united waters
let Attic ships along a new way be borne. Let
earth be changed; along new valleys let Ister run
and Tanaïs receive new channels. Give, give me,
O Jupiter, at least the gods to guard; there mayst
thou put aside thy thunderbolts where I shall be on
guard. Whether thou bidst me guard the icy pole,
whether the torrid zone, there count the gods secure.
Cirrha's shrine [3] and a place in heaven did Pean [4]
earn by one serpent's [5] slaughter—oh, how many
Pythons in the hydra lie o'erthrown ! Already have
Bacchus and Perseus reached the gods; but how
small a tract of earth was the conquered east, [6] or how
meagre a spoil was Gorgon ! [7] what son of thine and
of my stepdame has by his praises merited the
stars ? I seek the skies which I myself have borne. [8]

[He turns to LICHAS*]*

[99] But do thou, Lichas, comrade of the toils of
Hercules, proclaim his triumphs—the conquered
house of Eurytus, his kingdom overthrown. *[To the
other attendants.]* Do you with speed drive the

---

[3] *i.e.* Delphi.   [4] Apollo.   [5] The Python.
[6] *i.e.* India, the scene of Bacchus' conquests.
[7] Slain by Perseus.
[8] *i.e.* when he relieved Atlas of his burden.

qua templa tollens acta Cenaei Iovis
austro timendum spectat Euboicum mare.

CHORVS

Par ille est superis cui pariter dies
et fortuna fuit ; mortis habet vices
lente cum trahitur vita gementibus.
quisquis sub pedibus fata rapacia
et puppem posuit fluminis ultimi,
non captiva dabit bracchia vinculis
nec pompae veniet nobile ferculum ;   110
numquam est ille miser cui facile est mori.
illum si medio decipiat ratis
ponto, cum Borean expulit Africus
aut Eurus Zephyrum, cum mare dividunt,
non puppis lacerae fragmina conligit,
ut litus medio speret in aequore ;
vitam qui poterit reddere protinus,
solus non poterit naufragium pati.

Nos turpis macies et lacrimae tenent
et crinis patrio pulvere sordidus ;   120
nos non flamma rapax, non fragor obruit.
felices sequeris, mors, miseros fugis.
stamus, nec patriae [1] messibus [2] heu locus
at [3] silvis dabitur, lapsaque sordidae
fient templa casae ; iam gelidus Dolops
hac ducet pecudes qua tepet obrutus
stratae qui superest Oechaliae cinis.

---

[1] *So Richter, with A :* patriis *E.*
[2] messibus *N. Heinsius :* moenibus *A : Leo marks the line
corrupt, and conjectures* stamus nec patria est : messibus h. l.
[3] *Leo* et, *with w, corrected by Scaliger.*

herds to where the shore, lifting on high the shrine of Cenaean Jove,[1] looks out upon the Euboic sea, fearsome with southern gales.

[*Exit* HERCULES *on his way to the Cenaean Promontory, intending there to sacrifice to Jove.*]

CHORUS OF CAPTIVE OECHALIAN MAIDENS IN COMPANY
WITH IOLE

Mate of the gods is he whose life and fortune have gone side by side; but when 'tis slowly dragged out midst lamentations, life has the lot of death. Whoe'er has set beneath his feet the greedy fates, and the last river's barque,[2] he will not give his captive arms to bonds nor fare in the victor's train a noble spoil; ne'er is he wretched for whom to die is easy. Should his boat be wrecked far out upon the deep, where South with North-wind strives, and East with West, rending the sea asunder, he does not gather up the wreckage of his broken ship, that in mid-ocean he may hope for land; he who can straightway render up his life, he only from a wreck can suffer naught.

[119] But us, foul wasting claims, and tears, and hair defiled by the dust of fatherland; us nor greedy flame nor crashing wall has overwhelmed. The happy dost thou pursue, O Death, the wretched thou fleest. Here we stand, yet alas! the spot shall no more be given to our country's crops, but to forests wild, and squalid hovels shall our fallen shrines become. Here soon shall the chill Dolopian lead his flocks where the buried ashes, sole remnant of Oechalia's ruins, still are warm. Here in our very

---

[1] So called because his temple stood at Cenaeum, a lofty promontory on the north-west point of the island of Euboea.

[2] *i.e.* he who does not fear death.

ipso Thessalicus pastor in oppido
indocta referens carmina fistula
cantu nostra canet tempora flebili;   130
et dum pauca deus saecula contrahet,
quaeretur patriae quis fuerit locus.
felix incolui non steriles focos
nec ieiuna soli iugera Thessali;
ad Trachina vocor, saxa rigentia
et dumeta iugis horrida torridis,
vix gratum pecori montivago nemus.
at si quas melior sors famulas vocat,
illas aut volucer transferet Inachus
aut Dircaea colent moenia, qua fluit   140
Ismenos tenui flumine languidus;
hic mater tumidi nupserat Herculis.   142
    Falsa est de geminis fabula noctibus,[1]   147
aether cum tenuit sidera longius
commisitque vices Lucifer Hespero
et Solem vetuit Delia tardior.   150
quae cautes Scythiae, quis genuit lapis?   143
num Titana ferum te Rhodope tulit,
te praeruptus Athos, te fera Caspia,[2]
quae virgata tibi praebuit ubera?   146
nullis vulneribus pervia membra sunt;   151
ferrum sentit hebes, lentior est chalybs;
in nudo gladius corpore frangitur
et saxum resilit, fataque neglegit
et mortem indomito corpore provocat.
non illum poterant figere cuspides,
non arcus Scythica tensus harundine,
non quae tela gerit Sarmata frigidus
aut qui soliferae suppositus plagae
vicino Nabatae vulnera dirigit   160

---

[1] *The transposition of ll. 147-150 after l. 142 is Leo's.*
[2] *So Avantius, with a : caseta A : Leo Caspias, with E.*

city a Thessalian shepherd, on rude pipe going
o'er his songs, shall sing of our story with doleful
notes; and ere God shall bring a few more generations
to an end, men will be asking where our country lay.
Once I was blest; not barren the hearth nor hungry
the acres of Thessalian soil whereon I dwelt; but now
to Trachin am I called, to a rough and stony land, to
brambles bristling on her parched hills, to woods
which e'en the wandering goats disdain. But if
some captives by a milder fate are called, then either
swift Inachus will bear them o'er,[1] or within Dir-
caean[2] walls shall they abide, where flows slow
Ismenus with scanty stream, where the mother[3] of
haughty Hercules once was wed.[4]

[147] False is the story[5] of the double night, when
the stars lingered in the sky o'erlong, when Lucifer
changed place with Hesperus, and Delia,[6] too slow,
kept back the sun. What Scythian crag, what rocky
cliff begot thee? As some fierce Titan, did Rhodope
bring thee forth, or Athos rough? Did some wild
Caspian beast, some striped tigress give thee suck?
By no wounds may his limbs be assailed; iron he
feels blunt, steel is too dull; upon his naked body
swords are broken, and stones rebound; and so he
scorns the fates, and with body all invincible defies
mortality. Sharp spear-points could not pierce him,
nor Scythian arrows shot from bended bow, nor darts
which cold Sarmatians wield, or the Parthians who,
in the land of the rising sun, with surer aim than
ever Cretan's was, direct their shafts against the

---

[1] *i.e.* either to Argos or Mycenae.
[2] Theban, so called from the neighbouring fountain of
Dirce.   [3] Alcmena.   [4] *i.e.* to Amphitryon.
[5] See Index *s.v.* "Hercules," first part. The chorus means
to say that Hercules is not the son of Jove and Alcmena.
[6] The moon.

Parthus Cnosiacis certior ictibus.
muros Oechaliae corpore propulit,
nil obstare valet ; vincere quod parat
iam victum est.   quota pars vulnere concidit !
pro fato patuit vultus iniquior
et vidisse sat est Herculeas minas.
quis vastus Briareus, quis tumidus Gyas,
supra Thessalicum cum stetit aggerem
caeloque inseruit vipereas manus,
hoc vultu riguit ?   commoda cladibus   170
magnis magna patent : nil superest mali—
iratum miserae vidimus Herculem.

IOLE

 At ego infelix non templa suis
conlapsa deis sparsosve focos,
natis mixtos arsisse patres
hominique deos, templa sepulchris,
nullum querimur commune malum ;
alio nostras fortuna vocat
lacrimas, alias flere ruinas
me fata iubent.   quae prima querar ?   180
quae summa gemam ?   pariter cuncta
deflere iuvat— [1] nec plura dedit
pectora Tellus, ut digna sonent
verbera fatis.
 Me vel Sipylum flebile saxum
fingite, superi, vel in Eridani
ponite ripis, ubi maesta sonat
Phaetontiadum silva sororum ;

---

[1] *After* iuvat *D. Heinsius recognized a lacuna, which Gronovius thought should be filled as follows :* cur non oculos
plures nobis.

neighbouring Arabians. With his bare hands did he
o'erthrow Oechalia's walls, and naught can make
stand against him; for whate'er he plans to overcome is overcome already. How few the foes who
by his wounds have fallen! His angry countenance
was death in open view, and but to have seen the
threats of Hercules is enough.[1] What huge Briareus,
what Gyas, puffed with pride, when upon Thessalia's
mountain-heap[2] they stood and clutched at heaven
with snaky hands, had countenance inflexible as his?
But mighty ills have mighty recompense. No more
is left to suffer—we have seen, oh, woe! the angry
Hercules.

IOLE

But I, unhappy one, bewail not temples fallen on
their gods, or hearth-fires scattered, or fathers burned
in mingled heaps with sons, and gods with men,
temples with tombs,—nay, no common misfortune
do I mourn; elsewhither doth fortune call my tears,
for other ruins the fates bid me weep. What lament
shall I make first? What last shall I bewail? Equally
all things is it meet to mourn. Oh me, that Mother
Earth hath not given me more eyes for tears,[3] more
breasts, that blows worthy of my losses might
resound.

[185] Me to a weeping rock[4] on Sipylus, ye heavenly
gods, transform, or set me on the banks of Po, where
the woods give back the grief of Phaëthon's sad

---

[1] *i.e.* was enough to kill his opponent.
[2] The giants piled up Ossa, Pelion, and Olympus in their
effort to reach the skies.
[3] Translating the suggested insertion of Gronovius.
[4] She is thinking of the fate of Niobe.

me vel Siculis addite saxis,
ubi fata gemam Thessala Siren,   190
vel in Edonas tollite silvas
qualis natum Daulias ales
solet Ismaria flere sub umbra ;
formam lacrimis aptate meis
resonetque malis aspera Trachin.
Cyprias lacrimas Myrrha tuetur,
raptum coniunx Ceyca gemit,
sibi Tantalis est facta superstes ;
fugit vultus Philomela suos
natumque sonat flebilis Atthis :   200
cur mea nondum capiunt volucres
bracchia plumas ?   felix, felix,
cum silva domus nostra feretur
patrioque sedens ales in agro
referam querulo murmure casus
volucremque Iolen fama loquetur.

　　Vidi, vidi miseranda mei
fata parentis, cum letifero
stipite pulsus tota iacuit
sparsus in aula.   210
a si tumulum fata dedissent,
quotiens, genitor, quaerendus eras !
potuine tuam spectare necem,
nondum teneras vestite genas
necdum forti sanguine, Toxeu ?
quid vestra queror fata, parentes,
quos in tutum mors aequa tulit ?
mea me lacrimas fortuna rogat.
iam iam dominae captiva colus
fusosque legam.   pro saeve decor

---

[1] *i.e.* make me one of the number of the Sirens who haunt
those rocks.

[2] *i.e.* Thracian　　　[3] Procne. See Index *s.v.*

sisters; or add [1] me to the rocks of Sicily, where as
a Siren I may weep Thessalia's fate; or bear me to
Edonia's [2] woods where I may mourn as, beneath
Ismarian shade, the Daulian bird [3] ever mourns her
son. Give me a form to fit my tears, and let rough
Trachin reëcho with my woes. Myrrha, the Cyprian
maid, yet guards her tears; [4] the wife [5] of Ceyx
mourns his taking off; and Niobe lives on, surviving
e'en herself; her human form has Philomel escaped,
and still the Attic maid bewails her son. [6] Why not
yet do my arms become swift wings? Happy, ah,
happy shall I be when the woods shall be called my
home, and, in my native meadows resting, with
plaintive strains I shall recall my fate, and fame shall
tell of winged Iole.

[207] I saw, I saw my father's wretched fate, when,
beaten down by the death-dealing club, he lay in
scattered fragments throughout the hall. Ah me, if
fate had given him burial, how often, father, must
thou have been sought! How could I have looked
upon thy death, O Toxeus, [7] with thy boyish cheeks
as yet unbearded, and thy veins not yet filled with
manly vigour? But why do I lament your fates, my
parents, whom kindly death has to a place of safety
borne? 'Tis my own fortune that requires my tears.
Soon, soon in captive state shall I whirl the distaff
and the spindle of my mistress. O cruel beauty,

---

[4] The exuding gum of the myrrh tree into which the maid
was changed.

[5] Alcyone, still alive in feathered form.

[6] Itys was not the son of Philomela, but of her sister,
Procne.   [7] Her brother.

formaque mortem paritura mihi,   220
tibi cuncta domus concidit uni,
dum me genitor negat Alcidae
atque Herculeus socer esse timet.
sed iam dominae tecta petantur.

CHORUS

Quid regna tui clara parentis
casusque tuos respicis amens?
fugiat vultus fortuna prior.
felix quisquis novit famulum
regemque pati vultusque suos
variare potest.   rapuit vires   230
pondusque malis casus animo
qui tulit aequo.

NVTRIX

O quam cruentus feminas stimulat furor,
cum patuit una paelici et nuptae domus!
Scylla et Charybdis Sicula contorquens freta
minus timendae, nulla non melior fera est.
namque ut reluxit paelicis captae decus
et fulsit Iole qualis innubis dies
purisve clarum noctibus sidus micat,
stetit furenti similis ac torvum intuens   240
Herculea coniunx; feta ut Armenia iacens
sub rupe tigris hoste conspecto exilit
aut iussa thyrsum quatere conceptum ferens
Maenas Lyaeum, dubia quo gressus ferat
haesit parumper; tum per Herculeos lares
attonita fertur, tota vix satis est domus.
incurrit, errat, sistit, in voltus dolor
processit omnis, pectori paene intimo

---

[1] Lyaeus.

and form doomed to bring death to me, for thee alone is all my house undone, for that my sire refused me to Alcides and feared to have Hercules for son-in-law. But now must I betake me to a mistress' home.

CHORUS

Why dost thou, foolish one, ever look back upon thy sire's illustrious kingdom and thine own misfortunes? Banish from thy face thy former fortune. Happy is he whoever knows how to bear the estate of slave or king and can match his countenance with either lot. For he who bears his ills with even soul has robbed misfortune of its strength and heaviness.

[*The scene changes to the space before the palace of Hercules and Deïanira at Trachin. Enter* NURSE OF DEÏANIRA.]

NURSE

O how bloody is the rage that goads women on, when to mistress and to wife one house has opened! Scylla and Charybdis, whirling Sicilia's waves, are not more fearful, nor is any wild beast worse. For when her captive rival's beauty was revealed, and Iole shone like the unclouded day or a bright star in the clear night glittering, even as one distraught the wife of Hercules stood there with lowering gaze (as a tigress, lying big with young 'neath some Armenian rock, at sight of an enemy leaps forth; or as a maenad, bidden to toss the thyrsus, what time she bears the god[1] within her breast, in doubt where she shall take her way, stands still a while); then through the house of Hercules she madly dashed and scarce did all the house give space enough. Forward she rushes, wanders aimlessly, stands still. All her passion has come forth into her face; in her heart's

203

nihil est relictum ; fletus insequitur minas.
nec unus habitus durat aut uno furit   250
contenta voltu ; nunc inardescunt genae,
pallor ruborem pellit et formas dolor
errat per omnes ; queritur, implorat, gemit.
    Sonuere postes—ecce praecipiti gradu
secreta mentis ore confuso exerit.

DEÏANIRA

    Quamcumque partem sedis aetheriae premis,
coniunx Tonantis, mitte in Alciden feram
quae mihi satis sit. si qua fecundum caput
palude tota vastior serpens movet,
ignara vinci, si quid excessit feras   260
immane dirum horribile, quo viso Hercules
avertat oculos, hoc specu immenso exeat.
vel si ferae negantur, hanc animam precor
converte in aliquod—quodlibet possum malum
hac mente fieri. commoda effigiem mihi
parem dolori ; non capit pectus minas.
quid excutis telluris extremae sinus
orbemque versas ?   quid rogas Ditem mala ?
omnes in isto pectore invenies feras
quas timeat ; odiis accipe hoc telum tuis.   270
ego sim noverca. perdere Alciden potes ;
perfer manus quocumque. quid cessas, dea ?
utere furente—quod iubes fieri nefas ?

---

[1] i.e. the Hydra.

depths almost naught is left; tears follow hard on threats. Nor does one posture last, nor can one countenance contain her rage; now do her cheeks flame with wrath, now pallor drives the flush away, and from form to form her smarting anguish wanders; she wails, she begs, she groans.

²⁵⁴ The doors have sounded—behold, at headlong pace she comes, with confused words revealing all the secrets of her soul.

[Enter DEÏANIRA *from within the palace.]*

DEÏANIRA

Wife of the Thunderer, whatever portion of thy heavenly home thou treadest, send 'gainst Alcides a wild beast which shall suffice for me. If any serpent,[1] vaster than all the marsh, rears up its head, to conquest all unknown; if anything is worse than other beasts, monstrous, dire, horrible, from sight of which Hercules would turn away his eyes, let this from its huge den come forth. Or, if beasts be denied, change, I pray thee, this heart of mine into some—any evil thing there is can I with this present mind become. Give me a form to match my smarting grief; my breast cannot contain its rage. Why dost thou search out the folds of farthest earth, and overturn the world? Why dost ask ills of Dis? In such a breast thou'lt find all beasts to cause him dread; take thou this weapon for thy hate—let me be step-dame.[2] Thou canst destroy Alcides; use but these hands for any end thou wilt. Why dost thou hesitate, O goddess? Use me, the mad one—what

---

[2] She thinks of the possible children of Hercules by Iole and her chance for vengeance on them.

reperi.   quid haeres?   ipsa iam cesses licet,
haec ira satis est.

NVTRIX

Pectoris sani parum,
alumna, questus comprime et flammas doma;
frena dolorem.   coniugem ostende Herculis.

DEÏANIRA

Iole meis captiva germanos dabit
natis Iovisque fiet ex famula nurus?
non flamma cursus pariter et torrens feret   280
et ursa pontum sicca caeruleum bibet—
non ibo inulta.   gesseris caelum licet
totusque pacem debeat mundus tibi,
est aliquid hydra peius: iratae dolor
nuptae.   quis ignis tantus in caelum furit
ardentis Aetnae?   quidquid est victum tibi
hic vincet animus.   capta praeripiet toros?
adhuc timebam monstra, iam nullum est malum;
cessere pestes, in locum venit ferae
invisa paelex.   summe pro rector deum   290
et clare Titan, Herculis tantum fui
coniunx timentis; vota quae superis tuli
cessere captae, paelici felix fui,
illi meas audistis, o superi, preces,
incolumis illi remeat.—o nulla dolor
contente poena, quaere supplicia horrida,
incogitata, infanda, Iunonem doce
quid odia valeant; nescit irasci satis.
pro me gerebas bella, propter me vagas
Achelous undas sanguine infecit suo,   300

---

¹ See Index *s.v.* " Bears."

crime dost bid me do? Decide. Why dost thou
falter? Though now thou dost thyself shrink back,
this rage of mine suffices.

NURSE

Dear child, thy mad heart's plaints restrain, quench
passion's fire and curb thy grief. Show thyself wife
of Hercules.

DEÏANIRA

Shall captive Iole give brothers to my sons? Shall
a slave become daughter-in-law of Jove? Together
will flame and torrent never run, and the thirsty
Bear [1] from the blue sea ne'er will drink—nor will I
go unavenged. Though thou didst bear the heavens
up, though the whole world owes its peace to thee, a
worse pest than Hydra waits thee—the wrath of an
angered wife. What fire as hot as this rages to heaven
from burning Aetna? Whate'er has been conquered
by thy might, this passion of mine shall conquer.—
And shall a slave seize on my marriage bed? Till
now did I fear monsters, but now is no evil more;
the pests have vanished and in the place of beasts
has come the hated harlot. O most high ruler of the
gods, O lustrous Sun, I have been wife to Hercules
but in his perils; the prayers which to the heavenly
ones I raised have been granted to a slave; for a
harlot have I been fortunate; for her have ye heard
my prayers, O gods, for her is he safe returned.—O
grief that can be satisfied with no revenge, seek thee
some dreadful punishment, unthought, unspeakable;
teach Juno's self what hate can do; she knows not
to rage enough. For me didst thou do battle;
on my account did Acheloüs dye his wandering
waves with his own blood, when now he became a

cum lenta serpens fieret, in taurum trucem
nunc flecteret serpente deposita minas,
et mille in hoste vinceres uno feras.
iam displicemus, capta praelata est mihi—
non praeferetur ; qui dies thalami ultimus
nostri est futurus, hic erit vitae tuae.

  Quid hoc ?   recedit animus et ponit minas.
iam cessat ira ; quid miser langues dolor ?
perdis furorem, coniugis tacitae fidem
mihi reddis iterum.—quid vetas flammas ali ?   310
quid frangis ignes ? hunc mihi serva impetum,
pares eamus ¹—non erit votis opus ;
aderit noverca quae manus nostras regat
nec invocata.

NVTRIX

      Quod paras demens scelus ?
perimes maritum cuius extremus dies
primusque laudes novit et caelo tenus
erecta terras fama suppositas habet ?
Graiorum in istos terra consurget lares
domusque soceri prima et Aetolum genus
sternetur omne ; saxa iam dudum ac faces   320
in te ferentur, vindicem tellus suum
defendet omnis. una quot poenas dabis !
effugere terras crede et humanum genus
te posse—fulmen genitor Alcidae gerit.
iam iam minaces ire per caelum faces
specta et tonantem fulmine excusso diem.
mortem quoque ipsam, quam putas tutam, time ;

<hr>

¹ *So Leo and Richter, following an emendation of Madvig :*
patres erimus *E :* pares eramus *A.*

stubborn serpent, now to a fierce bull changed his threats, the serpent form discarded, and thou in that one foe didst conquer a thousand beasts. But now I please thee not; a captive is preferred to me—but she shall not be preferred; for that day which shall end our marriage joys shall end thy life.

[307] But what is this? My passion dies away and abates its threats. Now anger ceases; why dost thou languish, O wretched grief? Thou givest o'er thy madness, makest me again the faithful, uncomplaining wife.—Why dost forbid the feeding of the flames? Why checkest the fire? Keep but this passion in me; hand in hand let us go on—there will be no need of prayers; a step-dame[1] will be near to direct my hands and unbesought.

NURSE

What crime, distraught one, dost thou purpose? Wilt slay thy husband whose praises the evening and the morning[2] know full well, whose fame, towering to the sky, holds all the world beneath? The land of Greece will rise to defend that home, and this thy father's[3] house and the whole Aetolian race will be the first to be o'erthrown; soon rocks and firebrands will be hurled against thee, since every land will rally to its defender. How many penalties wilt thou, one woman, pay! Suppose thou canst escape the world and the race of men—the father of Alcides wields the thunder-bolt. Now, even now behold his threat'ning fires flashing athwart the sky, and the heavens thundering with the lightning shock. Even death itself, which thou deemest a place of safety,

---

[1] Juno.   [2] i.e. East and West.
[3] Deïanira's father, the father-in-law (socer) of Hercules.

dominatur illic patruus Alcidae tui.
quocumque perges, misera, cognatos deos
illic videbis.

DEÏANIRA

Maximum fieri scelus   330
et ipsa fateor, sed dolor fieri iubet.

NVTRIX

Moriere.

DEÏANIRA

Moriar Herculis nempe incluti
coniunx nec ullus nocte discussa dies
viduam notabit nec meos paelex toros
captiva capiet.   ante ab occasu dies
nascetur, Indos ante glacialis polus
Scythasve tepida Phoebus inficiet rota,
quam me relictam Thessalae aspiciant nurus.
meo iugales sanguine extinguam faces.
aut pereat aut me perimat ; elisis feris   340
et coniugem addat, inter Herculeos licet
me quoque labores numeret ; Alcidae toros
moritura certe corpore amplectar meo.
ire, ire ad umbras Herculis nuptam libet,
sed non inultam.   si quid ex nostro Hercule
concepit Iole, manibus evellam meis
ante et per ipsas paelicem invadam faces.
me nuptiali victimam feriat die
infestus, Iolen dum supra exanimem ruam—
felix iacet quicumque quos odit premit.   350

NVTRIX

Quid ipsa flammas pascis et vastum foves
ultro dolorem ?   misera, quid cassum times ?

---

fear; for there the uncle [1] of thine Alcides reigns. Turn where thou wilt, poor woman, there wilt thou see his kindred gods.

DEÏANIRA

That I am doing a fearful crime, e'en I myself confess; but passion bids me do it.

NURSE

Thou'lt die.

DEÏANIRA

Yea, truly, will I die, but the wife of glorious Hercules; neither shall any dawn, banishing night, brand me as widow; nor shall captive creature make capture of my bed. Sooner shall day be born in the western sky, sooner shall Indians grow pale 'neath the icy pole, or Scythians tan 'neath Phoebus' burning car, than shall the dames of Thessaly see me abandoned. With my own blood will I quench her [2] marriage torches. Either let him die or do me to death. To slaughtered beasts let him add wife as well, and let him count me, too, 'mongst the toils of Hercules; to Alcides' couch, aye with my dying body, will I cling. Ah, sweet, 'tis sweet to go to the shades as bride of Hercules,—but not without my vengeance. If Iole from my Hercules has conceived a child, with mine own hands will I tear it forth untimely, and by her very wedding torches' glare will I face the harlot. Let him in wrath slay me as victim on his nuptial day, so I but fall on the corpse of Iole. Happy he lies who crushes those he hates.

NURSE

Why dost thyself feed thy flames and wantonly foster an unmeasured grief? Poor soul, why dost thou cherish a needless fear? He did love Iole;

211

dilexit Iolen; nempe cum staret parens
regisque natam peteret. in famulae locum
regina cecidit; perdidit vires amor
multumque ab illa traxit infelix status.
illicita amantur, excidit quidquid licet.

DEÏANIRA

Fortuna amorem peior inflammat magis;
amat vel ipsum quod caret patrio lare,
quod nudus auro crinis et gemma iacet,   360
ipsas misericors forsan aerumnas amat;
hoc usitatum est Herculi, captas amat.

NVTRIX

Dilecta Priami nempe Dardanii soror
concessa famula est; adice quot nuptas prius,
quot virgines dilexit.   erravit vagus.
Arcadia nempe virgo, Palladios choros
dum nectit, Auge, vim stupri passa excidit,
nullamque amoris Hercules retinet notam.
referam quid alias?   nempe Thespiades vacant
brevique in illas arsit Alcides face.   370
hospes Timoli Lydiam fovit nurum
et amore captus ad leves sedit colus,
udum feroci stamen intorquens manu.
nempe illa cervix spolia deposuit ferae
crinemque mitra pressit et famulus stetit,
hirtam Sabaea marcidus myrrha comam.
ubique caluit, sed levi caluit face.

---

¹ Hesione.

but 'twas while yet her father reigned secure, and 'twas a king's daughter that he sought. The princess has now fallen to the place of slave; love has lost its power, and much from her charm her unhappy lot has stolen. What is forbidden we love; if granted it falls from our desire.

DEÏANIRA

Nay, but fallen fortunes fan hotter the flames of love; for this very cause he loves her, that she hath lost her father's house, that her hair lies stripped of gold and gems; out of pity, perchance, he loves her very woes; 'tis the wont of Hercules to love captive maids.

NURSE

'Tis true he loved the captive sister [1] of Dardanian Priam, but he gave her to another; [2] add all the dames, all the maids he loved before. A wanderer on earth, a wanderer in love was he. Why, the Arcadian maiden, Auge, while leading Pallas' sacred dance, suffered his lust's violence, but fell from his regard, and Hercules retains no trace of his love for her. Why mention others? The Thespiades are forgotten; for them with but a passing flame Alcides burned. When a guest on Timolus, he caressed the Lydian woman [3] and, daft with love, sat beside her swift distaff, twisting the moistened thread with doughty fingers. His shoulders, indeed, had laid aside the famous lion's-skin, a turban confined his hair, and there he stood like any slave, his shaggy locks dripping with Sabaean myrrh. Everywhere has he burned with love, but burned with feeble flame.

[2] *i.e.* to Telamon, who assisted him in the capture of Troy.
[3] Omphale, queen of Lydia.

DEÏANIRA

Haerere amantes post vagos ignes solent.

NVTRIX

Famulamne et hostis praeferet natam tibi?

DEÏANIRA

Vt laeta[1] silvas forma vernantes habet,   380
cum nemora nuda primus investit tepor,
at cum solutos expulit Boreas Notos
et saeva totas bruma discussit comas,
deforme solis aspicis truncis nemus;
sic nostra longum forma percurrens iter
deperdit aliquid semper et fulget minus,
nec illa vetus[2] est.   quidquid in nobis fuit
olim petitum cecidit, aut pariter labat.[3]
aetas citato senior eripuit gradu,[4]   390
materque multum rapuit ex illo mihi,   389
vides ut altum famula non perdat decus?   391
cessere cultus penitus et paedor sedet;
tamen per ipsas fulget aerumnas decor
nihilque ab illa casus et fatum grave
nisi regna traxit.   hic meum pectus timor,
altrix, lacessit, hic rapit somnos pavor.
praeclara totis gentibus coniunx eram
thalamosque nostros invido voto nurus
optabat omnis; quaeve mens quicquam deos
orabat ullos, nuribus Argolicis fui   400
mensura voti.   quem Iovi socerum parem,
altrix, habebo?   quis sub hoc mundo mihi

---

[1] alta *MSS.*, *corrected by Madvig.*
[2] *So Richter:* nec illa Venus *E:* haec illa Venus *Kiessling,*
followed by Leo.

DEÏANIRA

Oft after wandering fires lovers have clung to one.

NURSE

A slave and daughter of his foe shall he prefer to
thee?

DEÏANIRA

As a gladsome beauty covers the budding groves
when the first warmth of spring clothes the bare
forest trees, but, when the North-wind has put the
mild South to flight, and savage winter has shaken
off all the leaves, thou seest but a shapeless grove of
trunks alone; so does my beauty, pursuing a length-
ening way, lose something ever, and less brightly
gleams, nor is it as of yore. Whate'er in me was
sought in former days has vanished or is failing along
with me. Old age with hastening steps hath taken
much, and much of it hath motherhood stolen from
me. But seest thou how this slave hath not lost her
glorious charm? Gone are her adornings and squalor
clings close upon her; and yet through her very distresses beauty shines and naught have misfortune and
this hard stroke of fate stolen from her save her realm.
O nurse, this fear of her racks my heart; this dread
doth destroy my slumbers. I was a wife celebrated
in every land, and for marriage such as mine all
women prayed with envious prayer; or whatever
soul asked aught of any gods, for the prayers of
Grecian dames I was the measure. What father-in-
law like to Jove, O Nurse, shall I e'er have? Who
beneath these heavens will be given me as husband?

---

[3] *So Richter:* et . . . labat *E:* et partu labat *A: Leo conjectures* labor.   [4] *Leo deletes this line.*

dabitur maritus? ipse qui Alcidae imperat
facibus suis me iungat Eurystheus licet,
minus est. toris caruisse regnantis leve est:
alte illa cecidit quae viro caret Hercule.

NVTRIX

Conciliat animos coniugum partus fere.

DEÏANIRA

Hic [1] ipse forsan dividet partus toros.

NVTRIX

Famula illa trahitur interim donum tibi.

DEÏANIRA

Hic quem per urbes ire praeclarum vides   410
et fulva tergo spolia gestantem ferae,
qui regna miseris donat et celsis rapit,
vasta gravatus horridam clava manum,
cuius triumphos ultimi Seres canunt
et quisquis alius orbe concepto [2] iacet,—
levis est nec illum gloriae stimulat decor ;
errat per orbem, non ut aequetur Iovi
nec ut per urbes magnus Argolicas eat :
quod amet requirit, virginum thalamos petit.
si qua est negata, rapitur ; in populos furit,   420
nuptas ruinis quaerit et vitium impotens
virtus vocatur. cecidit Oechalia inclita
unusque Titan vidit atque unus dies
stantem et cadentem ; causa bellandi est amor.

---

[1] *So Richter after emendation of N. Heinsius:* sic *MSS.
and Leo.*

[2] *Leo* †concepto, *with* ΣA : consepto ς : *Grotius conjectures*
consumpto : *Gronovius* conpecto.

Though Eurystheus' self, who rules Alcides, should
wed me with his own torches, 'tis not enough. 'Tis
a trivial thing to have lost a royal couch; but from a
far height has she fallen who loses Hercules.

NURSE

Children ofttimes win back the love of husbands.

DEÏANIRA

These children themselves perchance will dissolve
the bond.[1]

NURSE

Meanwhile that slave is brought as gift to thee.

DEÏANIRA

He whom thou seest going, big with fame, from
town to town, wearing the spoil of a tawny lion on
his back; who gives kingdoms to the lowly and
takes them from the proud, his dread hand laden
with a massive club; whose triumphs the far off
Seres sing, and whoe'er besides dwells in the whole
known world,—he is a trifler, nor does the charm of
glory urge him on. He goes wandering o'er the
earth, not in the hope that he may rival Jove, nor
that he may fare illustrious through Grecian cities.
Some one to love he seeks; his quest is maidens'
chambers. If any is refused him, she is ravished;
against nations doth he rage, midst ruins seeks his
brides, and unrestrained excess is called heroic.
Oechalia, the illustrious, fell; one sun, one day
beheld her stand and fall; and passion was the

[1] *i.e.* if one woman's child holds her husband to her,
another's child (Iole's) will turn him from the old to his new
love.

totiens timebit Herculi natam parens
quotiens negabit, hostis est quotiens socer
fieri recusat; si gener non fit, ferit.
post haec quid istas innocens servo manus,
donec furentem simulet ac saeva manu
intendat arcus meque natumque opprimat?   430
sic coniuges expellit Alcides suas,
haec sunt repudia.   nec potest fieri nocens;
terris videri sceleribus causam suis
fecit novercam.   quid stupes, segnis furor?
scelus occupandum est; perage dum fervet manus.

NVTRIX

Perimes maritum?

DEÏANIRA

Paelicis certe meae.

NVTRIX

At Iove creatum.

DEÏANIRA

Nempe et Alcmena satum.

NVTRIX

Ferrone?

DEÏANIRA

Ferro.

NVTRIX

Si nequis?

DEÏANIRA

Perimam dolo.

mother of that strife. As oft as a father shall deny
his child to Hercules, and refuse to be the father of
his foe, so oft shall he have cause to fear; if he is
not accepted as a son, he smites. After all this, why
do I harmlessly keep back these hands until he feign
another fit of madness,[1] with deadly hand bend his
bow, and slay me and my son?[2] Thus does Alcides
put away his wives; such is his manner of divorce.
Yet naught can make him guilty! He has made the
world believe his step-dame answerable for his crimes.
Why art inactive then, thou sluggish rage? His
crime must be forestalled; act while thy hand is hot!

NURSE

Wilt slay thy husband?

DEÏANIRA

Truly, my rival's husband.

NURSE

But the son of Jove?

DEÏANIRA

Yes, but the son of Alcmena, too.

NURSE

With the sword?

DEÏANIRA

The sword.

NURSE

If thou canst not?

DEÏANIRA

I'll slay with guile.

[1] The reference is to the death of Megara and her sons at
the hands of mad Hercules. [2] Hyllus.

219

NVTRIX

Quis iste furor est?

DEÏANIRA

Quem meus coniunx docet.

NVTRIX

Quem nec noverca potuit, hunc perimes virum? 440

DEÏANIRA

Caelestis ira quos premit, miseros facit ;
humana nullos.

NVTRIX

Parce, miseranda, et time.

DEÏANIRA

Contempsit omnes ille qui mortem prius ;
libet ire in enses.

NVTRIX

Maior admisso tuus,

alumna, dolor est ; culpa par odium exigat.
cur saeva modicis statuis ?   ut laesa es dole.

DEÏANIRA

Leve esse credis paelicem nuptae malum ?
quidquid dolorem pascit, hoc nimium puta.

NVTRIX

Amorne clari fugit Alcidae tibi ?

---

[1] *i.e.* whatever else.

NURSE

What madness that?

DEÏANIRA

That which my husband teaches me.

NURSE

Whom e'en his step-dame could not slay—wilt thou slay him?

DEÏANIRA

Celestial wrath but makes wretched those on whom it falls; man's wrath makes them naught.

NURSE

Spare him, O wretched one, and fear.

DEÏANIRA

He has scorned all men, who first has scorn of death; 'tis sweet to go against the sword.

NURSE

Thy smart is too great for the offence, my child; let his fault claim but equal hate. Why dost so fiercely judge a light offence? According as thou hast been injured, grieve.

DEÏANIRA

Thinkst thou a mistress is light evil for a wife? Whatever [1] fosters anguish, count this [2] beyond all bounds.

NURSE

Has thy love for glorious Alcides fled away?

[2] *i.e.* the situation described in the preceding line.

DEÏANIRA

Non fugit, altrix, remanet et penitus sedet   450
fixus medullis, crede ; sed magnus dolor
iratus amor est.

NVTRIX

           Artibus magicis fere
coniugia nuptae precibus admixtis ligant.
vernare iussi frigore in medio nemus
missumque fulmen stare ; concussi fretum
cessante vento, turbidum explicui mare
et sicca tellus fontibus patuit novis ;
habuere motum saxa, discussi fores [1]
umbrasque Ditis,[2] et mea iussi prece
manes locuntur, tacuit infernus canis ;   460
nox media solem vidit et noctem dies [3] ;   462
mare terra caelum et Tartarus servit mihi   461
nihilque leges ad meos cantus tenet.
flectemus illum, carmina invenient iter.

DEÏANIRA

Quas Pontus herbas generat aut quas Thessala
sub rupe Pindus alit [4] ubi inveniam malum
cui cedat ille ?   carmine in terras mago
descendat astris Luna desertis licet
et bruma messes videat et cantu fugax
stet deprehensum fulmen et versa vice   470
medius coactis ferveat stellis dies :
non flectet illum.

---

[1] fores *ω : regarded as corrupt by Leo, who conjectures*
inferos : arbores *Birt.*
[2] *So Richter : Leo* umbrae stetistis, *with ω.*

HERCULES OETAEUS

DEÏANIRA

Not fled, dear Nurse; it still remains, believe me, deep-seated and fixed in my heart's core; but outraged love is poignant misery.

NURSE

By magic arts and prayers commingled do wives oft hold fast their husbands. I have bidden the trees grow green in the midst of winter's frost, and the hurtling lightning stand; I have stirred up the deep, though the winds were still, and have calmed the heaving sea; the parched earth has opened with fresh fountains; rocks have found motion; the gates have I rent asunder and the shades of Dis, and at my prayer's demand the spirits talk, the infernal dog is still; midnight has seen the sun, and day, the night; the sea, land, heaven and Tartarus yield to my will, and naught holds to law against my incantations. Bend him we will; my charms will find the way.

DEÏANIRA

What herbs does Pontus grow, or what does Pindus nourish 'neath the rocks of Thessaly,[1] wherein I may find a bane to conquer him? Though Luna should leave the stars and come down to earth, obedient to magic; though winter should see ripe grain; though the swift bolt should stand still, arrested by thy charm; though times be changed, and midday burn amid the crowding stars: 'twill not bend him.

[1] Where Medea, the famous witch, gathered magic herbs.

---

[3] Lines 461, 462 transposed by Bothe.
[4] Leo, †aluit, with E: corrected by Peiper, followed by Richter.

NVTRIX .

Vicit et superos Amor.

DEÏANIRA

Vincetur uni forsan et spolium dabit
Amorque summus fiet Alcidae labor.—
sed te per omne caelitum numen precor,
per hunc timorem : quidquid arcani apparo
penitus recondas et fide tacita premas.

NVTRIX

Quid istud est quod esse secretum petis ?

DEÏANIRA

Non tela sunt, non arma, non ignis minax.

NVTRIX

Praestare fateor posse me tacitam fidem,   480
si scelere careat ; interim scelus est fides.

DEÏANIRA

Circumspice agedum, ne quis arcana occupet,
partemque in omnem vultus inquirens eat.

NVTRIX

En locus ab omni tutus arbitrio vacat.

DEÏANIRA

Est in remoto regiae sedis loco
arcana tacitus nostra defendens specus.
non ille primos accipit soles locus,

NURSE

But love has conquered e'en heavenly gods.

DEÏANIRA

By one [1] alone, perchance, will he be conquered and yield his spoils, and Love become Alcides' crowning toil.—But thee by all the deities of heaven I pray, by this my fear: whatever secret thing I am preparing, hide it deep, and in faithful silence hold it fast.

NURSE

What is it that thou seekst to keep in secret?

DEÏANIRA

It is not spears, not arms, not threatening fire.

NURSE

That I can keep faithful silence I confess, if it be free from crime; but silence itself sometimes is criminal.

DEÏANIRA

Come, look about, lest someone grasp my secret, and in all directions turn thy questful glance.

NURSE

Behold the place is safe and free from all observers.

DEÏANIRA

In a remote corner of the royal dwelling is a recess that silently guards my secret. Neither the first rays of the sun can reach that spot, nor yet his

[1] Hercules.

non ille seros, cum ferens Titan diem [1]
lassum rubenti mergit Oceano iugum [2]
illic amoris pignus Herculei latet.   490
altrix, fatebor : auctor est Nessus mali
quem gravida Nephele Thessalo genuit duci,
qua celsus [3] astris inserit Pindus caput
ultraque nubes Othrys eductus riget.
namque ut subactus Herculis clava horridi
Achelous omnes facilis in species dari
tandem peractis omnibus patuit feris
unoque turpe subdidit cornu caput,
me coniugem dum victor Alcides habet,
repetebat Argos.   Forte per campos vagus   500
Euenos altum gurgitem in pontum ferens
iam paene summis turbidus silvis erat.
transire Nessus verticem solitus vadis
pretium poposcit.   meque iam dorso ferens
qua iungit hominem spina deficiens equo,
frangebat ipsas fluminis tumidi minas.
iam totus undis Nessus exierat ferox
medioque adhuc errabat Alcides vado,
vasto rapacem verticem scindens gradu,
at ille ut esse vidit Alciden procul :   510
" tu praeda nobis" inquit " et coniunx eris ;
prohibetur undis," meque complexus ferens
gressum citabat.   Non tenent undae Herculem :
" infide vector" inquit " immixti licet
Ganges et Hister vallibus iunctis eant,

---

[1] *Leo thinks there is a lacuna after line 488 and fills it thus :*
exurgit undis, cumque germanam vocans.

[2] *So Richter :* diem *Leo with* E.

[3] *So* A *:* †trepidus *Leo, with* E, *conjecturing* aetherius :
rigidus O. Rossbach.

226

last, when Titan, bringing the day to rest, plunges his weary yoke in the ruddy sea. There lurks the surety of Alcides' love. Nurse, I'll confess to thee: the giver of the baleful thing was Nessus, whom Nephele, heavy with child, to the Thessalian chieftain [1] bore, where lofty Pindus to the stars lifts up his head and Othrys stands stiff, towering above the clouds. For when Achelöus, forced by the club of dread Hercules to shift with ready ease from form to form, his beast-shapes all exhausted, at last stood forth and bowed his head, marred and with single horn,[2] victorious Hercules, with me, his bride, set out for Argos.

[500] It chanced that Evenus, wandering through the plains, rolling his deep eddies to the sea, was now in flood almost to the tree-tops' level. Nessus, accustomed to ford the whirling stream, offered to take me over for a price; and, bearing me on his back, where the backbone, leaving the equine enters the human form, soon was stemming even the threatening waves of the swollen flood. Now had wild Nessus entirely left the waters and Alcides was still wandering in mid-stream, cleaving the down-sweeping flood with his mighty strides; but when the centaur saw Alcides still afar, "Thou shalt be spoil of mine," he cried, "and wife; he is kept from thee by the waves"; and, clasping me in his arms as he bore me on, was galloping away.

[513] But the waves did not hold Hercules; "O faithless ferryman," he cried, "though Ganges and Hister commingled in united beds should flow, I

---

[1] Ixion.
[2] Hercules had wrenched away one horn from Achelöus while the latter was fighting in bull-form.

vincemus ambos, consequar telo fugam."
praecessit arcus verba ; tum longum ferens
harundo vulnus tenuit haerentem fugam
mortemque fixit.   ille, iam quaerens diem,
tabum fluentem[1] volneris dextra excipit   520
traditque nobis ungulae insertum suae,
quam forte saeva sciderat avolsam manu.
tunc verba moriens addit ; " hoc " inquit " magae
dixere amorem posse defigi malo ;
hoc docta Mycale Thessalas docuit nurus,
unam inter omnes Luna quam sequitur magas
astris relictis.   inlitas vestes dabis
hac " inquit " ipsa tabe, si paelex tuos
invisa thalamos tulerit et coniunx levis
aliam parenti dederit altisono nurum.   530
hoc nulla lux conspiciat, hoc tenebrae tegant
tantum remotae ; sic potens vires suas
sanguis tenebit."   verba deprendit quies
mortemque lassis intulit membris sopor.

   Tu, quam meis admittit arcanis fides,
perge ut nitentem virus in vestem datum
mentem per artus adeat et tacitum means[2]
intret medullas

NVTRIX

                    Ocius iussa exsequar,
alumna, precibus tu deum invictum advoca,
qui certa tenera tela dimittit manu.   540

----

[1] *So E : Leo* fluente : tabem fluentis *A*.
[2] *So Richter ·* tactus sinus *A :* tacitus mas *E : Leo* tactu
sinus.

shall o'ercome them both and with my shaft o'ertake
thy flight." His bow was swifter than his words.
Then the reedy shaft, wounding from afar, stayed
his hampered flight and implanted death. The
Centaur, now groping for light, in his right hand
caught the poison [1] flowing from the wound, and this
he gave me, pouring it into his hoof, which with
mad hand he had chanced to wrench away. Then
with his dying words he spoke : "By this charm
magicians have said love can be firmly fixed ; so were
Thessalian wives by the wise Mycale instructed,
whom only, midst all wonder-working crones, Luna
will forsake the stars and follow. A garment,
smeared with this very gore, shalt thou give to him,
if ever a hated mistress should usurp thy chamber,
and thy fickle husband should give another daughter
to his high-thundering sire. This let no light behold ; let darkness only, thick and hidden, cover it ;
so shall the potent blood retain its powers." Silence
seized on his words and to his weary limbs came the
sleep of death.

535 Now do thou, whom loyalty makes sharer of
my secret, haste thee that the poison, upon a
glittering robe besmeared, go through his heart
and limbs and, stealing silently, enter his very
marrow.

NURSE

With speed will I do thy bidding, dearest child ;
and do thou pray to the god [2] invincible, who with
tender hand doth send unerring shafts. [*Exit* NURSE.

[1] Communicated to the blood by the Hydra-poisoned arrow
of Hercules.
[2] Cupid.

229

DEÏANIRA

Te deprecor, quem mundus et superi timent
et aequor et qui fulmen Aetnaeum quatit,
timende matri te aliger saevae puer:
intende certa spiculum velox manu,
non ex sagittis levibus. e numero precor
graviore prome quod tuae nondum manus
misere in aliquem ; non levi telo est opus,
ut amare possit Hercules. rigidas manus
intende et arcum cornibus iunctis para.
nunc, nunc sagittam prome qua quondam hor-
    ridum   550
Iovem petisti, fulmine abiecto deus
cum fronte subita tumuit et rabidum mare
taurus puellae vector Assyriae scidit ;
immitte amorem, vincat exempla omnia—
amare discat coniugem. si quas decor
Ioles inussit pectori Herculeo faces,
extingue totas, perbibat formam mei.
tu fulminantem saepe domuisti Iovem,
tu furva nigri sceptra gestantem poli,
turbae ducem maioris et dominum Stygis ;   560
tuque o noverca gravior irata deus,
cape hunc triumphum solus et vince Herculem.

NVTRIX

Prolata vis est quaeque Palladia colu
lassavit omnem texta famularum manum.
nunc congeratur virus et vestis bibat

---

[1] The bolts of Jove were forged in Vulcan's smithy under
Aetna.   [2] Europa.

HERCULES OETAEUS

DEÏANIRA

Thee do I pray, by earth and heaven-dwellers held in fear, by sea, by him who wields Aetnaean [1] thunderbolts, and by thy ruthless mother to be feared, O winged boy; with unerring hand aim a swift shaft, and not of thy lighter arrows. Choose thee, I pray, one of thy heavier shafts, which thy hands have ne'er yet shot at any; for no light weapon must thou use that Hercules may feel the power of love. Stretch thy hands stiffly forth, and bend thy bow until the tips shall meet. Now, now that shaft let loose with which once thou aimedst at Jove the terrible, what time the god threw down his thunderbolt and as a bull, with horns quick-sprouting on his brow, clove through the boisterous sea, bearing the Assyrian maid. [2] Fill him with love; let him outstrip all precedents,—let him learn to love his wife. If Iole's beauty hath kindled fires in the breast of Hercules, extinguish them every one, and of my beauty let him deeply drink. Oft hast thou conquered Jove, the thunderer, oft him who wields the dark sceptre of the dusky world, king of the greater throng, and lord of Styx; and now, O god more dreadful than a step-dame's wrath, win thou this triumph all alone, and conquer Hercules.

[*Re-enter* NURSE, *with robe and charm.*]

NURSE

The charm has been brought out and a robe from Pallas' [3] distaff, at whose weaving thy maidens all have wrought with weary hands. Now let the poison be prepared and let the robe of Hercules

[3] The arts of spinning and weaving were of Pallas' invention.

Herculea pestem ; precibus augebo malum.

　In tempore ipso navus occurrit Lichas ;
celanda vis est dira, ne pateant doli.

DEÏANIRA

　O quod superbae non habent umquam domus,
fidele semper regibus nomen Licha,　　　　　　　　570
cape hos amictus, nostra quos nevit manus,
dum vagus in orbe fertur et victus mero
tenet feroci Lydiam gremio nurum,
dum poscit Iolen.　 sed iecur fors horridum
flectam merendo ; merita vicerunt malos.
non ante coniunx induat vestes iube
quam ture flammas pascat et placet deos,
cana rigentem populo cinctus comam.

　Ipsa in penates regios gressus feram
precibusque Amoris horridi matrem colam.　　　　580
vos, quas paternis extuli comites focis,
Calydoniae lugete deflendam vicem.

CHORVS

Flemus casus, Oenei, tuos
comitum primos turba per annos,

soak up its magic power; and by my incantations
will I increase the charm.

[*While they are occupying themselves with the robe,*
LICHAS *is seen approaching.*]

⁵⁶⁷ But in the nick of time the zealous Lichas
comes; the dire potency of the robe must be concealed lest our wiles be punished.

[*Enter* LICHAS.]

DEÏANIRA

O Lichas, name ever loyal to thy lords, though
loyalty proud houses ne'er possess, take thou this
garment which my hands have woven while he was
wandering o'er the earth, or, spent with wine, was
holding in his doughty arms the Lydian queen, or
seeking Iole. And yet, perchance, I may turn his
rough heart to me again by my deserving; for
deserts oft conquer those who work us ill. Before
my husband puts this garment on, bid him burn incense and appease the gods, his stiff locks wreathed
the while with hoary poplar.

[LICHAS *takes the robe and departs upon his mission.*]

⁵⁷⁹ I will myself pass within the royal palace and
with prayers worship the mother of relentless Love.

[*To her Aetolian attendants.*]

Do ye, whom I have brought as comrades from my
father's house, ye Calydonian maids, bewail the fortune that demands your tears.   [*Exit.*

CHORUS OF AETOLIAN WOMEN

O child of Oeneus, truly do we weep for thy
misfortunes, the band of thy companions through
thy childhood years, we weep thy couch dishonoured,

flemus dubios, veneranda, toros.
nos Acheloi tecum solitae
pulsare vadum, cum iam tumidas
vere peracto poneret undas
gracilisque gradu serperet aequo,
nec praecipitem volveret amnem   590
flavus rupto fonte Lycormas ;
nos Palladias ire per aras
et virgineos celebrare choros,
nos Cadmeis orgia ferre
tecum solitae condita cistis,
cum iam pulso sidere brumae
tertia soles evocat aestas
et spiciferae concessa deae
Attica mystas cludit Eleusin.
nunc quoque casum quemcumque times,   600
fidas comites accipe fatis ;
nam rara fides ubi iam melior
fortuna ruit.

  Tu quicumque es qui sceptra tenes,
licet omne tua vulgus in aula
centum pariter limina pulset ;
cum tot populis stipatus eas,
in tot populis vix una fides.
tenet auratum limen Erinys,
et cum magnae patuere fores,   610
intrant fraudes cautique doli
ferrumque latens ; cumque in populos
prodire paras, comes invidia est.

---

¹ Identified by Strabo with the Evenus, a neighbouring
river of Aetolia.
² The sacred objects used in the orgiastic worship of
Bacchus.
³ Called in the text Cadmaean from Cadmus, founder of
Thebes.

lady whom we revere. Often with thee have we splashed in Acheloüs' shallows, when now, the springtime passed, he allayed his swollen waters and, a slender stream, crept on with quiet course, and Lycormas [1] no longer rolled his headlong waters on, dark-hued with bursting fountains. Together were we wont to fare to Pallas' shrines and join in virgin dances, to bear the mysteries [2] in Theban [3] baskets hidden, when now the wintry star had fled, and each third summer [4] called forth the sun, and when the grain-giving goddess' [5] sacred seat, Attic Eleusis, shut in her mystic worshippers. Now too, whatever lot thou fearest, take us as trusted comrades of thy fates ; for rare is loyalty when now better fortune fails.

[604] O thou,[6] whoe'er thou art who the sceptre holdest, though all the people throng within thy hall, pressing together through its thousand doors ; though when thou walkst abroad whole nations hem thee round ; in all those nations scarce one man is true. Erinys keeps the gilded gate, and when the great doors have opened wide, there come in treacheries and cunning wiles and the lurking dagger ; and when amongst the people thou wouldst walk, envy walks by thy side. As often as dawn

----

[4] The festival of Bacchus was celebrated every third year in honour of his conquest of India.
[5] Ceres. The reference is to the Eleusinian mysteries. All these festivals these women had been wont to attend together in childhood.
[6] Addressed to kings in general.

noctem quotiens summovet Eos,
regem totiens credite nasci.
pauci reges, non regna colunt ;
plures fulgor concitat aulae.
cupit hic regi proximus ipsi
clarus latas ire per urbes ;
urit miserum gloria pectus.   620
cupit hic gazis implere famem ;
nec tamen omnis plaga gemmiferi
sufficit Histri nec tota sitim
Lydia vincit nec quae Zephyro
subdita tellus stupet aurato
flumine clarum radiare Tagum ;
nec si totus serviat Hebrus
ruraque dives iungat Hydaspes
intraque suos currere fines
spectet toto flumine Gangen.   630
avidis, avidis natura parum est.

 Colit hic reges regumque lares,
non ut presso vomere semper
numquam cesset curvus arator
vel mille secent arva coloni ;
solas optat quas ponat opes.
colit hic reges, calcet ut omnes
perdatque aliquos nullumque levet ;
tantum ut noceat, cupit esse potens.

 Quota pars moritur tempore fati ! 640
quos felices Cynthia vidit,
vidit miseros enata dies.
rarum est felix idemque senex.
caespes Tyrio mollior ostro
solet inpavidos ducere somnos ;

---

[1] *i.e.* so many dangers to the king's life lurk in the night
that if he survives these it is as if he were born anew in the
morning.

drives out the night, so often believe a king is born.[1]
Few worship kings and not their thrones; for 'tis the
glitter of the royal hall that stirs the most. One
man is eager to fare illustrious through broad towns
next to the king himself; for greed of glory burns
his wretched breast. Another longs with treasure
to appease his hunger; and yet not all gem-bearing
Hister's tract would satisfy, nor would the whole of
Lydia sate his thirst, nor the land [2] which, lying
'neath the west-wind, marvels to see bright Tagus
gleam with golden water; nor if all Hebrus were
his own, and rich Hydaspes should be added to his
fields, and he should gaze on Ganges flowing with all
its stream within his boundaries. For greed, for
greed all nature is too little.

[632] One man courts kings and homes of kings, not
that his ploughman, forever stooping o'er the deep-
driven share, may never cease his toil, or that the
peasantry may till his thousand fields; but wealth
alone, which he may hoard away, he seeks. Another
man courts kings that he may trample all, may ruin
many and establish none; he covets power only to
harm therewith.

[640] How few live out their allotted span! Whom
Cynthia [3] saw in happiness, the new-born day sees
wretched. 'Tis rare to find old age and happiness
in one. The couch of turf, softer than Tyrian
purple, oft soothes to fearless slumber; but gilded

---

[2] Spain.
[3] *i.e.* the moon of the previous night.

aurea rumpunt tecta quietem
vigilesque trahit purpura noctes
o si pateant pectora ditum!
quantos intus sublimis agit
fortuna metus! Bruttia Coro   650
pulsante fretum lenior unda est.
pectora pauper secura gerit;
tenet e patula pocula fago,
sed non trepida tenet illa manu;
carpit faciles vilesque cibos,
sed non strictos respicit enses.
aurea miscet pocula sanguis.

   Coniunx modico nupta marito
non disposito clara monili
gestat pelagi dona rubentis,   660
nec gemmiferas detrahit aures
lapis Eoa lectus in unda,
nec Sidonio mollis aeno
repetita bibit lana rubores,
nec Maeonia distinguit acu
quae Phoebeis subditus euris
legit Eois Ser arboribus.
quaelibet herbae tinxere colus
quas indoctae nevere manus;
sed non dubios fovet illa toros.   670
sequitur dira lampade Erinys
quarum populi coluere diem;
nec sibi felix pauper habetur
nisi felices cecidisse videt.

   Quisquis medium defugit iter
stabili numquam tramite currit.
dum petit unum praebere diem

---

[1] The north-west wind.
[2] The reference is to the story of the sword of Damocles.
See Index.

ceilings break our rest, and purple coverlets drag out
wakeful nights. Oh, if the hearts of rich men
were laid bare! What fears does lofty fortune stir
within! The waves of Bruttium, when Corus[1]
lashes up the sea, are calmer far. The poor man's
heart is free from care; he holds cups carved from
the wide-spreading beech, but holds them with hand
untrembling; he eats but cheap and common food,
yet sees no drawn sword[2] hanging o'er his head!
'Tis in golden cups that blood is mixed with wine.[3]

658 The wife who is wed to one of modest means
is not bedecked with necklaces of pearl, the red sea's
gift, nor do stones gathered on Orient shores weigh
down her gem-laden ears; for her no soft wool twice
dipped in Sidonian cauldrons drinks scarlet dyes;
not hers with Maeonian[4] needle to embroider stuffs
which Serians under sunlit skies gather[5] from eastern
trees. 'Tis but common herbs that dye the webs
which her unskilled hands have woven; but she
cherishes a marriage-couch all undisturbed. With
cruel torch doth Fury pursue the bride whose wed-
ding-day great throngs have celebrated; nor does the
poor man count himself full blest, unless he sees the
blessed fallen from their height.

675 Whoever has left the middle course fares never
in path secure. While for one day the youth[6] sought

---

[3] The author may have the story of Atreus and Thyestes
in mind.
[4] The Lydian (Maeonian) women were famous for their
skill in embroidery.
[5] The reference is to silk-culture, for which the Seres (the
Chinese) were well known among the ancients.
[6] Phaethon.

patrioque puer constitit axe
nec per solitum decurrit iter,
sed Phoebeis ignota petens   680
sidera flammis errante rota,
secum pariter perdidit orbem.
medium caeli dum sulcat iter,
tenuit placitas Daedalus oras
nullique dedit nomina ponto ;
sed dum volucres vincere veras
Icarus audet patriasque puer
despicit alas Phoeboque volat
proxumus ipsi, dedit ignoto
nomina ponto.   male pensantur   690
magna ruinis.

     Felix alius magnusque sonet ;
me nulla vocet turba potentem.
stringat tenuis litora puppis
nec magna meas aura phaselos
iubeat medium scindere pontum ;
transit tutos Fortuna sinus
medioque rates quaerit in alto,
quarum feriunt sipara nubes.

     Sed quid pavido territa vultu,   700
qualis Baccho saucia maenas,
fertur dubio [1] regina gradu ?
quae te rursus fortuna rotat ?
miseranda, refer : licet ipsa neges,
vultus loquitur quodcumque tegis.

DEÏANIRA

Vagus per artus errat excussos tremor,
erectus horret crinis, impulsis adhuc

---

[1] *So Gronovius :* †medio *Leo, with* E *:* rapido A *:* trepido
Rapheling : fert in medium . . . gradum *Richter.*

to furnish light and took his stand within his father's
car, and while he passed not o'er the accustomed
track, but sought the stars unknown to Phoebus' rays
with wandering wheel, himself he ruined and the
world, as well. Daedalus, cleaving his path midway
the heavens, reached peaceful shores and to no sea
gave his name; but while young Icarus dared rival
true birds in flight, looked down upon his father's
wings and soared aloft close to the sun itself, to an unknown sea[1] he gave his name. To our undoing,
high fortunes are by ruin balanced.

692 Let another be noised abroad as blest and great;
but let no throng hail me as powerful. Let my frail
craft keep close to shore, and let no strong wind
compel my bark to plough the mighty deep; misfortune passes by quiet ports, and seeks for ships
sailing the open sea, whose topsails smite the clouds.

[DEÏANIRA *appears hurrying distractedly from the palace.*]

700 But why in terror and with face of fear, like
some rage-smit Bacchante, comes the queen with
step uncertain?

[*Enter* DEÏANIRA]

What new reverse of fortune whirls thee about?
Poor lady, tell us. Though thou thyself sayst naught,
thy face speaks out whate'er thou hidest.

DEÏANIRA

Vague shivers steal through my trembling limbs,
my hair starts up in horror; fear sticks in my soul

[1] The Icarian sea.

stat terror animis et cor attonitum salit
pavidumque trepidis palpitat venis iecur.
ut fractus austro pontus etiamnum tumet,   710
quamvis quiescat languidis ventis dies,
ita mens adhuc vexatur excusso metu.
semel profecto premere felices deus
cum coepit, urget.   hos habent magna exitus.

NVTRIX

Quis tam impotens, miseranda, te casus rotat ?

DEÏANIRA

Vt missa palla est tabe Nessea inlita
thalamisque maerens intuli gressum meis,
nescio quid animus timuit [1] et fraudem struit ?
libet experiri.   solibus dirus ferum
flammisque Nessus sanguinem ostendi arcuit ;   720
hic ipse fraudes esse praemonuit dolus.

Et forte, nulla nube respersus iubar,
laxabat ardens fervidum Titan diem.—
vix ora solvi patitur etiam nunc timor.—
medios in ignes solis eiceram facem [2]
quo tincta fuerat palla vestisque inlita.
abiectus horret sanguis et Phoebi coma [3]
tepefactus ardet—vix queo monstrum eloqui.[4]
nives ut Eurus solvit aut tepidus Notus,
quas vere primo lucidus perdit Mimas,   730

---

[1] *Leo conjectures a lacuna here and suggests* an moriens
viro | poenas parat Centaurus : *Richter reads* timuit. an
fraudem struit ?

[2] †eiceram facem *Leo, with E, conjecturing* medios in ignes
vellus eieci madens : solis et claram facem *A*.

till now so passion-tossed; my heart leaps wildly and my quaking liver throbs with pulsing veins. As when the storm-tossed sea still heaves, though the skies are clear and the winds have died away, so is my soul still troubled, though my fear has been allayed. Surely when God has once begun to oppress the fortunate, he bears down hard. To such an end do mighty fortunes come.

NURSE

What headstrong fate, poor soul, whirls thee about?

DEÏANIRA

When I had sent away the robe anointed with Nessus' blood, and, sad at heart, betook me to my chamber, my soul feared I know not what—did the dying centaur 'gainst my husband plan revenge,[1] and plot some treachery? I was pleased to make the test. Dread Nessus forbade me to expose the wild blood to the sun's rays and to fire; and this artifice itself forewarned me of treachery.

[722] It chanced the burning sun, its radiance by no cloud dimmed, was setting free the day's fervid heat.—Even now my fear scarce suffers me to speak.— Right into the hot sunlight I had thrown the blood-soaked fleece[1] with which the robe had been moistened and the garment smeared. The bloody fleece I flung writhed horribly and, warmed with the sun's rays, burst aflame—I have scarce words to tell of the awful thing. As the East or the warm South-wind melts the snows which glistening Mimas

---

[1] Translating Leo's conjecture.

---

[3] So ς; Leo †comam.
[4] So A: Leo †astris vix quoque est. m. elocor.

utque evolutos frangit Ionio salo
opposita fluctus Leucas et lassus tumor
in litore ipso spumat, aut caelestibus
aspersa tepidis tura laxantur focis,
sic languet omne vellus et perdit comas.
dumque ista miror, causa mirandi perit ;
quin ipsa tellus spumeos motus agit
et quidquid illa tabe contactum est labat.[1]

   Natum paventem cerno et ardenti pede   740
gressus ferentem.   prome quid portes novi.[2]

HYLLVS

   I, profuge, quaere si quid ulterius patet
terris freto sideribus Oceano inferis,—
ultra labores, mater, Alcidae fuge !

DEÏANIRA

   Nescio quod animus grande praesagit malum.

HYLLVS

   Regnat, triumphat [3] ; templa Iunonis pete.
haec tibi patent ; delubra praeclusa omnia.

DEÏANIRA

   Effare quis me casus insontem premat.

[1] *Following line 738 in A stands the unintelligible line*
tumensque tacita sequitur et quassat caput.
[2] *Leo deletes lines 740, 741, assuming a considerable lacuna
between 738 and 742.*

loses in early spring; as 'gainst Leucadia's crags,
breasting the Ionian sea, the up-flung waves are
broken and with spent fury foam upon the shore, or
as incense sprinkled on holy shrines is melted in the
hot altar-fires; so all the wool withered and lost its
fleece. And while I stood wondering at it, the
object of my wonder disappears; nay, even the very
ground begins to foam, and whatever that poison
touched begins to shrink.

[HYLLUS *is seen approaching*]

740 But I see my son approaching with face of fear
and hurrying feet.

[*To* HYLLUS]

Speak out—what tidings dost thou bear?

HYLLUS [*hurrying upon the scene*]

Go! flee! seek out whatever place lies far away
on land, on sea, 'mongst stars, in Ocean, underworld—far beyond the labours of Alcides, mother,
flee!

DEÏANIRA

Some great disaster doth my mind presage.

HYLLUS

She [1] reigns, she triumphs; Juno's temple seek.
This sanctuary waits thee; closed is all refuge else.

DEÏANIRA

Tell what disaster my guiltless self o'erwhelms.

[1] *i.e.* Juno.

---

[3] *Leo's conjecture for* regna triumphi *of MSS.*

HYLLVS

Decus illud orbis atque praesidium unicum,
quem fata terris in locum dederant Iovis,   750
o mater, abiit. membra et Herculeos toros
urit lues nescio qua ; qui domuit feras,
ille ille victor vincitur maeret dolet.
quid quaeris ultra?

DEÏANIRA

        Miserias properant suas
audire miseri. fare, quo posita in statu
iam nostra domus est ? o lares, miseri lares !
nunc vidua, nunc expulsa, nunc ferar obruta.

HYLLVS

Non sola maeres Herculem, toto iacet
mundo gemendus. fata nec, mater, tua
privata credas : iam genus totum obstrepit.   760
hunc ecce luctu quem gemis cuncti gemunt,
commune terris omnibus pateris malum.
luctum occupasti : prima, non sola Herculem,
miseranda, maeres.

DEÏANIRA

        Quam prope a leto tamen
ede, ede quaeso iaceat Alcides meus.

HYLLVS

Mors refugit illum victa quae in regno suo
semel est nec audent fata tam vastum nefas
admittere. ipsas forsitan trepida colus
Clotho manu proiecit et fata Herculis

HERCULES OETAEUS

HYLLUS

That glory and sole guardian of the world, whom the fates had given to the lands in the place of Jove, O mother, is no more. The limbs and thews of Hercules a mysterious plague is wasting; and he who conquered monsters, he, he, the victor, is vanquished, is in grief, in agony. What more dost ask?

DEÏANIRA

The wretched are in haste to hear their wretchedness. Tell me: in what condition now stands our house? O home, O wretched home! Now truly am I widowed, exiled, overwhelmed.

HYLLUS

Not thou alone dost lament Hercules; low he lies for the whole world to mourn. And think not, mother, thine is a private loss; now the whole race is clamorous with woe. Lo, all men utter thy self-same groans of grief; common to all lands is the ill thou sufferest. Thou hast forestalled their grief; first, but not all alone, poor soul, dost thou mourn Hercules.

DEÏANIRA

Yet tell me, tell, I beg, how near to death does my Alcides lie.

HYLLUS

Death, who once in his own realm was overcome,[1] flees from him; nor do the fates dare countenance so great a crime. Perchance Clotho has thrown aside her very distaff from her trembling hand, and

---

[1] A probable reference to the struggle of Hercules with Death for the recovery of Alcestis.

timet peragere.   pro diem, infandum diem !   770
hocne ille summo magnus Alcides erit ?

DEÏANIRA

Ad fata et umbras adque peiorem polum
praecedere illum dicis ?   an possum prior
mortem occupare ?   fare, si nondum occidit.

HYLLVS

Euboica tellus vertice immenso tumens
pulsatur omni latere.   Phrixeum mare
scindit Caphereus, servit hoc Austro latus ;
at qua nivosi patitur Aquilonis minas,
Euripus undas flectit instabilis vagas
septemque cursus volvit et totidem refert,   780
dum lassa Titan mergat Oceano iuga.
hic rupe celsa, multa quam nubes ferit,
annosa fulgent templa Cenaei Iovis.
   Ut stetit ad aras omne votivum pecus
totumque tauris gemuit auratis nemus,
spolium leonis sordidum tabo exuit
posuitque clavae pondus et pharetra graves
laxavit umeros.   veste tum fulgens tua,
cana revinctus populo horrentem comam,
succendit aras ; " accipe has " inquit " focis   790
non false messes genitor et largo sacer
splendescat ignis ture, quod Phoebum colens
dives Sabaeis colligit truncis Arabs.
pacata tellus " inquit " et caelum et freta,

---

¹ *i.e.* the Aegaean.   See Index *s.v.* " Phrixus."
² Seneca's description in this passage of the topography of
Euboea is not correct.   The Cenaean Promontory is at the
far north-western point of the island, while the Strait of

is afraid to complete the fates of Hercules. O day,
O awful day! And shall this for the great Alcides
be the last?

DEÏANIRA

To the shades of death and to that darker world
dost say he has gone already? Can I not go before
and anticipate his death? Speak, if he is not yet
fallen.

HYLLUS

Euboea's shore, swelling with mighty headland,
on every side is beaten by the waves. Caphereus
cleaves the Phrixean[1] Sea, on this side the south-
wind blows; but on the side which feels the
blasts of snowy Aquilo, restless Euripus turns his
wandering waves, whose currents seven times flow
and seven times ebb again, till Titan plunges his
weary horses in the sea. Here on a lofty cliff, by
many a storm-cloud beaten, an ancient temple of
Cenaean Jove stands gleaming.[2]

[784] When all the votive herd stood at the altars,
and the whole grove was filled with the bellowing
of the gilded bulls, he[3] put off his lion's skin, all
stained with gore, laid down his heavy club and
freed his shoulders of the quiver's weight. Then
radiant in thy robe, his rough hair wreathed with
hoary poplar, he lit the altar-fires. "Accept these
gifts," he said, "upon thy shrine, O father, not
falsely claimed, and let thy sacred fire blaze brightly
with copious incense which the rich Arab gathers
from Sabaean trees, in worship of the Sun. Peace
has been given to earth, to sky, to sea; all monsters

Euripus is very nearly off the middle point. Caphereus,
moreover, is exposed not to the south but almost directly to
the east wind.   [3] *i.e.* Hercules.

feris subactis omnibus victor redi.
depone fulmen."
          Gemitus in medias preces
stupente et ipso cecidit ; hinc caelum horrido
clamore complet.   qualis impressa fugax
taurus bipenni volnus et telum ferens
delubra vasto trepida mugitu replet,   800
aut quale mundo fulmen emissum tonat,
sic ille gemitu sidera et pontum ferit,
et vasta Chalcis sonuit et voces Cyclas
excepit omnis ; hinc petrae Capherides,
hinc omne voces reddit Herculeas nemus.
flentem videmus.   volgus antiquam putat
rabiem redisse ; tum fugam famuli petunt.

  At ille voltus ignea torquens face
unum inter omnes sequitur et quaerit Lichan.
complexus aras ille tremibunda manu   810
mortem metu consumpsit et parvum sui
poenae reliquit.   dumque [1] tremibundum manu
tenuit cadaver : " hac manu, hac " inquit " ferar,
o fata, victus ?   Herculem vicit Lichas ?
ecce alia clades : Hercules perimit Lichan.
facta inquinentur ; fiat hic summus labor."
in astra missus fertur et nubes vago
spargit cruore.   talis in caelum exilit
harundo Getica visa dimitti manu
aut quam Cydon excussit : inferius tamen   820
et tela fugient.   truncus in pontum cadit,
in saxa vertex ; unus ambobus iacet.

         [1] *Leo conjectures* semianimum parens.

have I subdued and in triumph come again. Lay
down thy thunderbolt."

736 As he thus prayed a groan fell from his lips,
even he standing aghast; then with dreadful cries
he filled the air. As when a bull, fleeing the deep-
driven axe, bearing both wound and weapon, fills
with his huge bellowings the affrighted shrine, or as
the launched thunder crashes in the sky; so did he
with his roarings smite the stars and sea; towering
Chalcis reëchoed and all the Cyclades heard his
cries; then all Caphereus' crags and the whole
forest resounded with the cries of Hercules. We
saw him weep. The commons thought his ancient
madness had returned; then his attendants fled.

808 But he, his face writhing with pain of the
burning heat, pursued and sought out Lichas alone
among them all. The boy, embracing the altar with
trembling hands, through sheer terror tasted the
pangs of death, and left small part of his life for
punishment. Then Hercules, by his hand seizing
the quivering corpse, exclaimed: "By such a hand,
by such a hand as this, ye fates, shall I be said to
have been undone? Has Lichas conquered Hercules?
Behold another slaughter; Hercules in turn slays
Lichas. Be my deeds dishonoured; be this my
crowning task." To the stars the boy went hurtling
and sprinkled the clouds with his scattered blood.
So does a Getan arrow, from the hand let fly, go
speeding skyward, or the shaft a Cydonian has shot;
but far below[1] even these weapons will wing their
flight. His body falls into the sea, his head upon the
rocks; one youth lies slain in both.[2]

---

[1] *i.e.* below the height reached by Lichas.
[2] *i.e.* both head and body.

" Resistite " inquit " non furor mentem abstulit,
furore gravius istud atque ira malum est :
in me iuvat saevire." vix pestem indicat
et saevit ; artus ipse dilacerat suos
et membra vasta carpit avellens manu.
exuere amictus quaerit ; hoc solum Herculem
non posse vidi. trahere conatus tamen
et membra traxit ; corporis palla horridi   830
pars est et ipsa ; pestis immiscet cuti.[1]
nec causa dirae cladis in medio patet,
sed causa tamen est ; vixque sufficiens malo
nunc ore terram languidus prono premit,
nunc poscit undas—unda non vincit malum ;
fluctisona quaerit litora et pontum occupat ;
famularis illum retinet errantem manus—
o sortem acerbam ! fuimus Alcidae pares !
    Nunc puppis illum litore Euboico refert
Austerque lenis pondus Herculeum rapit ;   840
destituit animus membra, nox oculos premit.

DEÏANIRA

Quid, anime, cessas? quid stupes? factum est scelus.
natum reposcit Iuppiter, Iuno aemulum ;
reddendus orbi est. quod potes redde exhibe :
eat per artus ensis exactus meos.
sic, sic agendum est. tam levis poenas manus
tantas reposcit ? perde fulminibus, socer,

---

[1] *Following Richter's reconstruction :* pars (parum *E*) est et
ipsam (ipsa *A*) *MSS., for which Leo conjectures* ipsam pestis
immiscet cutem (*scil. pallae*).

---

[1] And not against others as heretofore.

823 "But hold!" said Hercules; "'tis not madness has robbed me of my wits; this bane is worse than madness and than rage; I am fain to rave against myself."[1] Scarce has he named the plague when lo, he raves, he tears his own flesh apart, with his own hand wounding and rending his huge limbs. He seeks to throw aside the robe; in this alone have I seen Alcides fail. Yet striving to tear the robe, he tears his limbs as well. The robe is part and parcel of his rugged body; the pest blends it with the skin. The cause of his dire suffering is hid, but still there is a cause; and, scarce able to endure his pain, now he lies spent, face down upon the ground, now calls for water—water checks not his pain; he seeks the wave-resounding shore and plunges in the sea, but a slave's hand restrains him wandering aimless there—oh, bitter lot! we were Alcides' equals![2]

839 And now a vessel is bringing him from Euboea's shore, and a gentle south wind wafts his huge bulk along; his spirit has left his body; night seals his eyes.

DEÏANIRA

Why, soul, dost hesitate? Why art amazed? The crime is done. Jupiter demands back his son of thee, Juno, her rival; yea, to the world must he be restored.[3] What still thou canst, give back, make restitution; let the sword, deep driven, through my body pass. So, so must it be done. But does so frail hand as this exact punishment so great? With thy thunderbolts, O sire, destroy thy guilty daughter.

---

[2] *i.e.* in the hero's present weakness, common men were able to control him.

[3] She has robbed the world of Hercules, and now must make such restitution as she may.

nurum scelestam.   nec levi telo manus
armetur; illud fulmen exiliat polo,
quo, nisi fuisset genitus Alcides tibi,   850
hydram cremasses.   pestem ut insolitam feri
et ut noverca potius irata malum.
emitte telum quale in errantem prius
Phaethonta missum est : perdidi in solo Hercule
et ipsa populos.

           Quid rogas telum deos ?
iam parce socero; coniugem Alcidae necem
optare pudeat; haec erit voto manus,
a me petatur; occupa ferrum ocius.
cur deinde ferrum?   quidquid ad mortem trahit
telum est abunde—rupe ab aetheria ferar.   860
haec, haec renatum prima quae poscit diem,
Oeta eligatur, corpus hinc mitti placet.
abrupta cautes scindat et partem mei
ferat omne saxum, pendeant lacerae manus
totumque rubeat asperi montis latus.
levis una mors est—levis?   at extendi potest.
eligere nescis, anime, cui telo incubes;
utinam esset, utinam fixus in thalamis meis
Herculeus ensis!   huic decet ferro inmori.
una perire dextera nobis sat est ?   870
coite, gentes, saxa et immensas faces
iaculetur orbis, nulla nunc cesset manus,
corripite tela, vindicem vestrum abstuli.
impune saevi sceptra iam reges gerent,
impune iam nascetur indomitum malum;
repetentur arae cernere assuetae hostiam
similem colenti.   sceleribus feci viam;

And with no common weapon let thy hand be armed;
let that bolt leap from heaven with which, had
Alcides not sprung from thee, thou wouldst have
scorched the Hydra. Destroy me as some strange
pest, as a scourge far worse than step-dame's wrath.
Launch such a bolt as once thou didst hurl at stray-
ing Phaëthon; for I, e'en I myself, in Hercules alone
have ruined nations.

855 But why dost ask weapons of the gods? At
last spare thy father.[1] The wife of Hercules should
be ashamed to pray for death; this hand shall grant
my prayer; from myself let death be sought. Then
quickly seize the sword.—Why then the sword?
Whatever brings to death is weapon all-sufficient—
from a sky-piercing cliff I'll cast me down. Let this,
this crag of Oeta, which is the first to greet the new-
born day, be chosen; from this 'tis well to fling me.
May its broken crags rend asunder, and every rock
take its share of me; may my mangled hands hang
there, and may the whole rough mountain-side run
red. One death is all too light—light? but still it
can be prolonged. Thou canst not choose, O soul,
on what weapon thou shalt fall. Oh, would that the
sword of Hercules were hanging in my chamber!
Upon that steel 'twere well for me to die. But is it
enough that by one right hand I perish? Come all
ye nations; let the world cast rocks and huge firebrands on me; let no hand shrink its task; seize
weapons, for your avenger have I done to death.
Now with impunity shall cruel kings wield sceptres;
yea, with impunity now fierce monsters shall be born;
again shall altars be found wont to behold victim
like to worshipper.[2] A highway to crime have I

---

[1] *i.e.* do not impose thy punishment on Jove.
[2] *i.e.* where human sacrifices are offered up.

ego vos tyrannis regibus monstris feris
saevisque rapto vindice opposui deis.
cessas, Tonantis socia? non spargis facem   880
imitata fratrem et mittis ereptam Iovi
meque ipsa perdis? laus tibi erepta incluta est,
ingens triumphus; aemuli, Iuno, tui
mortem occupavi.

HYLLVS

        Quid domum impulsam trahis?
erroris est hic omne quodcumque est nefas.
haut est nocens quicumque non sponte est nocens.

DEÏANIRA

Quicumque fato ignoscit et parcit sibi,
errare meruit. morte damnari placet.

HYLLVS

Nocens videri qui mori quaerit cupit.

DEÏANIRA

Mors innocentes sola deceptos facit.   890

HYLLUS

Titana fugiens—

DEÏANIRA

    Ipse me Titan fugit.

HYLLVS

Vitam relinques?

---

[1] *i.e.* the "nation" addressed in line 871.

prepared; I have exposed you[1] to tyrants, kings, monsters, wild beasts and cruel gods, by slaying your avenger. Dost shirk thy task, wife[2] of the thunderer? Why dost thou not, in imitation of thy brother,[2] scatter fire, snatch from Jove's hand his bolt, hurl it, and thyself destroy me? Illustrious praise and mighty triumph have been snatched from thee; I have forestalled thee, Juno, in thy rival's death.

HYLLUS

Why dost drag down a house already shaken? From error springs wholly whatever crime is here. He does no sin who sins without intent.

DEÏANIRA

Who casts the blame on fate and spares himself, has deserved to err. My sentence is for death.

HYLLUS

Fain would he seem guilty who seeks to die.

DEÏANIRA

'Tis death alone can make the beguiled[3] innocent.

HYLLUS

Fleeing the sun—

DEÏANIRA

The sun himself flees me.

HYLLUS

Wilt abandon life?

[2] Juno was both sister and wife of Jove.
[3] *i.e.* those who have been ensnared into sin.

257

DEÏANIRA

Miseram, ut Alciden sequar.

HYLLVS

Superest et auras ille caelestes trahit.

DEÏANIRA

Vinci Hercules cum potuit, hinc coepit mori.

HYLLVS

Natum relinques fataque abrumpes tua?

DEÏANIRA

Quamcumque natus sepelit haec vixit diu.

HYLLVS

Virum sequeris.

DEÏANIRA

Praegredi castae solent.

HYLLVS

Si te ipsa damnas, scelere te misera arguis.

DEÏANIRA

Nemo nocens sibi ipse poenas abrogat.

HYLLVS

Multis remissa est vita quorum error nocens,   900
non dextra fuerat.   fata quis damnat sua?

DEÏANIRA

Ay! a wretched life—that Alcides I may follow.

HYLLUS

But he still lives and breathes the air of heaven.

DEÏANIRA

When Hercules could be conquered, then he began to die.

HYLLUS

Wilt leave thy son? Wilt break thy thread of life?

DEÏANIRA

She whom her son has buried has lived long.

HYLLUS

Follow thy husband.[1]

DEÏANIRA

Faithful wives go before.

HYLLUS

It thou thyself dost doom thee, thou convictest thyself, unhappy one, of sin.

DEÏANIRA

No guilty one himself annuls his punishment.

HYLLUS

Life has been granted many whose guilt lay in wrong judgment, not in act. Who blames his own destiny?

[1] *i.e.* do not die until he is dead.

DEÏANIRA

Quicumque fata iniqua sortitus fuit.

HYLLVS

Hic ipse Megaram nempe confixam suis
stravit sagittis atque natorum indolem
Lernaea figens tela furibunda manu ;
ter parricida factus ignovit tamen
sibi, non furori.   fonte Cinyphio scelus
sub axe Libyco tersit et dextram abluit.
quo, misera, pergis ?   cur tuas damnas manus ?

DEÏANIRA

Damnat meas devictus Alcides manus.   910
placet scelus punire.

HYLLVS

            Si novi Herculem,
aderit cruenti forsitan victor mali
dolorque fractus cedet Alcidae tuo.

DEÏANIRA

Exedit artus virus ut fama est hydrae ;
immensa pestis coniugis membra abstulit.

HYLLVS

Serpentis illi virus enectae autumas
haut posse vinci qui malum vivum tulit ?
elisit hydram, dente cum infixo stetit [1]
media palude victor, effuso obrutus
artus veneno.   sanguis hunc Nessi opprimet,   920
qui vicit ipsas horridi Nessi manus ?

---

[1] *So Peiper, with A :* †cum fixo tenens *Leo, with* E, *and
conjectures* dum infecto tumet : *Richter conjectures* iam infixo
tumens.

260

HERCULES OETAEUS

DEÏANIRA

Whoever has fallen on unkind fates.

HYLLUS

But Hercules himself slew Megara, pierced by his arrows, and his own sons as well, shooting Lernaean shafts with furious hand; still, though thrice murderer, he forgave himself, but not his madness. At the source of Cinyps 'neath Libyan skies he washed away his guilt and cleansed his hands. Whither, poor soul, dost haste thee? Why dost condemn thy hands?

DEÏANIRA

'Tis Alcides' overthrow that doth condemn my hands. 'Tis well to punish crime.

HYLLUS

If I know Hercules, he will soon be here, perchance victorious o'er the cruel plague; and pain, subdued, will yield to thy Alcides.

DEÏANIRA

The hydra's poison, as report declares, hath consumed his frame; the deadly plague hath wasted his giant limbs.

HYLLUS

Thinkst thou the poison of a serpent, slain, cannot be overcome by him who met and overcame the monster, living? He crushed the hydra, and deep in the marsh, with the fangs fixed in his flesh, he stood victorious, while his limbs were bathed in venom. Shall Nessus' blood destroy the man who overcame e'en the hands of savage Nessus?

261

DEÏANIRA

Frustra tenetur ille qui statuit mori ;
proinde lucem fugere decretum est mihi.
vixit satis quicumque cum Alcide occidit.

NVTRIX

Per has aniles ecce te supplex comas
atque ubera ista paene materna obsecro :
depone tumidas pectoris laesi minas
mortisque dirae expelle decretum horridum.

DEÏANIRA

Quicumque misero forte dissuadet mori,
crudelis ille est ; interim poena est mori,   930
sed saepe donum ; pluribus veniae fuit.

NVTRIX

Defende saltem dexteram, infelix, tuam
fraudisque facinus esse, non nuptae, sciat.

DEÏANIRA

Defendar illic ; inferi absolvent ream,
a me ipsa damnor ; purget has Pluton manus.
stabo ante ripas immemor, Lethe, tuas
et umbra tristis coniugem excipiam meum.
Sed tu, nigrantis regna qui torques poli,
para laborem (scelera quae quisquam ausus est,
hic vincet error ; Iuno non ausa Herculem est   940
eripere terris) horridam poenam para.
Sisyphia cervix cesset et nostros lapis

HERCULES OETAEUS

DEÏANIRA

Vainly is he restrained who is bent on death; my will is fixed straightway to flee the light. Whoever has died with Hercules has lived enough.

NURSE

Lo, by these aged locks and by these breasts which were almost as a mother's to thee, I humbly pray; put by the wild threatenings of thy wounded heart, and banish thy dread resolve of cruel death.

DEÏANIRA

Whoever, perchance, dissuades the wretched from death, he is the cruel one; sometimes death is a punishment, but often 'tis a boon, and to many a way of pardon has it proved.

NURSE

At least absolve thy hand, unhappy one, that he may know that the deed was a treacherous foeman's, not his wife's.

DEÏANIRA

There[1] shall I be absolved; the lower gods will acquit the criminal, though I condemn myself. Let Pluto cleanse these hands. Upon thy banks, O Lethe, shall I stand, the past forgotten, and my grieving shade will welcome its lord again.

[938] But do thou, who torturest the realms of the dark under-world, prepare a toil—for this fault of mine outweighs all sins that man has ever dared; Juno was never bold enough to rob the world of Hercules—some dreadful toil prepare. Let Sisyphus' neck

---

[1] In the lower world.

impellat umeros ; me vagus fugiat latex
meamque fallax unda deludat sitim.
merui manus praebere turbinibus tuis,
quaecumque regem Thessalum torques rota ;
effodiat avidus hinc et hinc vultur fibras.
vacat[1] una Danais, has ego explebo vices—
laxate manes.   recipe me comitem tibi,
Phasiaca coniunx ; peior haec, peior tuo   950
utroque dextra est scelere, seu mater nocens
seu dira soror es ; adde me comitem tuis,
Threicia coniunx, sceleribus ; natam tuam,
Althaea mater, recipe, nunc veram tui
agnosce prolem—quid tamen tantum manus
vestrae abstulerunt ?   claudite Elysium mihi
quaecumque fidae coniuges nemoris sacri
lucos tenetis ; si qua respersit manus
viri cruore nec memor castae facis
stricto cruenta Belias ferro stetit,   960
in me suas agnoscat et laudet manus.
in hanc abire coniugum turbam libet—
sed et illa fugiet turba tam diras manus.

   Invicte coniunx, innocens animus mihi,
scelesta manus est.   pro nimis mens credula !
pro Nesse fallax atque semiferi doli !
auferre cupiens paelici eripui mihi.
recede, Titan, tuque quae blanda tenes
in luce miseros vita ; caritura Hercule
lux vilis ista est.   exigam poenas tibi   970
reddamque vitam—fata an extendo mea
mortemque, coniunx, ad tuas servo manus?

---

[1] *So Richter : Leo* vacet, *with* ω, *corrected by Raphcling.*

---

[1] The punishment of Tantalus.
[2] Ixion.   [3] Hypermnestra.
[4] Medea.   [5] Procne.

be eased and let his rock press hard upon my shoulders; let the inconstant water fly my lips, my thirst let the elusive waves deceive.[1] Unto thy whirlings have I deserved to give my hands, whatsoe'er wheel thou art which rackest Thessalia's king;[2] from every side let the greedy vulture tear my entrails out. There still lacks one[3] from the Danaïdes; I will fill up their number—ye ghosts make room for me. Take me as thy companion, O Phasian wife;[4] my deed is worse, far worse than both thy crimes, whether as mother or as cruel sister thou hast sinned; let me be comrade also to thy crimes, thou Thracian wife;[5] Althea, mother,[6] welcome thy daughter, now recognize in me thine own true child—yet what crime so great have your hands ever done? Shut Elysium against me, O all ye faithful wives who have your dwelling in its sacred grove; but if any has bespattered her hands with her husband's blood and her chaste marriage torch forgot, has stood with drawn sword like Belus' bloody child, in me let her recognize and praise her own handiwork. To such a company of wives 'tis well to pass—but e'en that company will shun hands so accursed.

[964] O my unconquered husband, my soul is innocent, though my hands have sinned. O mind too credulous! O Nessus, false and of half-bestial guile! Striving to snatch him from a concubine, I have snatched him from myself. Away! thou sun, and life, who by thy cozening arts dost keep the unhappy in the light of day; worthless that light without my Hercules. I will exact penalty for thee,[7] will give up my life—or shall I put off my fate, O husband, and save myself for death at thine own

[6] For Althaea's crime see Index.
[7] i.e. will see that he is avenged.

virtusne superest aliqua et armatae manus
intendere arcum tela missurum valent?
an arma cessant teque languenti manu
non audit arcus?   si potes letum dare,
animose coniunx, dexteram expecto tuam.
mors differatur; frange ut insontem Lichan,
alias in urbes sparge et ignotum tibi
inmitte in orbem.   perde ut Arcadiae nefas   980
et quidquid aliud cessit [1]; ab illis tamen,
coniunx, redisti.

HYLLVS

      Parce iam, mater, precor,
ignosce fatis; error a culpa vacat.

DEÏANIRA

Si vera pietas, Hylle, quaerenda est tibi,
iam perime matrem—trepida quid tremuit manus?
quid ora flectis?   hoc erit pietas scelus.
ignave dubitas?   Herculem eripuit tibi
haec, haec peremit dextra cui debes patri
avum Tonantem.   maius eripui decus,
quam in luce tribui.   si tibi ignotum est nefas,   990
a matre disce.   seu tibi iugulo placet
mersisse ferrum sive maternum libet
invadere uterum, mater intrepidum tibi
praebebit animum.   non erit tantum scelus
a te peractum; dextera sternar tua,
sed mente nostra.   natus Alcidae, times?
ita nulla perages iussa nec franges mala [2]

---

[1] †cessit *Leo, with E*: restitit *A*.
[2] *Line 998, omitted by E, deleted by Leo:* erres per orbem.
si qua nascetur fera.

266

hands? Hast still some strength, and can thy
armed hands still bend the bow and send the arrow
darting? Or do thy weapons fail thee, and does thy
bow no more heed thy enfeebled hand? If thou
canst deal destruction, O undaunted husband, I
await thy stroke. Let death be stayed awhile[1];
crush me as thou didst the unoffending Lichas; to
other cities scatter me, yea, hurl me to a world to
thee unknown. Destroy me as thou didst the
Arcadian monster,[2] and whatever else succumbed to
thee; yet from them, my husband, thou didst
return.

HYLLUS

Give o'er now, mother, I beseech thee, pardon thy
fate; an error is not counted as a crime.

DEÏANIRA

If, Hyllus, thou wouldst be truly filial, come, slay
thy mother—why does thy hand quake and tremble?
Why turnst thy face away? This crime will be
filial piety. Tamely dost hesitate? This hand
robbed thee of Hercules, yea, this right hand
destroyed him to whom as father thou owest descent
from Jove. Of greater glory have I robbed thee
than I gave thee at thy birth. If thou art unskilled in monstrous crime, learn from thy mother.
Whether in my throat it pleases thee to plunge the
sword, or 'tis thy will to assail thy mother's womb,
thy mother herself will give thee unshrinking
courage. Not by thee will this dreadful crime be
done; by thy hand, truly, shall I fall, but by my
will. Son of Alcides, art afraid? Wilt thou not do
as bidden, wilt not crush monsters, and so be like

---

[1] *i.e.* until she may die at her husband's hands.
[2] The Erymanthian boar, Hercules' fourth labour.

referens parentem? dexteram intrepidam para. 999
patet ecce plenum pectus aerumnis : feri ; 1000
scelus remitto, dexterae parcent tuae
Eumenides ipsae—verberum crepuit sonus.

Quaenam ista torquens angue vipereo[1] comam
temporibus atras[2] squalidis pinnas quatit?
quid me flagranti dira persequeris face,
Megaera? poenas poscis Alcidae? dabo.
iamne inferorum, dira, sedere arbitri?
sedent. reclusas[3] carceris video fores.
quis iste saxum immane detritis gerit
iam senior umeris? ecce iam victus lapis 1010
quaerit relabi? membra quis quatitur rota?
hic ecce pallens dira Tisiphone stetit,
causam reposcit. parce verberibus precor,
Megaera, parce, sustine Stygias faces ;
scelus est amoris.

             Sed quid hoc? tellus labat
et aula tectis crepuit excussis—minax
unde iste coetus? totus in voltus meos
decurrit orbis, hinc et hinc populi fremunt
totusque poscit vindicem mundus suum.
iam parcite, urbes. quo fugam praeceps agam? 1020
mors sola portus dabitur aerumnis meis.
testor nitentis flammeam Phoebi rotam
superosque testor : Herculem in terris adhuc
moritura linquo.

---

[1] †angue vipereo *Leo :* angui *E :* igne *N. Heinsius :* angue
vibrato *Peiper.*

thy sire? Thy dauntless hand make ready. Behold my breast, so full of cares, lies open: smite; I forgive the deed, the Eumenides themselves will acquit thy hand—but I hear their scourges hissing.

[1003] Oh, who is that in whose locks viperous serpents coil, who brandishes deadly shafts at her foul temples? Why dost pursue me, awful Megaera, with blazing torch? Penalty for Alcides' murder dost demand? I'll pay. Already, dread one, have the arbiters of hell passed judgment on me? They have. I see the prison doors opened wide. Who is that ancient[1] who bears a huge stone on his toil-worn back? But see! already does the mastered stone seek to roll back again? Whose [2] limbs on the wheel are racked? Look! here has Tisiphone taken her stand, ghastly and dread; she demands revenge. Oh, spare thy scourge, I pray thee, Megaera, spare! Keep back the Stygian torches; mine was the crime of love.

[1015] But what is this? The earth quakes, the palace resounds with the noise of crashing roofs— whence comes that threatening throng? The whole world comes rushing 'gainst me, on every side the nations rage and the whole universe demands of me its saviour. Oh, spare me now, ye cities. Whither shall I rush in headlong flight? Death alone will be granted as a haven for my cares. By gleaming Phoebus' flaming car I swear, I swear by the heavenly gods: though to my death I go, I leave Alcides still upon the earth.

[*She rushes wildly from the scene.*]

[1] Sisyphus. [2] Ixion.

---

[2] *So A : Leo* †hastas, *with E : Madvig* aptas.
[3] *So Richter : Leo, with A,* †sed ecce diras.

HYLLVS

Fugit attonita, ei mihi.
peracta iam pars matris est—statuit mori ;
nunc nostra superest, mortis auferre impetum.
o misera pietas ! si mori matrem vetas,
patri es scelestus ; si mori pateris, tamen
in matre peccas.   urget hinc illinc scelus.
inhibenda tamen est, verum ut eripiam scelus.   1030

CHORVS

Verum est quod cecinit sacer
Thressae sub Rhodopes iugis
aptans Pieriam chelyn
Orpheus Calliopae genus,
aeternum fieri nihil.
illius stetit ad modos
torrentis rapidi fragor,
oblitusque sequi fugam
amisit liquor impetum ;
et dum fluminibus mora est,   1040
defecisse putant Getae
Hebrum Bistones ultimi.
advexit volucrem nemus
et silva residens venit ;
aut si qua aera pervolat,
auditis vaga cantibus
ales deficiens cadit.
abrumpit scopulos Athos
Centauros obiter ferens
et iuxta Rhodopen stetit   1050
laxata nive cantibus ;
et quercum fugiens suam
ad vatem properat Dryas.
ad cantus veniunt tuos

HERCULES OETAEUS

Ah me! in frenzy has she fled. Already has my mother played her part—she has resolved on death; now does my part remain, to thwart her deadly purpose. O wretched plight of love! if thou forbidst thy mother's death, thou wrongst thy father; if thou sufferest her to die, still 'gainst thy mother dost thou sin. Crime drives from either hand; still must I check her, that from true [1] crime she may be saved.   [*Exit after his mother.*]

CHORUS

True sang the bard beneath the heights of Thracian Rhodope, fitting the word to his Pierian lyre, e'en Orpheus, Calliope's blest son, that naught for endless life is made. At his sweet strains the rushing torrents' roar was stilled, and, forgetful of their eager flight, the waters ceased their flow; and, while the river stayed to hear, the far Bistonians thought their Hebrus had failed the Getan. The woods came with their birds to him, yea, perched among the trees they came; or if, in the high air soaring, some wandering bird caught sound of the charming song, his drooping wings sank earthward. Athos broke off his crags, bringing the Centaurs as he came, and next to Rhodope he stood, his snows melted by the music; the Dryad, leaving her oaken haunts, sped to the singer's side. To hear thy song, with their very lairs the

---

[1] *i.e.* the true crime of her own death as contrasted with the fancied crime of her act against Hercules.

ipsis cum latebris ferae,
iuxtaque inpavidum pecus
sedit Marmaricus leo
nec dammae trepidant lupos
et serpens latebras fugit,
tunc oblita veneni.   1060

    Quin per Taenarias fores
manes cum tacitos adit
maerentem feriens chelyn,
cantu Tartara flebili
et tristes Erebi deos
vicit nec timuit Stygis
iuratos superis lacus.
haesit non stabilis rota
victo languida turbine ;
increvit Tityi iecur,   1070
dum cantu volucres tenet ;   1071
et vinci lapis improbus   1081
et vatem potuit sequi.[1]   1082
tunc primum Phrygius senex   1075
undis stantibus immemor
excussit rabidam sitim
nec pomis adhibet manus.   1078
audis tu[2] quoque, navita ;   1072
inferni ratis aequoris   1073
nullo remigio venit.   1074
sic cum vinceret inferos   1079
Orpheus carmine funditus,   1080
consumptos iterum deae   1083
supplent Eurydices colus.   1084
sed dum respicit immemor

[1] *The arrangement of lines 1070–1084 as they stand in Leo
following the MSS. is more or less illogical, besides presenting
syntactic difficulties. The re-arrangement of Richter has been
adopted here.*

272

wild beasts came, and close to the fearless herds the
Marmaric lion crouched; does felt no fear of wolves,
and the serpent fled her gloomy den, her venom at
last forgot.

[1061] Nay, when through the gates Taenarian to the
silent ghosts he came, smiting his mournful lyre,
with his sad song he conquered Tartarus and the
sullen gods of Erebus; nor was he daunted by the
pools of Styx, by which the high gods swear. The
never staying wheel[1] stood still, listless, with
conquered whirling; the liver of Tityus grew,
undevoured, while spell-bound the singer held the
birds. The impish stone[2] allowed defeat and
attended on the bard. Then first the aged Phrygian,[3]
though the waves stood still, banished his raging
thirst, forgetful quite, nor to the apples stretched
his hand. Thou also, ferryman,[4] didst hear, and thy
boat that plies the infernal sea came oarless on.
So when by his song Orpheus had utterly o'ercome
the infernal gods, then did the goddesses[5] renew
again Eurydice's exhausted thread. But while
Orpheus thoughtlessly looked back, all unbelieving

[1] On which Ixion was bound.
[2] Which Sisyphus was rolling.
[3] Tantalus.   [4] Charon.
[5] i.e. the fatal sisters, the Parcae.

---

[2] So Birt's emendation of the impossible MSS. reading audito
quoque: Richter's auditum quoque is also impossible.

nec credens sibi redditam
Orpheus Eurydicen sequi,
cantus praemia perdidit;
quae nata est iterum perit.

    Tunc, solamina cantibus   1090
quaerens, flebilibus modis
[1] haec Orpheus cecinit Getis:
leges in superos datas,
et qui tempora digerit
quattuor praecipites deus
anni disposuit vices
nulli non avidi colus
Parcas stamina nectere,
quod natum est, quod erit, mori.[2]

    Vati credere Thracio   1100
devictus iubet Hercules.
iam, iam legibus obrutis
mundo cum veniet dies,
australis polus obruet
quidquid per Libyam iacet
et sparsus Garamas tenet;
arctous polus obruet
quidquid subiacet axibus
et siccus Boreas ferit.
amisso trepidus polo   1110
Titan excutiet diem.
caeli regia concidens
ortus atque obitus trahet
atque omnes pariter deos
perdet mors aliqua et chaos,
et mors fata novissima
in se constituet sibi.
quis mundum capiet locus?

---

[1] *Leo is of the opinion that the beginning and the end of Orpheus' song have fallen out, and that lines 1097–1099 are to*

his Eurydice restored to him and following, he lost his singing's recompense ; and she had come to the verge of life only to die once more.

1090 Then, solace in song still seeking, in mournful measures Orpheus thus to the Getans sang : that the gods are under law, e'en he who rules the seasons, who has arranged the four changes of the flying year ; that for no one the Parcae spin again the threads of the greedy distaff, and that all which has been and shall be born shall die.[1]

1100 The overthrow of Hercules bids us believe the Thracian bard. Soon, soon, when to the universe shall come the day that law shall be o'erwhelmed, the southern skies shall fall upon Libya's plains and all that the scattered Garamantians possess ; the northern heavens shall overwhelm all that lies beneath the pole and that Boreas smites with withering blasts. Then from the lost sky the affrighted sun shall fall and banish day. The palace of heaven shall sink, dragging down East and West, and death in some form and chaos shall o'erwhelm all gods in one destruction ; and death shall at last bring doom upon itself. What place will then receive the world ? Will the gates of Tartarus

---

[1] Reading according to the arrangement of Richter. See critical note [2].

---

be joined with the following lines. Richter reads 1093-1099 as Orpheus' song.

[2] *Richter proposes* quod natum est, poterit mori.

discedet via Tartari,
fractis ut pateat polis ?   1120
an quod dividit aethera
a terris spatium sat est
et mundi nimium malis ?
quis tantum capiet (nefas)
fatum, quis superos locus ?
pontum Tartara sidera
regna unus capiet tria.
    Sed quis non modicus fragor
aures attonitas movet ?
est est Herculeus sonus.   1130

HERCVLES

Converte, Titan clare, anhelantes equos,
emitte noctem ; pereat hic mundo dies
quo morior, atra nube inhorrescat polus ;
obsta novercae. nunc, pater, caecum chaos
reddi decebat, hinc et hinc compagibus
ruptis uterque debuit frangi polus.
quid parcis astris ?   Herculem amittis, pater.
nunc partem in omnem, Iuppiter, specta poli,
ne quis Gyas Thessalica iaculetur iuga
et fiat Othrys pondus Encelado leve.   1140
laxabit atri carceris iam iam fores
Pluton superbus, vincula excutiet patri
caelumque reddet.   ille qui pro fulmine
tuisque facibus natus in terris eram,
ad Styga revertor ; surget Enceladus ferox
mittetque quo nunc premitur in superos onus ;
regnum omne, genitor, aetheris dubium tibi

---

¹ Let the world be shrouded in darkness, that Juno may
not see the death of Hercules.

spread wide, that room for the shattered heavens
may be found? Or is the space 'twixt heaven and
earth great enough (perchance too great) for the
evils of the world? What place will be great
enough to hold (oh, horrible!) a death so vast, what
place, the gods? Sea, Tartarus and heaven—three
kingdoms shall one place contain.

[1128] But what outrageous clamour this that assails
our startled ears? It is, it is the sound of Hercules.

[Enter HERCULES in the extremity of suffering.]

HERCULES

Turn back, O shining Sun, thy panting steeds, and
let loose the night; let this day wherein I die perish
for the world, and let heaven shudder in the pitchy
dark. So thwart[1] my stepdame. Now, father, were
it fitting to restore blind chaos; now this side and
that should heaven's frame be burst and both poles
rent asunder. Why dost thou spare the stars?
Thou art losing Hercules, O father. Now, Jupiter,
look well to every part of heaven, lest any Gyas
hurl Thessalian crags and Othrys become a slight
missile for Enceladus.[2] Now, now will haughty
Pluto open his dark prison gates, strike off his
father's[3] chains and give him back to heaven.
Since I thy son, who on earth have been in place of
thy bolt and lightning flash, am turning me back to
Styx, Enceladus, the fierce, will rise, and the mass
'neath which he now is crushed will he hurl against
the gods; yea, father, thy whole realm of air will
my death put to hazard. Then ere thou art utterly

---

[2] The reference is to the former battle of the Giants
against Jupiter. See Index *s.v.* "Giants."

[3] Saturn.

277

mors nostra faciet.   antequam spolium tui [1]
caelum omne fiat, conde me tota, pater,
mundi ruina, frange quem perdis polum.   1150

CHORVS

   Non vana times, nate Tonantis.
nunc Thessalicam Pelion Ossam
premet et Pindo congestus Athos
nemus aetheriis inseret astris ;
vincet scopulos inde Typhoeus
et Tyrrhenam feret Inarimen ;
feret Aetnaeos inde caminos
scindetque latus montis aperti
nondum Enceladus fulmine victus.
iam te caeli regna secuntur. [2]   1160

HERCVLES

  Ego qui relicta morte, contempta Styge
per media Lethes stagna cum spolio redi
quo paene lapsis excidit Titan equis,
ego quem deorum regna senserunt tria,
morior ; nec ullus per meum stridet latus
transmissus ensis, haut meae telum necis [3]
est totus Othrys, non truci rictu gigans   1168
Pindo cadaver obruit toto meum :
sine hoste vincor, quodque me torquet magis   1170
(o misera virtus !) summum Alcidae dies
nullum malum prosternit ; inpendo, ei mihi,
in nulla vitam facta.
        Pro mundi arbiter
superique quondam dexterae testes meae,
pro cuncta tellus, Herculem vestrum placet

[1] tibi *E.*   [2] signa sequentur *A.*
[3] *Leo deletes line 1167,* saxum est nec instar montis abrupti
latus.
278

despoiled of heaven, bury me, father, 'neath the whole ruined world; shatter the skies which thou art doomed to lose.

CHORUS

Not vain thy fears, son of the Thunderer. Soon now shall Pelion weigh down Thessalian Ossa, and Athos, on Pindus heaped, shall thrust his forests midst the heavenly stars; then shall Typhoeus overcome the crags[1] and upheave Tuscan Inarime; the Aetnean furnaces then shall Enceladus upheave, not yet by thy bolt o'ercome, and rend the gaping mountain's side. E'en now the kingdoms of the sky are following thee.[2]

HERCULES

Lo I, who have escaped from death, who scorned the Styx, who through the midst of Lethe's pool have returned with spoil,[3] at sight whereof Titan was almost flung from his falling car, I, whose presence three realms of gods have felt, am perishing. No deep-thrust sword grates through my side, nor is all Othrys the instrument of my death; no giant with fierce and gaping jaws has buried my body beneath the whole of Pindus; no, without enemy am I overcome and, thought which racks me more, (shame to my manhood!) the last day of Alcides has seen no monster slain. Ah, woe is me! I am squandering my life for no return.

1173 O thou ruler of the world, ye gods, once witnesses of my deeds, O earth entire, is it resolved

---

[1] Beneath which he is buried.
[2] *i.e.* Jupiter is falling and his kingdom with him.
[3] Cerberus.

morte hac perire ? [1]   dirus o nobis pudor,
o turpe fatum—femina Herculeae necis
auctor feretur !   morior Alcides quibus ?
invicta si me cadere feminea manu
voluere fata perque tam turpes colus   1180
mea mors cucurrit, cadere potuissem, ei mihi,
Iunonis odio.   feminae caderem manu,
sed caelum habentis.   si nimis, superi, fuit,
Scythico sub axe genita domuisset meas
vires Amazon.   feminae cuius manu
Iunonis hostis vincor ?   hinc gravior tibi,
noverca, pudor est.   quid diem hunc laetum vocas ?
quid tale tellus genuit iratae tibi ?
mortalis odia femina excessit tua.
adhuc ferebas esse te Alcidae imparem ;   1190
victa es duobus—pudeat irarum deos !
utinam meo cruore satiasset suos
Nemeaea rictus pestis aut centum anguibus
vallatus hydram tabe pavissem mea !
utinam fuissem praeda Centauris datus
aut inter umbras vinctus aeterno miser
saxo sederem !   spolia nunc traxi ultima
Fato stupente, nunc ab inferna Styge
lucem recepi, Ditis evici moras—
ubique mors me fugit, ut leto inclitae   1200
sortis carerem.   pro ferae, victae ferae !
non me triformis sole conspecto canis
ad Styga revexit, non sub Hesperio polo
Hibera vicit turba pastoris feri,

---

[1] *So N. Heinsius :* †morte ferire *Leo, with* E, *conjecturing*
inertem obire : mortem perire *A :* perire inertem *L. Müller.*

---

[1] He is thinking of the many monsters, beasts, tyrants,
whom he has slain, he who must now die by a woman's hand.
[2] *i.e.* than for me.

your Hercules should perish by such death as this?
Oh, cruel shame to me, oh, end most foul—a woman
will be called author of Alcides' death! And for
whom[1] is Alcides dying? If the fates unchanging
have willed that by a woman's hand I fall, if through
distaff so base the thread of my death has run, ah
me! that I might have fallen by Juno's hate! 'Twould
be by woman's hand, but of one who holds the
heavens. If, O ye gods, that were too much to
ask, the Amazon, born 'neath Scythian skies, might
have o'ercome my strength. But by what woman's
hand is Juno's foe o'ercome? This is for thee, my
stepdame, heavier[2] shame. Why callest thou this
day joyful? What monster such as this has earth
produced to sate thy wrath[3]? A mortal woman
has outdone thy hate. Till now thou deemdst
thyself by Alcides alone outmatched; by two hast
thou been surpassed—of such wrath let heaven be
ashamed! Oh, that the Nemean lion with my blood
had sated his gaping jaws, or that, hedged by a
hundred snakes, I had fed the hydra with my gore!
O that I had been given to the Centaurs as a prey,
or that midst the shades I, bound to an everlasting
rock, in wretchedness were sitting! But now have I
dragged here my latest spoil[4] while Death looked
on amazed; now from infernal Styx have I regained
the light, the bars of Dis I've conquered—on every
hand death shunned me, that I might lack at last
a glorious end. O beasts, O conquered beasts!
Neither did the three-formed dog, when he saw the
sun, drag me back to Styx, nor 'neath western skies
did the Spanish rout of the wild shepherd[5] conquer

[3] He counts Deïanira as worse than all monsters Juno has
sent against him. She has outdone even Juno's hate. Hence
Juno is put to shame.   [4] Cerberus.   [5] Geryon.

non gemina serpens—perdidi mortem, ei mihi,
totiens honestam! titulus extremus quis est?

CHORVS

Viden ut laudis conscia virtus
non Lethaeos horreat amnes?
pudet auctoris, non morte dolet;
cupit extremum finire diem   1210
vasta tumidi mole gigantis
et montiferum Titana pati
rabidaeque necem debere ferae.
sed tua causa est, miserande, manus,
quod nulla fera est nullusque gigas;
nam quis dignus necis Herculeae
superest auctor nisi dextra tui?

HERCVLES

Heu qualis intus scorpios, quis fervida
plaga revulsus cancer infixus meas
urit medullas? sanguinis quondam capax   1220
tumidi igne cor [1] pulmonis arentes fibras
distendit, ardet felle siccato iecur
totumque lentus sanguinem avexit vapor.
primam cutem consumpsit, hinc aditum nefas
in membra fecit, abstulit pestis latus,
exedit artus penitus et costas malum,
hausit medullas. ossibus vacuis sedet;
nec ossa durant ipsa, sed compagibus
discussa ruptis mole conlapsa fluunt.
defecit ingens corpus et pesti satis   1230
Herculea non sunt membra—pro quantum est malum
quod esse vastum fateor, o dirum nefas!

---

[1] *So Richter: Leo*, tumidi †iecur, *with* ω, *conjecturing*
tumet igne cor : tumidi cor en *N. Heinsius.*

me, nor the twain serpents [1]—ah, woe is me! how often have I missed a glorious death! My final claim to glory—what is it?

CHORUS

Seest thou how virtue, conscious of its fame, shrinks not from Lethe's stream? He grieves not at death but blushes for its cause; he longs 'neath some towering giant's vasty bulk to end the last day of life, to suffer some mountain-heaving Titan's weight, to owe his death to some wild, raging beast. But no, poor soul, because of thine own hand, there is no beast, no giant; for what worthy author of the death of Hercules is left save thy right hand?

HERCULES

Alas, what scorpion,[2] what crab,[2] torn from the torrid zone, burns deep fixed in my marrow? My heart, once filled with pulsing streams of blood, hotly distends the parched fibres of my lungs; my liver glows, its bile dried quite away, and a slow fire has exhausted all my blood. First did the dread plague feed upon my skin, next to my limbs it passed, devoured my sides, then deep in my joints and ribs the pest ate its way, and drank my very marrow. In my hollow bones it lurks; nor do my bones themselves retain their hardness, but, shattered with broken structure, fall in a crumbling mass. My huge frame has shrivelled, and even the limbs of Hercules sate not the pest.—Oh, how mighty the ill which I admit is great! Oh, cruel curse! Behold,

---

[1] Which Juno sent against him in his infancy.
[2] Pestilent creatures from among the constellations of the zodiac (*fervida plaga*).

en cernite, urbes, cernite ex illo Hercule
quid iam supersit.   Herculem agnoscis, pater?
hisne ego lacertis colla Nemeaei mali
elisa pressi?   tensus hac arcus manu
astris ab ipsis detulit Stymphalidas?
his ego citatam gressibus vici feram
radiante clarum fronte gestantem caput?
his fracta Calpe manibus emisit fretum?   1240
his tot ferae, tot scelera, tot reges iacent?
his mundus umeris sedit?   haec moles mea est,
haecne illa cervix?   hasne ego opposui manus
caelo ruenti?   quis mea custos manu
trahetur ultra Stygius?   ubi vires prius
memet sepultae?   quid patrem appello Iovem?
quid per Tonantem vindico caelum miser?
iam, iam meus credetur Amphitryon pater.

 Quaecumque pestis viscere in nostro lates,
procede—quid me vulnere occulto petis?   1250
quis te sub axe frigido pontus Scythes,
quae pigra Tethys genuit aut Maurum premens
Hibera Calpe litus?   o dirum malum!
utrumne serpens squalidum crista caput
vibrans an aliquod et mihi ignotum malum,
numquid cruore es genita Lernaeae ferae
an te reliquit Stygius in terris canis?
omne es malum nullumque—quis voltus tibi est?
concede saltem scire quo peream malo.
quaecumque pestis sive quaecumque es fera, 1260

ye cities, behold what now remains of that great Hercules. Dost recognize thy Hercules, my father? Was it with these arms I crushed and overwhelmed the Nemean plague? Was it with this hand I stretched the bow that brought down the Stymphalian birds from the very stars? With these feet did I o'ertake the swift-fleeing beast [1] with golden antlers gleaming on his head? By these hands shattered, did Calpe [2] let out the sea? So many beasts, so many monstrous things, so many kings, have these hands of mine brought low? Upon these shoulders did the heavens rest? Is this my massive frame, is this my neck? These hands did I oppose to the falling sky? What Stygian watch-dog will hereafter be dragged forth by my hand? Where are my powers, buried before my burial? Why on Jove as father do I call? Why, wretched man, by right of the Thunderer do I claim heaven? Now, now will Amphitryon be deemed my sire.

[1249] O pest, whate'er thou art that lurkest in my vitals, come forth—why dost attack me with a hidden smart? What Scythian Sea beneath the icy pole, what sluggish Tethys, what Spanish Calpe, crowding the Moorish coast, begot thee? O cursed bane! Art thou some serpent, brandishing his foul, full-crested head, or some evil thing even to me unknown? Art thou begotten of the Lernaean monster's [3] gore, or did the Stygian dog leave thee here on earth? Every ill thou art and yet no ill— what form hast thou? Grant me at least to know by what ill I am perishing. Whatever pest or what-

---

[1] The Arcadian stag.
[2] When Hercules rent the cliffs of Calpe and Abyla (the pillars of Hercules) asunder and gave outlet to the Mediterranean Sea.   [3] The hydra.

palam timere ! quis tibi in medias locum
fecit medullas ? ecce direpta cute
viscera manus detexit ; ulterior tamen
inventa latebra est—o malum simile Herculi !
   Unde iste fletus ? unde in has lacrimae genas ?
invictus olim voltus et numquam malis
lacrimas suis praebere consuetus (pudet)
iam flere didicit. quis dies fletum Herculis,
quae terra vidit ? siccus aerumnas tuli.
tibi illa virtus, quae tot elisit mala,   1270
tibi cessit uni ; prima et ante omnes mihi
fletum abstulisti ; durior saxo horrido
et chalybe voltus et vaga Symplegade
rictus meos infregit et lacrimam[1] expulit.[2]
flentem gementem, summe pro rector poli,
me terra vidit, quodque me torquet magis,
noverca vidit. urit ecce iterum fibras,
incaluit ardor—unde nunc fulmen mihi ?

CHORVS
   Quid non possit superare dolor ?
quondam Getico durior Haemo   1280
nec Parrhasio lenior axe
saevo cessit membra dolori
fessumque movens per colla caput
latus alterno pondere flectit,
fletum virtus saepe resorbet.
sic arctoas laxare nives
quamvis tepido sidere Titan
non tamen audet vincitque faces
solis adusti glaciale iubar.

      [1] lacrimas *E*.   [2] extulit *A*.

ever beast thou be, oppose me openly! Who gave
thee place within my inmost marrow? See, my hand
has ripped away the skin and the flesh uncovered;
yet deeper still must its lurking place be found—O
woe, invincible as Hercules!

1265 But whence this lamentation? Whence tears
upon these cheeks? My face, before unmoved, and
never wont to express its woes in tears, at last (oh,
shame!) has learned to weep. What day, what
country has seen the tears of Hercules? Dry-eyed
have I borne my cares. To thee [1] that strength,
which has crushed so many monsters, to thee alone
has yielded; thou first of all hast forced tears from
mine eyes; my face, harder than rough rock, harder
than steel and the wandering Symplegades, has relaxed my visage and driven forth my tears. Me,
weeping and groaning, O most high ruler of the
heaven, the earth has seen and, thought which
racks me more, my step-dame has seen. But lo,
again the scorching heat flames up and burns my
vitals. Oh, where is the lightning flash to bring
me death?

CHORUS

What may not suffering overcome? But now,
harder than Thracian Haemus' crags, than Parrhasian skies more calm, to dire agony has he
yielded him; his head drops wearily upon his neck,
from side to side he turns his mighty bulk and oft
does his fortitude drain back his tears. So, with
however fervent beam he shine, Titan avails not to
melt the arctic snows, whose icy splendour defies the
torches of the burning sun.

[1] Addressed to the hidden pest.

287

HERCVLES

Converte voltus ad meas clades, pater.   1290
numquam ad tuas confugit Alcides manus,
non cum per artus hydra fecundum meos
caput explicaret ; inter infernos lacus
possessus atra nocte cum Fato steti
nec invocavi ; tot feras vici horridas,
reges, tyrannos, nec tamen voltus meos
in astra torsi—semper haec nobis manus
votum spopondit ; nulla propter me sacro
micuere caelo fulmina—hic aliquid dies
optare iussit.   primus audierit preces   1300
idemque summus.   unicum fulmen peto ;
giganta crede.   non minus caelum mihi
asserere potui ; dum patrem verum puto,
caelo peperci.   sive crudelis, pater,
sive es misericors, commoda nato manum
properante morte et occupa hanc laudem tibi.

Vel si piget manusque detrectat nefas,
emitte Siculo vertice ardentes, pater,
Titanas in me, qui manu Pindon ferant
aut te, Ossa, qui me monte proiecto opprimant.[1]   1310
abrumpat Erebi claustra, me stricto petat
Bellona ferro ; mitte Gradivum trucem,
armetur in me dirus.   est frater quidem,
sed ex noverca.   tu quoque, Alcidae soror
tantum ex parente, cuspidem in fratrem tuum
iaculare, Pallas.   supplices tendo manus
ad te, noverca : sparge tu saltem, precor,

---

[1] *So A : Madvig* aut te, Ossa, quae me . . . opprimat : *Leo*
†aut Ossa qui . . . opprimat *with E, conjecturing* Ossamque
ut in me . . . opprimar.

288

HERCULES OETAEUS

HERCULES

O father, turn thou thine eyes on my calamity·
Never till now has Alcides fled to thee for aid, not
even when around my limbs the hydra entwined its
fertile heads. Midst the infernal pools, by the black
pall of night enfolded, I stood with Death nor did I
call upon thee. So many dreadful beasts have I
o'ercome, yea kings and tyrants; yet have I ne'er
lifted my face unto the stars. This hand of mine
has ever been surety for my prayers; no bolts for
my sake have flashed from the sacred sky—but this
day has bidden me ask somewhat of thee. 'Tis the
first to hear my prayers, 'twill be the last. Just one
thunderbolt I ask; count me a giant.[1] I could have
laid hands on heaven no less than they; but while I
thought thee my sire in very truth, I spared the
skies. Oh, whether thou be harsh, my sire, or
merciful, lay hands on thy son with speedy death
and claim thee this great renown.[2]

[1307] Or, if thy hand shrinks reluctant from the
impious task, 'gainst me release from Aetna's mount
the burning Titans, who in their hands may heave
Pindus up, or, Ossa, thee, and by the hurled mountain
overwhelm me quite. Let Bellona burst the bars of
Erebus and with drawn sword rush upon me; or
send fierce Mars; let the dread god 'gainst me be
armed. He is my brother, true, but of my step-
dame born. Thou too, Alcides' sister, but by our
sire alone, hurl thy spear, O Pallas, against thy
brother hurl. And to thee, my step-dame, do I
stretch suppliant hands; do thou at least, I pray, let

---

[1] Think of me as one of the old giants storming heaven, and
hurl a bolt at me.
[2] *i.e.* of killing Hercules ere Juno can do so.

telum (perire feminae possum manu)
iam fracta, iam satiata, quid pascis minas ?
quid quaeris ultra ? supplicem Alciden vides, 1320
et nulla tellus, nulla me vidit fera
te deprecantem. nunc mihi irata quidem [1]
opus est noverca—nunc tuus cessat dolor ?
nunc odia ponis ? parcis ubi votum est mori.
o terra et urbes, non facem quisquam Herculi,
non arma tradet ? tela subtrahitis mihi ?
ita nulla saevas terra concipiat feras
post me sepultum nec meas umquam manus
imploret orbis ; si qua nascentur mala,
nascatur ultor.[2] undique infelix caput 1330
mactate saxis, vincite aerumnas meas.
ingrate cessas orbis ? excidimus tibi ?
adhuc malis ferisque suppositus fores,
ni me tulisses. vindicem vestrum malis
eripite, populi ; tempus hoc vobis datur
pensare merita—mors erit pretium omnium.

ALCMENA

Quas misera terras mater Alcidae petam ?
ubi natus, ubinam ? certa si visus notat,
reclinis ecce corde anhelante aestuat ;
gemit; peractum est. membra conplecti ultima, 1340
o nate, liceat, spiritus fugiens meo
legatur ore ; bracchia, amplexus cape—
ubi membra sunt ? ubi illa quae mundum tulit
stelligera cervix ? quis tibi exiguam tui
partem reliquit ?

---

[1] So A : †pater Leo with E, conjecturing ac fera.
[2] So Richter : nascatur alius A : nascetur odium E : Leo
conjectures nascatur opifer.

fly thy bolt (I brook to perish by a woman's hand);
oh, at last yielding, at last glutted, why still feed thy
vengeance? What seekest thou further? Thou
seest Alcides suppliant; whereas no land, no monster
has ever seen me begging thee for quarter. Now
have I need of a wrathful, raging step-dame—now
has thy passion cooled? Now dost lay by thy hate?
Thou sparest me when my prayer is all for death.
O earth and cities of the earth, have ye none to
bring torches 'gainst your Hercules, none to bring
arms? Do ye withhold weapons from me? So[1]
may no land produce savage monsters more when I
am dead, and let the world ne'er ask for aid of
mine; if any evils rise, let avenger rise as well.
From every side crush out my luckless life with
stones, o'erwhelm my woes. O ungrateful world,
dost falter? Hast quite forgotten me? E'en now
wouldst thou be prey to ills and savage beasts hadst
thou not borne me. Then, O ye peoples, rescue your
champion from his woes. This chance is given you
to requite my services—death will be reward for all.

[*Enter* ALCMENA.]

ALCMENA

What lands shall Alcides' wretched mother seek?
Where is my son, oh, where? If mine eyes see
aright, yonder he lies, panting and fever-tossed; he
groans, his life is at an end. In a last embrace let
me enfold thee, O my son, and gather thy parting
spirit in my mouth; take my embracing arms to thine
—but where are thy limbs? Where is that star-
bearing neck which propped the heavens up? Who
is it has left to thee but a shadow of thyself?

[1] *i.e.* according as ye grant my prayer.

HERCVLES

Herculem spectas quidem,
mater, sed umbram et vile nescio quid mei.
agnosce, mater—ora quid flectis retro
voltumque mergis?   Herculem dici tuum
partum erubescis?

ALCMENA

Quis feram mundus novam,
quae terra genuit?   quodve tam dirum nefas   1350
de te triumphant?   victor Herculeus quis est?

HERCVLES

Nuptae iacentem cernis Alciden dolis.

ALCMENA

Quis tantus est qui vincat Alciden dolus?

HERCVLES

Quicumque, mater, feminae iratae sat est.

ALCMENA

Et unde in artus pestis aut ossa incidit?

HERCVLES

Aditum venenis palla femineis dedit.

ALCMENA

Vbinam ista palla est?   membra nudata intuor.

HERCVLES

Consumpta mecum est.

ALCMENA

Tantane inventa est lues?

HERCULES

Hercules thou seest indeed, my mother, but 'tis the shadow and the vile somewhat of myself. Behold me, mother—why dost thou turn thine eyes away and hide thy face? Art ashamed to have Hercules called thy son?

ALCMENA

What world, what land has given birth to a fresh monster? What so dread horror is triumphing over thee? Who is a victor over Hercules?

HERCULES

By his wife's wiles thou seest Alcides low.

ALCMENA

What wile is great enough to worst Alcides?

HERCULES

Whatever, mother, suffices a woman's wrath.

ALCMENA

And how gained the pest entrance to thy joints and bones?

HERCULES

A robe, poisoned by woman's hands, gave entrance to it.

ALCMENA

Where is that robe? I see but naked limbs.

HERCULES

'Twas consumed with me.

ALCMENA

Was so destructive pestilence ever found?

293

HERCVLES

Errare mediis crede visceribus meis,
o mater, hydram et mille cum Lerna feras.   1360
quae tanta nubes flamma Sicanias secat,
quae Lemnos ardens, quae plaga igniferi poli
vetans flagranti currere in zona diem ?
in ipsa me iactate, pro comites, freta
mediosque in amnes—quis sat est Hister mihi ?
non ipse terris maior Oceanus meos
franget vapores, omnis in nostris malis
deficiet umor, omnis arescet latex.
quid, rector Erebi, me remittebas Iovi ?
decuit tenere ; redde me tenebris tuis,   1370
talem subactis Herculem ostende inferis.
nil inde ducam, quid times iterum Herculem ?
invade, mors, non trepida ; iam possum mori.

ALCMENA

Compesce lacrimas saltem et aerumnas doma
malisque tantis Herculem indomitum refer
mortemque differ ; quos soles vince inferos.

HERCVLES

Si me catenis horridus vinctum suis
praeberet avidae Caucasus volucri dapem,
Scythia gemente flebilis gemitus mihi
non extitisset ; si vagae Symplegades   1380
utraque premerent rupe, redeuntis minax [1]

[1] *So Richter :* redeuntes †minas *Leo with* E, *suggesting*
silens.

---

[1] *i.e.* the hydra.
[2] He compares these flames with the fires of Aetna.

HERCULES OETAEUS

HERCULES

Believe me, mother, through my inmost parts the hydra is wandering and with the Lernaean one [1] a thousand savage beasts. What flames [2] as hot as these pierce the Sicilian clouds, what Lemnian fires, or heaven's burning tract, within whose scorching zone [3] the sun's path may not lie? O comrades, throw me into the sea itself, into the river's midst—alas! what Hister is enough for me? Though greater than all lands, the Ocean itself will not cool my burning pains; to ease my woe all water will dry up, all moisture fail. Why, ruler of Erebus, didst send me back to Jove? 'Twere more seemly to have held me fast. To thy glooms restore me, and show such Hercules as this to the ghosts [4] I conquered. Naught will I take away; why dost fear Hercules a second time? Assail me, Death, and fear not; now do I brook to die.

ALCMENA

Restrain thy tears, at least, master thy pains; even to such woes show Hercules invincible; put death away; conquer the lords of hell as is thy wont.

HERCULES

If rugged Caucasus should offer me, bound by its chains, as a feast to greedy birds,[5] while Scythia mourned around, no doleful cry would issue from my lips, should the wandering Symplegades crush me 'twixt both their cliffs, their returning rushes would

---

[3] *i.e.* the space between the ecliptic and the celestial equator.

[4] All the creatures he conquered on earth are now ghosts in the lower world.

[5] He is thinking of the sufferings of Prometheus.

ferrem ruinas ; Pindus incumbat mihi
atque Haemus et qui Thracios fluctus Athos
frangit Iovisque fulmen excipiens Mimas ;
non ipse si in me, mater, hic mundus ruat
superque nostros flagret incensus toros
Phoebeus axis, degener mentem Herculis
clamor domaret.   mille decurrant ferae
pariterque lacerent, hinc feris clangoribus
aetheria me Stymphalis, hinc taurus minax   1390
cervice tota pulset et quidquid fuit
solum quoque ingens ; surgat hinc illinc nemus
artusque nostros durus immittat Sinis :
sparsus silebo—non ferae excutient mihi,
non arma gemitus, nil quod impelli potest.

ALCMENA

Non virus artus, nate, femineum coquit,
sed dura series operis et longus tibi
pavit cruentos forsitan morbos labor.

HERCVLES

Vbi morbus, ubinam est ? estne adhuc aliquid mali
in orbe mecum ?   veniat ; huc aliquis mihi   1400
intendat arcus—nuda sufficiet manus.
procedat agedum huc.

ALCMENA

Ei mihi, sensum quoque
excussit ille nimius impulsans dolor.

HERCULES OETAEUS

I bear, defiant; were Pindus lying on me, and
Haemus, and Athos which resists the Thracian
waves, and Mimas which welcomes the bolts of
Jupiter; mother, if even this sky should fall upon
my head, and over my shoulders the fiery car of
Phoebus should go flaming, no coward cry would
subdue Alcides' soul. Though a thousand beasts at
once should rush against me and rend me sore;
though here from the skies Stymphalus' bird,
swooping with clangour wild, and there with full
strength the threatening bull should push upon me,
and whatever huge monster has sprung from earth;
though Sinis' groves should arise this side and that,
and the rough giant shoot my limbs[1] afar; rent limb
from limb, still will I hold my peace—no beasts, no
arms, naught that can be met and vanquished shall
extort one groan from me.

ALCMENA

Son, 'tis no woman's poison melts thy frame; but
thy hard round of labours, thine unceasing toil, perchance has fed some deadly disease in thee.

HERCULES

Disease? Where is it? Where is it, pray? Is
there still aught of evil in the world with me alive?
Let it come on; let some one reach hither my bow
to me—nay, my bare hands will be enough. Let it
come on, I say. [*He sinks into a deep, swoon-like
slumber.*]

ALCMENA

Alas! the too great shock of agony hath reft e'en
his sense away. [*To attendants.*] Remove his weapons,

[1] See Index *s.v.* "Sinis."

removete quaeso tela et infestas precor
rapite hinc sagittas : igne suffuso genae
scelus minantur.   quas petam latebras anus ?
dolor iste furor est : Herculem solus domat.
cur deinde latebras aut fugam vaecors petam ?
obire forti meruit Alcmene manu :
vel scelere pereat, antequam letum mihi   1410
ignavus aliquis mandet [1] ac turpis manus
de me triumphet.
     Ecce lassatus malis
sopore fessas alligat venas dolor
gravique anhelum pectus impulsu quatit.
favete, superi.   si mihi natum inclutum
miserae negastis, vindicem saltem precor
servate terris.   abeat excussus dolor
corpusque vires reparet Herculeum suas.

HYLLVS

Pro lux acerba, pro capax scelerum dies !
nurus Tonantis occidit, natus iacet,   1420
nepos supersum ; scelere materno hic perit,
fraude illa capta est.   quis per annorum vices
totoque in aevo poterit aerumnas senex
referre tantas ?   unus eripuit dies
parentem utrumque ; cetera ut sileam mala
parcamque fatis, Herculem amitto patrem.

ALCMENA

Compesce voces, inclutum Alcidae genus
miseraeque fato similis Alcmenae nepos :
longus dolorem forsitan vincet sopor.

---

[1] *So A :* mandat . . . triumphat *Leo with E.*

298

take these deadly shafts out of his reach, I pray you ;
his burning cheeks portend some violence. Where
shall an old woman hide herself? That is the smart
of madness ; it alone masters Hercules. But why
should I, foolish that I am, seek flight or hiding ? By
a brave hand Alcmena deserves to die ; so let me
perish even impiously, before some craven decree my
death, or a base hand triumph over me.

¹⁴¹² But see, all spent with woe, his pain holds his
worn heart fast bound in slumber, and his panting
chest heaves with laboured breathing. Help him, ye
gods ! If to my misery ye have denied my glorious
son, at least spare to the world, I pray, its champion.
May his smart be driven quite away, and the body of
Hercules renew its strength.

[*Enter* HYLLUS.]

HYLLUS

O bitter light, O crime-filled day! Dead is the
Thunderer's daughter,[1] his son lies dying, and I, his
grandson, still survive. By my mother's crime is he
perishing, but she was by guile ensnared. What
aged man, throughout his round of years, in his
whole life, will be able to recount woes so great ?
Both parents has one day taken off ; to say naught
of other ills and to spare the fates,[2] Hercules, my
father, am I losing.

ALCMENA

Restrain thy words, child of illustrious sire,
wretched Alcmena's grandson, like her in fate ; perchance long slumber will o'ercome his pains. But

---

[1] Deïanira, who has just killed herself off stage.
[2] *i.e.* not to speak too hardly of them by recounting all
their cruelty.

sed ecce, lassam deserit mentem quies   1430
redditque morbo corpus et luctum mihi.

HERCVLES

Quid hoc ?   rigenti cernitur Trachin iugo
aut inter astra positus evasi genus
mortale tandem ?   quis mihi caelum parat ?
te te, pater, iam video, placatam quoque
specto novercam.   quis sonus nostras ferit
caelestis aures ?   Iuno me generum vocat !
video nitentem regiam clari aetheris
Phoebique tritam flammea zonam rota.
cubile video Noctis ; hinc tenebrae vocant.[1]   1440

Quid hoc ?   quis arcem cludit et ab ipsis, pater,
deducit astris ?   ora Phoebeus modo
afflabat axis, iam prope a caelo fui—
Trachina video.   quis mihi terras dedit ?
Oete modo infra steterat ac totus fuit
suppositus orbis.   quam bene excideras, dolor !
cogis fateri—parce et hanc vocem occupa.

Hoc, Hylle, dona matris hoc munus parant.
utinam liceret stipite ingesto impiam
effringere animam quale Amazonium malum   1450
circa nivalis Caucasi domui latus.
o cara Megara, tune cum furerem mihi
coniunx fuisti ?   stipitem atque arcus date,

---

[1] *So Richter with MSS. order: Leo reads this line after
1444.*

see, repose is deserting his weary heart, and gives
back his frame to suffering, me to grief.

HERCULES [*awakening in delirium*]

Why, what is this? Do I see Trachin midst her
rugged hills, or have I, set 'mongst the stars, at last
left behind the race of men? Who opens heaven for
me? Thee, thee, my father, now do I behold, and
my step-dame also, at last appeased, I see. What
heavenly sound strikes on mine ears? Juno calls
me son! I see bright heaven's gleaming palace, and
the track worn by Phoebus' burning wheels. I see
Night's couch; her shadows call me hence.

[*Begins to come out of his delirium.*]

1441 But what is this? Who shuts heaven's gates
to me, O father, and draws me down even from the
stars? But now the car of Phoebus breathed hot
upon my face, now was I near to heaven—but I see
Trachin. Who has given me earth again? A
moment since, and Oeta stood below me, and the
whole world lay beneath my feet. How well, O
pain, hadst thou fallen from me! Thou compellest
me to confess—but stay, forestall that word.[1]

[*To* HYLLUS.]

1448 O Hyllus, this, this is thy mother's boon, her
gift to me. Would that with lifted club I might
crush out her wicked life just as I smote down the
Amazonian pest [2] upon the slopes of snowy Caucasus.
O well-loved Megara, wast *thou* wife [3] to me when
madness came upon me? Give me my club and

[1] He thus checks himself on the brink of an unmanly
confession of his weakness.
[2] *i.e.* the Amazons themselves.
[3] It should have been Deïanira.

dextra inquinetur, laudibus maculam imprimam,
summus legatur femina Herculeus labor.

HYLLVS

Compesce diras, genitor, irarum minas ;
habet, peractum est, quas petis poenas dedit ;
sua perempta dextera mater iacet.

HERCVLES

Cecidit dolose [1] ; manibus irati Herculis
occidere meruit ; perdidit comitem Lichas.   1460
saevire in ipsum corpus exanime impetus
atque ira cogit.   cur minis nostris caret
ipsum cadaver ?   pabulum accipiant ferae.

HYLLVS

Plus misera laeso doluit ; hinc aliquid quoque
detrahere velles.   occidit dextra sua,
tuo dolore ; plura quam poscis tulit.
sed non cruentae sceleribus nuptae iaces
nec fraude matris ; Nessus hos struxit dolos
ictus sagittis qui tuis vitam expuit.
cruore tincta est palla semiferi, pater,   1470
Nessusque nunc has exigit poenas sibi.

HERCVLES

Habet, peractum est, fata se nostra explicant ;
lux ista summa est.   quercus hanc sortem mihi

---

[1] *So Richter:* relicte dolor es *Leo:* caeci dolores *A :* recte
dolor es *E :* iacet? ei dolori est *Peiper.*

bow, let my right hand be defiled, let me put stain upon my glory, and let a woman be chosen as the last toil of Hercules.

HYLLUS

Check the dire threatenings of thy wrath, my father ; she has it,[1] 'tis over, the penalty which thou desirest she has paid ; slain by her own hand, my mother lies in death.

HERCULES

Treacherously has she fallen ; by the hands of enraged Hercules should she have died ; Lichas has lost a comrade. I am moved to rage e'en 'gainst her lifeless body, and wrath impels me. Why is even her corpse safe from my assaults ? Let the wild beasts make banquet on it.

HYLLUS

The unhappy woman has suffered more than him she injured ; somewhat still of this thou wouldst wish to lighten. By her own hand has she fallen, through grief for thee ; more suffering than thou demandest has she borne. But 'tis not by crimes of a murderous wife, nor by my mother's guile, thou liest low ; Nessus contrived this snare, who, by thine arrow smit, spewed out his life. Father, 'twas in that half-beast's gore the robe was dipped, and Nessus by these thy sufferings doth requite his own.

HERCULES

'Tis well,[2] 'tis over, my fate unfolds itself ; this is my last day on earth. This oracle the prophetic

---

[1] The formula of the gladiatorial contest when one of the contestants has received his death stroke.

[2] See note on l. 1457.

fatidica quondam dederat et Parnassio
Cirrhaea quatiens templa mugitu specus :
" dextra perempti victor, Alcide, viri
olim iacebis ; hic tibi emenso freta
terrasque et umbras finis extremus datur."
nil querimur ultra ; decuit hunc finem dari,
ne quis superstes Herculis victor foret.   1480
nunc mors legatur clara memoranda incluta,
me digna prorsus.   nobilem hunc faciam diem.
caedatur omnis silva et Oetaeum nemus
conripite, ut ingens Herculem accipiat rogus,
sed ante mortem.   tu, genus Poeantium,
hoc triste nobis, iuvenis, officium appara ;
Herculea totum flamma succendat diem.

Ad te preces nunc, Hylle, supremas fero.
est clara captas inter, in voltu genus
regnumque referens, Euryto virgo edita   1490
Iole.   tuis hanc facibus et thalamis para.
victor cruentus abstuli patriam lares
nihilque miserae praeter Alciden dedi ;
et ipse rapitur.   penset aerumnas suas,
Iovis nepotem foveat et natum Herculis ;
tibi illa pariat quidquid ex nobis habet.

Tuque ipsa planctus pone funereos, precor,
o clara genetrix ; vivit Alcides tibi.
virtute nostra paelicem feci tuam

---

¹ The oracle of the talking oaks, sacred to Jupiter, was at
Dodona, in Epirus ; the oracle of Apollo at Delphi was in
Phocis, on Mount Parnassus. The poet either means that

oak [1] once gave me, and the Parnassian grot,[1] shaking
the shrines of Cirrha with rumbling tones, declared:
" By the hand of one whom, conquering, thou hast
slain, Alcides, one day shalt thou lie low; this end,
when thou hast traversed seas and lands and shades,
awaits thee at the last." We complain no more;
such end was meet, that no living thing might
conquer Hercules. Now let me choose a death
glorious, renowned, illustrious, full worthy of myself.
This day will I make famous. Go, cut down all the
woods, heap Oeta's grove together, that a mighty
pyre may receive Hercules, and that before he dies.
Thou, son [2] of Poeas, dear youth, perform this sad
office for me; set the whole sky aglow with the
flames of Hercules.

[1488] And now to thee, Hyllus, I bring my latest
prayer. Among the captives is a beauteous maid, in
feature revealing her race and royal state, Iole,
daughter of king Eurytus. Lead her to thy
chamber with wedding torch. Victorious, blood-
stained, I robbed her of her fatherland and home,
and to the wretched girl gave naught except
Alcides; and now e'en he is reft from her. Let her
find recompense for her sorrows, and cherish Jove's
grandson and the son of Hercules; to thee be born
whatever seed she has conceived by me.

[To ALCMENA.]

[1497] Do thou thyself cease thy death-wails for me,
I pray, illustrious mother; thy Alcides lives; by my
heroic deeds have I made my step-dame seem but

two oracles foretold the same fate, or simply mingles the two
references by way of emphasis on the oracular utterance
itself.

[2] Philoctetes.

305

credi novercam.   sive nascente Hercule   1500
nox illa certa est sive mortalis meus
pater est—licet sit falsa progenies mei,[1]
merui parentem ; contuli caelo decus
materque me concepit in laudes Iovis.
quin ipse, quamquam Iuppiter, credi meus
pater esse gaudet.   parce iam lacrimis, parens ;
superba matres inter Argolicas eris.
quid tale Iuno genuit aetherium gerens
sceptrum et Tonanti nupta?   mortali tamen   1510
caelum tenens invidit, Alciden suum
dici esse voluit.

     Perage nunc, Titan, vices
solus relictus ; ille qui vester comes
ubique fueram, Tartara et manes peto.
hanc tamen ad imos perferam laudem inclutam,
quod nulla pestis fudit Alciden palam
omnemque pestem vicit Alcides palam.

CHORVS

  O decus mundi, radiate Titan,
  cuius ad primos Hecate vapores
  lassa nocturnae levat ora bigae,   1520
  dic sub Aurora positis Sabaeis,
  dic sub occasu positis Hiberis,
  quique sub plaustro patiuntur ursae
  quique ferventi quatiuntur axe,
  dic sub aeternos properare manes

---

[1] *Leo deletes l. 1503:* materna culpa cesset et crimen Iovis.

---

[1] By bearing such a son to Jove, Alcmena is proved to be
real wife, and Juno the mistress.

the concubine.[1]   Whether the tale[2] of the night of
Hercules' begetting be the truth, or whether my sire
be mortal [3]—though I be falsely called the son of
Jove, I have deserved to be his son; glory on heaven
have I conferred, and to Jove's glory did my mother
bring me forth.   Nay, he himself, though he be
Jupiter, is glad to be believed my sire.   Dry now
thy tears, my mother; proud 'mongst the Grecian
mothers shalt thou be.   What son like thine has
Juno borne, though she wield the sceptre of the
skies, and be the Thunderer's bride?   Still, though
queen of heaven, she envied a mortal woman, and
wished that Alcides might be called her own.

1512 Now, O Sun, must thou speed thy course
alone, for I, who have been thy companion everywhere, am bound for Tartarus and the land of
shades.   Yet to the depths shall I bear this glorious
fame, that no pest openly has laid Alcides low,
and that all pests openly has Alcides slain.

[*He goes out toward the pyre which has been prepared for
him.*]

CHORUS

O glory of the world, O ray-girt Sun, at whose
first warmth Hecate loosens the bits from the weary
steeds of her nocturnal car, tell the Sabaeans who
lie beneath the dawn, tell the Iberians who lie
beneath thy setting, tell those who suffer 'neath the
Wagon of the Bear,[4] and those who pant beneath
thy burning car: Hercules is hasting to the endless

---

[2] See Index *s.v.* "Hercules," at beginning.
[3] *i.e.* Amphitryon.
[4] This northern constellation is either the Wain (wagon)
or the Bear.   The poet confuses the two conceptions.

Herculem et regnum canis inquieti,
unde non umquam remeabit ille.[1]
sume quos nubes radios sequantur,
pallidus maestas speculare terras
et caput turpes nebulae pererrent.   1530
quando, pro Titan, ubi, quo sub axe
Herculem in terris alium sequeris?
quas manus orbis miser invocabit,
si qua sub Lerna numerosa pestis
sparget in centum rabiem dracones,
Arcadum si quis populis vetustis
fecerit silvas aper inquietas,
Thraciae si quis Rhodopes alumnus
durior terris Helices nivosae
sparget humano stabulum cruore?   1540
quis dabit pacem populo timenti,
si quid irati superi per orbem
iusserint nasci?   iacet omnibus par,
quem parem tellus genuit Tonanti.
planctus immensas resonet per urbes
et comas nullo cohibente nodo
feminae exertos feriant lacertos,
solaque obductis foribus deorum
templa securae pateant novercae.

Vadis ad Lethen Stygiumque litus,   1550
unde te nullae referent carinae;
vadis ad manes miserandus, unde
Morte devicta tuleras triumphum,
umbra nudatis veniens lacertis
languido vultu tenuique collo;
teque non solum feret illa puppis [2]

---

[1] *So Richter:* unde non umquam remeavit ullus *A:* Leo
†unde non numquam remeavit inde *with E,* Leo conjecturing
denuo numquam remeabit inde.

[2] *Peiper notes a lacuna after l. 1556, which Leo thus sup-
plies:* quae tulit solum metuitque mergi.

shades, to the realm of sleepless Cerberus, whence
he will never more return. Let thy bright rays be
overcast with clouds; gaze on the grieving world
with pallid face and let disfiguring mists roam o'er
thy head. When, O Titan, where, beneath what
sky wilt thou follow another Hercules on the earth?
To whose aid will the wretched world appeal if
within Lerna's swamp some many-headed pest in a
hundred snakes shall spread its poisonous rage; if
for the ancient tribes of Arcady some boar shall
disturb the quiet of the woods; if some son[1] of
Thracian Rhodope, harder than the ground of snow-
clad Helice, shall spatter his stalls with the blood of
men? Who to the trembling nations will give peace,
if the angry gods shall raise up new monsters o'er
the world? Level with all men he lies,[2] whom
earth produced level with the Thunderer. Through
countless cities let cries of brief resound; let
women with streaming hair smite their bare arms;
let the temples of all gods be closed save his step-
dame's only, for she only is free from care.

[1550] Thou farest to Lethe and the Stygian shore
whence no keel will ever bring thee back; thou
farest, lamented one, unto the ghosts whence, over-
coming Death, thou didst once return in triumph,
now but a shade, with fleshless arms, wan face and
drooping neck; nor will that skiff, which once bore
thee alone and feared 'twould be plunged beneath

---

[1] Like Diomedes, the bloody tyrant of Thrace.
[2] *i.e.* brought to the common level by death.

non tamen viles eris inter umbras,
Aeacon [1] inter geminosque Cretas
facta discernens, feriens tyrannos.
parcite, o dites, inhibete dextras.   1560
laudis est purum tenuisse ferrum,
cumque regnabas, minus in procellis
in tuas urbes licuisse fatis.

    Sed locum virtus habet inter astra.
sedis arctoae spatium tenebis
an graves Titan ubi promit aestus?
an sub occasu tepido nitebis,
unde commisso resonare ponto
audies Calpen?   loca quae sereni
deprimes caeli?   quis erit recepto   1570
tutus Alcide locus inter astra?
horrido tantum procul a leone
det pater sedes calidoque cancro,
ne tuo vultu tremefacta leges
astra conturbent trepidetque Titan.
vere dum flores venient tepenti
et comam silvis hiemes recident,
vel comam silvis revocabit aestas
pomaque autumno fugiente cedent,
nulla te terris rapiet vetustas;   1580
tu comes Phoebo, comes ibis astris.
ante nascetur seges in profundo
vel fretum dulci resonabit unda,
ante descendet glacialis ursae
sidus et ponto vetito fruetur,
quam tuas laudes populi quiescant.

    Te, pater rerum, miseri precamur:
nulla nascatur fera, nulla pestis,
non duces saevos miseranda tellus
horreat, nulla dominetur aula   1590

[1] *So Gronovius*: Aeacos *Leo with* E: Aeacumque *A*.

the waves,[1] bear thee alone. And yet thou shalt not dwell midst common shades ; midst Aeacus and the two Cretans[2] shalt thou be, sitting in judgment on men's deeds, scourging tyrannic kings. Spare, O ye mighty, restrain your hands. 'Tis thy praise to have kept the sword unstained and that, what time thou didst bear sway, fate midst its storms had less power against thy cities.

1564 But now has thy manhood place amongst the stars. Wilt occupy the spaces of the north, or where Titan sends forth his oppressive rays ? Or in the warm western sky wilt shine, where thou wilt hear Calpe resound with the charging sea ? What region of the cloudless heavens wilt thou weigh down ? What place, when Alcides comes, will be safe amidst the stars ? Only may Jove give thee thy seat far from the dread Lion and the burning Crab, lest at sight of thee the affrighted stars make turmoil of their laws and Titan tremble. While flowers shall bloom as the spring days grow warm ; while winter shall strip the foliage from the trees, and summer to the trees recall their foliage ; while fruits shall fall as autumn takes his flight, no lapse of time shall snatch thee from the world ; comrade of Phoebus, comrade of the stars, shalt thou pass on. Sooner shall wheat sprout from the surface of the deep ; sooner the roaring waves of the sea be sweet ; sooner shall the icy Bear come down and enjoy the forbidden waters, than shall the nations be silent of thy praise.

1587 To thee, father of all, in wretchedness we pray : let no dread beast be born, no pest ; from the fear of savage kings keep this poor world free ; let no one lord it in palace hall who deems it the sole

---

[1] Translating Leo's suggested line.
[2] Minos and Rhadamanthus.

qui putet solum decus esse regni
semper impensum tenuisse ferrum.
si quid in terris iterum timetur,
vindicem terrae petimus relictae.
   Heu quid hoc ? mundus sonat. ecce maeret,
maeret Alciden pater ; an deorum
clamor, an vox est timidae novercae ?
Hercule an viso fugit astra Iuno ?
passus an pondus titubavit Atlas ?
an magis diri tremuere manes   1600
Herculem et visum canis inferorum
fugit abruptis trepidus catenis ?
fallimur ; laeto venit ecce voltu
quem tulit Poeans umerisque tela
gestat et notas populis pharetras,
       Herculis heres.

Effare casus, iuvenis, Herculeos precor
voltuque quonam tulerit Alcides necem.

PHILOCTETES [1]

Quo nemo vitam.

CHORVS

          Laetus adeone ultimos
invasit ignes ?

PHILOCTETES

          Esse iam flammas nihil   1610
ostendit ille. quid sub hoc mundo Hercules
immune vinci liquit ? en domita omnia.

CHORVS

Inter vapores quis fuit forti locus ?

---

[1] *The dialogue throughout this scene is given by Leo and
Richter to Nuntius and Chorus, following E ; to Nutrix and
Philoctetes A ; since the messenger is obviously Philoctetes (see*

glory of his realm to have held the sword e'er threatening. If some dread thing should come again to earth, oh, give to forsaken earth a champion.

1595 But what is this? The universe resounds. Behold, he mourns, the father mourns Alcides; or is it the outcry of the gods or the voice of his frighted step-dame? At the sight of Hercules does Juno flee the stars? Under the mighty weight has Atlas staggered? Or is it that the awful ghosts have trembled and at sight of Hercules the hell-hound in affright has broken his chains and fled? No, we are wrong; behold with joyful face comes Poeas' son and on his shoulders he bears the shafts and the quiver known to all, the heir of Hercules.

[*Enter* PHILOCTETES.]

1607 Speak out, good youth, and tell the end of Hercules, I pray, and with what countenance Alcides bore his death.

PHILOCTETES

With such as none e'er bore his life.

CHORUS

So joyous did he mount his funeral pyre?

PHILOCTETES

He showed that now flames were as naught to him. What 'neath the heavens has Hercules left by defeat unscathed? Lo, all things have been subdued.

CHORUS

Midst the hot flames what room was there for valour?

---

l. 1604) and there is no pertinency in the introduction of the nurse, we have given the dialogue to Philoctetes and the Chorus.

313

PHILOCTETES

Quod unum in orbe vicerat nondum malum,
et flamma victa est ; haec quoque accessit feris :
inter labores ignis Herculeos abit.

CHORVS

Edissere agedum, flamma quo victa est modo?

PHILOCTETES

Vt omnis Oeten maesta corripuit manus,
huic fagus umbras perdit et toto iacet
succissa trunco, flectit hic pinum ferox   1620
astris minantem et nube de media vocat ;
ruitura cautem movit et silvam tulit
secum minorem.   Chaonis qualis loquax
stat vasta late quercus et Phoebum vetat
ultraque totos porrigit ramos manus ;
gemit illa multo volnere impresso minax
frangitque cuneos, resilit incussus chalybs
volnusque ferrum patitur et rigidum est parum.
commota tandem cum cadens latam sui
duxit ruinam, protinus radios locus   1630
admisit omnes ; sedibus pulsae suis
volucres pererrant nemore succiso diem
quaeruntque lassis garrulae pinnis domus.
iamque omnis arbor sonuit et sacrae quoque
sensere quercus horridam ferro manum
nullique priscum profuit luco nemus.
aggeritur omnis silva et alternae trabes
in astra tollunt Herculi angustum rogum :

---

[1] See Index s.v. "Chaonian Oaks."
[2] Oak-trees were especially sacred to Jove.

HERCULES OETAEUS

PHILOCTETES

The one enemy on earth which he had not o'ercome, e'en fire, is vanquished; this also has been
added to the beasts; fire has taken its place midst
the toils of Hercules.

CHORUS

But tell us, in what wise were the flames o'ercome?

PHILOCTETES

When the whole sorrowing band fell upon Oeta's
woods, by the hands of one the beech-tree lost its
shade and lay full length, hewn to the ground; one
fiercely felled a pine-tree, towering to the stars, and
from the clouds' midst he summoned it; in act to
fall, it shook the rocky slope and with itself brought
down the lesser woods. A huge oak stood, wide
spreading, such as Chaonia's oak[1] of prophecy, ex-
cluding the light of day and stretching its branches
far beyond all the grove. Threat'ning it groaned,
by many a blow beset, and broke the wedges; back
bounded the smiting steel; its edge was dulled, too
soft for such a task. When the tree, at last dislodged, falling, brings widespread ruin down, straightway the place lets in the sun's full rays; the birds,
driven from their perches, flit aimless through the
day midst the felled grove, and, loudly complaining,
with wearied wings seek for their nests. And now
every tree resounded, and even the sacred oaks[2] felt
the dread steel-armed hand, and its ancient woods
availed no holy grove.[3] The whole forest was piled
into a heap; and the logs, starward in layers rising,
made all too small a pyre for Hercules—the pine-

[3] A deep, primeval forest, for ages left untouched, had
acquired a special sanctity.

raptura flammas pinus et robur tenax
et brevior ilex silva ; sed complet rogum   1640
populea silva, frontis Herculeae decus.
   At ille, ut ingens nemore sub Nasamonio
aegro reclinis pectore immugit leo,
fertur—quis illum credat ad flammas rapi ?
voltus petentis astra, non ignes erat,
ut pressit Oeten ac suis oculis rogum
lustravit omnem. fregit impositus trabes.
arcus poposcit. "accipe haec " inquit, " sate
Poeante, dona et munus Alcidae cape.
has hydra sensit, his iacent Stymphalides   1650
et quidquid aliud eminus vici malum.
virtute felix,[1] iuvenis, has numquam irritas
mittes in hostem ; sive de media voles
auferre volucres nube, descendent aves
et certa praedae tela de caelo fluent,
nec fallet umquam dexteram hic arcus tuam.
librare tela didicit et certam dare
fugam sagittis, ipsa non fallunt iter
emissa nervo tela. tu tantum precor
accommoda ignes et facem extremam mihi.   1660
hic nodus" inquit " nulla quem cepit manus,
mecum per ignes flagret ; hoc telum Herculem
tantum sequetur. hoc quoque acciperes " ait
" si ferre posses. adiuvet domini rogum."
tum rigida secum spolia Nemeaei mali
arsura poscit ; latuit in spolio rogus.
   Ingemuit omnis turba nec lacrimas dolor
cuiquam remisit. mater in luctum furens
diduxit avidum pectus atque utero tenus

---

[1] *So Gronovius with* ς : †victrice felix *Leo with* E : victure
felix. has enim numquam irritas A : his utere felix *Peiper :
arguing from* sive (1653) *Leo thinks the other alternative must
have begun in l. 1652 with some such words as* sive eris in acie.

tree, quick to burn, the tough-fibred oak, the ilex of shorter trunk ; but poplar wood, whose foliage adorns Alcides' brow, filled out the pyre.

1642 But he, like some huge, suffering lion, which, in Libyan forest lying, roars out his pain, hurried along,—who would suppose him hasting to the flames ? His gaze was of one who seeks the stars, not fires of earth, when he set foot on Oeta and with his eyes surveyed the pyre complete. The great beams broke beneath him. Then for his shafts and bow he called, and said : " Take these, thou son of Poeas, take them as Alcides' gift and pledge of love. These did the Hydra feel ; by these the Stymphalian birds lie low, and all other pests which at distance I overcame. O youth with valour blest, never in vain shalt thou send these 'gainst a foe ; or if birds from the very clouds thou wouldst fetch away, birds will fall down, and out of the sky will thy shafts, sure of their prey, come floating ; and ne'er will this bow disappoint thy hand. Well has it learned to poise the feathered shafts and unerringly send them flying ; while the shafts themselves, loosed from the string, fail never to find their mark. Only do thou, I pray, apply the fire and set the last torch for me. Let this club," he said, " which no hand but mine has wielded, burn in the flames with me ; this weapon alone shall follow Hercules. This also shouldst thou have," said he, " if thou couldst wield it. Let it add fuel to its master's pyre." Then did he call for the Nemean monster's shaggy skin to burn with him ; 'neath the skin the pyre was hidden.

1667 The whole throng set up a lamentation, and sorrow filled the eyes of all with tears. His mother, passionate in grief, her eager bosom stript, and she

317

exerta vastos ubera in planctus ferit,   1670
superosque et ipsum vocibus pulsans Iovem
implevit omnem voce feminea locum.
" deforme letum, mater, Herculeum facis ;
compesce lacrimas" inquit, " introrsus dolor
femineus abeat. Iuno cur laetum diem
te flente ducat ? paelicis gaudet suae
spectare lacrimas. comprime infirmum iecur,
mater ; nefas est ubera atque uterum tibi
laniare, qui me genuit." et dirum fremens,
qualis per urbes duxit Argolicas canem,   1680
cum victor Erebi Dite contempto redit
tremente fato, talis incubuit rogo.
quis sic triumphans laetus in curru stetit
victor ? quis illo gentibus voltu dedit
leges tyrannus ? quanta pax habitum tulit !
haesere lacrimae, cecidit impulsus dolor
nobis quoque ipsis, nemo periturum ingemit.
iam flere pudor est ; ipsa quam sexus iubet
maerere, siccis haesit Alcmene genis
stetitque nato paene iam similis parens.   1690

CHORVS

Nullasne in astra misit ad superos preces
arsurus aut in vota respexit Iovem ?

PHILOCTETES

Iacuit sui securus et caelum intuens
quaesivit oculis, parte an ex aliqua pater
despiceret illum. tum manus tendens ait :
" quacumque parte prospicis natum pater
(iste est pater, cui nocte commissa dies

smote her breasts, naked e'en to the waist, in endless lamentation; and with her cries assailing the gods and Jove himself, she filled all the region round with womanish bewailings. "Mother," he said, "thou dost disgrace the death of Hercules; restrain thy tears and confine thy womanish grief within thy heart. Why for thy weeping should Juno count this day joyful? For she rejoices to see her rival's tears. Curb thy faint heart, my mother; 'tis a sin to tear the breasts and the womb that bore Alcides." Then with dread mutterings, as when through Argive towns he dragged the dog, what time, triumphant over hell, in scorn of Dis and trembling death he returned to earth, so did he lay him down upon the pyre. What victor ever stood in his chariot so joyfully triumphant? What tyrant king with such a countenance ever gave laws to nations? How calmly he bore his fate! Even our tears were stayed, grief's shock subsided, none grieves that he must perish. Now were we 'shamed to weep; Alcmena, herself, whose sex impels to mourning, stood with dry cheeks, a mother now well-nigh equal to her son.

CHORUS

Sent he no supplications heavenward to the gods e'er the fire was lit? Looked he not to Jove to hear his prayers?

PHILOCTETES

Careless of self he lay and, gazing at heaven, quested with his eyes whether from any quarter his sire looked down at him. Then, with hands outstretched, he spoke: "O father, from what quarter soe'er thou lookest on thy son, (he truly is my father, for whose sake night joined with day and one

319

quievit unus), si meas laudes canit
utrumque Phoebi litus et Scythiae genus
et omnis ardens ora quam torret dies,   1700
si pace tellus plena, si nullae gemunt
urbes nec aras impias quisquam inquinat,
si scelera desunt, spiritum admitte hunc precor
in astra. non me mortis infernae locus
nec maesta nigri regna conterrent Iovis ;
sed ire ad illos umbra, quos vici, deos,
pater, erubesco. nube discussa diem
pande, ut deorum voltus ardentem Herculem
spectet ; licet tu sidera et mundum neges,
ultro, pater, cogere—si voces dolor   1710
abstulerit ullas, pande tum Stygios lacus
et redde fatis ; approba natum prius.
ut dignus astris videar, hic faciet dies.
leve est quod actum est ; Herculem hic, genitor, dies
inveniet aut damnabit.''

      Haec postquam edidit, 1715
flammas poposcit. " hoc age, Alcidae comes 1717
non segnis '' inquit " corripe Oetaeam facem ;
noverca cernat quo feram flammas modo.[1] 1716
quid dextra tremuit ? num manus pavida impium 1719
scelus refugit ? redde iam pharetras mihi, 1720
ignave iners inermis—en nostros manus
quae tendat arcus ! quid sedet pallor genis ?
animo faces invade quo Alciden vides
voltu iacere. respice arsurum, miser.

 Vocat ecce iam me genitor et pandit polos.
venio, pater.'' voltusque non idem fuit.
tremente pinum dextera ardentem impuli ; [2]

---

[1] *Leo deletes this line with E : Richter, following Gronovius,
places it after l. 1718.*
[2] *So A : Leo* impulit *with E.*

320

day ceased to be,) if both the bounds of Phoebus sing my praise, the tribes of Scythia and every burning strand which daylight parches; if peace fills all the earth; if no cities groan and no man stains with sin his altar-fires; if crimes have ceased, admit this soul, I pray thee, to the stars. I have no fear of the infernal realm of death, nor do the sad realms of dusky Jove [1] affright me; but to go, naught but a shade, to those gods I overcame, O sire, I am ashamed. Dispel the clouds, spread wide the day, that the eyes of gods may gaze on burning Hercules. Though thou deny me stars and a place in heaven, O sire, thou shalt even be compelled—ah! if pain will excuse any words [2] of mine, then open the Stygian pools and give me to death again; but prove me first thy son. This day will make me seem worthy of the stars. Worthless is all that has been done; this day, my father, will bring Hercules to light or doom him."

[1715] When he had thus said, he called for fire. "Up now, Alcides' willing friend," said he, "catch up the Oetaean torch; let my step-dame see how I can bear the flames. Why did thy right hand tremble? Did thy hand shrink timid from such unholy deed? Then give me my quiver back, thou undaring, unskilled, unwarlike—*that* the hand to bend my bow! Why do thy cheeks grow pale? Come, seize on the torch with courage, with face thou seest on prone Alcides. Poor soul, have some regard for him who soon will burn.

[1725] But lo! now doth my father call me and he opens heaven. I come, O sire." Then was his face no more the same. With trembling hand I applied

---

[1] Pluto.

[2] *i.e.* the latest defiant word, "compelled."

refugit ignis et reluctantur faces
et membra vitant, sed recedentem Hercules
insequitur ignem. Caucasum aut Pindum aut
    Athon   1730
ardere credas ; nullus erumpit sonus,
tantum ingemescit ignis. o durum iecur !
Typhon in illo positus immanis rogo
gemuisset ipse quique convulsam solo
imposuit umeris Ossan Enceladus ferox.

    At ille medias inter exurgens faces,
semiustus ac laniatus, intrepidum tuens :
" nunc es parens Herculea ; sic stare ad rogum
te, mater," inquit, " sic decet fleri Herculem."
inter vapores positus et flammae minas   1740
immotus, inconcussus, in neutrum latus
correpta torquens membra adhortatur, monet,
gerit aliquid ardens. omnibus fortem addidit
animum ministris ; urere ardentem putes.
stupet omne volgus, vix habent flammae fidem,
tam placida frons est, tanta maiestas viro.
nec properat uri ; cumque iam forti datum
leto satis pensavit, igniferas trabes
hinc inde traxit, minima quas flamma occupat,
totasque in ignes vertit et quis plurimus   1750
exundat ignis repetit intrepidus ferox.
tunc ora flammis implet. ast illi graves
luxere barbae ; cumque iam voltum minax
appeteret ignis, lamberent flammae caput,
non pressit oculos.—sed quid hoc ? maestam intuor

the blazing pine; the flames shrunk back, the torch
resisted and would not touch his limbs; but Hercules
followed up the shrinking flames. Thou wouldst
suppose that Caucasus or Pindus or Athos was
ablaze; no sound burst forth, save that the fire
seemed groaning. O stubborn heart! Had huge
Typhon been lying on that pyre, he would have
groaned aloud, and fierce Enceladus who upon his
shoulders bore Ossa, uptorn from earth.

[1736] But Hercules, midst roaring flames upstarting,
all charred and mangled, gazed dauntless round and
cried: "Now art thou parent true of Hercules; thus
'tis meet that thou shouldst stand, my mother,
beside the pyre, and thus 'tis meet that Hercules be
mourned." Midst scorching heat and threat'ning
flames, unmoved, unshaken, to neither side turning
his tortured limbs, he encourages, advises, is active
still, though all aflame. To all his ministrants stout-
ness of soul he gives; you would deem him all on
fire to burn. The whole crowd stands in speechless
wonder and the flames have scarce belief,[1] so calm
his brow, the hero so majestic. Nor does he speed
his burning; but when now he deemed that courage
enough had been shown in death, from every side he
dragged the burning logs which the fire least fed
upon, and into that blazing mass he strode and
sought where the flames leaped highest, all unafraid,
defiant. Awhile he feasted his eyes upon the fires.
But now his heavy beard burned bright; and even
when threat'ning fire assailed his face and the hot
tongues licked about his head, he did not close his
eyes.—But what is this? I see the sad mother

---

[1] The people hardly believed that the fire was real.

sinu gerentem reliquias magni Herculis [1]
crinemque iactans squalidum Alcmene gemit.

ALCMENA

Timete, superi, fata! tam parvus cinis
Herculeus, huc huc ille decrevit gigans!
o quanta, Titan, ad nihil moles abit!   1760
anilis, heu me, recipit Alciden sinus,
hic tumulus illi est. ecce vix totam Hercules
complevit urnam; quam leve est pondus mihi,
cui totus aether pondus incubuit leve.
ad Tartara olim regnaque, o nate, ultima
rediturus ibas—quando ab inferna Styge
remeabis iterum? non ut et spolium trahas
rursusque Theseus debeat lucem tibi—
sed quando solus? mundus impositus tuas
compescet umbras teque Tartareus canis 1770
inhibere poterit? quando Taenarias fores
pulsabis, aut quas mater ad fauces agar
qua mors aditur? vadis ad manes iter
habiturus unum. quid diem questu tero?
quid misera duras vita? quid lucem tenes?
quem parere rursus Herculem possum Iovi?
quis me parentem natus Alcmenen suam
tantus vocabit? o nimis felix nimis,
Thebane coniunx, Tartari intrasti loca
florente nato teque venientem inferi   1780
timuere forsan, quod pater tantum Herculis,

---

[1] *Leo deletes ll. 1755, 1756, Richter 1755–1757: the last part
of the speech of Philoctetes is supposed to have fallen out.*

bearing in her bosom the remains of great Alcides, and Alcmena, tossing her squalid locks, bewails her son.

[*Enter* ALCMENA, *carrying in her bosom a funeral urn.*]

ALCMENA

Fear ye the fates, O powers above! (*Holding up the urn.*) See the scant dust of Hercules—to this, to this has that mighty body shrunk! O Sun, how great a mass has passed away to nothingness! Ah me, this aged breast can hold Alcides, this is a tomb for him. See, Hercules has scarce filled all the urn; how light for me his weight upon whose shoulders the whole heavens as a light weight rested. Once to the farthest realms of Tartarus, O son, didst thou go but to return—Oh, when from infernal Styx wilt thou come again? Not in such wise as to bring e'en spoil with thee, nor that Theseus again may owe thee the light of day,—but when, though all alone? Will the whole world, heaped on thee, hold thy shade, or the hell-hound avail to keep thee back? When wilt thou batter down the Taenarian[1] gates, or to what yawning jaws shall thy mother betake herself, where is the approach to death? Thou takest thy journey to the dead, and 'twill be thy only one. Why do I waste time in wailing? Why dost endure, O wretched life? Why clingest to the light? What Hercules can I again bring forth to Jove? What son so great will call me mother, will call me his Alcmena? Oh, too, too happy thou, my Theban husband,[2] for thou to the realms of Tartarus didst descend, thy son still living; at thy approach the infernal ones, perchance, were filled with fear, merely because thou wast the sire of Hercules, even

---

[1] See Index *s.v.* "Taenarus."   [2] Amphitryon.

vel falsus, aderas—quas petam terras anus,
invisa saevis regibus, si quis tamen
rex est relictus saevus ?   ei miserae mihi !
quicumque caesos ingemit natus patres,
a me petet supplicia, me cuncti obruent.
si quis minor Busiris aut si quis minor
Antaeus orbem fervidae terret plagae,
ego praeda ducar ; si quis Ismarius greges
Thracis cruenti vindicat, carpent greges   1790
mea membra diri.   forsitan poenas petet
irata Iuno ; totus huc verget [1] dolor ;
secura victo tandem ab Alcide vacat,
paelex supersum—a quanta supplicia expetet
ne parere possim !   fecit hic natus mihi
uterum timendum.

             Quae petam Alcmene loca ?
quis me locus, quae regio, quae mundi plaga
defendet aut quas mater in latebras agar
ubique per te nota ?   sic patriam petam
laresque miseros ?   Argos Eurystheus tenet.   1800
marita Thebas regna et Ismenon petam
thalamosque nostros, in quibus quondam Iovem
dilecta vidi ?   pro nimis felix, nimis,
si fulminantem et ipsa sensissem Iovem !
utinam meis visceribus Alcides foret
exectus infans !   nunc datum est tempus, datum est
videre natum laude certantem Iovi,
ut et hoc daretur, scire quid fatum mihi
eripere posset.

   [1] *So Richter with N. Heinsius : Leo reads* †uretur *with* ω,
and conjectures exurget.
326

though falsely called.—What lands shall an aged
woman seek, hated by savage kings, if spite of all
any savage king is left alive? Oh, woe is me! All
sons[1] who lament their murdered sires will seek
revenge from me; they all will overwhelm me. If
any young Busiris or if any young Antaeus terrifies
the region of the burning zone,[2] I shall be led off as
booty; if any Ismarian[3] seeks revenge for the herds
of the bloody king[4] of Thrace, upon my limbs
will his horrid herds be fed. Juno, perchance, in
anger will seek revenge; against me will the whole
force of her wrath incline; though her soul is no
more disturbed by Alcides, o'ercome at last, I, the
concubine, am left—ah! what punishments will she
inflict, lest I be again a mother! This son has made
my womb a thing of fear.

[1796] Whither shall Alcmena flee? What place,
what region, what quarter of the world will take my
part, or to what hiding-place shall thy mother betake
herself, known everywhere through thee? Shall I
seek my fatherland and my wretched home?
Eurystheus is king at Argos. Shall I seek Thebes,
my husband's kingdom, the Ismenus and my bridal
chamber, where once, greatly beloved by him, I
looked on Jove? Oh, happy, far too happy had I
been, if I myself, too,[5] had known Jove's thunderbolt! Oh, would that from my womb the infant
Alcides had been ripped! But now was the chance
given me, yea 'twas given to see my son vying in
praise with Jove, that this, too, might be given me—
to know of how much fate had power to rob me.

---

[1] *i.e.* whose fathers Hercules has slain.
[2] Both these enemies of Hercules had lived in Africa.
[3] *i.e.* Thracian.   [4] Diomedes.
   She is thinking of the experience of Semele.

Quis memor vivet tui,
o nate, populus? omne iam ingratum est genus. 1810
petam Cleonas? Arcadum populos petam
meritisque terras nobiles quaeram tuis?
hic dira serpens cecidit, hic ales fera,
hic rex cruentus, hic tua fractus manu
qui te sepulto possidet caelum leo.
si grata terra est, populus Alcmenen tuam
defendat omnis. Thracias gentes petam
Hebrique populos? haec quoque est meritis tuis
defensa tellus; stabula cum regno iacent.
hic pax cruento rege prostrato data est; 1820
ubi enim negata est?

Quod tibi infelix anus
quaeram sepulchrum? de tuis totus rogis
contendat orbis. reliquias magni Herculis
quis populus aut quae templa, quae gentes rogant?
quis, quis petit, quis poscit Alcmenes onus?
quae tibi sepulchra, nate, quis tumulus sat est?
hic totus orbis; fama erit titulus tibi.
quid, anime, trepidas? Herculis cineres tenes;
complectere ossa; reliquiae auxilium dabunt,
erunt satis praesidia, terrebunt tuae 1830
reges vel umbrae.

HYLLVS

Debitos nato quidem
compesce fletus, mater Alcidae incluti.
non est gemendus nec gravi urgendus prece,

---

[1] Lerna.   [2] The Stymphalian bird.

328

[1809] What people will live mindful of thee, O son?
Now is the whole race ungrateful. Shall I seek
Cleonae? seek the Arcadian tribes and hunt out the
lands made famous by thy righteous toils? Here [1]
fell the serpent dire, here the bird-monster,[2] here [3]
fell a bloody king, and here [4] by thy hand subdued,
the lion fell, who, while thou liest buried here, holds
a place in heaven. If earth is grateful, let every
people shield thine Alcmena. Shall I go to the
Thracian peoples, and to Hebrus' tribes? for this
land, too, was defended by thy toils; low do the
stables [5] with the kingdom lie. Here peace was
granted when the bloody king was overthrown; for
where has it not been granted?

[1821] What tomb for thee shall a luckless old woman
seek? Let the whole world contend for thy remains.
The ashes of mighty Hercules, what people or what
temples, what races desire to have? Who then, who
seeks, who demands Alcmena's burden [6]? What
sepulchre, O son, what tomb is great enough for
thee? Thy tomb is the whole wide world, and fame
shall be thine epitaph. Why, soul of mine, art fearful? Thou holdst the dust of Hercules; embrace
his bones; his mere dust will bring thee aid, will be
defence enough; even thy ghost will cause kings to
tremble.

HYLLUS [*who seems to have been present during the
preceding scene*]

Though truly they are due thy son, restrain thy
tears, mother of Alcides the illustrious. He is
neither to be mourned nor pursued with grievous

---

[3] Egypt, Thrace, or Libya, according as Busiris, Diomedes,
or Antaeus is in her mind.   [4] Nemea.   [5] *i.e.* of Diomedes.
[6] *i.e.* the urn containing the ashes of Hercules.

virtute quisquis abstulit fatis iter;
aeterna virtus Herculem fieri vetat.
fortes vetant maerere, degeneres iubent.[1]

ALCMENA

Sedabo questus vindice amisso parens?

HYLLVS

Terra atque pelagus quaque purpureus dies
utrumque clara spectat Oceanum rota[2]

ALCMENA

Quot misera in uno condidi natos parens!   1840
regno carebam, regna sed poteram dare.
una inter omnes terra quas matres gerit
votis perperci, nil ego a superis peti
incolume nato; quid dare Herculeus mihi
non poterat ardor?   quis deus quicquam mihi
negare poterat?   vota in hac fuerant manu;
quidquid negaret Iuppiter, daret Hercules.
quid tale genetrix ulla mortalis tulit?
deriguit aliqua mater ut toto stetit
succisa fetu bisque septenos gregem   1850
deplanxit una; gregibus aequari meus
quot ille poterat?   matribus miseris adhuc
exemplar ingens derat—Alcmene dabo.
cessate, matres, pertinax si quas dolor
adhuc iubet lugere, quas luctus gravis
in saxa vertit; cedite his cunctae malis.
agedum senile pectus, o miserae manus,
pulsate—et una funeri tanto sat es,

[1] *Leo deletes this line.*
[2] *Evidently there is a lacuna following this line. Leo suggests:* (non sola maeres) vindice amisso dolent.

prayers, whoe'er by his valour hath halted the march of fate; his deathless valour forbids to weep for Hercules. Brave men forbid to mourn, cowards command.

ALCMENA

When her deliverer is lost, shall a mother abate her grief?

HYLLUS

Both land and sea and where the shining sun from his bright car looks down upon both oceans, (not thou alone dost grieve) all mourn for their lost deliverer.[1]

ALCMENA

How many sons has his wretched mother buried in him alone! Kingdom I lacked, yet kingdoms could I give. I only, midst all the mothers whom the earth contains, refrained from prayer; naught from the gods I asked, while my son remained; for what could the love of Hercules not grant to me? What god could deny me aught? In my own hands were the answers to my prayers; whatever Jove denied, Hercules could bestow. What son like this has a mortal mother borne? Once a mother[2] stiffened into stone when, stripped of her whole brood, she stood and, one alone, lamented her twice seven children; but to how many broods like hers could my son be compared? Till now for mother's grief a measure vast enough was lacking—Alcmena will furnish it. Then cease, ye mothers, whom persistent woe still bids to mourn, whom crushing sorrow has transformed to stone; yield ye, yea, all of you, to these my woes. Then come, beat on this aged breast, O wretched hands,—and canst thou alone

---

[1] Translating Leo's conjecture.   [2] Niobe.

grandaeva anus defecta, quam totus brevi
iam quaeret[1] orbis?   expedi in planctus tamen 1860
defessa quamquam bracchia ; invidiam ut deis
lugendo facias, advoca in planctus genus.

Ite Alcmenae magnique Iovis
plangite natum, cui concepto
lux una perit noctesque duas
contulit Eos : ipsa quiddam
plus luce perit.
totae pariter plangite gentes,
quarum saevos ille tyrannos
iussit Stygias penetrare domos   1870
populisque madens ponere ferrum.
fletum meritis reddite tantis,
totus, totus personet orbis.
fleat Alciden caerula Crete,
magno tellus cara Tonanti ;
centum populi bracchia pulsent ;
nunc Curetes, nunc Corybantes
arma Idaea quassate manu ;
armis illum lugere decet ;
nunc, nunc funus plangite verum ;   1880
iacet Alcides non minor ipso,
Creta, Tonante.
flete Herculeos, Arcades, obitus,
nondum Phoebe nascente genus ;
iuga Parthenii Nemeaeque[2] sonent
feriatque graves Maenala planctus.
magno Alcidae poscit gemitum

---

[1] *Leo* †iam quaeret *with* **E**, *and conjectures* iam totus
brevi | concurret orbis : sequetur *N. Heinsius:* conveniet
Koetschau: iam peraget *Richter.*

[2] †Nemeaeque *Leo* with ω: Tegeaeque *de Wilamowitz:*
Pheneique *Richter.*

suffice for loss so vast, an aged spent old woman ?
Soon will the whole world unite to mourn with
thee.[1] Yet raise thy arms, however weary, in
lamentation; that by thy grief thou mayst stir
envy in the gods, summon the whole race of men
unto thy mourning.

[*Here follows* ALCMENA'S *formal song of mourning
accompanied by the usual Oriental gestures of
lamentation.*]

1863 Come ye, bewail Alcmena's son and mighty
Jove's, for whose conception one day was lost and
lingering dawn joined two nights in one; something
greater than the day itself is lost. Together lament,
ye nations all, whose cruel tyrants he bade descend
to the abodes of Styx and lay down the sword,
reeking with blood of peoples. To such deserts pay
tribute of your tears; let all, yea all, the world echo
to your laments. Alcides let sea-girt Crete bewail,
land to the great Thunderer dear; let its hundred
peoples beat upon their arms. Now Cretans, now
priests of Cybele, with your hands clash Ida's
cymbals; 'tis meet that with arms ye mourn him.
Now, now make him just funeral; low lies Alcides,
equal, O Crete, to the Thunderer himself. Weep
for Alcides' passing, O Arcadians, who were a people
ere yet the moon was born; let Parthenius' heights
and Nemea's hills resound and Maenalus smite heavy
blows of grief. The bristly boar, within your fields
laid low, demands lament for great Alcides, and the

---

[1] Translating Leo's conjecture. See critical note 1.

stratus vestris saetiger agris
alesque sequi iussa sagittas
totum pinna velante diem.   1890
flete Argolicae, flete, Cleonae ;
hic terrentem moenia quondam
vestra leonem fregit nostri
dextera nati ; date Bistoniae
verbera matres gelidusque sonet
planctibus Hebrus ; flete Alciden,
quod non stabulis nascitur infans
nec vestra greges viscera carpunt.
fleat Antaeo libera tellus
et rapta fero plaga Geryonae ;   1900
mecum miserae plangite gentes,
audiat ictus utraque Tethys.

   Vos quoque, mundi turba citati,
flete Herculeos, numina, casus ;
vestrum Alcides cervice meus
mundum, superi, caelumque tulit,
cum stelligeri vector Olympi
pondere liber spiravit Atlans.
ubi nunc vestrae, Iuppiter, arces ?
ubi promissi regia mundi ?   1910
nempe Alcides mortalis obit,
nempe sepultus.   quotiens telis
facibusque tuis ille pepercit,
quotiens ignis spargendus erat !
in me saltem iaculare facem
Semelenque puta.

   Iamne Elysias, o nate, domus,
iam litus habes ad quod populos
natura vocat ?
an post raptum Styx atra canem
praeclusit iter teque in primo   1920
limine Ditis fata morantur ?

huge bird whose wings hid all the sky, challenged [1]
to meet his shafts. Weep, Argive Cleonae, weep;
here long ago the lion who kept your walls in fear
my son's right hand destroyed. Ye Bistonian dames,
beat your breasts, and let cold Hebrus resound to
your beatings; weep for Alcides, for no more are
your children born for the stalls,[2] nor your offspring
as food for the herds. Weep thou, O land from
Antaeus delivered, ye regions from fierce Geryon
saved; yea, with me, ye unhappy nations, lament;
let both seas [3] re-echo your beatings.

[1903] You too, ye thronging deities of the whirling
heavens, bewail Hercules' fate; for my Alcides bore
your heavens upon his shoulders, your sky, ye gods
above, when Atlas, starry Olympus' prop, was eased
of his load awhile. Where now are thy heights,
O Jove? Where is the promised [4] palace in the sky?
Alcides, mortal, is dead! mortal, is buried! How
oft did he save thee thy lightnings, how seldom thy
fire needed hurling! [5] Against me at least brandish
thy lightning, and deem me Semele.

[1916] And now, O son, holdst thou the Elysian seats,
holdst now the shore whither nature calls all peoples?
Or after the dog was stolen has the dark Styx
barred thy way, and on the very threshold of Dis do
the fates delay thee? What confusion now, my

---

[1] Hercules roused the bird from its Stymphalian lair by
the noise of a great rattle.   [2] i.e. of Diomedes.
[3] i.e. the eastern and western limits of the sea.
[4] Jove had promised Hercules a place in heaven.
[5] i.e. Hercules had taken upon himself the punishment of
sinful men.

quis nunc umbras, nate, tumultus
manesque tenet?
fugit abducta navita cumba
et Centauris Thessala motis
ferit attonitos ungula manes
anguesque suos hydra sub undas
territa mersit teque labores,
o nate, timent?
fallor, fallor vaesana furens!   1930
nec te manes umbraeque timent,
non Argolico rapta leoni
fulva pellis contecta iuba
laevos operit dira lacertos
vallantque ferae tempora dentes;
donum pharetrae cessere tuae
telaque mittet iam dextra minor.
vadis inermis, nate, per umbras,
ad quas semper mansurus eris.

VOX HERCVLIS

Quid me tenentem regna siderei poli   1940
caeloque tandem redditum planctu iubes
sentire fatum?   parce; iam virtus mihi
in astra et ipsos fecit ad superos iter.

ALCMENA

Vnde, unde sonus trepidas aures
ferit?   unde meas inhibet lacrimas
fragor?   agnosco victum esse chaos.
   A Styge, nate, redis iterum mihi
fractaque non semel est mors horrida?
vicisti rursus mortis loca
puppis et infernae vada tristia?   1950

336

son, seizes the shadowy spirits? Does the boatman draw away his skiff in flight? Do Thessalian Centaurs with flying hoofs smite the affrighted ghosts? Does the hydra in terror plunge his snaky heads beneath the waves and do thy toils all fear thee, O my son? Fooled, fooled am I, distracted, mad! Nor ghosts nor shadows are afraid of thee; the fearsome pelt, stripped from the Argolic lion, with its tawny mane shields thy left arm no more, and its savage teeth hedge not thy temples; thy quiver thou hast given away and now a lesser hand will aim thy shafts. Unarmed, my son, thou farest through the shades, and with them forever shalt thou abide.

THE VOICE OF HERCULES [*from above.*]

Why, since I hold the realms of starry heaven and at last have attained the skies, dost by lamentation bid me taste of death? Give o'er; for now has my valour borne me to the stars and to the gods themselves.

ALCMENA [*bewildered.*]

Whence, oh, whence falls that sound upon my startled ears? Whence do the thunderous tones bid check my weeping? Now know I that chaos has been o'ercome.

1947 From the Styx, O son, art come again to me? Broken a second time is the power of grisly death? Hast escaped once more death's stronghold and the infernal skiff's dark pools? Is Acheron's wan stream

pervius est Acheron iam languidus
et remeare licet soli tibi
nec te fata tenent post funera ?
an tibi praeclusit Pluton iter
et pavidus regni metuit sibi ?
certe ego te vidi flagrantibus
impositum silvis, cum plurimus
in caelum fureret flammae metus.
arsisti—cur te, cur ultima
non tenuere tuas umbras loca ?   1960
quid timuere tui manes precor ?
umbra quoque es Diti nimis horrida ?

HERCVLES

Non me gementis stagna Cocyti tenent
nec puppis umbras furva transvexit meas ;
iam parce, mater, questibus ; manes semel
umbrasque vidi.   quidquid in nobis tui
mortale fuerat, ignis evictus tulit ;
paterna caelo, pars data est flammis tua.
proinde planctus pone, quos nato paret
genetrix inerti.   luctus in turpes eat ;   1970
virtus in astra tendit, in mortem timor.
praesens ab astris, mater, Alcides cano :
poenas cruentus iam tibi Eurystheus dabit ;
curru superbum vecta transcendes caput.
me iam decet subire caelestem plagam ;
inferna vici rursus Alcides loca.

ALCMENA

Mane parumper—cessit ex oculis, abit,
in astra fertur.   fallor an voltus putat
vidisse natum ?   misera mens incredula est—

retraceable and mayst thou alone recross it? And after thy death do the fates hold thee no more? Has Pluto barred thy way, and trembling feared for his own sovereignty? Surely upon the blazing logs I saw thee laid, when the vast, fearful flames raged to the sky. Thou wast consumed—why, why did the bottomless abyss not gain thy shade? What part of thee did the ghosts fear, I pray? Is e'en thy shade too terrible for Dis?

HERCULES [*his form now taking shape in the air above.*]

The pools of groaning Cocytus hold me not, nor has the dark skiff borne o'er my shade; then cease thy laments, my mother; once and for all have I seen the shadowy ghosts. Whate'er in me was mortal and of thee, vanquished has felt the fire; my father's part to heaven, thy part to the flames has been consigned. Cease then thy lamentations which to a worthless son might well be given. Let tears for the inglorious flow; valour fares starward, fear, to the realm of death. In living presence, mother, from the stars Alcides speaks; soon shall bloody Eurystheus make thee full recompense; o'er his proud head shalt thou in triumph ride. But now 'tis meet that I pass to the realm above; Alcides once again has conquered hell.

[*He vanishes from sight.*]

ALCMENA

Stay but a little!—he has vanished from my sight, is gone, to the stars faring. Am I deceived or do my eyes but deem they saw my son? My soul for very grief cannot believe it.—But no! thou art divine,

339

z 2

es numen et te mundus aeternum tenet ;　　　1980
credo triumphis.
　　　　　Regna Thebarum petam
novumque templis additum numen canam.

CHORVS

　　Numquam Stygias fertur ad umbras
inclita virtus.　　vivunt fortes
nec Lethaeos saeva per amnes
vos fata trahent, sed cum summas
exiget horas consumpta dies,
iter ad superos gloria pandet.
　　Sed tu, domitor magne ferarum
orbisque simul pacator, ades ;　　　　　　　1990
nunc quoque nostras respice terras,
et si qua novo belua voltu
quatiet populos terrore gravi,
tu fulminibus frange trisulcis—
fortius ipso genitore tuo
fulmina mitte.

and deathless the heavens possess thee. In thy triumphant entrance I believe.

1981 Now will I take me to the realm of Thebes and there proclaim the new god added to their temples.

[*Exit.*

CHORUS

Never to Stygian shades is glorious valour borne. The brave live on, nor shall the cruel fates bear you o'er Lethe's waters; but when the last day shall bring the final hour, glory will open wide the path to heaven.

1989 But do thou, O mighty conqueror of beasts, peace-bringer to the world, be with us yet; still as of old regard this earth of ours; and if some strange-visaged monster cause us with dire fear to tremble, do thou o'ercome him with the forked thunder-bolts—yea, more mightily than thy father's self the thunders hurl.

PHOENISSAE

DRAMATIS PERSONAE

OEDIPUS, *late king of Thebes.*

ANTIGONE, *daughter of Oedipus, constant to him in his misfortunes.*

JOCASTA, *wife and mother of Oedipus.*

POLYNICES,
ETEOCLES, } *sons of Oedipus and rivals for the throne.*

MESSENGER.

THE SCENE is laid, first in the wild country to which Oedipus, accompanied by Antigone, has betaken himself; then in Thebes; and lastly in the plain before Thebes.

THE TIME is three years after the downfall of Oedipus.

ARGUMENT

THE *stroke of fate, that has been threatening Oedipus since long before his birth, has fallen at last, and he has done the thing he feared to do. And now, self-blinded and self-exiled from his land, he has for three years wandered in rough and trackless places, attended by Antigone, his daughter, who, alone of all his friends, has condoned his fated sins and remained attached to him.*

Meanwhile his sons, though they agreed to reign alternate years, are soon to meet in deadly strife ; for Eteocles, although his year of royal power is at an end, refuses to give up the throne ; and now Polynices, who has in exile wed the daughter of Adrastus, king of Argos, is marching against the gates of Thebes, with seven great armies to enforce his rights.

[By a different version from the " Oedipus," Jocasta did not slay herself at once as in that tale, but still is living on in grief and shame, and strives to reconcile her sons.]

PHOENISSAE

OEDIPVS

Caeci parentis regimen et fessi unicum
lateris levamen, nata, quam tanti est mihi
genuisse vel sic, desere infaustum patrem.
in recta quid deflectis errantem gradum ?
permitte labi ; melius inveniam viam,
quam quaero, solus, quae me ab hac vita extrahat
et hoc nefandi capitis aspectu levet
caelum atque terras.   quantulum hac egi manu ?
non video noxae conscium nostrae diem,
sed videor.   hinc iam solve inhaerentem manum   10
et patere caecum qua volet ferri pedem.
ibo, ibo qua praerupta protendit iuga
meus Cithaeron, qua peragrato celer
per saxa monte iacuit Actaeon suis
nova praeda canibus, qua per obscurum nemus
silvamque opacae vallis instinctas deo
egit sorores mater et gaudens malo
vibrante fixum praetulit thyrso caput ;
vel qua cucurrit, corpus inlisum trahens,
Zethi iuvencus, qua per horrentes rubos   20

---

[1] In the corresponding Greek play a chorus of Phoenician
maidens on their way to Delphi chanced to be at Thebes.
This circumstance gives the play its name.

PHOENISSAE,[1] OR THEBAÏS

A FRAGMENT

OEDIPUS

[*To* ANTIGONE, *who has followed him into exile.*]

THOU guide of thy blind father's steps, his weary
side's sole stay, daughter, whose getting, even so,
was worth the cost to me, quit thou thy heaven-cursed
sire. Why into right paths wouldst turn aside my
wandering feet? Let me stumble on; better alone
shall I find the way I seek, the way which from this
life shall deliver me and free heaven and earth from
sight of this impious head. How little did I
accomplish with this hand! I do not see the light,
witness of my crime, but I am seen. Therefore,
now unclasp thy clinging hand and let my sightless
feet wander where they will. I'll go, I'll go where my
own Cithaeron lifts his rugged crags; where, speeding over the mountain's rocky ways, Actaeon lay at
last, strange quarry for his own hounds; where,
through the dim grove and woods of the dusky
glade, a mother[2] led her sisters, by the god impelled,
and, rejoicing in the crime, bore in advance the
head[3] fixed on a quivering thyrsus; or where
Zethus' bull rushed along, dragging a mangled
corpse, while through the thorny brambles the mad

[2] Agave, who with her sisters, in a frenzy inspired by
Bacchus, slew her son, Pentheus.

[3] *i.e.* of Pentheus.

tauri ferocis sanguis ostendit fugas ;
vel qua alta maria vertice immenso premit
Inoa rupes, qua scelus fugiens novum
novumque faciens mater insiluit freto
mersura natum seque.   felices quibus
fortuna melior tam bonas matres dedit.

    Est alius istis noster in silvis locus,
qui me reposcit, hunc petam cursu incito ;
non haesitabit gressus, huc omni duce
spoliatus ibo.   quid moror sedes meas ?   30
mortem, Cithaeron, redde et hospitium mihi
illud meum restitue, ut expirem senex
ubi debui infans.   recipe supplicium vetus.
semper cruente saeve crudelis ferox,
cum occidis et cum parcis, olim iam tuum
est hoc cadaver : perage mandatum patris,
iam et matris.   animus gestit antiqua exequi
supplicia.   quid me, nata, pestifero tenes
amore vinctum ?   quid tenes ?   genitor vocat.
sequor, sequor, iam parce—sanguinem gerens   40
insigne regni Laius rapti furit ;
en ecce, inanes manibus infestis petit
foditque vultus.   nata, genitorem vides ?
ego video.   tandem spiritum inimicum expue,
desertor anime, fortis in partem tui.
omitte poenae languidas longae moras,
mortemque totam admitte.   quid segnis traho
quod vivo ?   nullum facere iam possum scelus.
possum miser, praedico—discede a patre,
discede, virgo.   timeo post matrem omnia.   50

creature's flight was traceable in blood; or where
Ino's cliff juts out into the deep sea with towering peak, where, fleeing strange crime and yet
strange crime committing, a mother leaped into the
strait to sink both son and self.[1] Oh, happy they
whose better fortune has given such kindly mothers!

[27] There is another place within these woods, my
own place, which calls for me; I would fain hasten to
it; my steps will falter not; thither will I go bereft
of every guide. Why keep my own place waiting?
Death, O Cithaeron, give me back; restore me that
resting-place of mine, that I may die in age where I
should have died in infancy. Claim now that penalty
of old. O ever bloody, savage, cruel, fierce, both
when thou slayest and when thou sparest, this carcass
of mine long since belonged to thee; fulfil my father's
behest—aye, and now my mother's too. My soul
yearns to suffer the penalty of long ago. Why,
daughter, dost hold me bound by thy baleful love?
Why dost thou hold me? My father calls. I come,
I come; at last let me go[2]—Laius rages yonder,
wearing the blood-stained badge of his ravished
kingdom; see! behold! there he assails and seeks to
tear at my sightless countenance with his threatening
hands. Daughter, dost see my father? I surely see
him. [He soliloquizes.] At length spew out thy hateful
breath, O traitor soul, brave 'gainst but a portion of
thyself. Away with the slow delays of thy long-
due punishment; receive death wholly. Why do
I sluggishly drag on this life? Now can I do no
crime. I can, wretch that I am, this I forebode—away
from thy father, away, while still a maid. After my
mother I fear all happenings.

[1] See Index s.v. "Ino."
[2] i.e (to his daughter) "spare me thy further opposition."

ANTIGONA

Vis nulla, genitor, a tuo nostram manum
corpore resolvet, nemo me comitem tibi
eripiet umquam.   Labdaci claram domum,
opulenta ferro regna germani petant;
pars summa magno patris e regno mea est,
pater ipse.   non hunc auferet frater mihi
Thebana rapto sceptra qui regno tenet,
non hunc catervas alter Argolicas agens;
non si revulso Iuppiter mundo tonet
mediumque nostros fulmen in nexus cadat,   60
manum hanc remittam. prohibeas, genitor, licet;
regam abnuentem, dirigam inviti gradum.
in plana tendis?   vado; praerupta appetis?
non obsto, sed praecedo; quo vis utere
duce me: duobus omnis eligitur via.
perire sine me non potes, mecum potes.
hic alta rupes arduo surgit iugo
spectatque longe spatia subiecti maris,
vis hanc petamus?   nudus hic pendet silex,
hic scissa tellus faucibus ruptis hiat;   70
vis hanc petamus?   hic rapax torrens cadit
partesque lapsi montis exesas rotat;
in hunc ruamus?   dum prior, quo vis eo.
non deprecor, non hortor.   extingui cupis
votumque, genitor, maximum mors est tibi?
si moreris, antecedo; si vivis, sequor.
sed flecte mentem, pectus antiquum advoca
victasque magno robore aerumnas doma;
resiste; tantis in malis vinci mori est.
350

PHOENISSAE

ANTIGONE

No force, my father, shall loose my hold of thee;
no one shall ever tear me from thy side. The
sovereignty of Labdacus' noble house and all its
riches—let my brothers fight over these; the best
part of my father's mighty kingdom is my own, my
father's self. Him no brother shall take from me,
not he [1] who holds the Theban sceptre by stolen
right, not he [2] who is leading the Argive hosts;
no, though Jove should rend the universe with his
thunders, and his bolt fall 'twixt our embrace, I
will not let go my hands. Thou mayst forbid me,
father; I'll guide thee against thy will, I'll direct
thine unwilling feet. Wouldst go to the level plain?
I go. Wouldst seek the craggy mountains? I
oppose not, but I go before. Whither thou wilt,
use me as guide; by two will all paths be chosen.
Without me thou canst not perish; with me thou
canst. Here rises a cliff, lofty, precipitous, and looks
out upon the long reaches of the underlying sea;
wouldst have us seek it? Here is a bare rock over-
hanging, here the riven earth yawns with gaping
jaws; shall we go here? Here a raging torrent
falls and rolls along worn fragments of the fallen
mountains; shall we plunge to this? Where'er
thou wilt, I go, so it be first. I neither oppose nor
urge. Art eager to be destroyed, and is death,
father, thy highest wish? If thou diest, I go before
thee; if thou livest, I follow. But change thy
purpose; summon up thine old-time courage;
conquer thy sorrows and with all thy might be
master of them, resist them; amidst such woes, to
be conquered is to die.

[1] Eteocles.   [2] Polynices.

OEDIPVS

Vnde in nefanda specimen egregium domo ?   80
unde ista generi virgo dissimilis suo ?
Fortuna, credis ?   aliquis est ex me pius ?
non esset umquam, fata bene novi mea,
nisi ut noceret.   ipsa se in leges novas
natura vertit ; regeret in fontem citas
revolutus undas amnis, et noctem afferet
Phoebea lampas, Hesperus faciet diem ;
ut ad miserias aliquid accedat meas,
pii quoque erimus.   unica Oedipodae est salus,
non esse salvum.   liceat ulcisci patrem   90
adhuc inultum ; dextra quid cessas iners
exigere poenas ?   quidquid exactum est adhuc,
matri dedisti.   mitte genitoris manum,
animosa virgo ; funus extendis meum
longasque vivi ducis exequias patris.
aliquando terra corpus invisum tege ;
peccas honesta mente, pietatem vocas
patrem insepultum trahere.   qui cogit mori
nolentem in aequo est quique properantem impedit ;
occidere est vitare cupientem mori,[1]   100
nec tamen in aequo est ; alterum gravius reor.
malo imperari quam eripi mortem mihi.
desiste coepto, virgo ; ius vitae ac necis
meae penes me est.   regna deserui libens,
regnum mei retineo.   si fida es comes,
ensem parenti trade, sed notum nece
ensem paterna.   tradis ? an nati tenent
cum regno et illum ?   facinore ubicumque est opus,
ibi sit—relinquo ; natus hunc habeat meus,

[1] *Leo deletes this line.*

PHOENISSAE

OEDIPUS

Whence this rare type in a house so impious? Whence this maid so unlike her race? Is it fortune, thinkst thou? Has any dutiful child sprung from me? Never would it be so, for well I know my fate, save for harmful ends. Nature herself has reversed her laws; now will the river turn and bear its swift waters backward to their source, Phoebus' torch will bring in the night, and Hesperus herald the day; and, that something be added to my woes, I, too, shall become holy. For Oedipus the only salvation is not to be saved. Let me avenge my father, till now unavenged; why, sluggish hand, dost thou hesitate to exact penalty? All thou hast as yet exacted, to my mother hast thou given. Let go thy father's hand, courageous girl; thou dost but protract my burying, and prolong the funeral rites of a living sire. Bury in the earth at last this hateful body; thou wrongst me, though with kind intent, and thou deemst it piety to drag along an unburied father. 'Tis all one—to force him who shrinks from death, and stay him who seeks to die; 'tis the same as killing to forbid death to him who wants it; and yet 'tis not all one; the second course I count the worse. Rather would I have death enforced than snatched from me. Desist, girl, from thine attempt; the right to live or die is in my own hands. The sovereignty over my realm have I yielded gladly; the sovereignty over myself I keep. If thou art true comrade, hand thy sire a sword, but be it the sword made famous by his father's slaughter. Dost give it? or hold my sons that, too, together with my kingdom? Wherever is need of crime, there let it be —I relinquish it; let my son have it—nay, both my

353

sed uterque. flammas potius et vastum aggerem 110
compone; in altos ipse me immittam rogos,
haerebo ad ignes, funebri abscondar strue;
pectusque solvam durum et in cinerem dabo
hoc quidquid in me vivit.   ubi saevum est mare?
duc ubi sit altis prorutum saxis iugum,
ubi torva rapidus ducat Ismenos vada.[1]   116
si dux es, illuc ire morituro placet,   118
ubi sedit alta rupe semifero dolos
Sphinx ore nectens.   dirige huc gressus pedum, 120
hic siste patrem.   dira ne sedes vacet,
monstrum repone maius.   hoc saxum insidens
obscura nostrae verba fortunae loquar,
quae nemo solvat.   quisquis Assyrio loca
possessa regi scindis et Cadmi nemus
serpente notum, sacra quo Dirce latet,
supplex adoras, quisquis Eurotan bibis
Spartamque fratre nobilem gemino colis,
quique Elin et Parnason et Boeotios
colonus agros uberis tondes soli,   130
adverte mentem—saeva Thebarum lues
luctifica caecis verba committens modis
quid simile posuit?   quid tam inextricabile?
avi gener patrisque rivalis sui,
frater suorum liberum et fratrum parens;
uno avia partu liberos peperit viro,
sibi et nepotes.   monstra quis tanta explicat?
ego ipse, victae spolia qui Sphingis tuli,
haerebo fati tardus interpres mei.

*   *   *   *   *[2]

---

[1] *Leo deletes line 117:* duc ubi ferae sunt, ubi fretum, ubi
praeceps locus.

[2] *A speech of Antigone may have dropped out at this point,
or Oedipus may hark back to the earlier speech of Antigone*

PHOENISSAE

sons. Flames, if thou prefer, and a huge mound prepare; myself, will I fling me on the lofty pyre, embrace the flames, and hide in the funeral pile. There will I set free this stubborn soul and give up to ashes this—all that is left of me alive. Where is the raging sea? Lead me where some beetling crag juts out with its high, rocky cliff, or where swift Ismenus rolls his wild waters. If thou art my guide, thither would I go to die where on a high cliff the Sphinx once sat and wove crafty speech with her half-bestial lips. Guide my feet thither, there set thy father. Let not that dreadful seat be empty, but place thereon a greater monster. On that rock will I sit and propound the dark riddle of my fate which none may answer. All ye who till the fields once ruled by the Assyrian king,[1] who suppliant worship in the grove of Cadmus for the serpent famed, where sacred Dirce lies; all ye who drink of the Eurotas, who dwell in Sparta for its twin brethren [2] famous; ye farmers who reap Elis and Parnassus and Boeotia's fertile fields, give ear. That dire pest of Thebes, who wrapped death-dealing words in puzzling measures, what riddle like this did she ever propound? What maze so bewildering? *He was his grandfather's son-in-law and his father's rival, brother of his children and father of his brothers; at one birth the grandmother bore children to her husband and grandchildren to herself.* Who can unfold a coil so monstrous? Even I, who gained spoils from the conquered Sphinx, shall prove but slow in unriddling mine own doom.

*   *   *   *   *

[1] Cadmus.   [2] Castor and Pollux.

---

after a dramatic pause. Leo holds that the hiatus is, as Swoboda thinks, left by the poet himself.

    Quid perdis ultra verba?   quid pectus ferum   140
mollire temptas precibus?   hoc animo sedet
effundere hanc cum morte luctantem diu
animam et tenebras petere; nam sceleri haec meo
parum alta nox est; Tartaro condi iuvat,
et si quid ultra Tartarum est; tandem libet
quod olim oportet.   morte prohiberi haud queo.
ferrum negabis?   noxias lapsu vias
cludes et artis colla laqueis inseri
prohibebis?   herbas quae ferunt letum auferes?
quid ista tandem cura proficiet tua?   150
ubique mors est.   optume hoc cavit deus:
eripere vitam nemo non homini potest,
at nemo mortem; mille ad hanc aditus patent.
nil quaero.   dextra noster et nuda solet
bene animus uti—dextra, nunc toto impetu,
toto dolore, viribus totis veni.
non destino unum vulneri nostro locum—
totus nocens sum; qua voles mortem exige.
effringe pectus corque tot scelerum capax
evelle, totos viscerum nuda sinus.   160
fractum incitatis ictibus guttur sonet
laceraeque fixis unguibus venae fluant.
aut dirige iras quo soles; haec vulnera
rescissa multo sanguine ac tabe inriga,
hac extrahe animam duram, inexpugnabilem.
et tu, parens, ubicumque poenarum arbiter
adstas mearum—non ego hoc tantum scelus
ulla expiari credidi poena satis
umquam, nec ista morte contentus fui,
nec me redemi parte; membratim tibi   170

PHOENISSAE

[140] Why dost thou waste further words? Why dost try to soften my hard heart with prayers? My will is fixed to pour forth this life which has long been struggling with death, and to seek the nether darkness; for this deep night is not deep enough for my crime; in Tartarus would I be buried, or if there be aught deeper than Tartarus; 'tis pleasing to do at last what long ago I should have done. I cannot be kept from death. Wilt withhold the sword? Wilt bar paths where I might fall to death? Wilt keep my neck from the choking noose? Wilt remove death-bringing herbs? What, pray, will that care of thine accomplish? Death is everywhere. This hath God with wisdom excellent provided: of life anyone can rob a man, but of death no one; to this a thousand doors lie open. I ask for naught. This right hand, though bare, my soul hath practice to use well—O hand of mine, come now with all thy force, with all thy smarting rage, with all thy might. Not one spot only do I mark out for the wound—I am all sin; inflict death where thou wilt. Break through my breast and tear out my heart, which has room for so many crimes; lay bare my vitals, every nook; rain resounding blows upon my neck until it break, and let my veins flow, torn by my gouging fingers. Or aim thy mad attack at the accustomed place;[1] these wounds reopen; bathe them in streams of blood and gore; through this passage drag out my stubborn life, impregnable. And do thou, my father, where'er thou standst as arbiter of my sufferings—I have never deemed that this grievous crime of mine was sufficiently atoned by any suffering, nor have I been content with such death as this, nor have I bought my pardon with a portion of myself; limb by limb

[1] His eyes.

357

perire volui—debitum tandem exige.
nunc solvo poenas, tunc tibi inferias dedi.
ades atque inertem dexteram introrsus preme
magisque merge; timida tunc parvo caput
libavit haustu vixque cupientes sequi
eduxit oculos.   haeret etiam nunc mihi
ille animus, haeret, cum recusantem manum
pressere vultus.   audies verum, Oedipus:
minus eruisti lumina audacter tua,
quam praestitisti.   nunc manum cerebro indue;   180
hac parte mortem perage qua coepi mori.

ANTIGONA

Pauca, o parens magnanime, miserandae precor
ut verba natae mente placata audias.
non te ut reducam veteris ad speciem domus
habitumque regni flore pollentem inclito
peto aut ut iras, temporum haut ipsa mora
fractas, remisso pectore ac placido feras;
at hoc decebat roboris tanti virum,
non esse sub dolore nec victum malis
dare terga; non est, ut putas, virtus, pater   190
timere vitam, sed malis ingentibus
obstare nec se vertere ac retro dare.
qui fata proculcavit ac vitae bona
proiecit atque abscidit et casus suos
oneravit ipse, cui deo nullo est opus,
quare ille mortem cupiat aut quare petat?
utrumque timidi est; nemo contempsit mori
qui concupivit.   cuius haut ultra mala
exire possunt, in loco tuto est situs.

have I desired to die for thee—at length exact the
debt. Now am I paying my penalty; before, I did
but offer sacrifices to thy ghost. Come to my aid,
help me to plunge my nerveless hand deep down and
deeper; timidly, aforetime, and with but a meagre
outpouring did it sprinkle my head, when it scarce
drew forth the eyes that yearned to follow. Even
now this soul of mine halts, yes halts, when my face
has bent downward to my shrinking hands. Thou
shalt hear the truth, Oedipus: less boldly didst
thou pluck out thine eyes than thou didst undertake
to do. Thrust now thy hand e'en to the brain;
through that door whereby I began to die fulfil my
death.

ANTIGONE

Father, great-souled, I beseech thee that with
calm mind thou listen to some few words of thy
wretched daughter. I seek not to lead thee back
again to the splendours of thine ancient home, and
to thy royal estate, flourishing in power and fame;
nor do I ask that thou bear with calm and peaceful
soul that tempest of passion which has not been
allayed even by lapse of time; and yet 'twere fitting
that one so stalwart should not yield to pain nor
turn in flight, by disaster overcome. It is not manhood, father, as thou deemst it, to shrink from life,
but to make stand against mighty ills and neither
turn nor yield. He who has trodden destiny under
foot, who has torn off and thrown away life's blessings,
and himself piled up the burden of his woes, who has
no need of God, wherefore should he desire death, or
wherefore seek it? Each is a coward's act; no one
despises death who yet yearns for it. He whose
misfortunes can no further go, is safely lodged.

Quis iam deorum, velle fac, quicquam potest   200
malis tuis adicere?   iam nec tu potes
nisi hoc, ut esse te putes dignum nece.
non es nec ulla pectus hoc culpa attigit.
et hoc magis te, genitor, insontem voca,
quod innocens es dis quoque invitis.   quid est
quod te efferarit, quod novos suffixerit
stimulos dolori?   quid te in infernas agit
sedes, quid ex his pellit?   ut careas die?
cares.   ut altis nobilem muris domum
patriamque fugias?   patria tibi vivo perit.   210
natos fugis matremque?   ab aspectu omnium
fortuna te summovit, et quidquid potest
auferre cuiquam mors, tibi hoc vita abstulit.
regni tumultus?   turba fortunae prior
abscessit a te iussa—quem, genitor, fugis?

OEDIPVS

Me fugio, fugio conscium scelerum omnium
pectus, manumque hanc fugio et hoc caelum et deos;
et dira fugio scelera quae feci innocens.[1]
ego hoc solum, frugifera quo surgit Ceres,
premo?   has ego auras ore pestifero traho?   220
ego laticis haustu satior aut ullo fruor
almae parentis munere?   ego castam manum
nefandus incestificus exsecrabilis
attrecto?   ego ullus aure concipio sonos,
per quos parentis nomen aut nati audiam?
utinam quidem rescindere has quirem vias

---

[1] *Leo deletes this line.*

²⁰⁰ Who now of the gods, granting he wills it so, can add aught to thy misfortunes? Now not even canst thou add aught save this, to deem thyself worthy of death. Thou art not worthy, nor has any taint of guilt touched thy heart. And for this all the more, father, call thyself guiltless; for thou art guiltless, though even the gods willed otherwise. What is it which has so maddened thee, which has goaded thy grief afresh? What drives thee to the infernal regions? What forces thee out of these? That thou mayst avoid the light of day? Thou dost avoid it. That thou mayst flee thy noble palace with its high walls, and thy native land? Thy native land, though thou still livest, is dead to thee. Dost flee from thy sons and mother? From the sight of all men fate has removed thee, and whatever death can take away from any man, this has life taken from thee. Wouldst avoid the tumult around a throne? They who once in prosperity thronged around thee, at thy command have left thee. Whom dost thou flee, my father?

OEDIPUS

Myself I flee; I flee my heart conscious of all crimes; I flee this hand, this sky, the gods; I flee the dread crimes which I committed, though in innocence. Do I tread this earth from which whole-some grain springs up? This air do I inhale with pestilential lips? Does water quench my thirst, or do I enjoy any gift of kindly mother earth? Do I, impious, incestuous, accursed, touch thy pure hand? Do my ears take in sound by which I may still hear the name of parent or of son? I would indeed that I might destroy these paths and might

manibusque adactis omne qua voces meant
aditusque verbis tramite angusto patet
eruere possem ; nata, iam sensum tui,
quae pars meorum es criminum, infelix pater   230
fugissem.
       Inhaeret ac recrudescit nefas
subinde, et aures ingerunt quidquid mihi
donastis, oculi.   cur caput tenebris grave
non mitto ad umbras Ditis aeternas ?   quid hic
manes meos detineo ?   quid terram gravo
mixtusque superis erro ?   quid restat mali ?
regnum parentes liberi, virtus quoque
et ingeni sollertis eximium decus
periere, cuncta sors mihi infesta abstulit.
lacrimae supererant—has quoque eripui mihi.   240
  Absiste !   nullas animus admittit preces
novamque poenam sceleribus quaerit parem.
et esse par quae poterit ?   infanti quoque
decreta mors est.   fata quis tam tristia
sortitus umquam ?   videram nondum diem
uterique nondum solveram clausi moras,
et iam timebar.   protinus quosdam editos
nox occupavit et novae luci abstulit ;
mors me antecessit ; aliquis intra viscera
materna letum praecoquis fati tulit ;   250
sed numquid et peccavit ?   abstrusum, abditum
dubiumque an essem sceleris infandi reum
deus egit ; illo teste damnavit parens
calidoque teneros transuit ferro pedes
et in alta nemora pabulum misit feris

with my hands driven deep pluck out every part
where voices enter and where a narrow passage gives
access to the words of men; then, daughter, thy
wretched father would have escaped all consciousness
of thee, who art part and parcel of my crimes.

231 My guilt sticks fast within me, threatens each
moment to break out afresh, and my ears pour in upon
me all that you, my eyes, have bestowed.[1] Why do
I not plunge this life, weighted with gloom, down to
the everlasting shades of Dis? Why here do I detain
my ghost? Why do I burden the earth and wander
amongst the living? What evil is left for me? My
kingdom, parents, children, my manhood, too, and
the illustrious fame of my cunning wit—all these
have perished, all have been stripped from me by
hostile chance. Tears were still left me—of these,
too, have I robbed myself.

241 Stand off! My soul will not listen to any prayers
and seeks some new punishment to match its crimes.
And what match can there be? Even in my infancy
I was doomed to death. Who ever drew lot so sad?
I had not yet seen the light, was still imprisoned in
the womb, and already I was held in fear. Some
there are whom straightway at birth night hath
seized upon and snatched from their first dawn; but
on me death came ere birth. Some, while still
within the mother's womb, have suffered untimely
death; but have they sinned also? Hidden away,
confined, my very being in doubt, the god made
me guilty of a charge unspeakable. On that charge
my sire condemned me, spitted my slender ankles
on hot iron, and sent me to the deep forest as prey

---

[1] Oedipus paradoxically deems that his eyes in their blind-
ness bestow on him the boon of avoiding sight; but his ears
still bring Antigone to his consciousness.

avibusque saevis quas Cithaeron noxius
cruore saepe regio tinctas alit.
sed quem deus damnavit, abiecit pater,
mors quoque refugit.   praestiti Delphis fidem ;
genitorem adortus impia stravi nece.   260
hoc alia pietas redimet : occidi patrem,
sed matrem—amavi.   proloqui hymenaeum pudet
taedasque nostras.   has quoque invitum pati
te coge poenas ; facinus ignotum efferum
inusitatum effare quod populi horreant,
quod esse factum nulla non aetas neget,
quod parricidam pudeat : in patrios toros
tuli paterno sanguine aspersas manus
scelerisque pretium maius accepi scelus.

Leve est paternum facinus ; in thalamos meos   270
deducta mater, ne parum sceleris foret,
fecunda—nullum crimen hoc maius potest
natura ferre.   si quod etiamnum est tamen,
qui facere possunt dedimus.   abieci necis
pretium paternae sceptrum et hoc iterum manus
armavit alias ; optime regni mei
fatum ipse novi ; nemo sine sacro feret
illud cruore.   magna praesagit mala
paternus animus.   iacta iam sunt semina
cladis futurae ; spernitur pacti fides.   280
hic occupato cedere imperio negat,
ius ille et icti foederis testes deos
invocat et Argos exul atque urbes movet
Graias in arma.   non levis fessis venit
ruina Thebis ; tela flammae vulnera

PHOENISSAE

for wild beasts and savage birds which baleful
Cithaeron, oft stained with royal blood, doth breed.
Yet him whom God condemned, whom his sire cast
away, hath death also shunned. I kept faith with
Delphi; I assailed my father and with impious
death-stroke slew him. For this another act of
piety will atone; I killed my father, true, but my
mother—I loved. Oh, 'tis shame to speak of wedlock and my marriage torches. But this punishment
also force thyself to bear though against thy will;
proclaim thy crime, unheard of, bestial, unexampled,
at which nations would shudder, which no age
would believe ever befell, which would put even a
parricide to shame : *into my father's bed I bore hands*
smeared with my father's blood, and there, as the reward
of my crime, I did worse crime.

270 A trivial sin is my father's murder; my mother,
brought to my marriage chamber, that my guilt might
be complete, conceived—no greater crime than this
can nature brook. And yet, if there is even now
worse crime, we have given the world those who can
commit it. I have flung away the sceptre, price of
my father's murder, and this, again, has armed other
hands. I myself best know my kingdom's destiny;
no one unstained by sacred blood shall bear sway there.
Dire misfortunes my father-soul presages. Already
are sown the seeds of calamity to come; the plighted
pact[1] is scorned. The one will not retire from the
throne he has usurped; the other proclaims his right,
calls on the gods to witness the broken bond, and,
wandering in exile, is rousing Argos and the cities
of Greece to arms. 'Tis no light destruction that is
coming on weary Thebes; weapons, flames, wounds

---

[1] *i.e.* between Eteocles and Polynices.

instant et istis si quod est maius malum,—
ut esse genitos nemo non ex me sciat.

ANTIGONA

Si nulla, genitor, causa vivendi tibi est,
haec una abunde est, ut pater natos regas
graviter furentes. tu impii belli minas   290
avertere unus tuque vaecordes potes
inhibere iuvenes, civibus pacem dare,
patriae quietem, foederi laeso fidem.
vitam tibi ipse si negas, multis negas.

OEDIPVS

Illis parentis ullus aut aequi est amor,
avidis cruoris imperi armorum doli,
diris, scelestis, breviter ut dicam—meis?
certant in omne facinus et pensi nihil
ducunt, ubi ipsos ira praecipites agit,
nefasque nullum per nefas nati putant.   300
non patris illos tangit afflicti pudor,
non patria; regno pectus attonitum furit.
scio quo ferantur, quanta moliri parent,
ideoque leti quaero maturam viam
morique propero, dum in domo nemo est mea
nocentior me. nata, quid genibus meis
fles advoluta? quid prece indomitum domas?
unum hoc habet fortuna quo possim capi,
invictus aliis; sola tu affectus potes
mollire duros, sola pietatem in domo   310
docere nostra. nil grave aut miserum est mihi
quod te sciam voluisse; tu tantum impera;
366

press round her and a greater ill than these, if greater there be,—that all may know I have begotten sons.

ANTIGONE

If, my father, thou hast no other cause for living, this one is more than enough, that as father thou mayst restrain thy sons from their fatal frenzy. Thou alone canst avert the threats of impious war, canst check these mad youths, give peace to our citizens, rest to our land, faith to the broken pact. If life to thyself thou dost deny, to many dost thou deny it.

OEDIPUS

Have they any love for father or for right, they who lust for blood, power, arms, treachery, they the cruel, the accursed,—in brief, *my* sons? They vie one with the other in every crime, and have no scruple where passion drives them headlong; impiously born, they count nothing impious. No feeling for their stricken father, none for their fatherland, moves them; their hearts are mad with lust of empire. I know well whither they tend, what monstrous deeds they are planning, and for this cause I seek an early path to destruction, rush on my death, while still there is none in my house more guilty than myself. Daughter, why dost thou fall weeping at my knees? Why seekst with prayer to conquer my unconquerable resolve? This is the one means by which fortune can take me captive, invincible in all else; thou only canst soften my hard heart, thou only canst teach piety in our house. Nothing is heavy or grievous to me which I know thou 'hast desired. Do thou but command; I,

hic Oedipus Aegaea transnabit freta
iubente te, flammasque quas Siculo vomit
de monte tellus igneos volvens globos,
excipiet ore seque serpenti offeret,
quae saeva furto nemoris Herculeo furit ;
iubente te praebebit alitibus iecur—
iubente te vel vivet.

PHOENISSAE

Oedipus, at thy bidding will swim the Aegean sea, will drink the flames which earth from the Sicilian mountains belches forth, pouring down balls of fire, will beard the dragon still savagely raging in the grove at the theft of Hercules; at thy bidding will offer my liver to the birds—at thy bidding e'en will live.

The first episode seems to be complete here, except for the commenting chorus which would naturally follow. OEDIPUS *has temporarily yielded to his daughter's will.*

NUNTIUS [1]

*   *   *   *   *

Exemplum in ingens regia stirpe editum   320
Thebae paventes arma fraterna invocant
rogantque tectis arceas patriis faces.
non sunt minae, iam propius accessit malum ;
nam regna repetens frater et pactas vices
in bella cunctos Graeciae populos agit.
septena muros castra Thebanos premunt.
succurre, prohibe pariter et bellum et scelus.

OEDIPVS

Ego ille sum qui scelera committi vetem
et abstineri sanguine a caro manus
doceam ?   magister iuris et amoris pii   330
ego sum ?   meorum facinorum exempla appetunt,
me nunc secuntur ; laudo et agnosco libens,
exhortor, aliquid ut patre hoc dignum gerant.
agite, o propago cara, generosam indolem

---

[1] Leo, with E ψ, assigns this speech to Antigone : Richter,
with A, gives it to Nuntius.

PHOENISSAE

The following passage fittingly opens the second episode. Although some editors would assign it to ANTIGONE, *it seems more properly to belong to a messenger who has just arrived, for the double reason that it gives fresher information from Thebes than* ANTIGONE *would naturally possess; and that* OEDIPUS, *after the speech to his daughter with which the previous episode ended, would hardly address to her as rough a reply as he uses in his next speech.*

MESSENGER

Thee, sprung from regal ancestry to be our great exemplar, Thebes calls to her aid, trembling at fratricidal strife, and prays that thou fend off from thy country's homes the brands of war. These are no mere threats; already is destruction at our gates; for the brother [1] demands his turn to rule according to the bond, and is marshalling to war all the peoples of Greece. Seven bands are encamped against the walls of Thebes. Haste to our aid; prevent in one act both war and crime.

OEDIPUS

Am I one to forbid crime and teach hands to refrain from the blood of loved ones? Am I a teacher of righteousness and love of kin? 'Tis from my crimes they seek their pattern, 'tis my example they follow now. I praise them and gladly acknowledge them as sons; I urge them on to do something worthy of such a father. Go on, dear offspring, prove your noble breeding by your deeds; surpass

[1] Polynices.

371

probate factis, gloriam ac laudes meas
superate et aliquid facite propter quod patrem
adhuc iuvet vixisse.   facietis, scio :
sic estis orti.   scelere defungi haut levi,
haut usitato tanta nobilitas potest.
ferte arma, facibus petite penetrales deos   340
frugemque flamma metite natalis soli,
miscete cuncta, rapite in exitium omnia,
disicite passim moenia, in planum date,
templis deos obruite, maculatos lares
conflate, ab imo tota considat domus ;
urbs concrematur—primus a thalamis meis
incipiat ignis.

ANTIGONA

    Mitte violentum impetum
doloris ac te publica exorent mala,
auctorque placidae liberis pacis veni.

OEDIPVS

  Vides modestae deditum menti senem   350
placidaeque amantem pacis ad partes vocas ?
tumet animus ira, fervet immensus dolor,
maiusque quam quod casus et iuvenum furor
conatur aliquid cupio.   non satis est adhuc
civile bellum ; frater in fratrem ruat ;
nec hoc sat est ; quod debet, ut fiat nefas
de more nostro, quod meos deceat toros,
date arma matri.   nemo me ex his eruat
silvis ; latebo rupis exesae cavo
aut sepe densa corpus abstrusum tegam.   360
hinc aucupabor verba rumoris vagi
et saeva fratrum bella, quod possum, audiam.

372

my fame and praises and do some deed whereat your
father may rejoice that he has lived till now. You
will do it, I know: of such mind were you born; no
trivial, no common crime can such high birth perform. Forward your arms! With torches have at
your household gods; reap with fire the ripened
grain of your native land; confound all things, hurry
all to destruction; on all sides throw down the walls,
raze them to the ground; bury the gods beneath
their own temples; the defiled deities of your
hearths melt in the fire, and let our whole house
from its foundations fall; let the city be consumed
—and be my marriage chamber the first to feel the
flames.

ANTIGONE

Give o'er this raging storm of grief; let the
public calamities prevail with thee; go to thy sons
as the adviser of calm peace.

OEDIPUS

Seest thou an old man given to gentle thoughts?
dost summon me as lover of calm peace to take her
part? My heart swells with rage, my smarting grief
burns measureless, and I long for some crime more
dreadful than what the casual madness of young men
attempts. Not enough for me is war that as yet is
between citizens; let brother rush on brother. Nor
is that enough; that, as is due, a horror may be
wrought after my fashion, one that may befit my
marriage-couch, arm ye your mother. Let no one
drag me from these woods! I'll lurk in the cliffs'
wave-worn caves or hide away in the thick under-
brush. Here will I catch at vague rumours and
hear of the dire strife of brothers as I may.

IOCASTA

Felix Agaue! facinus horrendum manu,
qua fecerat, gestavit et spolium tulit
cruenta nati maenas in partes dati ;
fecit scelus, sed misera non ultro suo
sceleri occucurrit.   hoc leve est quod sum nocens ;
feci nocentes.   hoc quoque etiamnunc leve est ;
peperi nocentes.   derat aerumnis meis,
ut et hostem amarem.   bruma ter posuit nives   370
et tertia iam falce decubuit Ceres,
ut exul errat natus et patria caret
profugusque regum auxilia Graiorum rogat.
gener est Adrasti, cuius imperio mare
quod scindit Isthmos regitur ; hic gentes suas
septemque secum regna ad auxilium trahit
genero.   quid optem quidve decernam haut scio.
regnum reposcit ; causa repetentis bona est,
mala sic petentis.   vota quae faciam parens ?
utrimque natum video ; nil possum pie   380
pietate salva facere.   quodcumque alteri
optabo nato fiet alterius malo.
sed utrumque quamvis diligam affectu pari,
quo causa melior sorsque deterior trahit
inclinat animus semper infirmo favens.
miseros magis fortuna conciliat suis.

---

[1] *i.e.* Polynices, who has now become a public foe of
Thebes.

PHOENISSAE

It is possible that the following fragments belong to another play. The presence of ANTIGONE *in Thebes, notwithstanding her resolve to remain with her father, would strengthen this view.*

JOCASTA

Fortunate Agave! she carried her ghastly crime in the hand that wrought it, and as a bloody maenad bore spoil of her dismembered son. She wrought a crime, but not wantonly did the wretched woman go to meet her crime. 'Tis but a trivial thing that I am guilty; I have made others guilty. This, too, bad as it is, is trivial; I have borne guilty sons. 'Twas as yet lacking to my woes that I should love even my enemy.[1] Thrice have the snows of winter fallen, three harvests now have yielded to the sickle, while my son in exile wanders, expatriate, and as an outcast begs aid from the Greek kings. And now he is son-in-law of Adrastus, whose sway is over the waters which Isthmus cleaves, and who brings with him his own tribes and seven kingdoms to the aid of his son-in-law. What I should pray for, or which side espouse, I know not. He demands back the kingdom; to reseek it is an honest plea, but ill to seek it thus. What should be a mother's prayer? On either side I see a son; I can do nothing piously that is not impious. Whatever blessing I shall ask for one, to the other will prove a curse. But, though I love both equally, whither the better cause and the worse fortune draw, my heart inclines, which always takes the weaker side. Misfortune knits the wretched closer to their kin.

[*Enter* MESSENGER *in haste.*]

SATELLES

Regina, dum tu flebiles questus cies
terisque tempus, saeva nudatis adest
acies in armis ; aera iam bellum cient
aquilaque pugnam signifer mota vocat ;   390
septena reges bella dispositi parant,
animo pari Cadmea progenies subit,
cursu citato miles hinc atque hinc ruit.
viden ?   atra nubes pulvere abscondit diem
fumoque similes campus in caelum erigit
nebulas, equestri fracta quas tellus pede
summittit et, si vera metuentes vident,
infesta fulgent signa, subrectis adest
frons prima telis, aurea clarum nota
nomen ducum vexilla praescriptum ferunt.   400
i, redde amorem fratribus, pacem omnibus,
et impia arma matris oppositu impedi.

ANTIGONA

Perge, o parens, perge et cita celerem gradum,
compesce tela, fratribus ferrum excute,
nudum inter enses pectus infestos tene !
aut solve bellum, mater, aut prima excipe.

IOCASTA

Ibo, ibo et armis obvium opponam caput,
stabo inter arma ; petere qui fratrem volet,
petat ante matrem.   tela, qui fuerit pius,
rogante ponat matre ; qui non est pius   410
incipiat a me.   fervidos iuvenes anus
tenebo, nullum teste me fiet nefas ;
376

PHOENISSAE

O queen, whilst thou art uttering tearful complaints and wasting time, the fierce battle-line with bared swords is at hand; the trumpets' blare sounds to war, the standard-bearer with eagle advanced signals for contest; the kings, each in his place, are setting their sevenfold battle in array, while with equal courage Cadmus' race advances; at the double-quick the soldiers on either side rush on. Dost see them? A dark cloud of dust hides the day; the plain lifts heavenward dense, smoke-like billows which the earth, beaten by horses' hoofs, sends up; and, if terror-stricken eyes see aught aright, hostile standards are gleaming there; the front rank, with lifted spears, is close at hand, and the battle-flags have the leaders' names clearly limned in golden characters. Go, restore love to brothers, peace to us all, and let a mother be the barrier to stay unholy arms.

Hasten, mother, hasten on flying feet! hold back their weapons, strike the steel from my brothers' hands, set thy bared breast between their hostile swords! Either stop the war, mother, or be the first to feel it.

I go, I go, and my own life will I set against their arms; I'll stand between their arms; and he who shall wish to attack his brother must attack his mother first. Let the more filial lay down his arms at a mother's prayer; let the unfilial begin with me. These fiery youths, old though I be, will I restrain; there shall be no impious crime committed in my sight; or, if

377

aut si aliquod et me teste committi potest,
non fiet unum.

ANTIGONA

Signa collatis micant
vicina signis, clamor hostilis fremit;
scelus in propinquo est; occupa, mater, preces.
et ecce motos fletibus credas meis,
sic agmen armis segne compositis venit.

SATELLES

Procedit acies tarda, sed properant duces.

IOCASTA

Quis me procellae turbine insano vehens   420
volucer per auras ventus aetherias aget?
quae Sphinx vel atra nube subtexens diem
Stymphalis avidis praepetem pennis feret?
aut quae per altas aeris rapiet vias
Harpyia saevi regis observans famem
et inter acies proiciet raptam duas?

SATELLES

Vadit furenti similis aut etiam furit.
sagitta qualis Parthica velox manu
excussa fertur, qualis insano ratis
premente vento rapitur, aut qualis cadit   430
delapsa caelo stella, cum stringens polum
rectam citatis ignibus rumpit viam,
attonita cursu fugit et binas statim
diduxit acies.   victa materna prece
haesere bella, iamque in alternam necem

e'en in my sight one crime can be committed, it shall not be only one.

[*Exit towards the scene of conflict.*]

ANTIGONE [*looking after her*]

The opposing standards gleam face to face, the hostile battle-cry is sounding, the crime is near at hand; forestall it, mother, with thy prayers! And see, you might deem them moved by tears of mine, so sluggishly moves the line with weapons held at rest.

MESSENGER

The line advances slowly, but the leaders haste.

JOCASTA [*hurrying on*]

What swift wind with the storm-blast's mad whirl will carry me through the air of heaven? What Sphinx, what Stymphalian bird, with its dark cloud veiling day, will speed me headlong on eager wings? Or what Harpy, hovering over the barbarian king's [1] famished board, will hurry me along the highways of the air, hurry and fling me 'twixt the two battle-lines?

MESSENGER [*looking after her*]

She goes like a mad thing, or is mad indeed. Swift as a dart hurled by some Parthian's hand, or as a vessel driven on by wild, raging winds, or as a star, dislodged from the firmament, when, sweeping o'er the heavens, with swift fire it cleaves its unswerving way, so has the frenzied queen sped on and at once has parted the two battle-lines. Stayed by a mother's prayer the battle hangs; and now the bands, eager to

[1] See Index *s.v.* "Phineus."

illinc et hinc miscere cupientes manus
librata dextra tela suspensa tenent.
paci favetur, omnium ferrum iacet
cessatve tectum ; vibrat in fratrum manu.
laniata canas mater ostendit comas,   440
rogat abnuentes, inrigat fletu genas.
negare matri, qui diu dubitat, potest.

IOCASTA

In me arma et ignes vertite, in me omnis ruat
unam iuventus quaeque ab Inachio venit
animosa muro quaeque Thebana ferox
descendit arce ; civis atque hostis simul
hunc petite ventrem, qui dedit frates viro.
haec membra passim spargite ac divellite.
ego utrumque peperi—ponitis ferrum ocius ?
an dico et ex quo?   dexteras matri date,   450
date dum piae sunt.   error invitos adhuc
fecit nocentes, omne Fortunae fuit
peccantis in nos crimen ; hoc primum nefas
inter scientes geritur.   in vestra manu est,
utrum velitis : sancta si pietas placet,
donate matri pacem [1] ; si placuit scelus,
maius paratum est—media se opponit parens.
proinde bellum tollite aut belli moram.

---

[1] *So Leo and Richter, with* ω *:* matri pacta *L. Müller :* date
arma matri saeva *Tachau :* domate Martem pace *M. Müller.*

join from both sides in mutual slaughter, hold their
swords poised in lifted hands. They incline to peace,
the swords of all are lowered, or idly sheathed; but
they still quiver in the brothers' hands. The mother
shows them her hoary hair, tearing it, beseeching
them as they stubbornly refuse, and floods her cheeks
with weeping. Who wavers long may say his mother
" No ! "

[*The scene shifts to the field before Thebes, between the
battle-lines.*]

JOCASTA

[*Kneeling between her two hostile sons.*]

Against me turn your arms and torches; against
me only let every warrior charge, both those who
come with high courage from the city of Inachus,[1]
and those who from the Theban citadel descend
thirsting for the fray. Townsman and enemy, together attack this womb which bore my husband
brothers. Rend these limbs asunder and scatter
them everywhere. I bore you both—lay you not
down your arms with speed? Or shall I tell from
what father, too? Your right hands—to your mother
give them, give while they are still filial. Ignorance
till now against our will hath made us [2] guilty; the
whole crime was Fortune's, who sinned against us;
this is the first crime wrought between those who
know. It is yours to choose which thing you will:
if holy affection please you, grant to your mother
peace; if crime has pleased, a greater is to hand—
your mother sets herself between you. Therefore
rid ye of strife or of this stay of strife.[3]

[1] Argos.   [2] *i.e.* Oedipus and Jocasta especially.
[3] *i.e.* or kill me who stand between you to stay your
fighting.

Sollicita cui nunc mater alterna prece
verba admovebo? misera quem amplectar prius? 460
in utramque partem ducor affectu pari.
hic afuit ; sed pacta si fratrum valent,
nunc alter aberit. ego iam numquam duos
nisi sic videbo?

        Iunge complexus prior,
qui tot labores totque perpessus mala
longo parentem fessus exilio vides.
accede propius, clude vagina impium
ensem et trementem iamque cupientem excuti
hastam solo defige ; maternum tuo
coire pectus pectori clipeus vetat ;   470
hunc quoque repone. vinculo frontem exue
tegumenque capitis triste belligeri leva
et ora matri redde. quo vultus refers
acieque pavida fratris observas manum?
affusa totum corpus amplexu tegam,
tuo cruori per meum fiet via.
quid dubius haeres? an times matris fidem?

POLYNICES

Timeo ; nihil iam iura naturae valent.
post ista fratrum exempla ne matri quidem
fides habenda est.

IOCASTA

        Redde iam capulo manum,   480
astringe galeam, laeva se clipeo inserat ;
dum frater exarmatur, armatus mane.

---

[1] *i.e.* in enmity.

PHOENISSAE

459 To which of you now shall your anxious mother with alternate prayers address her words? Whom shall I in my wretchedness first embrace? To both sides am I drawn with equal love. This son has been absent from me; but if the brothers keep their pact, now will the other be away. And shall I never see you both, save thus?[1]

[*Turning to* POLYNICES]

464 Come thou first to thy mother's arms, thou who hast endured so many toils, so many misfortunes, and, worn with long exile, seest thy mother at last. Come nearer, sheathe thine impious sword, and thy spear, which is even now quivering and eager to be thrown, thrust it in the ground. Thy shield keeps thee from coming close to thy mother, breast to breast; put that by, too. Unbind thy brow, take the grim helmet from thy warlike head, and let thy mother see thy face. Why dost thou look away, and with fearful glance watch thy brother's hand? I will cover thy whole body with my protecting embrace and allow way to thy blood only through my own. Why dost thou still halt in doubt? Dost fear thy mother's pledge?

POLYNICES

I am in fear; no longer do nature's laws avail. Since this example of a brother's faithlessness, even a mother's pledge may not be trusted.

JOCASTA

Put now hand to hilt again, bind on thy helmet, let thy left hand clasp its shield; and while thy brother unarms, remain thou armed.

[*She turns to* ETEOCLES.]

Tu pone ferrum, causa qui ferri es prior.
si pacis odium est, furere si bello placet,
inducias te mater exiguas rogat,
ferat ut reverso post fugam nato oscula
vel prima vel suprema.   dum pacem peto,
audite inermes.   ille te, tu illum times?
ego utrumque, sed pro utroque.   quid strictum abnuis
recondere ensem?   qualibet gaude mora;   490
id gerere bellum cupitis, in quo est optimum
vinci.   vereris fratris infesti dolos?
quotiens necesse est fallere aut falli a suis,
patiare potius ipse quam facias scelus.
sed ne verere; mater insidias et hinc
et rursus illinc abiget.   exoro? an patri
invideo vestro?   veni ut arcerem nefas
an ut viderem propius?   hic ferrum abdidit,
reclinis hasta est, arma defixa incubant.

Ad te preces nunc, nate, maternas feram,   500
sed ante lacrimas.   teneo longo tempore
petita votis ora.   te profugum solo
patrio penates regis externi tegunt,
te maria tot diversa, tot casus vagum
egere.   non te duxit in thalamos parens
comitata primos, nec sua festas manu
ornavit aedes, nec sacra laetas faces
vitta revinxit; dona non auro graves
gazas socer, non arva, non urbes dedit;
dotale bellum est.   hostium es factus gener,   510
patria remotus hospes alieni laris,

PHOENISSAE

⁴⁸³ Do thou put by the sword, who art the sword's
first cause. If thou hatest peace, if 'tis thy pleasure
to rage in war, thy mother begs brief truce of thee,
that to her son returned from exile she may give a
kiss—the first, perchance the last. While I beg for
peace, hearken ye, unarmed. Doth he fear thee;
thou, him? I fear you both, but for the sake of
both. Why dost refuse to sheathe thy drawn sword?
Be glad of any delay; ye both seek to wage a war
wherein 'twere best to be o'ercome. Dost thou fear
thy hostile brother's wiles? When one must either
cheat or be cheated by one's own, do thou thyself
suffer rather than commit the crime. But do not
fear; thy mother will shield thee from snares on
either hand. Do I prevail? or must I envy ¹ your
father? Have I come to prevent crime? or to see
it done before my eyes? [ETEOCLES *yields to her.*] He
has sheathed his sword, his spear droops, his arms
are laid aside.

[*She turns back to* POLYNICES.]

⁵⁰⁰ Now to thee, son, thy mother will bring her
prayers, but her tears first. After a weary time I hold
the face I prayed to see. Thee, an outcast from thy
native soil, the gods of a foreign king protect; thee
many seas far distant, many fates have driven wandering. Thy mother, at thy side, did not lead thee
to thy first bridal chamber, nor with her own hand
deck the festal hall, nor with sacred fillets wreathe
the glad torches. As wedding gifts no rich golden
treasure, no fields, no cities did thy father-in-law
bestow: war is thy bridal gift. Thou hast become
thine enemy's son, far from thy land, guest of an

---

¹ *i.e.* his blindness, which would shield her from unhallowed
sights.

externa consecutus, expulsus tuis,
sine crimine exul.   ne quid e fatis tibi
desset paternis, hoc quoque ex illis habes,
errasse thalamis.
    Nate post multos mihi
remisse soles, nate suspensae metus
et spes parentis, cuius aspectum deos
semper rogavi, cum tuus reditus mihi
tantum esset erepturus, adventu tuo
quantum daturus : " quando pro te desinam "   520
dixi " timere ? "   dixit inridens d'eus :
"ipsum timebis."   nempe nisi bellum foret,
ego te carerem ; nempe si tu non fores,
bello carerem.   a, triste conspectus datur
pretium tui durumque, sed matri placet.
hinc modo recedant arma, dum nullum nefas
Mars saevus audet ; hoc quoque est magnum nefas,
tam prope fuisse.   stupeo et exanguis tremo,
cum stare fratres hinc et hinc video duos
sceleris sub ictu.   membra quassantur metu ;   530
quam paene mater maius aspexi nefas,
quam quod miser videre non potuit pater.
licet timore facinoris tanti vacem
videamque iam nil tale, sum infelix tamen
quod paene vidi.
     Per decem mensum graves
uteri labores perque pietatem inclitae
precor sororis et per irati sibi
genas parentis, scelere quas nullo nocens,
erroris a se dira supplicia exigens,
hausit—nefandas moenibus patriis faces   540
averte, signa bellici retro agminis
flecte.   ut recedas, magna pars sceleris tamen
vestri peracta est ; vidit hostili grege

alien house, seeking another's, driven from thine own,
exiled for no fault. That thou mightst lack nothing
of thy father's fates, this also thou hast of them, that
thou hast erred in marriage.

515 O son, returned to me after so many years, son,
fear and hope of thy anxious mother, for sight of
whom I have ever prayed the gods, though thy
return was destined to take as much from me as by
thy coming it could give: "When shall I cease to
fear for thee?" I cried; and the god, mocking me,
answered: "'Tis himself thou shalt fear." Surely if
there were no war, I should be without thee; surely
if thou wert not here, I should be free from war.
Oh, bitter price and hard, to pay for a sight of thee;
but thy mother pays it willingly. Only let thy hostile
hosts fall back while as yet savage Mars dares no
impious crime. Even this is an outrageous crime,
that they have come so near. I am appalled; pale
am I and I tremble to see two brothers stand, one
here, one there, 'neath guilt's o'erhanging stroke.
My limbs quake with fear: how near did I, thy
mother, come to seeing greater infamy than that
which thy wretched father could not bear to see.
Though I am free from fear of so great a crime, and
now see no such thing, still I am unhappy because I
almost saw it.

535 By the womb that bore thee for ten weary
months, by the devotion of thy noble sister, by thy
self-hating father's eyes which he, though innocent,
yet, seeking to inflict on himself dire punishment for
his mistake, tore from their sockets—save thy
country's walls from the accursed torch; turn back
again the standards of this warring host. Though
thou shouldst retire, still is the great part of your sin
already done; thy country has seen its plains o'errun

387

c c 2

campos repleri patria, fulgentes procul
armis catervas vidit, equitatu levi
Cadmea frangi prata et excelsos rotis
volitare proceres, igne flagrantes trabes
fumare, cineri quae petunt nostras domos,
fratresque (facinus quod novum et Thebis fuit)
in se ruentes. totus hoc exercitus,   550
hoc populus omnis; utraque hoc vidit soror
genetrixque vidi: nam pater debet sibi
quod ista non spectavit. occurrat tibi
nunc Oedipus, quo iudice erroris quoque
poenae petuntur. ne, precor, ferro erue
patriam ac penates neve, quas regere expetis,
everte Thebas. quis tenet mentem furor?
petendo patriam perdis? ut fiat tua,
vis esse nullam? quin tuae causae nocet
ipsum hoc quod armis uris infestis solum   560
segetesque adultas sternis et totos fugam
edis per agros. nemo sic vastat sua;
quae corripi igne, quae meti gladio iubes
aliena credis. rex sit ex vobis uter,
manente regno quaerite. haec telis petis
flammisque tecta? poteris has Amphionis
quassare moles? nulla quas struxit manus
stridente tardum machina ducens onus,
sed convocatus vocis et citharae sono
per se ipse summas venit in turres lapis—   570
haec saxa franges? victor hinc spolia auferes
vinctosque duces patris aequales tui,
matresque ab ipso coniugum raptas sinu
saevus catena miles imposita trahet?
adulta virgo, mixta captivo gregi,
Thebana nuribus munus Argolicis eat?

by hostile hordes, has seen armed squadrons gleaming
from afar, the Cadmean meadows trampled by flying
hoofs, princes in their chariots careering high, the
smoke and flames of blazing torches which seek to burn
our homes, and brothers (a crime new even to Thebes)
rushing upon each other. This crime the whole army
saw, this, all the people, this, both thy sisters saw and I,
thy mother, saw—for thy father owes it to his own act
that he beheld not such deeds. Let Oedipus stand
before thee now, in whose judgment even for error
is penalty demanded. Do not, I beg of thee, with
the sword destroy thy country and thy household
gods, nor overthrow Thebes, which thou seekst to
rule. What madness holds thee? By seeking thy
land wouldst wreck it? to make it thine, wouldst
have it no land at all? Nay, thou harmst thine own
cause in this very act of harrying the land with
hostile arms, trampling the full-grown crops, and
spreading terror through the whole country-side.
No one works such havoc on his own; what thou
bidst be plundered with fire and reaped with sword,
thou deemst another's. Question whether of you
be king, but let the kingdom stand. These homes
dost thou seek with sword and fire? Wilt have the
heart to batter these walls which Amphion built,
whose stones no hand set in place, moving the slow
weight with creaking crane, but, marshalled by
sound of singing and of lyre, each stone of its own
accord came to the turrets' top—wilt batter down
these stones? Wilt thou bear spoils hence as victor,
and shall conquered chieftains, thy father's friends,
and matrons torn from their husbands' very arms, be
led off in chains by thy rough soldiery? Shall
Thebes' grown maidens, mingled with the captive
herd, go as gifts to the dames of Argos? Or shall

an et ipsa, palmas vincta post tergum datas,
mater triumphi praeda fraterni vehar?
potesne cives leto et exitio datos
videre passim?   moenibus caris potes   580
hostem admovere, sanguine et flamma potes
implere Thebas?   tam ferus durum geris
saevumque in iras pectus?   et nondum imperas—
quid sceptra facient?   pone vaesanos, precor,
animi tumores teque pietati refer.

POLYNICES

Vt profugus errem?   semper ut patria arcear
opemque gentis hospes externae sequar?
quid paterer aliud, si fefellissem fidem?
si peierassem?   fraudis alienae dabo
poenas, at ille praemium scelerum feret?   590
iubes abire; matris imperio obsequor.
da quo revertar.   regia frater mea
habitet superbus, parva me abscondat casa,
hanc date repulso, liceat exiguo lare
pensare regnum.   coniugi donum datus
arbitria thalami dura felicis feram
humilisque socerum lixa dominantem sequar?
in servitutem cadere de regno grave est.

IOCASTA

Si regna quaeris nec potest sceptro manus
vacare saevo, multa quae possunt peti   600
in orbe toto quaelibet tellus dabit.
hinc nota Baccho Tmolus attollit iuga
qua lata terris spatia frugiferis iacent,
390

PHOENISSAE

I myself, with hands bound behind my back, thy
mother, be borne as prize in thy triumph o'er a
brother? Canst thou bear to see thy countrymen
given to death and destruction on every hand?
Against these dear walls canst thou lead the enemy,
canst fill Thebes with blood and fire? Art thou so
wild, is thy heart so hard, so full of savage rage?
And thou art not yet a king—what will the sceptre
do? Oh, I beseech thee, allay the mad ferment of
thy soul, and come back to duty's ways.

POLYNICES

That I may wander outcast? That I may be for
ever shut out from my country and as a stranger
look to the bounty of an alien race? What worse
should I suffer if I had broken faith, if I had forsworn
myself? Am I to pay the penalty of another's sin,
while he enjoys the profit of his crimes? Thou
bidst me go; I bend to my mother's will. Show
me whither I shall get me back. Let my haughty
brother dwell in my palace, let a little hut hide me
away; this grant to the banished brother, let it be
mine to match a kingdom with a paltry hearth. A
wife's mere chattel, shall I bear the harsh sway of a
rich bride and, like a humble camp-follower, attend
upon her domineering father? To fall from a king's
estate to slavery is hard.

JOCASTA

It thou seekst a king's estate, and the harsh
sceptre thy hand cannot forego, any land in the
whole world will offer many kingdoms to be won.
Here Tmolus lifts his ridges, the Wine-god's haunts,
where stretch broad plains of grain-producing lands,

et qua trahens opulenta Pactolus vada
inundat auro rura ; nec laetis minus
Maeandros arvis flectit errantes aquas,
rapidusque campos fertiles Hermus secat.
hinc grata Cereri Gargara et dives solum
quod Xanthus ambit nivibus Idaeis tumens ;
hinc qua relinquit nomen Ionii mare [1]   610
faucesque Abydo Sestos opposita premit ;
aut qua latus [2] iam propior orienti dedit
tutamque crebris portibus Lyciam videt.
haec regna ferro quaere, in hos populos ferat
socer arma fortis, has tuo sceptro paret
tradatque gentes.   hoc adhuc regnum puta
tenere patrem.   melius exilium est tibi
quam reditus iste.   crimine alieno exulas,
tuo redibis.   melius istis viribus
nova regna nullo scelere maculata appetes.   620
quin ipse frater arma comitatus tua
tibi militabit.
　　　　　　　Vade et id bellum gere
in quo pater materque pugnanti tibi
favere possint.   regna cum scelere omnibus
sunt exiliis graviora.   nunc belli mala
propone, dubias Martis incerti vices :
licet omne tecum Graeciae robur trahas,
licet arma longe miles ac late explicet,
fortuna belli semper ancipiti in loco est,
quodcumque Mars decernit.   exaequat duos,   630
licet impares sint, gladius ; et spes et metus
Fors caeca versat.   praemium incertum petis,
certum scelus.   favisse fac votis deos

---

[1] So *Richter* : *Leo*, with ω, maris : *Bücheler conjectures*
Ionium Thetis : *Wilamowitz* qua reliqui nomen Inois mari.
[2] So *Leo*, with ω : *Richter* quae : *N. Heinsius* aut qua
Thetis se.

and where Pactolus, rolling his rich waves, o'erflows
the fields with gold; nor does Meander through
meadows less joyful bend his wandering waters, and
swift Hermus cleaves the fertile plains. Here is
Gargara, beloved of Ceres, and the soil which rich
Xanthus compasses, swollen by Ida's snows; here the
land where the Ionian sea gives up its name, and
Sestos, over against Abydos, hugs the narrow strait[1];
or where, now nearer to the east, it curves and sees
Lycia secure with its many harbours. These kingdoms
seek thou with the sword; against these peoples let
thy brave father in-law bear arms; these tribes let him
acquire and deliver to thy sway. As for this kingdom, deem that thy father still holds it fast. Better
is exile for thee than such return as this. Through
another's sin thou livest in exile, through thine
own wilt thou return. With yonder forces, 'twere
better to seek new realms, stained by no crime.
Nay, thy brother's self, accompanying thine arms,
will fight for thee.

[622] Go thou, then, and wage such warfare that,
as thou fightest, thy father and thy mother may
pray for thy success. Kingdoms won by crime are
heavier than any exile. Now picture to thyself war's mishaps, the wavering chances of uncertain Mars: though thou bring with thee the
whole strength of Greece, though thy armed soldiery
spread far and wide, the fortune of war hangs ever
in doubtful scale, according as Mars determines. The
sword makes two warriors equal though they be ill-
matched; both hope and fear are in blind Fortune's
hand. The prize thou seekst is uncertain; certain,
the crime. Grant that all the gods have been

---

[1] The Hellespont.

omnes tuis ; cessere et aversi fugam
petiere cives, clade funesta iacens
obtexit agros miles—exultes licet
victorque fratris spolia deiecti geras,
frangenda palma est.   quale tu hoc bellum putas,
in quo execrandum victor admittit nefas,
si gaudet?   hunc quem vincere infelix cupis,   640
cum viceris, lugebis.   infaustas age
dimitte pugnas, libera patriam metu,
luctu parentes.

POLYNICES

Sceleris et fraudis suae
poenas nefandus frater ut nullas ferat ?

IOCASTA

Ne metue.   poenas et quidem solvet graves :
regnabit.   est haec poena.   si dubitas, avo
patrique crede ; Cadmus hoc dicet tibi
Cadmique proles.   sceptra Thebano fuit
impune nulli gerere, nec quisquam fide
rupta tenebit illa.   iam numeres licet   650
fratrem inter istos.

ETEOCLES

Numeret, est tanti mihi
cum regibus iacere.   te turbae exulum
ascribo.

IOCASTA

Regna, dummodo invisus tuis.

favourable to thy prayers; grant that the citizens have given way, that they have turned and fled, that soldiers, lying in bloody heaps, cover the fields—though thou shouldst triumph and as victor bear off the spoils of thy conquered brother, broken must be the victor's palm. What manner of war deemst thou that, wherein the conqueror takes on him the curse of guilt if he rejoices? Him whom, unhappy man, thou art so eager to o'ercome, when thou hast o'ercome thou wilt lament. Oh, then, forego this unhallowed strife, free thy country from fear, from agony thy parents.

POLYNICES

That my cursed brother may receive no penalty for his crime and treachery?

JOCASTA

Have no fear. Penalty, yes, heavy penalty shall he pay: he shall reign. That is the penalty. If thou dost doubt it, believe thy grandsire and thy sire; Cadmus will tell thee this, and the race of Cadmus. No Theban hath e'er borne sceptre without penalty, nor will any hold it who has broken faith. Now mayst thou count thy brother amongst these.

ETEOCLES

So let him count me; 'tis worth the price, methinks, to lie with kings.

[*To* POLYNICES.]

652 Thee I enrol amongst the exiled throng.

JOCASTA

Reign, then, but hated by thy people.

ETEOCLES

Regnare non vult esse qui invisus timet ;
simul ista mundi conditor posuit deus,
odium atque regnum. regis hoc magni reor,
odia ipsa premere. multa dominantem vetat
amor suorum ; plus in iratos licet.
qui vult amari, languida regnat manu.

IOCASTA

Invisa numquam imperia retinentur diu.   660

ETEOCLES

Praecepta melius imperi reges dabunt ;
exilia tu dispone.   pro regno velim—

IOCASTA

Patriam penates coniugem flammis dare ?

ETEOCLES

Imperia pretio quolibet constant bene.

*   *   *   *   *

PHOENISSAE

ETEOCLES

To reign he hath no will who feareth to be hated;
the god who made the world set those two things
together, hatred and sovereignty. This is the part
of a great sovereign, I think, to tread e'en hatred
under foot. A people's love forbids a ruler many
things; against their rage he has more rights. Who
would be loved reigns with a nerveless hand.

JOCASTA

But hated sovereignty is never long retained.

ETEOCLES

The rules for sovereignty kings will better give;
do thou make rules for exiles. For sovereignty I
would fain—

JOCASTA

Give country, home, wife to the flames?

ETEOCLES

Sovereignty is well bought at any price.

*　　*　　*　　*　　*

OCTAVIA

OCTAVIA

A FABULA PRAETEXTA

THE ONLY EXTANT ROMAN HISTORICAL DRAMA

Introduction

THE Roman historical drama had a place among the earliest products of Roman literature, and seems to have enjoyed a degree of popularity through all succeding periods. That Roman literary genius did not find a much fuller expression through this channel was not due to a lack of national pride and patriotism, nor yet to a dearth of interesting and inspiring subjects in Roman history. The true reason is probably to be found in the fact that by the time national conditions were ripe for the development of any form of literature, the Greeks had already worked, and well worked, nearly all available fields, and had produced a mass of literature which dazzled the Roman mind when at last circumstances brought these two nations into closer contact.

The natural and immediate result was an attempt on the part of the Romans to imitate these great models. And hence we have in drama, both in tragedy and in comedy, a wholesale imitation of the Greek dramas, oftentimes nothing more than a translation of these, with only here and there an attempt to produce something of a strictly native character, entirely independent of the Greek influence.

This imitative impulse was augmented by the fact

401

that the Romans were following the line of least resistance, since it is always easier to imitate than to create. Furthermore, they had as yet developed no national pride of literature to hold them to their own lines of national development; they had no forms of their own so well established that the mere force of literary momentum would carry them steadily on toward a fuller development, in spite of the disturbing effects of the influx of other and better models. They had, indeed, developed a native Saturnian verse which, had it been allowed a free field, might have reached a high pitch of literary excellence. But it speedily gave way at the approach of the more elegant imported forms.

The overwhelming influence of Greek tragedy upon the Roman dramatists can be seen at a glance as we review the dramatic product of the Roman tragedians. We have titles and fragments of nine tragedies by Livius Andronicus, seven by Naevius, twenty-two by Ennius, thirteen by Pacuvius, forty-six by Accius, and many fragments from each of these, unassignable to definite plays, which indicate numerous other plays of the same character. To these should be added additional fragments from nearly a score more of Roman writers during the next two hundred years after Accius. All the above-mentioned plays are on Greek subjects; and most of those whose fragments are sufficiently extensive to allow us to form an opinion of their character are either translations or close imitations of the Greeks, or are so influenced by these as to be decidedly Greek rather than Roman in character.

And what of the genuine Roman dramatic product? Speaking for the *fabula praetexta*, or Roman historical drama, alone, the entire output, so far as our records go, is contained in the following list of authors and titles.

OCTAVIA

From Naevius (265–204 B.C.) we have the *Clastidium*,
written in celebration of the victory of Marcellus (at
Clastidium in 222 B.C.) over Vidumarus, king of the
Transpadane Gauls, whom Marcellus slew and stripped
of his armour, thus gaining the rare *spolia opima*. The
play was probably written for the especial occasion
either of the triumph of Marcellus or of the celebration of his funeral.

We have also from Naevius a play variously entitled
Lupus or *Romulus* or *Alimonium Remi et Romuli*,
evidently one of those dramatic reproductions of
scenes in the life of a god, enacted as a part of the
ceremonies of his worship. This play is comparable
to dramatic representations among the Greeks in the
worship of Dionysus.

The *Ambracia* and the *Sabinae* of Ennius (239–169
B.C.) are ordinarily classed as *fabulae praetextae*,
although Lucian Müller classes the fragments of
the *Ambracia* among the *Saturae* of Ennius ; while
Vahlen puts the *Ambracia* under the heading *Comoe-
diarum et ceterorum carminum reliquiae*, and classifies
the fragments of the *Sabinae* under *ex incertis satur-
arum libris*. The *Ambracia* is evidently called after
the city of that name in Epirus, celebrated for the
long and remarkable siege which it sustained against
the Romans under M. Fulvius Nobilior. That general
finally captured the city in 189 B.C. If the piece is
to be considered as a play, it was, like the *Clastidium*,
written in honour of the Roman general, and acted on
the occasion either of his triumph or of his funeral.

We have four short fragments from the *Paulus* of
Pacuvius (220–130 B.C.), written in celebration of the
exploits of L. Aemilius Paulus who conquered Perseus,
king of Macedonia, in the battle of Pydna, 168 B.C.

The fragments of the plays already mentioned

403

are too brief to afford any adequate idea of their character or content. But in the *Brutus* of Accius (b. 170. B.C.), which centres around the expulsion of the Tarquins and the establishment of the Republic, we have a larger glimpse into the play through two most interesting fragments consisting of twelve iambic trimeters and ten trochaic tetrameters, respectively. In the first, King Tarquin relates to his seer an ill-ominous dream which he has had; the second is the seer's interpretation of this dream, pointing to Tarquin's dethronement by Brutus. Other short fragments give glimpses of the outrage of Lucretia by Sextus at Collatia, and the scene in the forum where Brutus takes his oath of office as first consul. This play, unlike its predecessors, was not written at the time of the events which it portrays, but may still be classed with them, so far as its object is concerned, since it is generally thought to have been written in honour of D. Junius Brutus, who was consul in 138 B.C., and with whom the poet enjoyed an intimate friendship.

Another *praetexta* of Accius is preserved, the *Decius*, of which eleven short fragments remain. This play celebrates the victory of Quintus Fabius Maximus and P. Decius Mus over the Samnites and Gauls at Sentinum in 295 B.C. The climax of the play would be the self-immolation of Decius after the example of his father in the Latin war of 340 B.C.

In addition to these plays of the Roman dramatists of the Republic, we have knowledge of a few which date from later times. There was a historical drama entitled *Iter*, by L. Cornelius Balbus, who dramatized the incidents of a journey which he made to Pompey's camp at Dyrrachium at the opening of civil war in 49 B.C. Balbus was under commission from Caesar to treat with the consul, L. Cornelius Lentulus, and other optimates who had fled from Rome, concerning their return to the city. The journey was a complete fiasco, so far as results were concerned; but the vanity of Balbus was so flattered by this (to him) important mission that he must needs dramatize his experiences and present the play under his own direction in his native city of Gades.

We have mention also of an *Aeneas* by Pomponius Secundus, and of two *praetextae* by Curiatius Maternus, entitled *Domitius* and *Cato*.

These eleven historical plays are, as we have seen, for the most part, plays of occasion, and would be at best of but temporary interest, born of the special circumstances which inspired them. They are in no way comparable with such historical dramas on Roman subjects as Shakespeare's *Julius Caesar* or *Coriolanus*, whose interest is for all times.

We have still a twelfth play of this class, which enjoys the unique distinction of being the only Roman historical drama which has come down to us in its complete form—the *Octavia*. Its authorship is unknown, although tradition gives it a place among the tragedies of Seneca, the philosopher. The general opinion of modern critics, however, is against this tradition, chiefly because one passage in the play, in the form of a prophecy, too circumstantially describes the death of Nero, which occurred three years after the death of Seneca. It is generally agreed that the play must have been written soon after the death of Nero, and by some one, possibly Maternus, who had been an eye-witness of the events, and who had been inspired by his sympathies for the unfortunate Octavia to write this story of her sufferings.

THE TRAGEDIES OF SENECA

Summary of the Imperial Family History which forms a Background to the *Octavia* and to which References are made throughout the Play.

Tiberius Claudius Drusus Nero Caesar Germanicus, more commonly known as Claudius, fourth emperor of Rome, had taken for his third wife the daughter of M. Valerius Messala, Messalina, who bore to him two children, Britannicus and Octavia. Always notorious for her profligacy and licentiousness, Messalina crowned her career by publicly marrying C. Silius at Rome during the temporary sojourn of her imperial husband at Ostia. Claudius long wavered as to her punishment, but at last, through the influence of his favourite, Narcissus, he signed her death warrant, and she was executed by a tribune of the guards in 48 A.D.

In the following year, through the intrigue of the freedman Pallas, Claudius married his brother's daughter, Agrippina, who brought with her into the emperor's household Lucius Domitius, her son by her first husband, Cn. Domitius Ahenobarbus.

Immediately Agrippina began to plot for the succession of her son to the throne of the Caesars. In 50 A.D. she prevailed upon Claudius to adopt, to the prejudice of Britannicus, her own son, who was thereafter known as Nero. She had already caused Seneca, who had been exiled at the instance of Messalina, to be recalled that he might serve as

406

Nero's tutor. In 53 A.D. she further advanced her plans by compassing the marriage of her son to Octavia, the emperor's daughter. Octavia had already been betrothed by Claudius to L. Silanus, who now, to escape the vengeance of Agrippina, committed suicide.

Her plans being now fully laid for the final act, Agrippina secretly poisoned Claudius on October 12th, 54 A.D., and on the following day Nero succeeded to the throne, being then seventeen years of age. In the following year, by the joint plotting of mother and son, the young Britannicus, also, was poisoned.

Because of the youth and inexperience of her son Agrippina enjoyed four years of practically imperial power ; but at last, in 59 A.D., Nero, tired of his mother's ascendancy, caused her to be assassinated, after an unsuccessful attempt upon her life by means of a treacherous vessel, in which death-trap he had sent her to sea.

Nero had long since become enamoured of Poppaea, a beautiful profligate, who had left her husband, Rufinus Crispinus, to live with Otho, and who now became mistress of the emperor. Aspiring to be his wife, she had plotted to bring about the death of Agrippina and later the divorce of Octavia. Through these machinations of his mistress and Nero's own more than ready acquiescence, Octavia was falsely accused of adultery and in 62 A.D. she was banished to Pandataria, where she was shortly afterwards put to death.

Poppaea herself died in 65 A.D. as the result, it was said, of a kick by her brutal husband when she was far advanced in pregnancy. In the same year, at the command of the emperor, Seneca committed suicide; and three years thereafter, in 68 A.D., Nero himself, deposed by the praetorian guards, who had espoused the cause of Galba, and condemned to death by the Senate, fled from Rome and, after vain efforts to escape, received his death-stroke by his own request at the hands of a faithful attendant who had fled with him.

DRAMATIS PERSONAE

OCTAVIA, *step-sister and wife of Nero.*

NURSE *of Octavia.*

POPPAEA, *mistress and afterward wife of Nero.*

NURSE *of Poppaea.*

GHOST OF AGRIPPINA, *mother of Nero, slain by him.*

NERO, *Emperor of Rome.*

SENECA, *former tutor of Nero, and later one of his chief counsellors.*

PREFECT OF ROMAN SOLDIERS.

MESSENGER.

CHORUS OF ROMANS, *sympathetic with Octavia.*

CHORUS, *attached to the interests of the court.*

THE SCENE is laid throughout in different apartments of the palace of Nero, and is concerned with the events of the year 62 A.D.

OCTAVIA

Iam vaga caelo sidera fulgens
Aurora fugat, surgit Titan
radiante coma mundoque diem
reddit clarum.
age, tot tantis onerata malis,
repete assuetos iam tibi questus
atque aequoreas vince Alcyonas,
vince et volucres Pandionias;
gravior namque his fortuna tua est.
semper, genetrix, deflenda mihi,   10
prima meorum causa malorum,
tristes questus natae exaudi,
si quis remanet sensus in umbris.
utinam ante manu grandaeva sua
mea rupisset stamina Clotho,
tua quam maerens vulnera vidi
oraque foedo sparsa cruore!
o lux semper funesta mihi,
tempore ab illo
lux es tenebris invisa magis!   20
tulimus saevae iussa novercae,
hostilem animum vultusque truces.
illa illa meis tristis Erinys
thalamis Stygios praetulit ignes
teque extinxit, miserande pater,
modo cui totus paruit orbis
ultra Oceanum

OCTAVIA

Now doth flushing dawn drive the wandering stars
from heaven; with radiant beams the sun arises and
gives the world once more the light of day. On
then, with all thy woes weighed down, resume thy
now accustomed plaints and out-wail the sea-bred
Halcyons,[1] out-wail the birds[2] of old Pandion's
house; for more grievous is thy lot than theirs.
O mother, constant source of tears to me, first
cause of my misfortunes, hearken to thy daughter's
sad complaints, if any consciousness remains among
the shades. Oh, that the ancient Clotho with her
own hand had clipped my threads before sadly I saw
thy wounds, thy face with foul gore besmeared! O
light, ever calamitous to me, from that time, O light,
thou art more hateful than the dark! We have
endured a cruel step-dame's[3] orders, her hostile
spirit and her aspect fierce. 'Twas she, 'twas she,
the baleful fury, who bore the Stygian torches to my
bridal chamber, and quenched thy light, O wretched
father, whom but yesterday the whole world obeyed,
even beyond Ocean's bounds, before whom the

---

[1] See Index *s.v.* " Ceyx."
[2] See Index *s.v.* " Philomela."
[3] Agrippina.

cuique Britanni terga dedere,
ducibus nostris ante ignoti
iurisque sui.   30
coniugis, heu me, pater, insidiis
oppresse iaces servitque domus
cum prole tua capta tyranno.

NVTRIX

Fulgore primo captus et fragili bono [1]
fallacis aulae quisquis attonitus stupet,
subito [2] latentis ecce Fortunae impetu
modo praepotentem cernat eversam domum
stirpemque Claudi, cuius imperio fuit
subiectus orbis, paruit liber diu
Oceanus et recepit invitus rates.   40
en qui Britannis primus imposuit iugum,
ignota tantis classibus texit freta
interque gentes barbaras tutus fuit
et saeva maria, coniugis scelere occidit ;
mox illa nati ; cuius extinctus iacet
frater venenis.   maeret infelix soror
eademque coniunx nec graves luctus valet
ira coacta tegere crudelis viri ;
quem sancta refugit semper, atque odio pari
ardens maritus impia flagrat face.   50
animum dolentis nostra solatur fides
pietasque frustra ; vincit immitis dolor
consilia nostra nec regi mentis potest
generosus ardor, sed malis vires capit.
heu quam nefandum prospicit noster timor
scelus, quod utinam numen avertat deum.

---

[1] *So Richter : Leo conjectures* facie nova.
[2] *So Richter : Leo* sub uno, *with* ΠΦ, *but conjectures* subito involantis.

Britons [1] fled, erstwhile to our leaders all unknown
and unsubdued. Alas, my father, by thy wife's plots
thou liest crushed, and thy house together with thy
child [2] bends to a tyrant's [3] will.

[*Exit to her chamber. Enter* NURSE.]

NURSE

Whoso, o'erpowered by the novel splendour and
the frail blessings of deceitful royalty, stands awe-
struck and amazed, lo, 'neath the sudden blow of
lurking Fate, let him behold, o'erthrown, the house
and stock of Claudius, but now all powerful, under
whose rule the whole world was brought, whom the
Ocean, long to sway unknown, obeyed and, all un-
willingly, received his ships. Lo, he who first on
the Britons set a yoke, who covered unknown floods
with his mighty fleets, who was safe midst tribes
barbaric, midst raging seas, by his wife's [4] crime is
fallen ; she soon by her son's hand fell ; and by his
poison lies my brother [5] slain. The unhappy sister, [6]
yea, the unhappy wife grieves on, nor can she hide
her bitter sufferings, forced to the angry will of her
cruel husband. From him ever the pure girl recoils,
and her husband, though by equal hate inspired,
with incestuous passion burns. Our fond love strives
in vain to console her grieving heart ; her cruel
smart o'ercomes our counsels, nor can the noble passion of her soul be governed, but from her woes she
draws new strength. Alas ! how my fears forbode
some desperate deed, which may the gods forbid.

[1] Claudius had made an expedition to Britain in 43 A.D.
[2] *i.e.* herself.   [3] Nero.
[4] Agrippina.   [5] Britannicus.
[6] *i.e.* step-sister, Octavia ; she was also Nero's sister by
adoption.

OCTAVIA

O mea nullis aequanda malis
fortuna, licet
repetam luctus, Electra tuos.
tibi maerenti caesum licuit   60
flere parentem,
scelus ulcisci vindice fratre,
tua quem pietas hosti rapuit
texitque fides ;
me crudeli sorte parentes
raptos prohibet lugere timor
fratrisque necem deflere vetat,
in quo fuerat spes una mihi
totque malorum breve solamen.
nunc in luctus servata meos   70
magni resto nominis umbra.

NVTRIX

Vox en nostras perculit aures
tristis alumnae ; cesset thalamis
inferre gradus tarda senectus ?

OCTAVIA

Excipe nostras lacrimas, nutrix,
testis nostri fida doloris.

NVTRIX

Quis te tantis solvet curis,
miseranda, dies ?

OCTAVIA

Qui me Stygias mittet ad umbras.

NVTRIX

Omina quaeso sint ista procul.   80

OCTAVIA

OCTAVIA [*heard speaking from her chamber*]

O fate of mine, to be matched by no misfortunes, though I recall thy woes, Electra. Thou couldst weep out thy grief for thy father's murder, couldst take vengeance on the crime with thy brother as avenger, whom thy love snatched from the foe and thy faithful care protected ; but me fear forbids to mourn my parents reft from me by cruel fate, forbids to bewail my brother's taking off, in whom was my sole hope, the fleeting solace of my many woes. And now, saved but to my suffering, I remain, the shadow of a noble name.

NURSE

Hark ! the voice of my sad foster-child strikes on mine ears. Does thy slow age take thee to her chamber with lagging steps ?
[*She advances toward the chamber, but is met by Octavia, coming forth.*]

OCTAVIA

Receive my tears, dear nurse, thou trusty witness of my suffering.

NURSE

What day will free thee from thy mighty cares, poor child ?

OCTAVIA

The day that sends me to the Stygian shades.

NURSE

Far from us be the omen of that word, I pray.

415

OCTAVIA

Non vota meos tua nunc casus,
sed fata regunt.

NVTRIX

Dabit afflictae meliora deus
tempora mitis ; tu modo blando
vince obsequio placata virum.

OCTAVIA

Vincam saevos ante leones
tigresque truces, fera quam saevi
corda tyranni.
odit genitos sanguine claro,
spernit superos hominesque simul,   90
nec fortunam capit ipse suam
quam dedit illi per scelus ingens
infanda parens.   licet ingratum
dirae pudeat munere matris
hoc imperium cepisse, licet
tantum munus morte rependat,
feret hunc titulum post fata tamen
femina longo semper in aevo.

NVTRIX

Animi retine verba furentis,
temere emissam comprime vocem.

OCTAVIA

Toleranda quamvis patiar, haud umquam que-
            ant   100
nisi morte tristi nostra finiri mala.
genetrice caesa, per scelus rapto patre,
orbata fratre, miseriis luctu obruta,
maerore pressa, coniugi invisa ac meae

OCTAVIA

OCTAVIA

No longer is it thy prayers that shape my life but the fates.

NURSE

God in his mercy will bring to thine affliction better days. Do thou but be soothed, and win thy husband with gentle courtesy.

OCTAVIA

Sooner shall I win savage lions and fierce tigers, than that savage tyrant's brutal heart. He hates all born of noble blood, scorns gods and men alike ; nor can he of himself wield his high fortune which by a monstrous crime his impious mother bestowed on him. Yes! though the ungrateful wretch count it shame to take this empire as his cursed mother's gift, though he requite her mighty gift with death, still will the woman even after death win the fame thereof for ever through unending age.

NURSE

Check thou the utterance of thy raging heart ; repress the words thou hast poured forth too rashly.

OCTAVIA

Though I should endure what must be borne, ne'er could my woes be ended, save by gloomy death. With my mother slain, my father by crime snatched from me, robbed of my brother, by wretchedness and grief o'erwhelmed, by sorrow crushed, by my husband

417

subiecta famulae luce non grata fruor,
trepidante semper corde non mortis metu
sed sceleris—absit crimen a fatis meis,
mori iuvabit ; poena nam gravior nece est
videre tumidos et truces miserae mihi
vultus tyranni iungere atque hosti oscula,   110
timere nutus cuius obsequium meus
haud ferre posset fata post fratris dolor
scelere interempti, cuius imperium tenet
et sorte gaudet auctor infandae necis.
quam saepe tristis umbra germani meis
offertur oculis, membra cum solvit quies
et fessa fletu lumina oppressit sopor.
modo facibus atris armat infirmas manus
oculosque et ora fratris infestus petit,
modo trepidus idem refugit in thalamos meos ;   120
persequitur hostis atque inhaerenti mihi
violentus ensem per latus nostrum rapit.
tunc tremor et ingens excutit somnos pavor
renovatque luctus et metus miserae mihi.
adice his superbam paelicem, nostrae domus
spoliis nitentem, cuius in munus suam
Stygiae parentem natus imposuit rati,
quam dira post naufragia superato mari
ferro interemit saevior pelagi fretis.
quae spes salutis post nefas tantum mihi ?   130
inimica victrix imminet thalamis meis
odioque nostri flagrat et pretium stupri
iustae maritum coniugis poscit caput.
emergere umbris et fer auxilium tuae
natae invocanti, genitor, aut Stygios sinus
tellure rupta pande, quo praeceps ferar.

---

[1] *i.e.* Acte. See line 197, note.
[2] Nero, in divorcing Octavia, alleged adultery as the cause.

hated, and set beneath my slave,[1] the sweet light brings no joy to me; for my heart is ever trembling, not with the fear of death, but of crime [2]—be crime but lacking to my misfortunes, death will be delight. For 'tis a punishment far worse than death to look in the tyrant's face, all swollen with rage 'gainst wretched me, to kiss my foe, to fear his very nod, obedience to whom my smarting grief could not endure after my brother's death, most sinfully destroyed, whose throne he usurps, and rejoices in being the worker of a death unspeakable. How oft does my brother's sad shade appear before my eyes when rest has relaxed my body, and sleep weighed down my eyes, weary with weeping. Now with smoking torches he arms his feeble hands, and with deadly purpose aims at his brother's eyes and face; and now in trembling fright takes refuge in my chamber; his enemy pursues and, e'en while the lad clings in my embrace, savagely he thrusts his sword through both our bodies. Then trembling and mighty terror banish my slumbers, and bring back to my wretched heart its grief and fear. Add to all this the proud concubine, bedecked with our house's spoil, as gift for whom the son set his own mother on the Stygian bark; and, when she had o'ercome dread shipwreck and the sea, himself more pitiless than ocean's waves, slew her with the sword. What hope of safety, after crime so great, have I? My victorious foe threatens my chamber, blazes with hate of me, and, as the reward of her adultery, demands of my husband his lawful consort's head. Arise thou, my father, from the shades and bring help to thy daughter who calls on thee; or else, rending the earth, lay bare the Stygian abyss, that I may plunge thither headlong.

419

Frustra parentis invocas manes tui,
miseranda, frustra, nulla cui prolis suae
manet inter umbras cura ; qui nato suo
praeferre potuit sanguine alieno satum   140
genitamque fratris coniugem pactus sibi
toris nefandis flebili iunxit face.
hinc orta series facinorum—caedes, doli,
regni cupido, sanguinis clari sitis ;
mactata soceri concidit thalamis gener
victima, tuis ne fieret hymenaeis potens.
pro facinus ingens ! feminae est munus datus
Silanus et cruore foedavit suo
patrios penates, criminis ficti reus.
intravit hostis, ei mihi, captam domum,   150
dolis novercae principis factus gener
idemque natus, iuvenis infandi ingeni,
scelerum capacis, dira cui genetrix facem
accendit et te iunxit invitam metu.
tantoque victrix facta successu ferox
ausa imminere est orbis imperio sacri.
quis tot referre facinorum formas potest
et spes nefandas feminae et blandos dolos
regnum petentis per gradus scelerum omnium ?
tunc sancta Pietas extulit trepidos gradus   160
vacuamque Erinys saeva funesto pede
intravit aulam, polluit Stygia face
sacros penates, iura naturae furens
fasque omne rupit.   miscuit coniunx viro
venena saeva, cecidit atque eadem sui
mox scelere nati ; tu quoque extinctus iaces,
deflende nobis semper infelix puer,
modo sidus orbis, columen augustae domus,
Britannice, heu me, nunc levis tantum cinis

OCTAVIA

In vain dost thou call upon thy father's ghost,
poor girl, in vain, for no care for his child abides
amidst the shades with him who to his own son
could prefer one born of other blood, and, taking his
brother's child to wife, wed her with couch incestuous
and gloomy torch.   Thence sprung a train of crimes
—murders, deceits, the lust for empire, thirst for
illustrious blood ; as victim offered to the father's
marriage-bed the son-in-law was slain, lest, wedded
to thee he might become too strong.   Oh, monstrous
crime !   To a woman was Silanus given as a boon
and with his blood defiled the ancestral gods, charged
with a crime that was not his.   Then entered the
foe, ah me ! into the conquered palace, by a step-
mother's wiles made an emperor's son-in-law and
son withal, a youth of bent unnatural, fertile in crime,
whose passion thy cruel mother fanned, and forced
thee by fear to wed him, 'gainst thy will.   Triumphant
and emboldened by such success, she dared aspire to
the awful empire of the world.   Who can rehearse
the various forms of crime, the wicked hopes, the
cozening wiles of her who by all crimes would mount
to empire round by round ?   Then holy Piety with
trembling step withdrew, and raging Fury with baleful feet entered the empty palace, defiled with
Stygian torch the holy household-gods, and in mad
rage rent nature's laws and all things sacred.   The
wife for her husband mingled deadly poison, and
soon by her son's crime the same wife fell.   Thou
too dost lie dead, unhappy youth, ever to be mourned
by us, but late the world's star, the prop of a noble
house, Britannicus, and now, ah me ! only light ashes

et tristis umbra ; saeva cui lacrimas dedit   170
etiam noverca, cum rogis artus tuos
dedit [1] cremandos membraque et vultus deo
similes volanti funebris flamma abstulit. [2]

OCTAVIA

Extinguat et me, ne manu nostra cadat !

NVTRIX

Natura vires non dedit tantas tibi.

OCTAVIA

Dolor ira maeror miseriae luctus dabunt.

NVTRIX

Vince obsequendo potius immitem virum.

OCTAVIA

Vt fratrem ademptum scelere restituat mihi ?

NVTRIX

Incolumis ut sis ipsa, labentem ut domum
genitoris olim subole restituas tua.   180

OCTAVIA

Expectat aliam principis subolem domus ;
me dira miseri fata germani trahunt.

NVTRIX

Confirmet animum civium tantus favor.

---

[1] So the MSS.: Leo, with Buecheler, dedi.
[2] Some editors suggest a lacuna of thirty or more lines following 173.

and a mournful shade, o'er whom e'en thy step-mother wept, when on the pyre she gave thy body to be burned, and when thy limbs and features, that were like a winged god's, were by the mournful flame consumed.

OCTAVIA

Let him [1] destroy me also, lest by my hand he fall.

NURSE

Nature has not bestowed on thee such strength.

OCTAVIA

Anguish, anger, sorrow, wretchedness, grief will bestow it.

NURSE

By compliance, rather, win thine unfeeling lord.

OCTAVIA

That he may give back to me my brother, wickedly destroyed?

NURSE

That thou mayst be thyself unharmed, that one day thou mayst restore thy father's tottering house with sons of thine.

OCTAVIA

The royal house expects another son ; [2] me my poor brother's cruel fates drag down.

NURSE

Let thy soul be strengthened by the citizens' great love.

[1] Nero.
[2] *i.e.* Nero's by Poppaea.

OCTAVIA

Solatur iste nostra, non relevat mala.

NVTRIX

Vis magna populi est.

OCTAVIA

Principis maior tamen.

NVTRIX

Respiciet ipse coniugem.

OCTAVIA

Paelex vetat.

NVTRIX

Invisa cunctis nempe.

OCTAVIA

Sed cara est viro.

NVTRIX

Nondum uxor est.

OCTAVIA

Iam fiet, et genetrix simul.

NVTRIX

Iuvenilis ardor impetu primo furit,
languescit idem facile nec durat diu   190
in Venere turpi, ceu levis flammae vapor ;
amor perennis coniugis castae manet.
violare prima quae toros ausa est tuos
animumque domini famula possedit diu,
iam metuit eadem—

424

OCTAVIA

That comforts my woes but does not lighten them.

NURSE

The people's power is mighty.

OCTAVIA

But the emperor's mightier.

NURSE

Of himself will he respect his wife.

OCTAVIA

His concubine forbids.

NURSE

Surely she is scorned by all.

OCTAVIA

But to her husband, dear.

NURSE

She is not yet a wife.

OCTAVIA

But soon will be, and a mother, too.

NURSE

Youthful passion burns fierce at the first rush but readily grows dull, nor long endures in foul adultery, like heat of flickering flame ; but a chaste wife's love remains perpetual. She who first dared profane thy bed, and, though a slave, has long held in thrall her master's heart, already herself fears—

OCTAVIA

Nempe praelatam sibi.

NVTRIX

subiecta et humilis, atque monimenta extruit
quibus timorem fassa testatur suum.
et hanc levis fallaxque destituet deus
volucer Cupido; sit licet forma eminens,
opibus superba, gaudium capiet breve.   200

Passa est similes ipsa dolores
regina deum,
cum se formas vertit in omnes
dominus caeli divumque pater,
et modo pennas sumpsit oloris
modo Sidonii cornua tauri,
aureus idem fluxit in imbri;
fulgent caelo sidera Ledae,
patrio resident Bacchus Olympo,
deus Alcides possidet Heben   210
nec Iunonis iam timet iras,
cuius gener est qui fuit hostis.
vicit sapiens tamen obsequium
coniugis altae pressusque dolor;
sola Tonantem tenet aetherio
secura toro maxima Iuno,
nec mortali captus forma
deserit altam Iuppiter aulam.
tu quoque, terris altera Iuno,
soror Augusti coniunxque, graves   220
vince dolores.

---

[1] It is the opinion of Gruterus that the common interpretation of this whole passage is wrong in its assumption
that the poet has Poppaea in mind; he would have it that
the freed-woman, Acte, is the concubine referred to here,

426

OCTAVIA

Aye ! a more favoured mistress.

NURSE

—subdued and humble, and gives signs by which she confesses her own great fear.[1] Even her shall winged Cupid, false and fickle god, betray ; though she be passing fair, boastful in power, hers shall be but a transitory joy.

[201] The queen of the gods herself like sorrows suffered, when the lord of heaven and father of the gods into all forms changed, and now wings of a swan [2] put on, now the horns of a bull [3] of Sidon, and again in a golden shower [4] poured down ; the stars of Leda glitter in the sky, Bacchus [5] on his father's Olympus dwells, Alcides [5] as a god possesses Hebe and now no more fears Juno's wrath ; he is her son-in-law who was her enemy. Yet wise compliance and controlled wrath won victory for the queenly wife ; without rival, without care does Juno hold the Thunderer on her heavenly couch, and no more does Jupiter, by mortal beauty smitten, desert the court of heaven. Thou too, on earth a second Juno, Augustus' [6] wife and sister, thy grievous woes o'ercome.

[2] In which form he came to Leda.
[3] Thus he appeared to Europa.
[4] Thus he appeared to Danaë.
[5] Son of Jove and a mortal woman. See Index.
[6] A surname not only of the first, but of all the Roman emperors. Here, Nero.

427

OCTAVIA

Iungentur ante saeva sideribus freta
et ignis undae, Tartaro tristi polus,
lux alma tenebris, roscidae nocti dies,
quam cum scelesti coniugis mente impia
mens nostra, semper fratris extincti memor,
utinam nefandi principis dirum caput
obruere flammis caelitum rector paret,
qui saepe terras fulmine infesto quatit
mentesque nostras ignibus terret sacris   230
novisque monstris; vidimus caelo iubar
ardens cometam pandere infestam facem,
qua plaustra tardus noctis aeterna vice
regit Bootes, frigore Arctoo rigens.
en ipse diro spiritu saevi ducis
polluitur aether, gentibus clades novas
minantur astra, quas regit dux impius.
non tam ferum Typhona neglecto Iove
irata Tellus edidit quondam parens;
hic gravior illo pestis, hic hostis deum   240
hominumque templis expulit superos suis
civesque patria, spiritum fratri abstulit,
hausit cruorem matris—et lucem videt
fruiturque vita noxiam atque animam trahit!
pro summe genitor, tela cur frustra iacis
invicta totiens temere regali manu?
in tam nocentem dextra cur cessat tua?
utinam suorum facinorum poenas luat
Nero insitivus, Domitio genitus patre,
orbis tyrannus, quem premit turpi iugo   250
morumque vitiis nomen Augustum inquinat!

---

[1] A comet actually did appear at this time (Tacitus, *Annales*, xiv. 22). The appearance of a comet was portentous, and was supposed to prelude the death of a king.

OCTAVIA

Sooner shall savage seas unite with stars, water with fire, heaven with sad Tartarus, the kindly light with darkness, day with the dewy night, than with my accursed husband's impious soul this soul of mine, that ever broods upon my brother's death. And oh, that the lord of the heaven-dwellers, who often shakes the lands with deadly bolt and terrifies our souls with awful fires and portents strange, would make ready to whelm with flames this impious prince. We have seen a glowing radiance in the sky, a comet [1] spreading its baleful trail, where slow Boötes, numb with Arctic chill, with endless, nightlong wheeling, guides his wain. Lo, by the pestilential breath of this destructive leader the very air is tainted ; the stars threaten unheard disasters for the nations which this godless leader rules. Not such a pest was Typhon, whom wrathful mother Earth produced in scorn of Jove ; this scourge, worse than he, this enemy of gods and men, has driven the heavenly ones from their shrines, and citizens from their country, from his brother has he reft the breath of life, and drained his mother's blood—and he still sees the light of day, still lives and draws his baneful breath ! O high exalted father, why vainly, why so oft at random dost thou hurl thy darts invincible with thine imperial hand ? 'Gainst one so criminal why is thy right hand stayed ? Would that he might pay penalty for his crimes, this spurious [2] Nero, son of Domitius, tyrant of a world he burdens with his shameful yoke, and with foul ways pollutes the name Augustus !

[2] Referring to the fact that Nero was not the true son and rightful heir of Claudius.

NVTRIX

Indignus ille, fateor, est thalamis tuis ;
sed cede fatis atque fortunae tuae,
alumna, quaeso neve violenti move
iram mariti.   forsitan vindex deus
existet aliquis, laetus et veniet dies.

OCTAVIA

Gravi deorum nostra iam pridem domus
urgetur ira, prima quam pressit Venus
furore miserae dura genetricis meae,
quae nupta demens nupsit incesta face,   260
oblita nostri, coniugis, legum immemor.
illi soluta crine, succincta anguibus
ultrix Erinys venit ad Stygios toros
raptasque thalamis sanguine extinxit faces ;
incendit ira principis pectus truci
caedem in nefandam ; cecidit infelix parens,
heu, nostra ferro meque perpetuo obruit
extincta luctu ; coniugem traxit suum
natumque ad umbras, prodidit lapsam domum.

NVTRIX

Renovare luctus parce cum fletu pios,   270
manes parentis neve sollicita tuae,
graves furoris quae sui poenas dedit.

CHORVS

Quae fama modo venit ad aures ?
utinam falso credita perdat
frustra totiens iactata fidem,

---

[1] *i.e.* C. Silius.

430

OCTAVIA

NURSE

Unworthy he, I do confess it, to mate with thee;
but yield thee to the fates and to thy lot, my child,
I beg, nor rouse thy violent husband's wrath. Perchance some god will arise as thine avenger, and a
day of happiness will come again.

OCTAVIA

Long since has the heavy wrath of the gods
pursued our house, which harsh Venus first o'erwhelmed in my poor mother's madness; for she,
already wed, in mad folly wed another [1] with unholy torch, of me, of her husband forgetful, and re-
gardless of the laws. Against her to that hellish
couch, with streaming hair and girt about with snakes,
came the avenging Fury and quenched those stolen
wedding fires in blood; with rage she inflamed the
cruel emperor's heart to impious murder; my ill-
starred mother fell, alas, and, by the sword destroyed,
o'erwhelmed me in endless suffering; her husband
and her son did she drag down to death [2] and shame-
fully betrayed our fallen house.

NURSE

Forbear with weeping to renew thy filial griefs, and
vex not thy mother's spirit, who for her madness has
grievously atoned.   [*Exeunt.*

CHORUS

What rumour has but now come to our ears?
May it prove false and gain no credence though
vainly told o'er and o'er; and may no new wife the

[2] Because, after Messalina's death, Claudius married
Agrippina who was responsible for the death of Claudius
and Britannicus.

nec nova coniunx nostri thalamos
principis intret teneatque suos
nupta penates Claudia proles ;
edat partu pignora pacis
qua tranquillus gaudeat orbis   280
servetque decus Roma aeternum.
fratris thalamos sortita tenet
maxima Iuno ; soror Augusti
sociata toris cur a patria
pellitur aula ?   sancta quid illi
prodest pietas divusque pater,
quid virginitas castusque pudor ?
nos quoque nostri sumus immemores
post fata ducis, cuius stirpem
prodimus aegro [1] suadente metu.   290
vera priorum virtus quondam
Romana fuit verumque genus
Martis in illis sanguisque viris.
illi reges hac expulerunt
urbe superbos ultique tuos
sunt bene manes,
virgo, dextra
caesa parentis, ne servitium
paterere grave et improba ferret
praemia victrix dira libido.   300
te quoque bellum triste secutum est,[2]
mactata tua miseranda manu,
nata Lucreti, stuprum saevi
passa tyranni.
dedit infandi sceleris poenas
cum Tarquinio Tullia coniunx,
quae per caesi membra parentis
egit saevos impia currus
laceroque seni violenta rogos
nata negavit.

emperor's chamber enter, and may his bride, the child of Claudius, keep her rightful home, and bring forth sons, pledges of peace, wherein the untroubled world may rejoice and Rome preserve her everlasting glory. Her brother's bridal chamber mightiest Juno won and holds; why is Augustus's sister, made partner of his couch, driven from her father's house? Of what avail to her is pure devotion, a father deified, virginity, unblemished chastity? We too, after his death have quite forgot our leader, and betray his child at the bidding of sick fear. Right Roman virtue of old our fathers had; in such men was the true race and blood of Mars. They from this city arrogant kings expelled, and well did they avenge thy ghost, O virgin,[1] slain by thy father's hand lest thou shouldst suffer slavery's heavy load, and lest cruel lust, victorious, should gain its shameless prize. Thee [2] also a sad war followed, daughter of Lucretius, slain, poor girl, by thine own hand, by a brutal tyrant outraged. With Tarquin Tullia, his wife, paid penalty for crime unspeakable, who, over the body of her murdered father heartlessly drove her cruel car, and, mad daughter, refused the mangled old man a funeral-pyre.

[1] Virginia. See Index.
[2] Lucretia. See Index.

---

[1] *So Richter: Leo* †aevo : *A* sevo : ψ evo : *Peiper* eheu.
[2] *Leo deletes lines 297–301.*

Haec quoque nati videre nefas   310
saecula magnum, cum Tyrrhenum
rate ferali princeps captam
fraude parentem misit in aequor.
properant placidos linquere portus
iussi nautae, resonant remis
pulsata freta.
fertur in altum provecta ratis,
quae resoluto robore labens
pressa dehiscit sorbetque mare.
tollitur ingens clamor ad astra   320
cum femineo mixtus planctu.
mors ante oculos dira vagatur ;
quaerit leti sibi quisque fugam ;
alii lacerae puppis tabulis
haerent nudi fluctusque secant,
repetunt alii litora nantes ;
multos mergunt fata profundo.
scindit vestes Augusta suas
laceratque comas rigat et maestis
fletibus ora.   330
Postquam spes est nulla salutis,
ardens ira, iam victa malis :
" haec " exclamat " mihi pro tanto
munere reddis praemia, nate ?
hac sum, fateor, digna carina,
quae te genui, quae tibi lucem
atque imperium nomenque dedi
Caesaris amens.   exere vultus
Acheronte tuos poenisque meis
pascere, coniunx ;   340
ego causa tuae, miserande, necis
natoque tuo funeris auctor
en, ut merui, ferar ad manes
inhumata tuos, obruta saevis
aequoris undis."

310 This age as well has seen a son's dire crime, when in a deadly bark the prince[1] sent his mother out on the Tyrrhene sea, by a trick ensnared. At his bidding the sailors make haste to leave the peaceful port and, smit by the oars, the sea resounds. The vessel is borne far out upon the deep; and there, with loosened timbers, sinking, overwhelmed, it yawns wide and drinks in the sea. A mighty outcry rises to the stars, mingled with shrieks of women. Death stalks dire before the eyes of all; each for himself seeks refuge from destruction; some cling naked to planks of the broken ship and face the floods, while others, swimming, seek to gain the shore; fate plunges many into the depths below. Augusta[2] rends her garments and tears her hair and waters her cheeks with grieving tears.

331 At last, with hope of safety gone, blazing with anger and now o'ercome with woe, she cries; "Such reward as this for my great boon, O son, dost thou return me? Worthy am I of this ship, I do confess, who brought thee forth, who gave thee light and empire and the name of Caesar, fool that I was. Thrust forth thy face from Acheron, and glut thee with my punishment, O husband; I caused thy death, poor soul, was the author of thy son's destruction, and lo, as I have merited, to thy ghost am I now borne unburied, whelmed in the cruel waters of the sea."

[1] Nero.   [2] *i.e.* Agrippina.

435

Feriunt fluctus ora loquentis,
ruit in pelagus rursumque salo
pressa resurgit, pellit palmis
cogente metu freta, set cedit
fessa labori. mansit tacitis   350
in pectoribus spreta tristi
iam morte fides. multi dominae
ferre auxilium pelago fractis
viribus audent, bracchia quamvis
lenta trahentem voce hortantur
manibusque levant. quid tibi saevi
fugisse maris profuit undas?
ferro es nati moritura tui,
cuius facinus vix posteritas,
tarde semper saecula credent.   360
furit ereptam pelagoque dolet
vivere matrem
impius, ingens geminatque nefas;
ruit in miserae fata parentis
patiturque moram sceleris nullam.
missus peragit iussa satelles;
reserat dominae pectora ferro.
caedis moriens illa ministrum
rogat infelix, utero dirum
condat ut ensem: 370
" hic est, hic est fodiendus" ait
" ferro, monstrum qui tale tulit."
post hanc vocem
mixtam gemitu cum supremo
animam tandem per fera tristem
vulnera reddit.

SENECA

Quid me, potens Fortuna, fallaci mihi
blandita vultu, sorte contentum mea
436

[346] E'en while she speaks the waves wash o'er her lips, and down into the deep she plunges; anon she rises from the briny weight and with her hands, fear driving her, lashes the sea; but soon, outwearied, gives o'er the struggle. There still lived in secret hearts[1] fidelity which scorned the grim fear of death. Many to their mistress dare bring aid, when her strength is exhausted by the sea, and, as she drags her arms, though sluggishly, along, with their voices cheer her and lift her with their hands. But what availed it to have escaped the waters of the cruel sea? By the sword of thine own son thou art to die, to whose crime scarce will posterity, slowly will all future ages, give belief. He rages and grieves that his mother, snatched from the sea, still lives, the impious monster, and heaps huge guilt on guilt; bent on his wretched mother's death, he brooks no stay of crime. Sent to the task, his creature works his will, and with the sword lays open his mistress' breast. The unhappy woman, dying, begs her murderer to sheathe his fell sword within her womb: "'Tis this, 'tis this that must with the sword be pierced, which gave such monster birth!" After such utterance, with a dying groan commingled, at length through the cruel wound she yielded her sad ghost.

SENECA [*alone*]

Why, potent Fortune, with false, flattering looks, hast high exalted me when contented with my lot,

[1] *i.e.* of some of her servants.

alte extulisti, gravius ut ruerem edita
receptus arce totque prospicerem metus?　　　380
melius latebam procul ab invidiae malis
remotus inter Corsici rupes maris,
ubi liber animus et sui iuris mihi
semper vacabat studia recolenti mea.
o quam iuvabat, quo nihil maius parens
Natura genuit, operis immensi artifex,
caelum intueri, solis et currus sacros
mundique motus,[1] solis alternas vices
orbemque Phoebes, astra quem cingunt vaga,
lateque fulgens aetheris magni decus ;　　　390
qui si senescit, tantus in caecum chaos
casurus iterum, tunc adest mundo dies[2]
supremus ille, qui premat[3] genus impium
caeli ruina, rursus ut stirpem novam
generet renascens melior, ut quondam tulit
iuvenis, tenente regna Saturno poli.
tunc illa virgo, numinis magni dea,
Iustitia, caelo missa cum sancta Fide
terris regebat mitis humanum genus.
non bella norant, non tubae fremitus truces,　　400
non arma gentes, cingere assuerant suas
muris nec urbes : pervium cunctis iter,
communis usus omnium rerum fuit ;
et ipsa Tellus laeta fecundos sinus
pandebat ultro, tam piis felix parens
et tuta alumnis.

　　　　　　Alia sed suboles, minus
experta mitis, tertium sollers genus
novas ad artes extitit, sanctum tamen ;
mox inquietum, quod sequi cursu feras

----

[1] *Leo deletes* solis . . . motus.
[2] *So Richter with MSS.*: *Leo* casurus iterum est—nunc ades
mundo, dies.　　　[3] *So Richter with MSS.*: *Leo* premas.

that, raised to a lofty pinnacle, in heavier ruin I might fall, and might look out upon so many fears? Better was I hid, far out of the reach of envy's sting, midst the crags of Corsica, facing on the sea, where my spirit, free and its own lord, had ever time to contemplate my favourite themes. Oh, 'twas joy— a joy surpassing anything to which mother Nature, contriver of this fabric infinite, hath given birth, to gaze upon the heavens, the sun's sacred chariot, the motions of the universe and the sun's recurring rounds, and the orb of Phoebe, which the wandering stars encircle, and the far effulgent glory of the mighty sky. If this sky is growing old, doomed wholly once more to fall into blind nothingness, then for the universe is that last day at hand which shall crush sinful man beneath heaven's ruin, that so once more a reborn and better world may bring forth a new race such as she bore in youth, when Saturn[1] held the kingdoms of the sky. Then did that virgin, Justice,[2] goddess of mighty sway, from heaven sent down with holy Faith to earth, rule with mild sway the race of men. No wars the nations knew, no trumpet's threatening blasts, no arms, nor were they used to surround their cities with a wall : open to all was the way, in common was the use of every thing ; and the glad Earth herself willingly laid bare her fruitful breast, a mother happy and safe amid such duteous nurslings.

406 But another race arose which proved less gentle; another yet, cunning in unknown arts, but holy still ; then came a restless race, which dared

---

[1] In the Golden Age.   [2] *i.e.* Astraea.

auderet acres, fluctibus tectos gravi 410
extrahere pisces rete vel calamo levi,
decipere volucres [1]
tenere laqueo, premere subiectos iugo
tauros feroces, vomere immunem prius
sulcare terram, laesa quae fruges suas
interius alte condidit sacro sinu.
sed in parentis viscera intravit suae
deterior aetas; eruit ferrum grave
aurumque, saevas mox et armavit manus;
partita fines regna constituit, novas 420
extruxit urbes, tecta defendit sua,
aliena telis aut petit praedae imminens.
neglecta terras fugit et mores feros
hominum et cruenta caede pollutas manus
Astraea virgo, siderum magnum decus.
cupido belli crevit atque auri fames
totum per orbem, maximum exortum est malum
luxuria, pestis blanda, cui vires dedit
roburque longum tempus atque error gravis.
collecta vitia per tot aetates diu 430
in nos redundant; saeculo premimur gravi,
quo scelera regnant, saevit impietas furens,
turpi libido Venere dominatur potens,
luxuria victrix orbis immensas opes
iam pridem avaris manibus, ut perdat, rapit.
    Sed ecce, gressu fertur attonito Nero
trucique vultu.   quid ferat mente horreo.

NERO

Perage imperata; mitte, qui Plauti mihi
Sullaeque caesi referat abscisum caput.

[1] *Leo conjectures a lacuna, and suggests* <turbidos forti
canes>.

440

pursue the wild beasts in the chase, draw fish from their coverts 'neath the sea with weighted net or slender rod, catch birds, on a strong leash hold unruly dogs,[1] force headstrong bullocks to endure the yoke, furrow the earth which had never felt the plough, and which, now thus outraged, had hidden her fruits deeper in her sacred bosom. But into its mother's bowels did that degenerate age intrude ; it dug out heavy iron and gold, and soon did it arm savage hands for war. Marking out boundaries, it established kingdoms, built cities, hitherto unknown, guarded its own dwellings or, bent on booty, with weapons attacked another's. Away from earth that scorned her, from the wild ways of men and hands defiled with bloody slaughter, fled the maid, Astraea, chief glory of the firmament. Lust for war increased and hunger for gold throughout the world; luxury arose, deadliest of ills, a luring pest, which acquired strength and force by long use and grievous error. These sins, through many ages gathering, are o'er-flowing upon us; a heavy age weighs us down, wherein crime is regnant, impiety runs mad, all-potent lust lords it with shameless love, and triumphant luxury has long with greedy hands been clutching the world's unbounded stores—that she may squander them.

[NERO *is seen approaching.*]

[436] But see, with startled step and savage mien Nero approaches. At thought of what he brings I tremble.

[*Enter* NERO, *followed by a Prefect.*]

NERO [*to Prefect*]

Go do my bidding ; send one to slay me Plautus and Sulla and bring back their severed heads.

---

[1] Translating Leo's conjecture.

PRAEFECTVS

Iussa haud morabor : castra confestim petam.

SENECA

Nihil in propinquos temere constitui decet. 440

NERO

Iustum esse facile est cui vacat pectus metu.

SENECA

Magnum timoris remedium clementia est.

NERO

Extinguere hostem maxima est virtus ducis.

SENECA

Servare cives maior est patriae patri.

NERO

Praecipere mitem convenit pueris senem.

SENECA

Regenda magis est fervida adolescentia.

NERO

Aetate in hac sat esse consilii reor.

SENECA

Vt facta superi comprobent semper tua.

NERO

Stulte verebor, ipse cum faciam, deos.

PREFECT

Thy bidding will I do : to the camp forthwith I'll take me.   *[Exit.*

SENECA

'Tis not becoming to proceed rashly 'gainst one's friends.

NERO

'Tis easy to be just when the heart is free from fear.

SENECA

A sovereign cure for fear is clemency.

NERO

To destroy foes is a leader's greatest virtue.

SENECA

For the father of his country to save citizens, is greater still.

NERO

A mild old man should give schooling to boys.

SENECA

More needful 'tis that fiery youth be ruled.

NERO

I deem that at this age we are wise enough.

SENECA

May thy deeds be ever pleasing to the gods.

NERO

Foolish I'd be to fear the gods, when I myself make them.[1]

---

[1] Referring to his own act in deifying the late Claudius.

SENECA

Hoc plus verere quod licet tantum tibi, 450

NERO

Fortuna nostra cuncta permittit mihi.

SENECA

Crede obsequenti parcius; levis est dea.

NERO

Inertis est nescire quid liceat sibi.

SENECA

Id facere laus est quod decet, non quod licet.

NERO

Calcat iacentem vulgus.

SENECA

Invisum opprimit.

NERO

Ferrum tuetur principem.

SENECA

Melius fides.

NERO

Decet timeri Caesarem.

SENECA

At plus diligi.[1]

NERO

Metuant necesse est—

[1] *Leo deletes* decet . . . diligi.

OCTAVIA

SENECA

Fear thou the more, that so great power is thine.

NERO

My fortune doth allow all things to me.

SENECA

Indulgent fortune trust more cautiously; she is a fickle goddess.

NERO

'Tis a dullard's part not to know what he may do.

SENECA

'Tis praiseworthy to do, not what one may, but what one ought.

NERO

Him who lies down the crowd trample on.

SENECA

Him whom they hate, they crush.

NERO

The sword protects the prince.

SENECA

Still better, loyalty.

NERO

A Caesar should be feared.

SENECA

But more be loved.

NERO

But men must fear—

445

SENECA

Quidquid exprimitur grave est.

NERO

Iussisque nostris pareant.

SENECA

Iusta impera—

NERO

Statuam ipse.

SENECA

Quae consensus efficiat rata.   460

NERO

Respectus [1] ensis faciet.

SENECA

Hoc absit nefas.

NERO

An patiar ultra sanguinem nostrum peti,
inultus et contemptus ut subito opprimar?
exilia non fregere summotos procul
Plautum atque Sullam, pertinax quorum furor
armat ministros sceleris in caedem meam,
absentium cum maneat etiam ingens favor
in urbe nostra, qui fovet spes exulum.
tollantur hostes ense suspecti mihi,
invisa coniunx pereat et carum sibi   470
fratrem sequatur.   quidquid excelsum est cadat.

SENECA

Pulcrum eminere est inter illustres viros,
consulere patriae, parcere afflictis, fera

---

[1] *So Buecheler and Richter: Leo, with the MSS.,* Despectus:
Wilamowitz despectum ut ensis feriat?

OCTAVIA

SENECA

What is compelled is burdensome.

NERO

Let them obey our orders.

SENECA

Give righteous orders—

NERO

I shall myself decide.

SENECA

which all men may respect.

NERO

The sword will force respect.

SENECA

May heaven forbid !

NERO

Shall I then go on suffering them to seek my blood,
that, unavenged and scorned, I may suddenly be
crushed ?   Exile has not broken Plautus and Sulla,
though far removed, whose persistent rage arms the
agents of their guilt to work my death, since still,
though absent, great is the favour they enjoy in this
our city, which nurtures the exiles' hopes.   Let the
sword remove foemen whom I suspect ; let my hateful
wife perish and follow the brother whom she loves.
Whatever is high exalted, let it fall.

SENECA

'Tis glorious to tower aloft amongst great men, to
have care for father-land, to spare the downtrodden,

caede abstinere tempus atque irae dare,
orbi quietem, saeculo pacem suo.
haec summa virtus, petitur hac caelum via.
sic ille patriae primus Augustus parens
complexus astra est colitur et templis deus.
illum tamen Fortuna iactavit diu
terra marique per graves belli vices,   480
hostes parentis donec oppressit sui ;
tibi numen incruenta summisit suum
et dedit habenas imperi facili manu
nutuque terras maria subiecit tuo.
invidia tristis victa consensu pio
cessit ; senatus, equitis accensus favor ;
plebisque votis atque iudicio patrum
tu pacis auctor, generis humani arbiter
electus orbem iam sacra specie regis
patriae parens ; quod nomen ut serves petit   490
suosque cives Roma commendat tibi.

NERO

Munus deorum est, ipsa quod servit mihi
Roma et senatus quodque ab invitis preces
humilesque voces exprimit nostri metus.
servare cives principi et patriae graves.
claro tumentes genere—quae dementia est,
cum liceat una voce suspectos sibi
mori iubere ? Brutus in caedem ducis,
a quo salutem tulerat, armavit manus ;
invictus acie, gentium domitor, Iovi   500
aequatus altos ipse per honorum gradus
Caesar nefando civium scelere occidit.
quantum cruoris Roma tum vidit sui,
lacerata totiens ! ille qui meruit pia
virtute caelum, divus Augustus, viros

to abstain from cruel bloodshed, to be slow to wrath, give quiet to the world, peace to one's time. This is virtue's crown, by this way is heaven sought. So did that first Augustus, his country's father, gain the stars, and is worshipped in the temples as a god. Yet him did Fortune toss for long on land and sea in battle's deadly chances, until his father's foes he overwhelmed. But to thee hath she yielded her divinity, unstained of blood; hath with easy hand given thee the reins of government, and to thy nod subjected lands and seas. Sour hate, o'ercome, hath yielded in loyal harmony; the senate's favour and the knights' is warm toward thee; and by the people's prayers and the judgment of the Fathers, thou art the source of peace, the arbiter of human destinies, chosen to rule the world with godlike mien, the country's father. This name Rome prays thee to preserve, and to thy care commends her citizens.

NERO

'Tis the gift of heaven that Rome herself and the senate are subject unto me, and that from unwilling lips prayers and servile words are extorted by fear of me. To preserve citizens, to ruler and father-land alike oppressive, puffed up with pride of race— what folly is't, when with a word one may give to death those he suspects? Brutus for the murder of his chief, to whom he owed his safety, armed his hands; and Caesar, invincible in battle shock, tamer of nations, walking, a very Jove, along the upward path of honours, died by the unspeakable crime of *citizens*. What streams of her own blood did Rome then behold, so often rent with strife! He who earned heaven by piety, the deified Augustus, how

449

quot interemit nobiles, iuvenes senes
sparsos per orbem, cum suos mortis metu
fugerent penates et trium ferrum ducum,
tabula notante deditos tristi neci !
exposita rostris capita caesorum patres   510
videre maesti, flere nec licuit suos,
non gemere dira tabe polluto foro,
stillante sanie per putres vultus gravi.
nec finis hic cruoris aut caedis stetit :
pavere volucres et feras saevas diu
tristes Philippi, hausit et Siculum mare
classes virosque [1] saepe cedentes ; suis
concussus orbis viribus.   magnus ducum
superatus acie, puppibus Nilum petit
fugae paratis, ipse periturus brevi ;   520
hausit cruorem incesta Romani ducis
Aegyptus iterum ; nunc leves umbras tegit.
illic sepultum est impie gestum diu
civile bellum.   condidit tandem suos
iam fessus enses victor hebetatos feris
vulneribus, et continuit imperium metus.
armis fideque militis tutus fuit,
pietate nati factus eximia deus,
post fata consecratus et templis datus.
nos quoque manebunt astra, si saevo prior   530
ense occuparo quidquid infestum est mihi
dignaque nostram subole fundaro domum.

---

[1] *The text here is hopelessly corrupt and has been variously
emended.   Schroeder's emendation is at least intelligible.   Leo
reads*

            saepe cedentes suos
      concussus orbis viribus magnus ducum
      superatus, *etc.*

many nobles did he put to death, young men and old,
scattered throughout the world, when they fled their
own homes through fear of death and the sword of
the three banded chiefs [1]—all by the accusing list [2]
delivered to grim destruction! The grieving fathers
saw the heads of the slain set out upon the rostra,
but dared not weep their dead nor groan, while the
forum reeked with foul corruption, and sluggish gore
dripped down the rotting faces. Nor was this the
end of slaughter and of blood : long did grim Philippi
feed birds and beasts of prey, and the Sicilian sea
engulfed fleets and men often retreating ; the world [3]
was shaken by its own contending forces. The great [4]
commander, by the leaders' array o'ercome, with his
ships prepared for flight, hied him to the Nile, himself doomed soon to perish ; incestuous [5] Egypt a
second [6] time drank a Roman leader's blood, and
now covers his flitting shade. There civil strife is
buried, waged impiously and long. At last the
victor [7] now weary, sheathed his sword, blunted with
savage blows, and maintained his sway by fear. Safe
under the protection of his loyal guards he lived, and
when he died, by the surpassing piety of his son [8]
was made a god, hallowed and enshrined. Me, too,
shall the stars await, if with relentless sword I first
destroy whate'er is hostile to me, and on a worthy
offspring found my house.

[1] The Second Triumvirate, Lepidus, Antonius, and
Octavius.   [2] The proscription lists.
[3] *i.e.* the world of the Roman Empire.
[4] Evidently referring to Marcus Antonius, as the context
shows.
[5] Because of the marriage of Cleopatra with her brother,
Ptolemy.
[6] The implied first was Cn. Pompeius.   [7] Octavius.
[8] Tiberius, the adopted son of Augustus.

SENECA

Implebit aulam stirpe caelesti tuam
generata divo Claudiae gentis decus,
sortita fratris more Iunonis toros.

NERO

Incesta genetrix detrahit generi fidem,
animusque numquam coniugis iunctus mihi.

SENECA

Teneris in annis haud satis clarus ferest,[1]
pudore victus cum tegit flammas, amor.

NERO

Hoc equidem et ipse credidi frustra diu,   540
manifesta quamvis pectore insociabili
vultuque signa proderent odium mei ;
tandem quod ardens statuit ulcisci dolor.
dignamque thalamis coniugem inveni meis
genere atque forma, victa cui cedat Venus
Iovisque coniunx et ferox armis dea.

SENECA

Probitas fidesque coniugis, mores pudor
placeant marito ; sola perpetuo manent
subiecta nulli mentis atque animi bona ;
florem decoris singuli carpunt dies.   550

NERO

Omnes in unam contulit laudes deus
talemque nasci fata voluerunt mihi.

---

[1] clara est fides *A, emended by Leo, and with reason, for
the* fides *of line 536 is not in question, but the* amor *implicit in
line 537.*

OCTAVIA

With stock celestial will she [1] fill thy halls, she,
the daughter of a god,[2] the Claudian race's glory,
who has, like Juno, gained her brother's bed.

NERO

A harlot mother [3] brings her birth in doubt;—
and the soul of my wife was never linked with mine.

SENECA

In tender years rarely is love revealed, when, by
modesty o'ercome, it hides its fires.

NERO

This truly I, too, myself have vainly trusted long,
although clear signs from her unloving heart and
face betrayed her hate of me; which to avenge at
last my hot grief has resolved. And now I have
found a wife worthy of my bed in birth and beauty, to
whom Venus, outshone, would yield, and the wife of
Jove and the goddess [4] bold in battle.

SENECA

But honour, wifely faith, virtue and modesty,
should please a husband; for 'tis these only, the
treasures of mind and heart, that, subject to none,
abide perpetual; but beauty's flower each passing
day despoils.

NERO

All charms upon one woman has God bestowed,
and such was she born,—so have the fates decreed,—
for me.

[1] Octavia.
[2] Claudius, by courtesy and custom called *divus* after
death.   [3] Messalina.   [4] Minerva.

SENECA

Recedet a te (temere ne credas) amor.

NERO

Quem summovere fulminis dominus nequit,
caeli tyrannum, saeva qui penetrat freta
Ditisque regna, detrahit superos polo?

SENECA

Volucrem esse Amorem fingit immitem deum
mortalis error, armat et telis manus
arcuque sacras, instruit saeva face
genitumque credit Venere, Vulcano satum.   560
vis magna mentis blandus atque animi calor
Amor est; iuventa gignitur, luxu otio
nutritur inter laeta Fortunae bona;
quem si fovere atque alere desistas, cadit
brevique vires perdit extinctus suas.

NERO

Hanc esse vitae maximam causam reor,
per quam voluptas oritur; interitu caret,
cum procreetur semper humanum genus
Amore grato, qui truces mulcet feras.
hic mihi iugales praeferat taedas deus   570
iungatque nostris igne Poppaeam toris.

SENECA

Vix sustinere possit hos thalamos dolor
videre populi, sancta nec pietas sinat.

NERO

Prohibebor unus facere quod cunctis licet?

454

OCTAVIA

SENECA

Love will depart from thee, be not too credulous.

NERO

What? He whom the lightning's lord cannot put off? Heaven's tyrant, who enters the savage seas and the realm of Dis, and draws gods from the sky?

SENECA

'Tis our human ignorance fashions Love a winged god, implacable, and arms with shafts and bow his sacred hands, equips him with blazing torch, and counts him the son of Venus, Vulcan's seed. This "Love" is a mighty force of mind, a fond heat of the soul; 'tis born of youth, 'tis nursed by luxury and ease midst the glad gifts of Fortune; and if thou cease to feed and foster it, it falls away and quickly is its power dead and lost.

NERO

This do I deem the chiefest source of life, whence pleasure hath its birth; 'tis a deathless thing, since the human race is evermore renewed by pleasing Love, who softens e'en savage beasts. May this god bear before me the wedding torch, and with his fire join Poppaea to my bed.

SENECA

The people's grief could scarce endure to see such marriage, nor would holy reverence allow it.

NERO

Shall I alone be forbidden what all may do?

SENECA

Maiora populus semper a summo exigit.

NERO

Libet experiri, viribus fractus meis
an cedat animis temere conceptus favor.

SENECA

Obsequere potius civibus placidus tuis.

NERO

Male imperatur, cum regit vulgus duces.

SENECA

Nihil impetrare cum valet, iuste dolet.   580

NERO

Exprimere ius est, ferre quod nequeunt preces?

SENECA

Negare durum est.

NERO

Principem cogi nefas.

SENECA

Remittat ipse.

NERO

Fama sed victum feret.

SENECA

Levis atque vana.

NERO

Sit licet, multos notat.

OCTAVIA

SENECA

Greatest from highest ever the state exacts.

NERO

Fain would I make trial whether, broken by my might, this rashly cherished regard would not vanish from their hearts.

SENECA

Bend, rather, peacefully to thy people's will.

NERO

Ill fares the state when commons govern kings.

SENECA

He justly chafes who naught avails by prayer.

NERO

Is it right to extort what prayer cannot obtain

SENECA

To refuse is harsh.

NERO

To force a prince is outrage.

SENECA

He should himself give way.

NERO

But rumour will report him conquered.

SENECA

A trivial and empty thing is rumour.

NERO

E'en so, it disgraces many.

457

SENECA

Excelsa metuit.

NERO

Non minus carpit tamen.

SENECA

Facile opprimetur.   merita te divi patris
aetasque frangat coniugis, probitas pudor.

NERO

Desiste tandem, iam gravis nimium mihi,
instare ; liceat facere quod Seneca improbat.
iam pridem et ipse vota Poppaeae moror,[1]   590
cum portet utero pignus et partem mei.
quin destinamus proximum thalamis diem ?

AGRIPPINA

Tellure rupta Tartaro gressum extuli,
Stygiam cruenta praeferens dextra facem
thalamis scelestis.   nubat his flammis meo
Poppaea nato iuncta, quas vindex manus
dolorque matris vertet ad tristes rogos.
manet inter umbras impiae caedis mihi
semper memoria, manibus nostris gravis
adhuc inultis.   reddita est meritis meis   600
funesta merces puppis et pretium imperi
nox illa qua naufragia deflevi mea ;
comitum necem natique crudelis nefas
deflere votum fuerat—haud tempus datum est

---

[1] *So Buecheler.   Leo reads* et ipse populi vota iam pridem
moror.   populi *is impossible in view of the next line.*

458

OCTAVIA

SENECA

It fears the high exalted.

NERO

But none the less maligns.

SENECA

'Twill easily be crushed. Let the merits of thy
sainted father [1] break thy will,[2] and thy wife's youth,
her faith, her chastity.

NERO

Have done at last; already too wearisome has thy
insistence grown; permit me to do what Seneca
disapproves. Long since am I myself Poppaea's
prayers delaying, since in her womb she bears a
pledge and part of me. Why not appoint to-morrow
for the wedding day? [*Exeunt.*

[*Enter Ghost of* AGRIPPINA *bearing a flaming torch.*]

AGRIPPINA

Through the rent earth from Tartarus have I come
forth, bringing in bloody hand a Stygian torch to
these curst marriage rites. With these flames let
Poppaea wed my son, which a mother's avenging
hand and grief shall turn to grim funeral pyres.
Ever amidst the shades the memory of my impious
murder abides with me, burdening my ghost still
unavenged. The payment I received for all my
services was that death-fraught ship, and the reward
of empire, that night wherein I mourned my wreck.
My comrades' murder and my son's heartless
crime I would have wept—no time was given for

---

[1] *i.e.* his adoptive father, Claudius.
[2] In the matter of Poppaea.

lacrimis, sed ingens scelere geminavit nefas.
perempta ferro, foeda vulneribus sacros
intra penates spiritum effudi gravem
erepta pelago, sanguine extinxi meo
nec odia nati.   saevit in nomen ferus
matris tyrannus, obrui meritum cupit,   610
simulacra, titulos destruit mortis [1] metu
totum per orbem quem dedit poenam in meam
puero regendum noster infelix amor.

  Extinctus umbras agitat infestus meas
flammisque vultus noxios coniunx petit,
instat, minatur, imputat fatum mihi
tumulumque nati, poscit auctorem necis.
iam parce ; dabitur, tempus haud longum peto.
ultrix Erinys impio dignum parat
letum tyranno, verbera et turpem fugam   620
poenasque quis et Tantali vincat sitim,
dirum laborem Sisyphi, Tityi alitem
Ixionisque membra rapientem rotam.
licet extruat marmoribus atque auro tegat
superbus aulam, limen armatae ducis
servent cohortes, mittat immensas opes
exhaustus orbis, supplices dextram petant
Parthi cruentam, regna divitias ferant ;
veniet dies tempusque quo reddat suis
animam nocentem sceleribus, iugulum hostibus 630
desertus ac destructus et cunctis egens.

  Heu, quo labor, quo vota ceciderunt mea ?

      [1] *So A.   Leo, following Buecheler, matris.*

---

[1] Britannicus.   [2] Nero.
[3] It is the following passage which forms the chief argu-

460

tears, but with crime he doubled that awful crime. Though saved from the sea, yet by the sword undone, loathsome with wounds, midst the holy images I gave up my troubled ghost. Still my blood quenched not the hatred of my son. Rages the mad tyrant against his mother's name, longs to blot out her merits; my statues, my inscriptions he destroys by threat of death throughout the world—the world which, to my own punishment, my ill-starred love gave to a boy's government.

[*She seems to see her husband's ghost.*]

614 Wrathfully doth my dead husband harass my ghost, and with torches attacks my guilty face; pursues me, threatens, charges to me his death and his son's[1] burial mound, demands the author[2] of the murderous deed. Have done; he shall be given; 'tis no long time I seek. The avenging Fury plans for the impious tyrant a worthy doom[3]; blows and base flight and sufferings whereby he may surpass e'en Tantalus' thirst, the dread toil of Sisyphus, the bird of Tityus and the wheel which whirls Ixion's limbs around. Though in his pride he build him marble palaces and roof them in with gold, though armed guards stand at their chieftain's door, though the beggared world send him its boundless riches, though Parthians in suppliance seek his bloody hand, though kingdoms bring wealth to him; the day and the hour will come when for his crimes he shall pay his guilty soul, shall give his throat to his enemies, abandoned and undone and stripped of all.

632 Alas! to what end my labour and my prayers?

ment of those who deny the Senecan authorship of this play, on the ground that it gives in the form of prophecy a circumstantial account of the death of Nero, in 68 A.D., whereas Seneca died in 65.

quo te furor provexit attonitum tuus
et fata, nate, cedat ut tantis malis
genetricis ira quae tuo scelere occidit ?
utinam antequam te parvulum in lucem edidi
aluique, saevae nostra lacerassent ferae
viscera ; sine ullo scelere, sine sensu innocens
meus occidisses ; iunctus atque haerens mihi
semper quietam cerneres sedem inferum,   640
proavos patremque, nominis magni viros,
quos nunc pudor luctusque perpetuus manet
ex te, nefande, meque quae talem tuli.
quid tegere cesso Tartaro vultus meos,
noverca coniunx mater infelix meis ?

OCTAVIA

 Parcite lacrimis urbis festo
laetoque die, ne tantus amor
nostrique favor principis acres
suscitet iras vobisque ego sim
causa malorum. non hoc primum 650
pectora vulnus mea senserunt ;
graviora tuli ; dabit hic nostris
finem curis vel morte dies.
non ego saevi cernere cogar
coniugis ora,
non invisos intrare mihi
thalamos famulae ;
soror Augusti, non uxor ero.
absint tantum tristes poenae
letique metus. 660
scelerum diri, miseranda, viri
potes hoc demens sperare memor ?
hos ad thalamos servata diu

462

OCTAVIA

Hath thy frenzy carried thee so far in madness, and
thy destiny, my son, that the wrath of a mother
murdered by thy hand gives way before such woes?
Would that, ere I brought thee, a tiny babe, to light,
and suckled thee, savage beasts of prey had rent
my vitals; then without crime, without sense and
innocent, thou wouldst have died—my own; close
clinging to my side, thou wouldst forever see the
quiet seats of the underworld, thy grandsires and
thy sire, heroes of glorious name, whom now shame
and grief perpetual await because of thee, thou
monster, and of me who bore such son. But why
delay to hide my face in Tartarus, as step-dame,
mother, wife, a curse unto my own?

[*The Ghost vanishes. Enter* OCTAVIA.]

OCTAVIA [*to the Chorus*]

Restrain your tears on this glad, festal day of
Rome, lest your great love and care for me arouse
the emperor's sharp wrath, and I be cause of
suffering to you. This wound [1] is not the first my
heart has felt; far heavier have I borne; but this
day shall end my cares e'en by my death. No more
shall I be forced to look on my brutal husband's face,
nor to enter a slave's chamber which I hate;
Augustus' sister shall I be, not wife. Only may I
be spared dire punishments and fearful death.—
And canst thou, poor, foolish girl, remembering thy
cruel husband's crimes, yet hope for this? Long
kept back for this marriage-festival, thou shalt fall

---

[1] *i.e.* her divorce and disgrace.

victima tandem funesta cades.
sed quid patrios saepe penates
respicis udis confusa genis?
propera tectis efferre gradus,
linque cruentam principis aulam.

CHORVS

En illuxit suspecta diu,
fama totiens iactata dies.   670
cessit thalamis Claudia diri
pulsa Neronis, quo iam victrix
Poppaea tenet, cessat pietas
dum nostra gravi compressa metu
segnisque dolor.
ubi Romani vis est populi,
fregit claros quae saepe duces,
dedit invictae leges patriae,
fasces dignis civibus olim,
iussit bellum pacemque, feras   680
gentes domuit,
captos reges carcere clausit?
gravis en oculis undique nostris
iam Poppaeae fulget imago,
iuncta Neroni!
affligat humo violenta manus
similes nimium vultus dominae
ipsamque toris detrahat altis,
petat infestis mox et flammis
telisque feris principis aulam.

NVTRIX POPPAEAE

Quo trepida gressum coniugis thalamis tui   690
effers, alumna, quidve secretum petis

---

[1] *i.e.* Octavia.

at last, an ill-starred victim. But why so often to thy father's house dost look back with streaming eyes? Haste thee to leave this roof; abandon the blood-stained palace of the emperor.   [*Exit.*

CHORUS

Lo, now has dawned the day long dim foreseen, so oft by rumour bruited. Departed is Claudia[1] from cruel Nero's chamber, which e'en now Poppaea holds in triumph, while lags our love by grievous fear repressed, and grief is numb. Where is the Roman people's manhood now, which oft in olden times hath crushed illustrious chiefs, given laws to an unconquered land,[2] the fasces to worthy citizens, made war and peace at will, conquered wild races and imprisoned captive kings? Lo, grievous to our sight, on every hand now gleams Poppaea's image, with Nero's joined! Let violent hands throw them to the ground, too like their mistress' features; let them drag her down from her lofty couch, and then with devouring flames and savage spears attack the palace of the emperor.   [*Exit* CHORUS.

[*Enter* POPPAEA'S NURSE *and* POPPAEA *herself, who appears, distraught, coming out of her chamber.*]

NURSE

Whither, dear child, dost pass all trembling from the chamber of thy lord, or what hidden place seekst

[2] *i.e.* withstood all outside enemies and righteously ruled within the father-land.

turbata vultu ?   cur genae fletu madent ?
certe petitus precibus et votis dies
nostris refulsit ; Caesari iuncta es tuo
taeda iugali, quem tuus cepit decor,
contempta [1] Senecae tradidit vinctum tibi
genetrix Amoris, maximum numen, Venus.
o qualis altos quanta pressisti toros
residens in aula !   vidit attonitus tuam
formam senatus, tura cum superis dares   700
sacrasque grato spargeres aras mero,
velata summum flammeo tenui caput ;
et ipse lateri iunctus atque haerens tuo
sublimis inter civium laeta omina
incessit habitu atque ore laetitiam gerens
princeps superbo.   talis emersam freto
spumante Peleus coniugem accepit Thetin,
quorum toros celebrasse caelestes ferunt,
pelagique numen omne consensu pari.
quae subita vultus causa mutavit tuos ?   710
quid pallor iste, quid ferant lacrimae doce.

POPPAEA

Confusa tristi proximae noctis metu
visuque, nutrix, mente turbata feror,
defecta sensu.   laeta nam postquam dies
sideribus atris cessit et nocti polus,
inter Neronis iuncta complexus mei
somno resolvor ; nec diu placida frui
quiete licuit.   visa nam thalamos meos
celebrare turba est maesta ; resolutis comis
matres Latinae flebiles planctus dabant ;   720
inter tubarum saepe terribilem sonum
sparsam cruore coniugis genetrix mei
vultu minaci saeva quatiebat facem.

---

[1] et culpa Senecae *A*, *variously emended : by Leo as above.*

466

thou with troubled face? Why are thy cheeks wet
with weeping? Surely the day sought by our prayers
and vows has dawned; to thy Caesar art thou joined
by the marriage torch, him whom thy beauty snared,
whom Venus hath delivered in bonds to thee, Venus,
of Seneca flouted, mother of Love, most mighty
deity. Oh, how beautiful and stately wast thou on
the high couch reclining in the hall! The senate
looked on thy beauty in amaze, when incense to the
gods thou offeredst and with pleasing wine didst
sprinkle the sacred shrines, thy head covered with
filmy marriage-veil, flame-coloured. And close beside
thee, majestic midst the favouring plaudits of the
citizens, walked the prince himself, showing, in look
and bearing, his joy and pride. So did Peleus take
Thetis for his bride, risen up from Ocean's foam,
to whose marriage, they say, the heaven-dwellers
thronged, and with equal joy each sea divinity.
What cause so suddenly has changed thy face?
Tell me what mean thy pallor and thy tears.

POPPAEA

My sad heart, dear nurse, is confused and troubled
by a fearful vision of yester-night, and my senses
reel. For, after joyful day had to the dark stars
yielded, and the sky to night, held close in my Nero's
arms I lay relaxed in slumber. But not long was it
granted to enjoy sweet rest; for my marriage chamber
seemed thronged with many mourners; with streaming hair did Roman matrons come, making tearful
lamentations; midst oft repeated and fearful trumpet
blasts, my husband's mother,[1] with threatening mien
and savage, brandished a blood-spattered torch.

---

[1] Agrippina.

quam dum sequor coacta praesenti metu,
diducta subito patuit ingenti mihi
tellus hiatu ; lata quo praeceps toros
cerno iugales pariter et miror meos,
in quis residi fessa.   venientem intuor
comitante turba coniugem quondam meum
natumque ; properat petere complexus meos   730
Crispinus, intermissa libare oscula ;
irrupit intra tecta cum trepidus mea
ensemque iugulo condidit saevum Nero.
tandem quietem magnus excussit timor ;
quatit ossa et artus horridus nostros tremor
pulsatque pectus ; continet vocem timor,
quam nunc fides pietasque produxit tua.
heu quid minantur inferum manes mihi
aut quem cruorem coniugis vidi mei ?

NVTRIX

Quaecumque mentis agitat intentus [1] vigor   740
ea per quietem sacer et arcanus refert
veloxque sensus.   coniugem thalamos toros
vidisse te miraris amplexu novi
haerens mariti ?   sed movent laeto die
pulsata palmis pectora et fusae comae ?
Octaviae discidia planxerunt sacros
inter penates fratris et patrium larem.
fax illa, quam secuta es, Augustae manu
praelata clarum nomen invidia tibi
partum ominatur.   inferum sedes toros   750
stabiles futuros spondet aeternae domus.
iugulo quod ensem condidit princeps tuus,
bella haud movebit, pace sed ferrum teget.

----

[1] *So Gronovius : Leo, with A,* infestus.

----

[1] Crispinus.

While I was following her, driven by urgent fear,
suddenly the earth yawned beneath me in a mighty
chasm. Downward through this I plunged and there,
as on earth, beheld my wedding-couch, wondering
to behold it, whereon I sank in utter weariness. I
saw approaching, with a throng around him, my
former husband[1] and my son.[2] Crispinus[3] hastened
to take me in his arms, to kiss me as long ago; when
hurriedly into my chamber Nero burst and buried
his savage sword in the other's throat. At length a
mighty fear roused me from slumber; my bones and
limbs shook with a violent trembling; my heart beat
wildly; fear checked my utterance, which now thy
love and loyalty have restored to me. Alas! What
do the spirits of the dead threaten me, or what means
the blood of my husband that I saw?

NURSE

Whate'er the mind's waking vigour eagerly pursues, a mysterious, secret sense, swift working, brings
back in sleep. Dost marvel that thou didst behold
husband and marriage-bed, held fast in thy new
lord's arms? But do hands beating breasts and
streaming hair on a day of joy trouble thee? 'Twas
Octavia's divorce they mourned midst her brother's
sacred gods and her father's house. That torch
which thou didst follow, borne in Augusta's[4] hand,
foretells the name that thou shall gain illumed by
envy. Thy abode in the lower world[5] promises the
stablished marriage-bed of a home unending. Whereas thine emperor buried his sword in that other's
throat, wars shall he not wage, but in peace shall

[2] Rufrius Crispinus. For his fate, see Index.
[3] *i.e.* her husband.   [4] *i.e.* Agrippina's.
[5] Since in that world all things are changeless.

469

recollige animum, recipe laetitiam, precor,
timore pulso redde te thalamis tuis.

POPPAEA

Delubra et aras petere constitui sacras,
caesis litare victimis numen deum,
ut expientur noctis et somni minae
terrorque in hostes redeat attonitus meos.
tu vota pro me suscipe et precibus piis   760
superos adora, maneat ut praesens status.

CHORVS

Si vera loquax fama Tonantis
furta et gratos narrat amores
(quem modo Ledae pressisse sinum
tectum plumis pennisque ferunt,
modo per fluctus raptam Europen
taurum tergo portasse trucem),
quae regit et nunc deseret astra,
petet amplexus, Poppaea, tuos,
quos et Ledae praeferre potest   770
et tibi, quondam cui miranti
fulvo, Danae, fluxit in auro.
formam Sparte iactet alumnae
licet et Phrygius praemia pastor
vincet vultus haec Tyndaridos
qui moverunt horrida bella
Phrygiaeque solo regna dedere.
Sed quis gressu ruit attonito
aut quid portat pectore anhelo?

NVNTIVS

Quicumque tectis excubat miles ducis,   780
defendat aulam cui furor populi imminet.

sheathe his sword. Take heart again, recall thy
joy, I pray; banish thy fear and return thee to thy
chamber.

POPPAEA

Rather am I resolved to seek the shrines and
sacred altars, and with slain victims sacrifice to the
holy gods, that the threats of night and sleep may be
averted, and that my crazed terror may turn against
my foes. Do thou make vows for me and with pious
prayers implore the gods of heaven that my present
lot may be abiding. [*Exeunt.*

CHORUS [*of Roman women in sympathy with* POPPAEA]

If truly speaks babbling rumour of the Thunderer's
sweet stolen loves, (who now, they say, in feathery
plumage hid, held Leda in his embrace, now over
the waves, in fierce bull-form, the stolen Europa
bore,) e'en now will he desert the stars o'er which
he rules and seek thy arms, Poppaea, which even to
Leda's he might prefer, and to thine, O Danaë,
before whose wondering eyes in olden time he
poured down in yellow gold. Let Sparta vaunt the
beauty of her daughter,[1] and let the Phrygian
shepherd[2] vaunt his prize; she[3] will outshine the
face of Tyndaris,[4] which set dread war on foot and
levelled Phrygia's kingdom with the ground.

778 But who comes running with excited steps?
What tidings bears he in his heaving breast?

[*Enter* MESSENGER.]

MESSENGER

Whatever guard holds watch o'er our leader's
house, let it defend the palace which the people's

---

[1] Helen.   [2] Paris.   [3] Poppaea.   [4] Helen.

471

trepidi cohortes ecce praefecti trahunt
praesidia ad urbis, victa nec cedit metu
concepta rabies temere, sed vires capit.

CHORUS

Quis iste mentes agitat attonitus furor?

NVNTIVS

Octaviae favore percussa agmina
et efferata per nefas ingens ruunt.

CHORVS

Quid ausa facere quove consilio doce.

NVNTIVS

Reddere penates Claudiae divi parant
torosque fratris, debitam partem imperi.   790

CHORVS

Quos iam tenet Poppaea concordi fide?

NVNTIVS

Hic urit animos pertinax nimium favor
et in furorem temere praecipites agit.
quaecumque claro marmore effigies stetit
aut aere fulgens, ora Poppaeae gerens,
afflicta vulgi manibus et saevo iacet
eversa ferro; membra per partes trahunt
deducta laqueis, obruunt turpi diu
calcata caeno.   verba conveniunt feris
immixta factis quae timor reticet meus.   800
sepire flammis principis sedem parant,

fury threatens. See, in trembling haste the captains
are bringing cohorts to defend the town; nor does
the mob's madness, rashly roused, give place, o'ercome with fear, but gathers strength.

CHORUS

What is that wild frenzy which stirs their hearts?

MESSENGER

Smitten with love for Octavia and beside themselves with rage, the throngs rush on, in mood for
any crime.

CHORUS

What do they dare to do, or what is their plan,
tell thou.

MESSENGER

They plan to give back to Claudia [1] her dead father's
house, her brother's bed and her due share of empire.

CHORUS

Which even now Poppaea shares with her lord in
mutual loyalty?

MESSENGER

'Tis this too stubborn love [2] that inflames their
minds and into rash madness drives them headlong.
Whatever statue was set up of noble marble or of
gleaming bronze, which bore the features of Poppaea,
lies low, cast down by base-born hands and by
relentless bars o'erturned; the limbs, pulled down by
ropes, they drag piecemeal, trample them o'er and
o'er and cover them with foul mud. Commingled
curses match their savage acts, which I am afraid to
tell of. They make ready to hem the emperor's

---

[1] Octavia. [2] *i.e.* for Octavia.

populi nisi irae coniugem reddat novam,
reddat penates Claudiae victus suos.
ut noscat ipse civium motus, mea
voce haud morabor iussa praefecti exequi.

CHORVS

Quid fera frustra bella movetis?
invicta gerit tela Cupido ;
flammis vestros obruet ignes
quibus extinxit fulmina saepe
captumque Iovem caelo traxit.   810
laeso tristes dabitis poenas
sanguine vestro.   non est patiens
fervidus irae facilisque regi ;
lle ferocem iussit Achillem
pulsare lyram, fregit Danaos,
fregit Atridem, regna evertit
Priami, claras diruit urbes ;
et nunc animus quid ferat horret
vis immitis violenta dei.

NERO

O lenta nimium militis nostri manus   820
et ira patiens post nefas tantum mea,
quod non cruor civilis accensas faces
extinguit in nos, caede nec populi madet
funerea Roma quae viros tales tulit.   824 [1]
at illa, cui me civium subicit furor,   827
suspecta coniunx et soror semper mihi,
tandem dolori spiritum reddat meo
iramque nostram sanguine extinguat suo.   830
admissa sed iam morte puniri parum est.
graviora meruit impium plebis scelus ;

 [1] *The inverted order of the following lines is that of Richter.*

474

house with flames should he not yield to the people's wrath his new-made bride, not yield to Claudia the home that is her own. That he himself may know of the citizens' uprising, with my own lips will I hasten to perform the prefect's bidding. [*Exit.*

CHORUS

Why do you stir up dire strife in vain? Invincible the shafts that Cupid bears; with his own flames will he o'erwhelm your fires, with which he oft has quenched thunderbolts and dragged Jove as his captive from the sky. To the offended god [1] dire penalties shall you pay e'en with your blood. Not slow to wrath is the glowing boy, nor easy to be ruled; 'twas he who bade the fierce Achilles smite the lyre, broke down the Greeks, broke down Atrides, the kingdoms of Priam overthrew, and famed cities utterly destroyed; and now my mind shudders at the thought of what the unchecked power of the relentless god will do.

[*Enter* NERO.]

NERO

Oh, too slow are my soldiers' hands, and too patient my wrath after such sacrilege as this, seeing that the blood of citizens has not quenched the fires they kindled 'gainst me, and that with the slaughter of her people mourning Rome reeks not, who bore such men as these. But she for whose sake the citizens rage at me, my sister-wife whom with distrust I ever look upon, shall give her life at last to sate my grief, and quench my anger with her blood. But now death is too light a punishment for her deeds. Heavier doom has the people's unhallowed

[1] Cupid.

mox tecta flammis concidant urbis meis,   831
ignes ruinae noxium populum premant
turpisque egestas, saeva cum luctu fames.
exsultat ingens saeculi nostri bonis
corrupta turba nec capit clementiam
ingrata nostram ferre nec pacem potest,
sed inquieta rapitur hinc audacia,
hinc temeritate fertur in praeceps sua.
malis domanda est et gravi semper iugo
premenda, ne quid simile temptare audeat   840
contraque sanctos coniugis vultus meae
attollere oculos ; fracta per poenas metu
parere discet principis nutu sui.
   Sed adesse cerno rara quem pietas virum
fidesque castris nota praeposuit meis.

PRAEFECTVS

Populi furorem caede paucorum, diu
qui restiterunt temere, compressum affero.

NERO

Et hoc sat est ?   sic miles audisti ducem ?
compescis ? haec vindicta debetur mihi ?

PRAEFECTVS

Cecidere motus impii ferro duces.   850

NERO

Quid illa turba, petere quae flammis meos
ausa est penates, principi legem dare,
476

guilt deserved. Quickly let Rome's roofs fall beneath my flames; let fires, let ruins crush the guilty populace, and wretched want, and grief and hunger dire. The huge mob grows riotous, distempered by the blessings of my age, nor hath it understanding of my mercy in its thanklessness nor can it suffer peace; but here 'tis swept along by restless insolence and there by its own recklessness is headlong borne. By suffering must it be held in check, be ever pressed beneath the heavy yoke, that it may never dare the like again, and against my wife's sacred countenance lift its eyes; crushed by the fear of punishment, it shall be taught to obey its emperor's nod.

844 But here I see the man whose rare loyalty and proven faith have made him captain of my royal guards.

[*Enter* PREFECT.]

PREFECT

The people's rage by slaughter of some few, who recklessly long resisted, is put down: such is my report.

NERO

And is this enough? Is't thus a soldier has obeyed his chief? "Put down," sayst thou? Is this the vengeance due to me?

PREFECT

The guilty ring-leaders of the mob have fallen by the sword.

NERO

But the mob itself, that dared to attack my household with their torches, dictate to the emperor, from

abstrahere nostris coniugem tantam toris,
violare quantum licuit incesta manu
et voce dira? debita poena vacat?

PRAEFECTVS

Poenam dolor constituet in cives tuos ?

NERO

Constituet, aetas nulla quam famae eximat.

PRAEFECTVS

Quam[1] temperet non ira, non noster timor ?

NERO

Iram expiabit prima quae meruit meam.

PRAEFECTVS

Quam poscat ede, nostra ne parcat manus.   860

NERO

Caedem sororis poscit et dirum caput.

PRAEFECTVS

Horrore vinctum trepidus astrinxit rigor.

NERO

Parere dubitas ?

PRAEFECTVS

Cur meam damnas fidem ?

NERO

Quod parcis hosti.

     [1] *Reading with Schroeder.   Leo* tua . . . nos.

my very bed to drag my noble wife, to offer her violence, so far as lay in their power, with hands unclean and voices insolent? Are they still without due punishment?

PREFECT

Shall angry grief determine penalty against thy citizens?

NERO

It shall determine, the tale of which no age shall banish from men's lips.

PREFECT

Which neither wrath nor fear of us can hold in check?

NERO

She first shall appease who has first deserved my wrath.

PREFECT

Whom it demands tell thou, that my hand may spare not.

NERO

The slaughter of my sister it demands, and her hateful head.

PREFECT

Fearful, benumbing horror holds me fast.

NERO

Does thy obedience falter?

PREFECT

Why dost condemn my faith?

NERO

Because thou spar'st my foe.

479

PRAEFECTVS

Femina hoc nomen capit ?

NERO

Si scelera cepit.

PRAEFECTVS

Estne qui sontem arguat ?

NERO

Populi furor.

PRAEFECTVS

Quis regere dementes valet ?

NERO

Qui concitare potuit.

PRAEFECTVS

Haud quemquam reor.

NERO

Mulier, dedit natura cui pronum malo
animum, ad nocendum pectus instruxit dolis.

PRAEFECTVS

Sed vim negavit.

NERO

           Vt ne inexpugnabilis   870
esset, sed aegras frangeret vires timor
vel poena ; quae iam sera damnatam premet
diu nocentem.
         Tolle consilium ac preces
et imperata perage : devectam rate
480

OCTAVIA

PREFECT

       Call'st thou a woman foe?

NERO

If crime she has committed.

PREFECT

       Who charges her with guilt?

NERO

The people's rage.

PREFECT

       But who can check their madness?

NERO

She who could rouse it.

PREFECT

       Not any one, I think.

NERO

Woman, to whom nature has given a mind to mischief prone, and equipped her heart with wiles to work us ill.

PREFECT

But strength it has denied her.

NERO

That so she might not be impregnable, but that fear or punishment might break her feeble strength, a punishment which now, though late, shall crush the criminal, who has too long been guilty.
873 But have done with advice and prayers, and do my bidding: let her be borne by ship to some far

481

procul in remotum litus interimi iube,
tandem ut residat pectoris nostri timor.

CHORVS

O funestus multis populi
dirusque favor, qui cum flatu
vela secundo ratis implevit
vexitque procul, languidus idem   880
deserit alto saevoque mari.
flevit Gracchos miseranda parens,
perdidit ingens quos plebis amor
nimiusque favor genere illustres,
pietate fide lingua claros,
pectore fortes, legibus acres.
te quoque, Livi, simili leto
Fortuna dedit, quem neque fasces
texere suae nec tecta domus.
plura referre prohibet praesens   890
exempla dolor.   modo cui patriam
reddere cives aulam et fratris
voluere toros, nunc ad poenam
letumque trahi flentem miseram
cernere possunt.   bene paupertas
humili tecto contenta latet ;
quatiunt altas saepe procellae
aut evertit Fortuna domos.

OCTAVIA

Quo me trahitis quodve tyrannus
aut exilium regina iubet,   900
si mihi vitam fracta remittit
tot iam nostris et victa malis ?
sin caede mea cumulare parat
luctus nostros, invidet etiam

482

distant shore and there be slain, that at last the terror at my heart may be at rest.   [*Exeunt.*

Oh, dire and deadly to many has the people's favour proved, that has filled their vessels' sails with prosperous breeze and borne them out afar, then, languishing, has failed them on the deep and dangerous sea.   The wretched mother [1] of the Gracchi wept her sons, whom, though nobly born, for loyal faith and eloquence renowned, though brave in heart, keen in defence of law, the great love and excessive favour of the citizens destroyed.   Thee also, Livius, [2] to fate like theirs did fortune give, whom neither his lictors' rods nor his own house protected.   But present grief forbids us to rehearse more instances.   Her, to whom but now the citizens decreed the restoration of her father's house, her brother's bed, now may they see dragged out in tears and misery to punishment and death.   Oh, blessed poverty, content to hide beneath a lowly roof, while lofty homes the storm-blasts oft-times shatter, or fortune overthrows.

[*Enter* OCTAVIA *in the custody of the palace guards, who are dragging her roughly away.*]

OCTAVIA

Oh, whither do ye drag me ?   What exile does the tyrant or his queen ordain, if, softened and o'ercome by all my miseries, she grants me life ?   But if by death she is ready to crown my sufferings, why, cruel, does

---

[1] Cornelia.   [2] Livius Drusus.   See Index.

cur in patria mihi saeva mori ?
sed iam spes est nulla salutis—
fratris cerno miseranda ratem.
hac en cuius vecta carina
quondam genetrix, nunc et thalamis
expulsa soror miseranda vehar.   910
nullum Pietas nunc numen habet
nec sunt superi ; regnat mundo
tristis Erinys.
quis mea digne deflere potest
mala ? quae lacrimis nostris questus
reddat aedon ?   cuius pennas
utinam miserae mihi fata darent !
fugerem luctus sublata meos
penna volucri procul et coetus
hominum tristes caedemque feram   920
sola in vacuo nemore et tenui
ramo pendens querulo possem
gutture maestum fundere murmur.

CHORVS

Regitur fatis mortale genus,
nec sibi quisquam spondere potest
firmum et stabilem vitae cursum [1]
per quem casus volvit varios
semper nobis metuenda dies.
animum firment exempla tuum,
iam multa domus quae vestra tulit.   930
quid saevior est Fortuna tibi ?
    Tu mihi primum
tot natorum memoranda parens,
nata Agrippae, nurus Augusti,

---

[1] *Reading with Richter's proposed emendation. Leo with
the MSS. reads* firmum et stabile * * *per quae. The
lacuna has been variously filled and the passage variously
emended.*

she e'en grudge me death at home?   But now is no
hope of safety—ah, woe is me, I see my brother's
ship.   And lo, on that vessel on which his mother
once was borne, now, driven from his chamber, his
wretched sister, too, shall sail away.   Now Piety no
longer has divinity, nor are there any gods; grim
Fury reigns throughout the universe.   Who worthily
can lament my evil plight?   What nightingale can
match my tears with her complaints?   Whose wings
would that the fates might grant to wretched me!
Then on swift pinions borne, would I leave my
grievous troubles far behind, the dismal haunts of
men, and cruel slaughter.   There, all alone, within
some solitary wood, perched on a slender bough,
might I pour forth from plaintive throat my song
of woe.

CHORUS

Our mortal race is ruled by fate, nor may any
promise to himself that the path of life will be sure
and steadfast, along which each coming day with its
continual fears brings ever-shifting chances.   Comfort
now thy heart with the many sufferings which thine
own house has borne.   In what has fortune been
more harsh to thee?

⁹³² And thee first must I name, the mother of so
many sons, Agrippa's child,[1] Augustus'[2] daughter-

---

[1] Agrippina, (1) daughter of M. Vipsanius Agrippa and of
Julia, d. of Augustus; married Germanicus, son of Tiberius
Augustus, and bore to him nine sons.
[2] *i.e.* Tiberius.

485

Caesaris uxor, cuius nomen
clarum toto fulsit in orbe,
utero totiens enixa gravi
pignora pacis, mox exilium
verbera, saevas passa catenas,
funera, luctus, tandem letum   940
cruciata diu.   felix thalamis
Livia Drusi natisque ferum
ruit in facinus poenamque suam.
Iulia matris fata secuta est ;
post longa tamen tempora ferro
caesa est, quamvis crimine nullo.
quid non potuit quondam genetrix
tua quae rexit principis aulam
cara marito partuque potens ?
eadem famulo subiecta suo   950
cecidit diri militis ense.
quid cui licuit regnum in caelum
sperare, parens tanta Neronis ?
non funesta violata manu
remigis ante,
mox et ferro lacerata diu
saevi iacuit victima nati ?

OCTAVIA

Me quoque tristes mittit ad umbras
ferus et manes ecce tyrannus.
quid iam frustra miseranda moror ?   960
rapite ad letum quis ius in nos
Fortuna dedit.   testor superos—
quid agis, demens ? parce precari

---

[1] *i.e.* Germanicus.

[2] She was banished by Tiberius, who was jealous of the
people's favour toward her, to the island of Pandataria,
where she died three years afterward.

in-law, a Caesar's [1] wife, whose name shone bright
throughout the world, whose teeming womb brought
forth so many hostages of peace; yet thou wast
doomed to suffer exile, blows and galling chains, loss
of thy friends, and bitter grief, and at last a death of
lingering agony.[2]   And Livia,[3] blest in her Drusus'
chamber, in her sons, fell into brutal crime—and
punishment.   Julia met her mother's fate; though
after long delay, yet she was slain by the sword,
though no man called her guilty.   What power once
was thy mother's,[4] who ruled the palace of the emperor,[5] dear to her husband, and in her son [6] secure?
Yet she was made subject to her slave,[7] and fell
beneath a brutal soldier's sword.   And what of her
who might have hoped for the very throne of heaven,
the emperor's great mother?   Was she not first by
a murderous boatman's hand abused, then, mangled
by the sword, lay she not long the victim of her
cruel son?

OCTAVIA

Me also to the gloomy shades and ghosts, the
cruel tyrant, see, is sending.   Why do I now make
vain and pitiable delay?   Hurry me on to death, ye
to whose power fortune hath given me.   Witness, ye
heavenly gods—what wouldst thou, fool?   Pray not

[3] See Index.   [4] Messalina.
[5] Claudius.   [6] Britannicus.
[7] The freedman, Narcissus.

quibus invisa es numina divum.
Tartara testor
Erebique deas scelerum ultrices
et te, genitor [1] dignum tali
morte et poena.   non invisa est
mors ista mihi.
armate ratem, date vela fretis   970
ventisque petat puppis rector
Pandatariae litora terrae.

CHORVS

Lenes aurae zephyrique leves,
tectam quondam nube aetheria
qui vexistis raptam saevae
virginis aris Iphigeniam,
hanc quoque tristi procul a poena
portate, precor, templa ad Triviae.
urbe est nostra mitior Aulis
et Taurorum barbara tellus :   980
hospitis illic caede litatur
numen superum ;
civis gaudet Roma cruore.

---

[1] *Leo suggests* perde tyrannum *between* genitor *and* dignum.

OCTAVIA

to deities who scorn thee. Witness, O Tartarus, ye goddesses of Erebus who punish crime, and thou, O father : destroy the tyrant,[1] worthy such death and punishment. [*To her guards.*] I dread not the death you threaten. Put your ship in readiness, set sail upon the deep, and let your pilot speed before the winds to Pandataria's shore.

[*Exit* OCTAVIA *with her guards.*]

CHORUS

Ye gentle breezes and ye zephyrs mild, that once caught Iphigenia wrapped in an airy cloud, and bore her from the altar of the cruel maid,[2] this maiden, too, far from her dire punishment bear ye, I pray, to the shrine of Trivia. More merciful than Rome is Aulis and the Taurians' barbarous land : there by the blood of strangers are the gods appeased ; but Rome's delight is in her children's blood.

[1] Translating Leo's suggestion.   [2] Diana.

COMPARATIVE ANALYSES

OF THE TRAGEDIES IN THIS VOLUME AND THE CORRESPONDING GREEK DRAMAS

The *Phoenissae*, if, indeed, these fragments are to be considered as belonging to one play, has no direct correspondent in Greek drama ; although, in the general situations and in some details, it is similar to parts of three plays : *The Seven against Thebes* of Aeschylus, the *Oedipus at Colonus* of Sophocles, and the *Phoenician Damsels* of Euripides. The *Thyestes* is without a parallel in extant Greek drama ; and the *Octavia*, of course, stands alone.

COMPARATIVE ANALYSES

THE GREEK DRAMAS

THE *AGAMEMNON* OF AESCHYLUS

Prologue.—A watchman, stationed upon the palace roof at Argos, laments the tedium of his long and solitary task ; and prays for the time to come when, through the darkness of the night, he shall see the distant flashing of the beacon fire, and by this sign know that Troy has fallen and that Agamemnon is returning home. And suddenly he sees the gleam for which he has been waiting so long. He springs up with shouts of joy and hastens to tell the queen. At the same time he makes dark reference to that which has been going on within the palace, and which must now be hushed up.

Parode, or chorus entry.—A chorus of twelve Argive elders sings of the Trojan war, describing the omens with which the Greeks started on their mission of vengeance. They dwell especially upon the hard fate which forced Agamemnon to sacrifice his daughter. And in this they unconsciously voice one of the motives which led to the king's own death.

First episode.—Clytemnestra appears with a stately procession of torch-bearers, having set the whole city in gala attire, with sacrificial incense burning on all the altars. The chorus asks the meaning of this. Has she had news from Troy ? The queen replies that this very night she has had news, and describes at length how the signal

492

COMPARATIVE ANALYSES

SENECA'S TRAGEDIES

THE *AGAMEMNON* OF SENECA

Prologue.—The ghost of Thyestes coming from the lower regions recites the *motif* of the play : how he had been most foully dealt with by Agamemnon's father, Atreus, and how he had been promised revenge by the oracle of Apollo through his son Aegisthus, begotten of an incestuous union with his daughter.   The ghost announces that the time for his revenge is come with the return of Agamemnon from the Trojan war, and urges Aegisthus to perform his fated part.

Parode, or chorus entry.—The chorus of Argive women complains of the uncertain condition of exalted fortune, and recommends the golden mean in preference to this.

First episode.—Clytemnestra, conscious of guilt, and fearing that her returning husband will severely punish her on account of her adulterous life with Aegisthus, resolves to add crime to crime and murder Agamemnon as soon as he comes back to his home.   She is further impelled to this action by his conduct in the matter of her daughter,

493

fires had gleamed, and thus the news had leaped from height to height, all the long way from Troy to Argos,

> "And this sure proof and token now I tell thee,
>   Seeing that my lord hath sent it me from Troy."

She expresses the hope that the victors in their joy will do nothing to offend the gods and so prevent their safe return :

> " May good prevail beyond all doubtful chance !
>   For I have got the blessing of great joy."

With these words she covers up the real desires of her own false heart, while at the same time voicing the principle on which doom was to overtake the Greeks.

The chorus receives Clytemnestra's news with joy and prepares to sing praises to the gods, as the queen with her train leaves the stage.

First choral interlude.—The chorus sings in praise of Zeus, who has signally disproved the sceptic's claim that

> " The gods deign not to care for mortal men
>   By whom the grace of things inviolable
>   Is trampled under foot."

The shameful guilt of Paris is described, the woe of the wronged Menelaüs, and the response of all Greece to his cry for vengeance. But, after all, the chorus is in doubt as to whether the good news can be true—when a herald enters with fresh news.

Second episode.—The herald describes to the chorus the complete downfall of Troy, which came as a punishment for the sin of Paris and of the nation which upheld him in it. At the same time the sufferings of the Greeks during the progress of the war are not forgotten. Clytemnestra, entering, prompted by her own guilty conscience, bids the herald tell Agamemnon to hasten home, and take to him her own protestation of absolute faithfulness to him :

> " who has not broken
>   One seal of his in all this length of time."

The herald, in response to further questions of the chorus, describes the great storm which wrecked the Greek fleet upon their homeward voyage.

Iphigenia, and by his own unfaithfulness to her during his long absence. Throughout this scene the nurse vainly tries to dissuade her.

Clytemnestra is either influenced to recede from her purpose by the nurse, or else pretends to be resolved to draw back in order to test Aegisthus, who now enters. In the end, the two conspirators withdraw to plan their intended crime.

First choral interlude.—The chorus sings in praise of Apollo for the victory over Troy. To this are added the praises of Juno, Minerva, and Jove. In the end the chorus hails the approach of the herald Eurybates.

Second episode.—Eurybates announces to Clytemnestra the return and approach of Agamemnon, and describes the terrible storm which overtook the Greeks upon their homeward voyage. At the command of the queen victims are prepared for sacrifice to the gods, and a banquet for the victorious Agamemnon. At last the captive Trojan women, headed by Cassandra, are seen approaching.

THE TRAGEDIES OF SENECA

Second choral interlude.—The chorus sings of Helen as the bane of the Trojans:

> "Dire cause of strife with bloodshed in her train."

And now

> "The penalty of foul dishonour done
> To friendship's board and Zeus"

has been paid by Troy, which is likened to a man who fosters a lion's cub, which is harmless while still young, but when full grown "it shows the nature of its sires," and brings destruction to the house that sheltered it.

Third episode.—Agamemnon is seen approaching in his chariot, followed by his train of soldiers and captives. The chorus welcomes him, but with a veiled hint that all is not well in Argos. Agamemnon fittingly thanks the gods for his success and for his safe return, and promises in due time to investigate affairs at home.

Clytemnestra, now entering, in a long speech of fulsome welcome, describes the grief which she has endured for her lord's long absence in the midst of perils, and protests her own absolute faithfulness to him. She explains the absence of Orestes by saying that she has entrusted him to Strophius, king of Phocis, to be cared for in the midst of the troublous times. She concludes with the ambiguous prayer:

> "Ah, Zeus, work out for me
> All that I pray for ; let it be thy care
> To look to that thou purposest to work."

Agamemnon, after briefly referring to Cassandra and bespeaking kindly treatment for her, goes into the palace, accompanied by Clytemnestra.

Third choral interlude.—The chorus, though it sees with its own eyes that all is well with Agamemnon, that he is returned in safety to his own home, is filled with sad forebodings of some hovering evil which it cannot dispel.

Exode.—Clytemnestra returns and bids Cassandra, who still remains standing in her chariot, to join the other slaves in ministering at the altar. But Cassandra stands motionless, paying no heed to the words of the queen, who leaves the scene saying:

> "I will not bear the shame of uttering more."

COMPARATIVE ANALYSES

Second choral interlude.—A chorus of captive Trojan women sings the fate and fall of Troy; while Cassandra, seized with fits of prophetic fury, prophesies the doom that hangs over Agamemnon.

Third episode.—Agamemnon comes upon the scene, and, meeting Cassandra, is warned by her of the fate that hangs over him; but she is not believed.

Third choral interlude.—Apropos of the fall of Troy, the chorus of Argive women sing the praises of Hercules, whose arrows had been required by fate for the destruction of Troy.

Exode.—Cassandra, either standing where she can see within the palace, or else by clairvoyant power, reports the murder of Agamemnon, which is being done within.

Electra urges Orestes to flee before his mother and Aegisthus shall murder him also. Very opportunely, Strophius comes in his chariot, just returning as victor from

497

Cassandra now descends from her chariot and bursts into wild and woeful lamentations. By her peculiar clairvoyant power she foresees and declares to the chorus the death of Agamemnon at the hands of Clytemnestra and Aegisthus, as well as the manner of it; she also foretells the vengeance which Orestes is destined to work upon the murderers. Her own fate is as clearly seen and announced, as she passes through the door into the palace.

Soon the chorus hears the death-cry of Agamemnon, that he is "struck down with deadly stroke." They are faint-heartedly and with a multiplicity of counsel discussing what it is best to do, when Clytemnestra, with bloodstained garments and followed by a guard of soldiers, comes out from the palace. The corpses of Agamemnon and Cassandra are seen through the door within the palace. The queen confesses to, describes, and exults in the murder of her husband. The chorus makes elaborate lamentation for Agamemnon, and prophesies that vengeance will light on Clytemnestra. But she scorns their threatening prophecies. In the end Aegisthus enters, avowing that he has plotted this murder and has at last avenged his father, Thyestes, upon the father of Agamemnon, Atreus, who had so foully wronged Thyestes. The chorus curses him and reminds him that Orestes still lives and will surely avenge his father.

THE MAIDENS OF TRACHIN OF SOPHOCLES

Prologue.—In the courtyard of her palace in Trachin, Deianira recounts to her attendants and the chorus of Trachinian maidens how her husband had won her from the river god, Acheloüs, and how, during all these years, she has lived in fear and longing for her husband, who has been kept constantly wandering over the earth by those who hold him in their power; and even now he has been for many months absent, she knows not where.

An old servant proposes that she send her son, Hyllus, abroad to seek out his father. This the youth, who enters at this juncture, readily promises to do, especially on

COMPARATIVE ANALYSES

the Olympic games. Electra entrusts her brother to his care, and betakes her own self to the altar for protection.

Electra, after defying and denouncing her mother and Aegisthus, is dragged away to prison and torture, and Cassandra is led out to her death.

THE *HERCULES OETAEUS* OF SENECA

Prologue.—Hercules, about to sacrifice to Cenaean Jove after having conquered Eurytus, king of Oechalia, recounts at length his mighty toils on earth, and prays that now at last he may be given his proper place in heaven. He dispatches his herald, Lichas, home to Trachin, to tell the news of his triumph, and to conduct the train of captives thither.

499

K K 2

hearing from his mother that the oracle declares this is the year in which his father shall end his life,

> " Or, having this his task accomplished,
> Shall, through the coming years of all his life,
> Rejoice and prosper."

Parode, or chorus entry.—The chorus prays to Helios, the bright sun-god, for tidings of Hercules, for Deianira longs for him, and " ever nurses unforgetting dread as to her husband's paths." Hercules is tossed upon the stormy sea of life, now up, now down, but ever kept from death by some god's hands. Deianira should, therefore, be comforted :

> " For who hath known in Zeus forgetfulness
> Of those he children calls ? "

First episode.—Deianira confides to the chorus her special cause for grief : she feels a strong presentiment that Hercules is dead ; for, when he last left home, he left a tablet, as it were a will, disposing of his chattels and his lands,

> " and fixed a time,
> That when for one whole year and three months more
> He from his land was absent, then 'twas his
> Or in that self-same hour to die, or else,
> Escaping that one crisis, thenceforth live with life unvexed."

At this moment, however, a messenger enters and announces the near approach of Hercules, accompanied by his spoils of victory.

First choral interlude.—The chorus voices its exultant joy over this glad and unexpected news.

Parode, or chorus entry.—The place of the chorus entry, which should be filled by the chorus proper, composed of Aetolian maidens, is taken by the band of captive Oechalian maidens. They bewail their lot and long for death ; they dwell upon the utter desolation of their fatherland, and upon the hard-heartedness of Hercules, who has laid it waste.

Iole, their princess, joins in their lamentations, recalls the horrors of her native city's overthrow, and looks forward with dread to her captivity.

First episode.—During the interval just preceding this episode the captives have been led to Trachin ; Deianira has seen the beauty of Iole, and learned of Hercules' infatuation for her. She has by this news been thrown into a mad rage of jealousy, and takes counsel with her nurse as to how she may wreak vengeance upon her faithless husband, while the nurse vainly advises moderation.

The nurse at last suggests recourse to magic, professing herself to be proficient in these arts. This suggests to Deianira the use of that blood of Nessus which the dying centaur had commended to her as an infallible love-charm. She takes occasion to relate at length the Nessus incident. She at once acts upon her decision to use the charm ; and speedily, with the nurse's aid, a gorgeous robe is anointed with the blood, and this is sent by Lichas' hand to Hercules.

First choral interlude.—The chorus of Aetolian women, who have followed Deianira from her girlhood's home to this refuge in Trachin, now tender to her their sympathy in her present sufferings. They recall all their past intercourse with her, and assure her of their undying fidelity.

This suggests the rarity of such fidelity, especially in the courts of kings, and they discourse at large upon the sordidness and selfishness of courtiers in general. The moral of their discourse is that men should not aspire to great wealth and power, but should choose a middle course in life, which alone can bring happiness.

Second episode.—Lichas, the personal herald of Hercules, now enters, followed by Iole and a company of captive women. He explains to Deianira how Hercules had been driven on by petty persecutions to slay Iphitus, the son of Eurytus, treacherously; how he had for this been doomed by Zeus to serve Omphale, queen of Lydia, for a year; and how in revenge he has now slain Eurytus, and even now is sending home these Oechalian captives as spoil; Hercules himself is delaying yet a little while in Euboea, until he has sacrificed to Cenacan Jove.

Deianira looks in pity upon the captives, praying that their lot may never come to her or hers; and is especially drawn in sympathy to one beautiful girl, who, however, will answer no word as to her name and state.

As all are passing into the palace, the messenger detains Deianira and tells her the real truth which Lichas has withheld: that this seemingly unknown girl is Iole, daughter of Eurytus; that it was not in revenge, but for love of Iole, that Hercules destroyed her father's house, and that he is now sending her to his own home, not as his slave, but as his mistress, and rival of his wife.

Lichas, returning from the palace, on being challenged by the messenger and urged by Deianira to speak the whole truth, tells all concerning Hercules' love for Iole.

Deianira receives this revelation with seeming equanimity and acquiescence.

Second choral interlude.—The chorus briefly reverts to the battle of Acheloüs and Hercules for the hand of Deianira.

Third episode.—Deianira tells to the chorus the story of how Nessus, the centaur, had once insulted her, and for this had been slain by Hercules with one of his poisoned

COMPARATIVE ANALYSES

Second episode.—Deianira comes hurrying distractedly out of the palace, and relates her discovery as to the horrible and deadly power of the charm which she has sent to her husband.

While she is still speaking, Hyllus rushes in and cries out to his mother to flee from the wrath of Hercules, whose dreadful sufferings, after putting on the robe which his wife had sent to him, the youth describes at length. He narrates also the death of Lichas. The suffering hero is even now on his way by sea from Euboea, in a death-like swoon, and will soon arrive at Trachin.

Deianira, smitten with quick repentance, begs Jupiter to destroy her with his wrathful thunderbolts. She resolves on instant self-destruction, though Hyllus and the nurse vainly try to dissuade her, and to belittle her responsibility for the disaster ; and in the end she rushes from the scene, Hyllus following.

Second choral interlude.—The chorus, contemplating the changing fates of their prince's house, is reminded of the saying of Orpheus, "that naught for endless life is made." This leads to an extended description of Orpheus' sweet music and its power over all things, both animate and inanimate, and suggests the story of his unsuccessful attempt to regain Eurydice.

Returning to the original theme, the chorus speculates upon the time when all things shall fall into death, and chaos resume her primeval sway.

It is startled out of these thoughts by loud groans, which prove to be the outcries of Hercules, borne home to Trachin.

Third episode.—Hercules in his ravings warns Jove to look well to his heavens, since now their defender is perishing. The giants will be sure to rise again and make

arrows; how, also, the centaur in dying had given her a portion of his blood, saying this would be a charm able to restore to her her husband's wandering love. She now resolves to use this charm. She anoints a gorgeous robe with the blood which she has preserved through all these years, and bids Lichas carry this to her lord as a special gift from her. He is to wear it as he offers his sacrifices to Cenaean Jove. Lichas departs upon this mission.

another attempt upon the skies. He bitterly laments that he, who has overcome so many monsters, must die at last, slain by a woman's hand, and that woman not Juno, nor even an Amazon :

> " Ah, woe is me,
> How often have I 'scaped a glorious death !
> What honour comes from such an end as this ? "

His burning pains coming on again, he cries out in agony, and describes the abject misery and weakness that have come upon him. Are these the shoulders, the hands, the feet, that were once so strong to bear, so terrible to strike, so swift to go? He strives to apprehend and tear away the pest that is devouring him, but it is too deep-hidden in his frame. He curses the day that has seen him weep, and beseeches Jove to smite him dead with a thunderbolt.

Alcmena enters, and while she herself is full of grief, she strives to soothe and comfort her suffering son. He falls into a delirium, and thinks that he is in the heavens, looking down upon Trachin. But soon he awakes, and, realizing his pains once more, calls for the author of his misery, that he may slay her with his own hands.

Hyllus, who has just entered from the palace, now informs his father that Deianira is already dead, and by her own hand ; that it was not her fault, moreover, but by the guile of Nessus, that Hercules is being done to death. The hero recognizes in this the fulfilment of an oracle once delivered to him :

> " By the hand of one whom thou hast slain, some day,
> Victorious Hercules, shalt thou lie low."

And he comforts himself with the reflection that such an end as this is meet, for

> " Thus shall no conqueror of Hercules
> Survive to tell the tale."

He now bids Philoctetes prepare a mighty pyre on neighbouring Mount Oeta, and there take and burn his body while still alive. Hyllus he bids to take the captive princess, Iole, to wife. He calls upon his mother, Alcmena, to comfort her grief by pride in her great son's deeds on earth, and the noble fame which he has gained thereby.

THE TRAGEDIES OF SENECA

Third choral interlude.—The chorus prays for the early and safe return of Hercules from where he lingers:

> "Thence may he come, yea, come with strong desire,
>   Tempered by suasive spell
> Of that rich unguent, as the monster spake."

Fourth episode.—Deianira discovers by experiment, now that it is too late, the destructive and terrible power of the charm which she has sent, and is filled with dire forebodings as to the result.

Her lamentations are interrupted by Hyllus, who comes hurrying in; he charges his mother with the murder of his father, and curses her. He then describes the terrible sufferings that have come upon the hero through the magic robe, and how Hercules, in the madness of pain, has slain Lichas, as the immediate cause of his sufferings. He has brought his father with him from Euboea to Trachin. Deianira withdraws into the palace, without a word, in an agony of grief.

Fourth choral interlude.—The chorus recalls the old oracle that after twelve years the son of Zeus should gain rest from toil, and sees in his impending death the fulfilment of this oracle. They picture the grief of Deianira over her act, and foresee the great changes that are coming upon their prince's house.

Fifth episode.—The nurse rushes in from the palace, and tells how Deianira has slain herself with the sword, bewailing the while the sufferings which she has unwittingly brought on Hercules; and how Hyllus repents him of his harshness towards his mother, realizing that she was not to blame.

Fifth choral interlude.—The chorus pours out its grief for the double tragedy. And now it sees Hyllus and attendants bearing in the dying Hercules.

Exode.—Hercules, awaking from troubled sleep, laments the calamity that has befallen him; he chides the lands which he has helped, that now they do not hasten to his aid; and prays Hyllus to kill him with the sword, and so put him out of his misery.

506

COMPARATIVE ANALYSES

Third choral interlude.—The chorus bids all nature mourn the death of Hercules. Verily the earth is bereft of her defender, and there is no one left to whom she may turn if again harassed by monsters. They speculate upon the place of the departed Hercules. Shall he sit in judgment among the pious kings of Crete in Hades, or shall he be given a place in heaven? At least on earth he shall live in deathless gratitude and fame.

Exode.—Philoctetes enters and, in response to the questions of the nurse, describes the final scene on Oeta's top. There a mighty pyre had been built, on which Hercules joyfully took his place. There he reclined, gazing at the heavens, and praying his father, Jupiter, to take him thither, in

He denounces Deianira because she has brought suffering and destruction upon him which no foe, man or beast, has ever been able to bring. He curses his own weakness, and laments that he must weep and groan like a woman.

He marvels that his mighty frame, which for years has withstood so many monsters, his encounters with which he describes, can now be so weak and wasted. Reverting to his wife, he bids her to be brought to him that he may visit punishment upon her.

Hyllus informs his father that Deianira has died by her own hand, for grief at what she has unwittingly brought upon her dear lord. It was, indeed, through Nessus' guile that the deed was done.

Hercules, on hearing this, recognizes the fulfilment of the oracle :

> "Long since it was revealèd of my sire
>   That I should die by hand of none that live,
>   But one who, dead, had dwelt in Hades dark."

He exacts an oath of obedience from Hyllus, and then bids him take him to Mount Oeta, and there place him upon a pyre for burning. Hyllus reluctantly consents in all but the actual firing of the pyre. The next request is concerning Iole, that Hyllus should take her as his wife. This mandate he indignantly refuses to obey, but finally yields assent. And in the end Hercules is borne away to his burning, while the chorus mournfully chants its concluding comment :

> "What cometh no man may know ;
>   What is, is piteous for us,
>   Base and shameful for them
> And for him who endureth this woe,
>   Above all that live hard to bear."

compensation for his service on the earth. His prayer seemed
to be answered, and he cried aloud :

> " ' But lo, my father calls me from the sky,
>   And opens wide the gates. O sire, I come ! '
>   And as he spake his face was glorified."

He presented his famous bow and arrows to Philoctetes,
bidding him for this prize apply the torch and light the pyre,
which his friend most reluctantly did. The hero courted the
flames, and eagerly pressed into the very heart of the burning mass.

In the midst of this narrative Alcmena enters, bearing in
her bosom an urn containing the ashes of Hercules. The
burden of her lament is that so small a compass and so
pitiful an estate have come to the mighty body of her son,
which one small urn can hold. But when she thinks upon
his deeds, her thoughts fly to the opposite pole :

> " What sepulchre, O son, what tomb for thee
>   Is great enough ?   Naught save the world itself."

Then she takes up in quickened measures her funeral song
of mourning, in the midst of which the deified Hercules,
taking shape in the air above, speaks to his mother, bidding
her no longer mourn, for he has at last gained his place in
heaven.

The chorus strikes a fitting final note, that the truly brave
are not destined to the world below :

> " But when life's days are all consumed,
>   And comes the final hour, for them
>   A pathway to the gods is spread
>   By glory."

INDEX

INDEX

[References are to the lines of the Latin text. If the passage is longer than one line, only the first line is cited. Line citations to passages of especial importance to the subject under discussion are starred. The names of the characters appearing in these tragedies are printed in large capitals, with the name of the tragedy in which the character occurs following in parentheses.]

513

INDEX

AEACUS, son of Jupiter and Europa, father of Peleus; for his just rule on earth was made a judge in Hades, *H. Oet.* 1558; *H. Fur.* 734. See under JUDGES IN HADES

AEËTES, king of Colchis, son of Phoebus and Persa, father of Medea, *Med.* 210; grandeur, extent, and situation of kingdom, *ibid.* 209; its wealth, *ibid.* 483; had a wonderful robe as proof that Phoebus was his father; this Medea anoints with magic poison and sends to Creüsa, *ibid.* 570; was despoiled of realm through theft of golden fleece, *ibid.* 913

AEGEUS, see THESEUS

AEGISTHUS (*Agamemnon*), son of incestuous union of Thyestes and his daughter. His birth the result of Apollo's advice to Thyestes, *Agam.* 48, 294; recognises that the fatal day is come for which he was born, *ibid.* 226; lived in guilty union with Clytemnestra, wife of Agamemnon, *ibid. passim*

AEGOCEROS, poetical expression for *Capricornus*, constellation of the Goat, *Thy.* 864

AEGYPTUS, see DANAÏDES

AESCULAPIUS, son of Apollo and the nymph Coronis; was versed in medicine, was deified, and worshipped at Epidaurus, *Hip.* 1022

AETNA, volcano in Sicily, *Phoen.* 314; its fires, *Hip.* 102; *H. Oet.* 285; seat of Vulcan's forge, *H. Fur.* 106; lay upon the buried Titan's breast, *Med.* 410

AGAMEMNON (*Troades, Agamemnon*), king of Mycenae, son of Atreus, brother of Menelaüs, commander of the Greeks at Troy. He and Menelaüs used by Atreus to entrap Thyestes, *Thy.* 325; tamed by love, *Oct.* 815; took captive Chryseïs, *Agam.* 175; compelled to give her up, he took Bryseïs from Achilles, *ibid.* 186; attempts to dissuade Pyrrhus from the sacrifice of Polyxena, *Tro.* *203; loved Cassandra, *Agam.* 188, 255; his power magnified *ibid.* 204; his homeward voyage and wreck of his fleet, *ibid.* *421; returns to Mycenae, *ibid.* 782; his murder described by Cassandra, *ibid.* *867. See CASSANDRA, CLYTEMNESTRA, IPHIGENIA, PYRRHUS

AGĀVE, daughter of Cadmus and Harmonia, mother of Pentheus, king of Thebes. She and her sisters, in Bacchic frenzy, slew Pentheus on Cithaeron, and bore his head to Thebes, *Oed.* 1006; *Phoen.* 15, 363; her shade appears from Hades, *Oed.* 616. See PENTHEUS

AGRIPPINA I, daughter of M. Vipsanius Agrippa and Julia, daughter of Augustus, mother of Caligula. Died in exile at Pandataria, *Oct.* *932

AGRIPPINA II (*Octavia*), daughter of the preceding, wife of Cn. Domitius Ahenobarbus, mother of Nero. Married Claudius, whom she poisoned, *Oct.* 26, 45, 165, 340; was stepmother of Octavia, and cause of all her woes, *ibid.* 22; plotted murder of Silanus, betrothed lover of Octavia, and forced her to marry Nero, *ibid.* 150; sought in all this her own power, *ibid.* 155, 612; was murdered by her son, Nero, *ibid.* 46, 95, 165; her murder attributed to Poppaea's influence, *ibid.* 126; described in full detail, *ibid.* *310, *600; former high estate and pitiable death contrasted, *ibid.* 952; her ghost appears to curse Nero, *ibid.* *593

AJAX, son of Oïleus, called simply Oïleus; his death described, *Med.* 660; for his defiance of the gods was destroyed by Pallas and Neptune in storm which wrecked the Greek fleet, *Agam.* *532

AJAX, son of Telamon, crazed with rage because the armour of Achilles was awarded to Ulysses, *Agam.* 210

ALCESTIS, wife of Admetus, king of Pherae, to save whose life she resigned her own, *Med.* 662

ALCIDES, see HERCULES

ALCMĒNA (*Hercules Oetaeus*), wife of Amphitryon, a Theban prince, beloved of Jupiter, mother by

514

INDEX

CENTAURS, race in Thessaly, half man, half horse, *H. Oet.* 1049, 1195, 1925; their fight with Lapithae, *H. Fur.* 778; the centaur Nessus killed by Hercules, *H. Oet.* *503. See CHIRON, NESSUS

CERBERUS, three-headed dog, guardian of Hades, *Thy.* 16; *H. Oet.* 23; *H. Fur.* 1107; his existence denied, *Tro.* 404; said to have broken out of Hades and to be abroad in the Theban land, *Oed.* 171; his clanking chains heard on earth, *ibid.* 581; Hercules brought him to the upper world, *H. Oet.* 1245; *Agam.* 859; *H. Fur.* *50, 547; Theseus describes him and tells how he was brought to the upper world by Hercules, *ibid.* *760; his actions in the light of day, *ibid.* *813. See HERCULES

CERES, daughter of Saturn, sister of Jupiter, mother of Proserpina, and goddess of agriculture; her vain and anxious search for her daughter, *H. Fur.* 659; taught Triptolemus the science of agriculture, *Hip.* 838; mystic rites of her worship, *H. Fur.* 300, 845. Her name used by metonymy for grain. See ELEUSIN, PROSERPINA, TRIPTOLEMUS

CEYX, king of Trachin, suffered death by shipwreck. His wife, Alcyone, mourned him incessantly; finally both were changed into kingfishers, *H. Oet.* 197; *Agam.* 681; *Oct.* 7

CHAONIAN OAKS, sacred grove in Chaonia of Epirus containing a temple and oracle of Jupiter, said to be oldest oracle in Greece; oracles supposed to be given out by the oaks themselves, endowed with speech, or by the doves which resorted there. "Chaonian trees" used for tall trees in general, *Oed.* 728; the "talking oak" of Chaonia, *H. Oet.* 1623. See DODONA

CHARON, aged ferryman of the Styx, *H. Fur.* 555; *Agam.* 752; his personal appearance, *ibid.* *764; forced by Hercules to bear him across the Lethe (not Styx),

ibid. *770; overwearied by transporting throngs of Theban dead, *Oed.* 166; charmed by music of Orpheus, *H. Oet.* 1072

CHARYBDIS, whirlpool between Italy and Sicily, opposite Scylla, *Med.* 408; *H. Oet.* 235; *Thy.* 581. See SCYLLA

CHIMAERA, monster combining lion, dragon, and goat, vomited forth fire, *Med.* 828

CHIRON, centaur dwelling in a cavern on Pelion, famous for his knowledge of medicine and divination. To his training were entrusted Jason, Hercules, Aesculapius, and Achilles, *H. Fur.* 971; *Tro.* 832; set in the sky as zodiacal constellation of Sagittarius, *Thy.* 860

CHRYSEÏS, daughter of Chryses, priest of Apollo at Chrysa. Taken captive, she fell to the lot of Agamemnon, who, forced to give her up, claimed Briseïs, captive maid of Achilles. Hence arose strife between the two, *Tro.* 223. See ACHILLES

CIRRHA, ancient town in Phocis, near Delphi, *Oed.* 269; *H. Oet.* 92, 1475

CITHAERON, mountain near Thebes where the infant Oedipus was exposed, *Phoen.* 13; the scene of many wild and tragic deeds, see ACTAEON, AGAVE, DIRCE, PENTHEUS

CLAUDIUS, fourth Roman emperor, father of Octavia, murdered by his second wife, Agrippina, *Oct.* 26, 45, 269.

CLOTHO, one of the three fates or Parcae, supposed to hold the distaff and spin the thread of life, *H. Oet.* 768; *Oct.* 16; *Thy.* 617

CLYTEMNESTRA (*Agamemnon*), daughter of Tyndareus and Leda, sister of Helen, wife of Agamemnon, mother of Orestes, Iphigenia, and Electra; called Tyndaris, *Agam.* 897. During her husband's absence engaged in conspiracy with Aegisthus to murder Agamemnon. Deliberates whether to give up her course of crime or carry it through, *ibid.* 108; tests Aegisthus' courage and deter-

INDEX

DISCORD, a Fury, summoned by Juno from Hades to drive Hercules to madness, *H. Fur.* 93 ; her abode, *ibid.* *93

DODŌNA, city of Chaonia in Epirus, famous for ancient oracle of Jupiter, in a grove of oaks, which had the gift of speech, *H. Oet.* 1473 ; when Minerva aided in the construction of the Argo, she set in its prow timber cut from the speaking oak of Dodona, and this piece had oracular power ; the Argo's "voice" was lost through fear of the Symplegades, *Med.* 349. See CHAONIAN OAKS

DOMITIUS, father of Nero, *Oct.* 249

DRAGON, (1) guardian of the apples of the Hesperides, slain by Hercules, and afterwards set in the heavens as constellation Draco, between the two Bears, *Thy.* 870 ; *Med.* 694 ; (2) of Colchis, guardian of the golden fleece, put to sleep by Medea's magic, *Med.* 703 ; (3) dragon sacred to Mars killed by Cadmus near the site of his destined city of Thebes. From the teeth of this dragon, sown by Cadmus, armed men sprang up, *Oed.* **725 ; *H. Fur.* 260 ; some of these teeth were sown by Jason in Colchis with a similar result, *Med.* 469 ; the brothers who sprang up against Cadmus are described as living in Hades, *Oed.* 586

DRUSUS, Livius, the fate of, *Oct.* 887, 942

DRYADS, race of wood-nymphs, *H. Oet.* 1053 ; *Hip.* 784

E

ECHO, nymph who pined away to a mere voice for unrequited love of Narcissus. She dwells in mountain caves, and repeats the last words of all that is said in her hearing, *Tro.* 109

ELECTRA (*Agamemnon*), daughter of Agamemnon and Clytemnestra, sister of Orestes ; gives her brother to Strophius, king of Phocis, to save him from Clytemnestra and Aegisthus, *Agam.*

910 ; defies her mother and Aegisthus, *ibid.* 953 ; is taken away to imprisonment, *ibid.* 1000 ; Octavia compares her woes with Electra's, to the advantage of the latter, *Oct.* 60

ELEUSIN (Eleusis), ancient city of Attica, famous for its mysteries of Ceres, *H. Oet.* 599 ; *Tro.* 843 ; *H. Fur.* 300 ; *Hip.* 838 ; the mysteries described, *H. Fur.* *842. See CERES, TRIPTOLEMUS

ELYSIUM, abode of the blest, *Tro.* 159, 944 ; *H. Oet.* 956, 1916 ; *H. Fur.* 744

ENCELADUS, one of the Titans who attempted to dethrone Jove, overthrown and buried under Sicily, *H. Fur.* 79 ; *H. Oet.* 1140, 1145, 1159, 1735

ERIDANUS, mythical and poetical name of the Po, *H. Oet.* 186. See PHAËTHONTIADES

ERINYES, the Furies, *H. Fur.* 982 ; *Med.* 952 ; *Oed.* 590 ; *Agam.* 83 ; *Thy.* 251 ; *H. Oet.* 609, 671 ; *Oct.* 23, 161, 263, 619, 913. See FURIES

ERYX, son of Butes and Venus, famous boxer, overcome by Hercules, *H. Fur.* 481 ; mountain in Sicily, said to have been named from the preceding, *Oed.* 600

ETEOCLES (*Phoenissae*), one of the two sons of Oedipus and Jocasta. After Oedipus abandoned the throne of Thebes (*Phoen.* 104), Eteocles and Polynices agreed to reign alternately. Eteocles, the elder, ascended the throne, but when his year was up refused to give way to his brother, *Phoen.* 55, 280, 389 ; *H. Fur.* 389. See POLYNICES

EUMENIDES (" the gracious ones "), a euphemistic name for the Furies, *H. Fur.* 87 ; *H. Oet.* 1002

EURŌPA, daughter of Agenor, king of Tyre, beloved of Jupiter, who, as a bull, carried her away to Crete, *Oct.* 206, 766 ; *H. Oet.* 550 ; this episode immortalised by the constellation of Taurus, *H. Fur.* 9 ; sought in vain by her brother Cadmus, *Oed.* 715 ; the continent of Europe named after her, *Agam.* 205, 274 ; *Tro.* 896

INDEX

EURYBATES (*Agamemnon*), messenger of Agamemnon who announces victory of Greeks at Troy and the hero's near approach to Mycenae, *Agam.* 392; relates the sufferings of the Greek fleet on the homeward voyage, *ibid.* *421

EURYDICE, wife of Orpheus, slain by a serpent's sting on her wedding day; story of Orpheus' quest for her in Hades, *H. Fur.* *569; rescued by Orpheus from the lower world, but lost again, *H. Oet.* *1084. See ORPHEUS

EURYSTHEUS, son of Sthenelus, grandson of Perseus, who, by a trick of Juno, was given power over Hercules, and, at Juno's instance, laid upon Hercules his various labours, *H. Oet.* 403; *H. Fur.* 43, 78, 479, 526, 830; lord of Argos and Mycenae, *ibid.* 1180; *H. Oet.* 1800; his punishment predicted, *ibid.* 1973

EURYTUS, king of Oechalia and father of Iole, *H. Oet.* 1490; he and his house destroyed by Hercules because he refused the latter's suit for Iole, *ibid.* 100, 207, 221; *H. Fur.* 477. See HERCULES

F

FESCENNINE, of Fescennia, ancient town of Etruria, famous for a species of coarse dialogues in verse which bear its name, *Med.* 113

FORTUNE, goddess of fate, ruling over affairs of men, *H. Fur.* 326, 524; *Tro.* *259, 269, 697, 735; *Phoen.* 82, 308, 452; *Med.* 159, 176, 287; *Hip.* 979, 1124, 1143; *Oed.* 11, 86, 674, 786, 825, 934; *Agam.* 28, 58, 72, 89, 101, 248, 594, 698; *H. Oet.* 697; *Oct.* 36, 377, 479, 563, 888, 898, 931, 962; *Thy.* 618

FURIES, avenging goddesses, dwelling in Hades, set to punish and torment men both on earth and in the lower world; described and appealed to, *Med.* 13; Juno plots to summon them from

Hades to make Hercules mad, *H. Fur.* 86; described, *ibid.* 87; described by Cassandra, *Agam.* *759; move in bands, *Thy.* 78, 250; *Med.* 958; a Fury used as a character in prologue, driving on Thyestes' ghost to perform his mission, *Thy.* *23. See EUMENIDES, ERINYES, MEGAERA, TISIPHONE

G

GEMINI, zodiacal constellation of the Twins, Castor and Pollux, *Thy.* 853

GERYON, mythical king in Spain, having three bodies; Hercules slew him and brought his famous cattle to Eurystheus as his tenth labour, *H. Fur.* 231, 487, 1170; *Agam.* 837; *H. Oet.* 26, 1204, 1900. See HERCULES

GHOSTS. The ghost appears as a *dramatis persona* in the following plays: *Agamemnon*, in which the ghost of Thyestes appears in the prologue to urge Aegisthus on to fulfil his mission; *Thyestes*, in which the ghost of Tantalus similarly appears in the prologue; *Octavia*, in which the ghost of Agrippina appears. In the following plays the ghost affects the action though not actually appearing upon the stage: *Troades*, in which the ghost of Achilles is reported to have appeared to the Greeks and demanded the sacrifice of Polyxena, 168 ff.; Andromache also claims to have seen the ghost of Hector warning her of the impending fate of Astyanax, 443 ff.; *Oedipus*, in which the ghost of Laïus and other departed spirits are described as set free by the necromancy of Tiresias, 582 ff.; *Medea*, in which the mangled ghost of Absyrtus seems to appear to the distracted Medea, 963; ghosts appear larger than mortal forms, *Oed.* 175

GIANTS, monstrous sons of Earth, made war upon the gods, scaling heaven by piling mountains one on another, *Tro.* 829; *Thy.* 804,

IRIS, messenger of Juno, goddess of the rainbow, *Oed.* 315

ITYS, son of Tereus, king of Thrace, and Procne, who, to punish her husband for his outrage upon her sister, Philomela, slew and served Itys at a banquet to his father. The sisters, changed to birds, ever bewail Itys, *H. Oet.* 192 ; *Agam.* 670

IXION, for his insult to Juno whirled on a wheel in Hades, *Hip.* 1236 ; *Thy.* 8 ; *Agam.* 15 ; *Oct.* 623 ; *H. Fur.* 750 ; *H. Oet.* 945, 1011 ; *Med.* 744 ; his wheel stood still at music of Orpheus, *ibid.* 1068. See NEPHELE

J

JASON (*Medea*), son of Aeson, king of Thessaly, nephew of the usurping king, Pelias. Was persuaded by Pelias to undertake the adventure of the Golden Fleece, for which he organised and led the Argonautic expedition. Through Medea's aid performed the tasks in Colchis set by Aeëtes : tamed the fire-breathing bull, *Med.* 121, 241, 466 ; overcame the giants sprung from the serpent's teeth, *ibid.* 467 ; put to sleep the dragon, *ibid.* 471. Had no part in murder of Pelias, for which he and Medea were driven out of Thessaly, *ibid.* 262 ; but this and all Medea's crimes had been done for his sake, *ibid.* *275 ; living in exile in Corinth, is forced by Creon into marriage with the king's daughter, Creüsa, *ibid.* 137 ; Medea curses him, *ibid.* 19 ; he laments the dilemma in which he finds himself, *ibid.* 431 ; decides to yield to Creon's demands for the sake of his children, *ibid.* 441

JOCASTA (*Oedipus, Phoenissae*), wife of Laïus, king of Thebes, mother and afterwards wife of Oedipus ; on learning that Oedipus is her son, kills herself, *Oed.* 1024. According to another version, she is still living after Oedipus goes into exile ; bewails the strife between her sons, Eteocles and Polynices, *Phoen.* 377 ; rushing between the two hosts, tries to reconcile her sons, *ibid.* *443

JUDGES IN HADES, Aeacus, Minos, and Rhadamanthus, weep when they hear Orpheus' strains, *H. Fur.* 579 ; Theseus describes their persons and judgments, the moral law under which the souls of men are judged, the punishments and rewards meted out, *ibid.* **727

JULIA, daughter of Drusus and Livia Drusilla, exiled and afterwards slain, *Oct.* 944

JUNO (*Hercules Furens*), reveals her motive in persecuting Hercules ; recounts Jove's infidelities and relates her struggles with Hercules ; she cannot overcome him by any toil, *H. Fur.* *1 ff. ; type of wife who, by wise management, won back her husband's love, *Oct.* *201 ; hymn in praise of, *Agam.* 340 ; Argos is dear to her, *ibid.* 809

JUPITER, lord of Olympus, ruler of the skies and seasons, *Hip.* *960 ; ruler of heaven and earth, to whom victors consecrate their spoils, *Agam.* *802 ; his mother, Rhea, brought him forth in Crete and hid him in a cave of Ida, lest his father, Saturn, should discover and destroy him, *H. Fur.* 459 ; hymn in praise of, *Agam.* 381 ; his thunderbolts forged in Aetna, *Hip.* 156 ; his amours with mortals : with Leda, to whom he appeared as a swan, *Hip.* 301 ; *H. Fur.* 14 ; with Europa, as a bull, *Hip.* 303 ; *H. Fur.* 9 ; *H. Oet.* 550 ; with Danaë, as a golden shower, *H. Fur.* 13 ; with Callisto, *ibid.* 6 ; with the Pleiades (Electra, Maia, Taygete), *ibid.* 10 ; with Latona, *ibid.* 15 ; with Semele, *ibid.* 16 ; with Alcmena, *ibid.* 22. For his ancient oracle in Epirus, see DODONA ; see also HERCEAN JOVE and CENAEUM

JUSTICE (*Justitia*), the goddess Astraea, who once lived on earth

aegis, *Agam.* 530 ; her gall used by Medea in magic, *Med.* 831

MEGAERA, one of the Furies, summoned by Juno to drive Hercules to madness, *H. Fur.* 102 ; appears to the maddened Medea with scourge of serpents, *Med.* 960 ; seems to appear to the distracted Deianira, *H. Oet.* 1006, 1014 ; summoned by Atreus to assist him in his revenge upon his brother, *Thy.* 252. See FURIES

MEGARA (*Hercules Furens*), daughter of Creon, king of Thebes, wife of Hercules, *H. Fur.* 202 ; laments her husband's constant absence from home, *ibid.* *205 ; scorns the advances of Lycus, *ibid.* *372 ; slain by her husband in a fit of madness brought on by Juno, *ibid.* 1010 ; *H. Oet.* 429, 903, 1452

MELEAGER, son of Oeneus, king of Calydon, and Althaea ; his tragic death caused by his mother's wrath because he had killed her brothers, *Med.* 644, 779. See ALTHAEA

MELICERTA, see INO

MEMNON, son of Aurora, slain by Achilles, *Tro.* 10, 239 ; *Agam.* 212

MENELAUS, son of Atreus, brother of Agamemnon, husband of Helen, king of Sparta, employed by his father to trick his uncle, Thyestes, *Thy.* 327 ; Helen looks forward with fear to his judgment, *Tro.* 923 ; pardoned Helen for her desertion of him, *Agam.* 273

MEROPE, wife of Polybus, king of Corinth ; adopted Oedipus and reared him to manhood as her own child, *Oed.* 272, 661, 802

MESSALINA, wife of Claudius, mother of Octavia, *Oct.* 10 ; cursed by Venus with insatiate lust, *ibid.* 258 ; openly married Silius in the absence of Claudius, *ibid.* *260 ; slain for this by order of Claudius, *ibid.* 265 ; her death, *ibid.* *974

MIMAS, one of the giants, *H. Fur.* 981. See GIANTS

MINOS, son of Jupiter, king of Crete ; father of Phaedra, *Hip.* 149 ; father of Ariadne, *ibid.* 245 ;

powerful monarch, *ibid.* 149 ; no daughter of Minos loved without sin, *ibid.* 127 ; because of his righteousness on earth, made a judge in Hades, *Agam.* 24 ; *Thy.* 23 ; *H. Fur.* 733. See JUDGES IN HADES

MINOTAUR, hybrid monster, born of the union of Pasiphaë, wife of Minos, and a bull ; called brother of Phaedra, *Hip.* 174 ; confined in the labyrinth in Crete, *ibid.* 649, 1171

MOPSUS, Thessalian soothsayer, Argonaut, killed by the bite of a serpent in Libya, *Med.* 655

MULCIBER, name of Vulcan. Gave to Medea sulphurous fires for her magic, *Med.* 824

MYCALE, witch of Thessaly, *H. Oet.* 525

MYCENAE, city of Argolis ; its walls built by the Cyclopes, *Thy.* 407 ; *H. Fur.* 997 ; ruled by the house of Pelops, *Thy.* 188, 561, 1011 ; *Tro.* 855 ; favourite city of Juno, *Agam.* 351 ; home of Agamemnon, *ibid.* 121, 251, 757, 871, 967, 998 ; *Tro.* 156, 245

MYRRHA, daughter of Cinyras ; conceived an unnatural passion for her father. Pursued by him, she was changed into the myrrh tree, whose exuding gum resembles tears, *H. Oet.* 196

MYRTILUS, son of Mercury, charioteer of Oenomaüs. Bribed by Pelops, suitor of Hippodamia, daughter of Oenomaüs, he secretly withdrew the linch-pins of his master's chariot, thus wrecking his master's car in the race which was to decide the success of Pelops' suit. His sin and fate, *Thy.* 140 ; the wrecked chariot preserved as a trophy in palace of Pelopidae, *ibid.* 660

N

NAIDES, deities, generally conceived as young and beautiful maidens, inhabiting brooks and springs. *Hip.* 780. See HYLAS

NAUPLIUS, son of Neptune, king of Euboea ; to avenge death of

531

his son, Palamedes, lured the Greek fleet to destruction by displaying false beacon fires off Euboea, *Agam.* *567; when Ulysses, whom he hated most, escaped, threw himself from the cliff, *Med.* 659. See PALAMEDES

NECROMANTĪA, necromancy. Practised by Tiresias in order to discover Laïus' murderer, *Oed.* **530

NEMEAN LION, slain by Hercules near Nemea, a city of Argolis, first of his twelve labours, *Agam.* 830; *H. Fur.* 224; *H. Oet.* 1193, 1235, 1665, 1885; set in the heavens as a zodiacal constellation, *Oed.* 40. See LEO

NEPHELE, cloud form of Juno, devised by Jupiter, upon which Ixion begot the centaur Nessus, in the belief that it was Juno herself, *H. Oet.* 492

NEPTUNE, son of Saturn, brother of Jupiter and Pluto, with whom, after the dethronement of Saturn, he cast lots for the three great divisions of his father's realm: the second lot, giving him the sovereignty over the sea, fell to Neptune, *Med.* 4, 597; *H. Fur.* 515, 599; *Oed.* 266; *Hip.* 904, 1159; rides over the sea in his car, *Oed.* 254; sends a monster to destroy Hippolytus in answer to Theseus' prayer, *Hip.* 1015; assists Minerva to destroy Ajax, son of Oïleus, in the storm which assailed the Greek fleet, *Agam.* 554; father of Theseus, to whom he gave three wishes, *ibid.* 942; other sons were Cycnus, *Agam.* 215; *Tro.* 183; Periclymenus, *Med.* 635

NEREUS, sea-deity, used often for the sea itself, *Oed.* 450, 508; *H. Oet.* 4; *Hip.* 88; father by Doris of Thetis and the other Nereïds, *Tro.* 882; *Oed.* 446; even they feel the fires of love, *Hip.* 336

NERO (*Octavia*), son of Cn. Domitius Ahenobarbus and Agrippina, *Oct.* 249; married his stepsister, Octavia, whom he treated with great cruelty; his character depicted by her, *ibid.* 86; em-

peror from A.D. 54 until his death in 68; murdered his mother, *ibid.* 46, 95, 243; lauds beauty of Poppaea and proclaims her his next wife, *ibid.* 544; his death prophesied by ghost of Agrippina, *ibid.* **618; decrees banishment and death of Octavia, *ibid.* 861

NESSUS, centaur, son of Ixion and Nephele, *H. Oet.* 492; insults Deianira, is slain by Hercules; dying gives his blood, poisoned by the arrow of Hercules, to Deianira as a charm which shall recall her husband's wandering affections, *ibid.* *500; some of this blood is in Medea's collection of charms, *Med.* 775; the power of this blood tested by Deianira after she has sent the fatal robe to Hercules, *H. Oet.* 716; Nessus conceived the plot against Hercules, Deianira the innocent instrument, *ibid.* 1468

NIOBE, daughter of Tantalus, wife of Amphion, king of Thebes; punished by the loss of her seven sons and seven daughters by Diana for her defiance of Latona, mother of the goddess, *Agam.* 392; changed to stone, she still sits on Mt. Sipylus and mourns her children, *Agam.* 394; *H. Fur.* 390; *H. Oet.* 185, 1849; her shade comes up from Hades, still proudly counting her children's shades, *Oed.* 613

NYCTELIUS, epithet of Bacchus, because his mysteries were celebrated at night, *Oed.* 492

O

OCTAVIA (*Octavia*), daughter of the Emperor Claudius and Messalina, *Oct.* 10, 26, 45; became first the stepsister and then the wife of Nero, *ibid.* 47; with whom she led a most wretched life, *ibid.* *100; had been betrothed to Silanus, *ibid.* 145, who was murdered to make way for Nero, *ibid.* 154; beloved by her people, *ibid.* 183; is compared with Juno, sister and wife of her husband, *ibid.* 282; doomed

INDEX

(see TANTALUS) ; Pelops and Tantalus, *ibid.* 242 ; his house doomed to sin, *ibid.* 22 ; degenerate, *ibid.* 625 ; came from Phrygia and settled Peloponnesus (whence its name), *H. Fur.* 1165 ; *Tro.* 855 ; *Agam.* 563 ; his palace, *Thy.* *641

PELŌRUS, promontory of Sicily opposite Italy, *H. Oet.* 81 ; Scylla dwelt under it, *Med.* 350

PENTHESILĒA, queen of Amazons, came to aid Priam ; armed with battle-axe and moon-shaped shield, *Agam.* 217 ; her struggles in battle, *Tro.* 12, 672 ; slain by Achilles, *ibid.* 243

PENTHEUS, king of Thebes, son of Echion and Agave ; opposed worship of Bacchus ; spying upon his mother and her sisters, was torn in pieces by them in their Bacchic madness, *Phoen.* 15, 363 ; *Oed.* 441, 483 ; his shade comes up from Hades, *ibid.* 618

PERICLYMENUS, son of Neptune, who could assume various shapes ; Argonaut, slain by Hercules, *Med.* 635

PERSEUS, son of Danaë and Jove, *H. Fur.* 13 ; earned a place in heaven by slaying the Gorgon, *H. Oet.* 51, 94

PHAEDRA (*Hippolytus* or *Phaedra*), daughter of Minos, king of Crete, and Pasiphaë, daughter of the Sun, *Hip.* 155, 156, 678, 688, 888 ; sister of the Minotaur, *ibid.* 174 ; of Ariadne, *ibid.* 245, 760 ; bewails her exile from Crete, and her marriage to Theseus, *ibid.* 85 ; her unnatural passion for Hippolytus, *ibid.* 113, 640 ; is scorned by him, *ibid.* *671 ; confesses her sin to her husband and slays herself, *ibid.* 1159

PHAËTHON, son of Clymene and Phoebus ; driving his father's chariot, was hurled from the car, *Hip.* 1090 ; slain by Jove's thunderbolt, *H. Oet.* 854 ; a warning against ambition and impious daring, *ibid.* 677 ; *Med.* 599 ; gave magic fire to Medea, *ibid.* 826

PHAËTHONTIADES, sisters of Phaëthon, wept for him on the banks

of the Po, and were changed into poplar trees, *H. Oet.* 188

PHASIS, river of Colchis, *Med.* 44, 211, 451, 762 ; *Hip.* 907 ; *Agam.* 120 ; Medea named from the river, *H. Oet.* 950

PHERAE, city in Thessaly, ruled over by Admetus, husband of Alcestis, *Med.* 663 ; here Apollo kept Admetus' flocks, *H. Fur.* 451

PHILOCTĒTES (*Hercules Oetaeus*), Thessalian prince, son of Poeas, friend of Hercules, *H. Oet.* 1604 ; receives bow and arrows of Hercules, *ibid.* 1648, to whose pyre he applies the torch, *ibid.* 1727 ; describes death of Hercules, *ibid.* *1610 ; Hercules' arrows used a second time against Troy, *Tro.* 136 and note

PHILIPPI, city of Thrace ; there Antony and Octavianus conquered forces of Brutus and Cassius, *Oct.* 516

PHILOMĒLA, daughter of Pandion, king of Athens, sister of Procne, who had married Tereus, king of Thrace ; outraged by Tereus, she and Procne punished Tereus by slaying and serving to him his son Itys ; she was changed into a nightingale, who ever mourns for Itys, *Agam.* 670 ; *H. Oet.* 199 ; *Thracia pellex*, used simply as a nightingale singing at sunrise and hovering over her young, *H. Fur.* 149

PHINEUS, king of Salmydessus in Thrace ; blind and tormented by the Harpies, *Thy.* 154 ; tormented in Hades, *H. Fur.* 759

PHLEGETHON, fiery river in the lower world, *Oed.* 162 ; *Thy.* 73, 1018 ; encircles the guilty, *Hip.* 1227 ; the river over which Charon rows his boat, *Agam.* 753 ; for Hades in general, *Hip.* 848

PHLEGRA, vale in Thrace where the giants fought with the gods, *Thy.* 810 ; Hercules assisted the gods, *H. Fur.* 444

PHOEBUS, one of Apollo's names ; most frequently conceived of as the sun-god, driving his fiery chariot across the sky, seeing all

535

INDEX

les and Deïdamia, daughter of Lycomedes, king of Scyros ; born on island of Scyros, *Tro.* 339 ; quarrelled with Ulysses inside the wooden horse, *Agam.* 635 ; slew old Priam, *Tro.* 44, 310

PYTHON, huge serpent that sprang from the slime of the earth when the flood subsided ; slain by Apollo, *H. Oet.* 93 ; *Med.* 700

R

RHADAMANTHUS, son of Jupiter and Europa, brother of Minos ; was made one of three judges in Hades, *H. Fur.* 734

RHESUS, king of Thrace, who came, late in Trojan War, to Priam's aid ; oracle that Troy could never be taken if horses of Rhesus should drink of the Xanthus and feed upon grass of Trojan plain was frustrated by Ulysses and Diomedes, *Agam.* 216 ; *Tro.* 8

S

SATURN, son of Coelus and Terra, succeeded to his father's kingdom of heaven and earth ; golden age was said to have been in his reign, *Oct.* 395 ; dethroned by his three sons, Jupiter, Neptune, and Pluto, who divided up his kingdom ; kept chained in Hades by Pluto, *H. Oet.* 1141 ; Hercules threatens to unchain him against Jove unless the latter grant him a place in heaven, *H. Fur.* 965

SCALES (*Libra*), zodiacal constellation marking the autumnal equinox, *H. Fur.* 842

SCIRON, robber in Attica, who threw his victims over cliffs into sea ; was slain by Theseus, *Hip.* 1023, 1225

SCORPION, one of the zodiacal constellations, *Thy.* 859

SCYLLA, one of the two shipwrecking monsters in Sicilian Strait, *H. Fur.* 376 ; *H. Oet.* 235 ; *Med.* 350, 407 ; *Thy.* 579. See CHARYBDIS

SCYTHIA, a portion of northern Asia of indefinite extent ; its nomadic tribes, frozen streams, *H. Fur.* *533

SEMELE, Theban princess, daughter of Cadmus, beloved of Jove, by whom she became mother of Bacchus, *H. Fur.* 16 ; was blasted by a thunderbolt while Bacchus was still unborn, *H. Fur.* 457 ; *H. Oet.* 1804. See BACCHUS

SENECA (*Octavia*), introduced into the play as Nero's counsellor, *Oct.* 377 ; recalls his life in exile in Corsica, and considers it happier and safer than his present life, *ibid.* 381 ; strives in vain to prevent marriage of Nero and Poppaea, *ibid.* 695

SERES, nation of Asia, supposed to be the Chinese ; they gather silken threads (spun by the silkworm) from trees, *H. Oet.* 666 ; *Hip.* 389 ; *Thy.* 379

SILĀNUS, L. Junius, praetor in A.D. 49 ; was betrothed to Octavia, but slain that Octavia might marry Nero, *Oct.* 145

SILĒNUS, demigod, foster-father and constant attendant of Bacchus, *Oed.* 429

SINIS, giant robber of the Isthmus of Corinth, who bent down treetops and, fixing his victims to these, shot them through the air ; was slain by Theseus, *H. Oet.* 1393 ; *Hip.* 1169, 1223

SINON, Greek warrior, who deceived the Trojans as to character and purpose of wooden horse, and so procured downfall of Troy, *Tro.* 39 ; *Agam.* *626

SIPYLUS, mountain in Phrygia, on which Niobe, changed to stone, was said to sit and weep eternally over her lost children, *H. Oet.* 185 ; *Agam.* 394 ; *H. Fur.* 391. See NIOBE

SIRENS, mythical maidens dwelling on an island of the ocean, whose beautiful singing lured sailors to destruction, *H. Oet.* 190 ; were passed in safety by Argonauts because Orpheus played sweeter music .*Med.* 355

SISYPHUS, son of Aeolus, founder of ancient Corinth, father of

INDEX

Creon, *Med.* 512, 776 ; *Oed.* 282 ; for disobedience to the gods was set to rolling a huge stone up a hill in Hades, which ever rolled back again, *Med.* 746 ; *Hip.* 1230 ; *Agam.* 16 ; *H. Fur.* 751 ; *Thy.* 6 ; *Oct.* 622 ; *H. Oet.* 942, 1010 ; the stone followed the music of Orpheus, *ibid.* 1081

SMINTHEUS, epithet of Phoebus Apollo, *Agam.* 176

SOL, the Sun personified as sun-god, *H. Fur.* 37, 61 ; *Med.* 29, 210 ; *Thy.* 637, 776, 789, 822, 990, 1035 ; *Hip.* 124, 1091 ; *H. Oet.* 150

SOMNUS, god of sleep, brother of Death, *H. Fur.* 1069 ; called son of Astraea, *ibid.* 1068 ; characteristics, symbols, and powers, *ibid.* *1065

SPHINX, fabulous monster with face of a woman, breast, feet, and tail of a lion, and wings of a bird ; sent to harass Thebes, slaying everyone who could not answer her riddle, *Oed.* 246 ; *Phoen.* 120, 131 ; Oedipus' encounter with her, *Oed.* *92 ; slain by Oedipus, *ibid.* 641 ; seen by Creon in Hades, called by him the "Ogygian" (*i.e.* Boeotian or Theban) pest, *ibid.* 589 ; type of winged speed, *Phoen.* 422

STROPHIUS (*Agamemnon*), see PYLADES

STYMPHALIAN BIRDS, monstrous creatures haunting a pool near town of Stymphalus in Arcadia ; were killed by Hercules as his sixth labour, *H. Fur.* 244 ; *Med.* 783 ; *Agam.* 850 ; *H. Oet.* 17, 1237, 1890 ; type of winged speed, *Phoen.* 422

STYX, river of Hades, *H. Fur.* 780 ; *Oed.* 162, over which spirits pass into nether world, river of death ; in Seneca, this conception is not confined to Styx, but is used of that river in common with Acheron, *H. Fur.* *713 ; *Hip.* 1180 ; *Agam.* 608 ; with Lethe, *Hip.* 148 ; *H. Oet.* 1161, 1550 ; with Phlegethon, *Agam.* *750 ; by the Styx the gods swear their inviolable oaths, *H. Fur.* 713 ; *Hip.* 944 ; *Thy.* 666 ;

H. Oet. 1066 ; comes to mean death itself, *H. Fur.* 185, 558 ; most frequently the river signifies the lower world in general, the land of the dead ; so are found Stygian "shades," "homes," "caverns," "ports," "gates," "borders," "torches," "fires," etc., *H. Fur.* 54, 90, 104, 1131 ; *Tro.* 430 ; *Med.* 632, 804 ; *Hip.* 477, 625, 928, 1151 ; *Oed.* 396, 401, 621 ; *Agam.* 493 ; *Thy.* 1007 ; *H. Oet.* 77, 560, 1014, 1145, 1198, 1203, 1711, 1766, 1870, 1919, 1983 ; *Oct.* 24, 79, 135, 162, 263, 594 ; Cerberus is the "Stygian dog" and "Stygian guardian," *Agam.* 13 ; *Hip.* 223 ; *H. Oet.* 79, 1245 ; the "deep embrace of Styx" is the pit which Andromache prays may open up beneath Hector's tomb and hide Astyanax, *Tro.* 520 ; the boat on which Agrippina was to meet her death is called the Stygian boat, *Oct.* 127

SYMPLEGADES (the "clashers"), two rocks or crags at entrance of Euxine Sea, which clashed together when an object passed between them, *H. Fur.* 1210 ; *H. Oet.* 1273, 1380 ; escaped by the Argo, *Med.* 341, 456, 610

T

TAENARUS, promontory on the southernmost point of Peloponnesus, near which was a cave, said to be entrance to the lower world, *Tro.* 402 ; *H. Fur.* 587, *663, 813 ; *Oed.* 171 ; *Hip.* 1203 ; *H. Oet.* 1061, 1771

TAGUS, river of Spain, celebrated for its golden sands, *H. Fur.* 1325 ; *Thy.* 354 ; *H. Oet.* 626

TANTALUS (*Thyestes*) (1), king of Lydia, son of Jupiter and the nymph Pluto, father of Pelops and Niobe, *H. Fur.* 390 ; *Oed.* 613 ; *Med.* 954 ; *Agam.* 392 ; *H. Oet.* 198 ; because of his sin against the gods (see PELOPS) was doomed to suffer in Hades endless pangs of hunger and thirst with fruit and water almost within reach of his lips, *H. Fur.*

INDEX

THESPIADES, fifty daughters of Thespius, loved by Hercules, *H. Oet.* 369

THETIS, sea-goddess, daughter of Nereus; was given as wife to Peleus, *Med.* 657; *Oct.* 707; became by him mother of Achilles, *Tro.* 346, 880; *Agam.* 616; to keep her son from Trojan War hid him disguised in girl's garments at the court of Lycomedes, *Tro.* 213; this ruse discovered and exposed by Ulysses, *ibid.* 569

THULE, farthest known land; all lands one day will be known, and there will be no *ultima Thule*, *Med.* 379

THYESTES (*Thyestes, Agamemnon*), see ATREUS

TIPHYS, pilot of the Argo, *Med.* 3, 318; his management of the vessel, *ibid.* *318; grew pale at sight of Symplegades, *ibid.* 346; death, *617

TIRESIAS (*Oedipus*), prophet of Thebes, father of Manto; attempts to discover the murderer of Laïus, *Oed.* 288; practises *pyromantia, capnomantia, hieroscopia,* and later *necromantia, ibid.* *307; discovers by the last process that Oedipus himself slew Laïus, *ibid.* *530

TISIPHONE, one of the Furies, who seems to appear to Deianira, *H. Oet.* 1012; seems to appear to Hercules, *H. Fur.* 984. See FURIES

TITANS, sons of Coelus and Terra, one of whom was Hyperion, identified by Homer with the Sun. Warred against one of their own number, Saturn, who had succeeded to his father's throne. Frequently confounded with the Giants, who banded together to dethrone Jove; they piled up mountains in their attempt to scale heaven, but were overthrown by Jove's thunderbolt and buried under Sicily, *H. Fur.* 79, 967; *Med.* 410; *Agam.* 340; *H. Oet.* 144, 1212, 1309 :in all other passages in Seneca Titan means the Sun, more or less completely personified as the

sun-god, *H. Fur.* 124, 133, 443, 1060, 1333; *Med.* 5; *Tro.* 170; *Hip.* 678, 779; *Oed.* 1, 40; *Thy.* 120, 785, 1095; *Agam.* 460, 908; *H. Oet.* 42, 291, 423, 488, 723, 781, 891, 968, 1111, 1131, 1163, 1287, 1512, 1518, 1566, 1575, 1760; *Oct.* 2. See GIANTS, PHOEBUS

TITYUS, giant, son of Earth, who offered violence to Latona; for this he was punished in Hades, where a vulture kept feeding upon his ever-renewed vitals, *H. Fur.* 756, 977; *H. Oet.* 947; *Hip.* 1233; *Agam.* 17; *Thy.* 9, 806; *Oct.* 622; relieved for a while by music of Orpheus, *H. Oet.* 1070

TMOLUS, mountain in Lydia, haunt of Bacchus, *Phoen.* 602

TOXEUS, youth slain by Hercules, *H. Oet.* 214

TRIPTOLEMUS, son of the king of Eleusis, through whom Ceres gave the arts of agriculture to mankind, *Hip.* 838

TRITONS, sea-deities; they sang the marriage chorus of Achilles, *Tro.* 202

TRIVIA, epithet of Diana, because she presided over places where three roads meet, *Agam.* 382; *Oct.* 978; applied by association to Luna, the heavenly manifestation of Diana, *Med.* *787

TROÏLUS, son of Priam, slain by Achilles, *Agam.* 748

TROY, ancient city of Troas; its walls built by Neptune and Apollo, *Tro.* 7; first destroyed in reign of Laomedon, father of Priam, by Hercules and Telamon, because of the perfidy of Laomedon, *Agam.* 614, 862; *Tro.* 135, *719; its second fall was after ten years of siege by the Greeks, *Tro.* 74; her festal day turned out to be a day of doom, *Agam.* 791; it was Sinon who destroyed Troy, by deceiving the Trojans about the wooden horse, *ibid.* 615; mourning for the fall of Troy, *ibid.* 589; smouldering ruins as seen from the Greek vessels, *ibid.* 456

TULLIA, daughter of Servius Tul-

541

INDEX

lius, king of Rome; her impious sin and its punishment, *Oct.* 304

TYNDARIDAE, Castor and Pollux, sons of Jupiter and Leda, but falsely named from Tyndareus, husband of Leda; their stars give help to sailors, *H. Fur.* 14, 552; *Oct.* 208. See CASTOR, LEDA

TYNDARIS, Clytemnestra, *Agam.* 897

TYPHOEUS, one of the Giants who fought against Jove, *Med.* 773; *Thy.* 809; he is supposed to be buried under the island of Inarime, *H. Oet.* 1155

TYPHON, giant, apparently the same as Typhoeus, *H. Oet.* 1733; *Oct.* 238

TYRRHENE, epithet applied to Phoenician pirates who attempted to kidnap Bacchus, *Oed.* 249; to the dolphin, because these pirates were changed into dolphins by Bacchus, *Agam.* 451; to the Tuscan Sea, because the Etrurians were supposed to have been of Tyrrhenian stock, *Oct.* 311; to Inarime, an island, possibly to be identified with Ischia, lying in the Tyrrhene Sea off Campania, *H. Oet.* 1156

U

ULYSSES (*Troades*), *Tro. passim*

V

VENUS, goddess, sprung from the foam of the sea, *Hip.* 274; goddess of love, *ibid.* 417, 576, 910; *Oct.* 545; mother of Cupid, *Hip.* 275; *H. Oet.* 543; *Oct.* 697; called Erycina, because Mt. Eryx in Sicily was sacred to her, *Hip.* 199; persecuted the stock of Phoebus (*i.e.* Pasiphaë and Phaedra) because that god had published her amours with Mars, *ibid.* 124; cursed Messalina with insatiate lust, *Oct.* 258; effect upon the world which the cessation of Venus' power would produce, *Hip.* **469; has no existence, but is used as an excuse for men's lust, *ibid.* 203; used frequently for the passion of love, either lawful or unlawful, *ibid.* 211, 237, 339, 447, 462, 721, 913; *Agam.* 183, 275, 927; *Oct.* 191, 433

VIRGINIA, daughter of Virginius, slain by her father to save her from the lust of Appius Claudius, *Oct.* 296

VIRGO, zodiacal constellation of the Virgin, Astraea, daughter of Jove and Themis, who left the earth last of all the gods on account of man's sin, *Thy.* 857

VULCAN, god of fire; forges thunderbolts of Jove, *Hip.* 190; is pierced by Cupid's darts, *ibid.* 193; father of Cupid and husband of Venus, *Oct.* 560

Z

ZETES, winged son of Boreas, who, together with his brother Calaïs, was a member of Argonautic expedition; they were slain by Hercules, *Med.* 634; they had previously driven away the Harpies from Phineus, *ibid.* 782

ZETHUS, Theban prince, son of Antiope, niece of Lycus, king of Thebes; he and his twin brother, Amphion, exposed in infancy on Cithaeron, but were saved by shepherds. Arrived at manhood, they killed Lycus and Dirce, his wife, on account of their cruelties to Antiope, and together reigned in Thebes. Reference is made to their rustic life in *H. Fur.* 916; the shade of Zethus comes up from Hades, still holding by the horn the wild bull to which he had tied Dirce, *Oed.* 610. See DIRCE

PRINTED IN GREAT BRITAIN BY R. CLAY AND SONS, LTD.,
BRUNSWICK STREET, STAMFORD STREET, S.E., AND BUNGAY, SUFFOLK.

THE LOEB CLASSICAL LIBRARY.

VOLUMES ALREADY PUBLISHED.

Latin Authors.

APULEIUS. The Golden Ass. (Metamorphoses.) Trans. by W. Adlington (1566). Revised by S. Gaselee. 1 Vol.

CAESAR: CIVIL WARS. Trans. by A. G. Peskett. 1 Vol.

CATULLUS. Trans. by F. W. Cornish; TIBULLUS. Trans. by J. P. Postgate; PERVIGILIUM VENERIS. Trans. by J. W. Mackail. 1 Vol.

CICERO: DE FINIBUS. Trans. by H. Rackham. 1 Vol.

CICERO: DE OFFICIIS. Trans. by Walter Miller. 1 Vol.

CICERO: LETTERS TO ATTICUS. Trans. by E. O. Winstedt. Vols I and II.

CONFESSIONS OF ST. AUGUSTINE. Trans. by W. Watts (1631). 2 Vols.

HORACE: ODES AND EPODES. Trans. by C. E. Bennett. 1 Vol.

OVID: HEROIDES AND AMORES. Trans. by Grant Showerman. 1 Vol.

OVID: METAMORPHOSES. Trans. by F. J. Miller. 2 Vols.

PETRONIUS. Trans. by M. Heseltine; SENECA: APOCOLOCYNTOSIS. Trans. by W. H. D. Rouse. 1 Vol.

PLAUTUS. Trans. by Paul Nixon. Vol. I.

PLINY: LETTERS. Melmoth's Translation revised by W. M. L. Hutchinson. 2 Vols.

PROPERTIUS. Trans. by H. E. Butler. 1 Vol.

SENECA: EPISTULAE MORALES. Trans. by R. M. Gummere. Vol. I.

SENECA: TRAGEDIES. Trans. by F. J. Miller. 2 Vols.

SUETONIUS. Trans. by J. C. Rolfe. 2 Vols.

TACITUS: DIALOGUS. Trans. by Sir Wm. Peterson; AGRICOLA AND GERMANIA. Trans. by Maurice Hutton. 1 Vol.

TERENCE. Trans. by John Sargeaunt. 2 Vols.

Greek Authors.

ACHILLES TATIUS. Trans. by S. Gaselee. 1 Vol.

APOLLONIUS RHODIUS. Trans. by R. C. Seaton. 1 Vol.

THE APOSTOLIC FATHERS. Trans. by Kirsopp Lake. 2 Vols.

APPIAN'S ROMAN HISTORY. Trans. by Horace White. 4 Vols.

DAPHNIS AND CHLOE. Thornley's Translation revised by J. M. Edmonds; PARTHENIUS. Trans. by S. Gaselee. 1 Vol.

DIO CASSIUS: ROMAN HISTORY. Trans. by E. Cary. Vols. I, II, III, IV, and V.

EURIPIDES. Trans. by A. S. Way. 4 Vols.

GALEN: ON THE NATURAL FACULTIES. Trans. by A. J. Brock. 1 Vol.

THE GREEK ANTHOLOGY. Trans. by W. R. Paton. Vols. I, II, III, and IV.

THE GREEK BUCOLIC POETS (THEOCRITUS, BION, MOSCHUS). Trans. by J. M. Edmonds. 1 Vol.

HESIOD AND THE HOMERIC HYMNS. Trans. by H. G. Evelyn White. 1 Vol.

JULIAN. Trans. by Wilmer Cave Wright. Vols. I and II.

LUCIAN. Trans. by A. M. Harmon. Vols. I and II.

MARCUS AURELIUS. Trans. by C. R. Haines. 1 Vol.

PHILOSTRATUS: THE LIFE OF APOLLONIUS OF TYANA. Trans. by F. C. Conybeare. 2 Vols.

PINDAR. Trans. by Sir J. E. Sandys. 1 Vol.

PLATO: EUTHYPHRO, APOLOGY, CRITO, PHAEDO, PHAEDRUS. Trans. by H. N. Fowler. 1 Vol.

PLUTARCH: THE PARALLEL LIVES. Trans. by B. Perrin. Vols. I, II, III, and IV.

PROCOPIUS. Trans. by H. B. Dewing. Vols. I and II.

QUINTUS SMYRNAEUS. Trans. by A. S. Way. 1 Vol.

SOPHOCLES. Trans. by F. Storr. 2 Vols.

ST. JOHN DAMASCENE: BARLAAM AND IOASAPH. Trans. by the Rev. G. R. Woodward and Harold Mattingly. 1 Vol.

STRABO: GEOGRAPHY. Trans. by Horace L. Jones. Vol. I.

THEOPHRASTUS: ENQUIRY INTO PLANTS. Trans. by Sir Arthur Hort, Bart. 2 Vols.

XENOPHON: CYROPAEDIA. Trans. by Walter Miller. 2 Vols.

DESCRIPTIVE PROSPECTUS ON APPLICATION.

London = (= **WILLIAM HEINEMANN.**
New York = \ = = **G. P. PUTNAM'S SONS.**